# zoom español 2

## Teacher Book

Kirsty Thathapudi

**With answers, transcripts and additional material by:**

Abigail Hardwick
Isabel Alonso de Sudea
María Isabel Isern Vivancos

OXFORD
UNIVERSITY PRESS

OXFORD
UNIVERSITY PRESS

Great Clarendon Street, Oxford OX2 6DP

Oxford University Press is a department of the University of Oxford. It furthers the University's objective of excellence in research, scholarship, and education by publishing worldwide in

Oxford New York

Auckland Cape Town Dar es Salaam Hong Kong Karachi Kuala Lumpur Madrid Melbourne Mexico City Nairobi New Delhi Shanghai Taipei Toronto

With offices in

Argentina Austria Brazil Chile Czech Republic France Greece Guatemala Hungary Italy Japan Poland Portugal Singapore South Korea Switzerland Thailand Turkey Ukraine Vietnam



First published 2012



British Library Cataloguing in Publication Data

Data available

ISBN-13: 978-0-19-912766-5

10 9 8

Printed in Great Britain by Ashford Colour Press Ltd, Gosport

Paper used in the production of this book is a natural, recyclable product made from wood grown in sustainable forests. The manufacturing process conforms to the environmental regulations of the country of origin.

**Acknowledgements**
The authors and publishers would like to thank the following people for their help and advice: Julie Green (course consultant), Jaime Veiga Perez (language consultant)

Cover illustration by: Oxford Designers & Illustrators

# Contents



**Symbols used in this Teacher Book:**

- a pairwork activity
- a groupwork activity
- a video activity
- a listening activity – audio on accompanying CD
- AT X.X reference to a National Curriculum Attainment Level
- L&S 1.1 reference to a Framework Objective
- PLTS an activity has been selected as an example of particular Personal Learning and Thinking Skills
- Core activities are highlighted in pale grey (see **Course progression**, page 9)

| Summary of Unit Contents | | | | | |
|---|---|---|---|---|---|
| | **Contexts/Objectives** | **Grammar** | **Language learning** | **Cultural focus** | **Renewed Framework References** |
| **Unit 0** | **Meeting new people**<br>• Meeting and greeting people<br>• Saying how you feel<br>• Saying if you get on with your friends and family<br>• Buying cinema tickets; accepting and refusing invitations<br>• Making excuses | • Questions<br>• The verbs *ser* and *estar to describe character and mood*<br>• *me llevo bien con .../me cae mal ..., conmigo/contigo/ con él/ con ella*, etc.<br>• the personal *a* | • Greeting people formally and informally<br>• Being aware of false friends<br>• Revising opinions<br>• Accepting/refusing politely<br>• Responding politely | • Meeting new Spanish-speaking people; going out | L&S 1.1, 1.2, 1.3, 1.4, 1.5; R&W 2.1, 2.2, 2.4, 2.5; IU 3.2; KAL 4.1, 4.3, 4.5; LLS 5.1, 5.4, 5.5, 5.7, 5.8 |
| **Unit 1A** | **Staying in Spain**<br>• Discuss differences in daily routines<br>• Saying what you do and have to do to help at home<br>• Revising mealtimes and saying what you prefer to eat<br>• Discussing recipes, ingredients and local dishes<br>• Talking about life in different regions and countries | • The verb *soler*<br>• Frequency adverbs<br>• The present continuous<br>• The present tense of radical-changing verbs<br>• Quantities and large numbers<br>• Revision of the present tense including *hay* and *no hay* | • Adapting previously learnt language<br>• Using a dictionary<br>• Memorising verb patterns<br>• Expressing opinions<br>• Extending sentences | • Daily life in Spain | L&S 1.1, 1.2, 1.3, 1.4, 1.5; R&W 2.1, 2.2, 2.4, 2.5; IU 3.1, 3.2; KAL 4.1, 4.3, 4.4, 4.5; LLS 5.1, 5.3, 5.4, 5.5, 5.6, 5.8 |
| **Unit 1B** | **Fashion**<br>• Talking about clothes and giving your opinion on them<br>• Discussing different styles and eras of fashion<br>• Buying clothes, saying what size you are and how well clothes fit<br>• Discussing different types of shops<br>• Describing clothes for different activities and occasions | • Opinions<br>• The imperfect tense<br>• Demonstrative adjectives<br>• Comparatives and superlatives<br>• Singular and plural verb forms (revision) | • Transferring previous knowledge to new situations<br>• Using cognates<br>• Working out the meaning of new vocabulary<br>• Understanding Spanish clothes sizes<br>• Revising numbers<br>• Making choices<br>• Evaluating options<br>• Understanding and producing descriptions | • Fashion and clothes | L&S 1.1, 1.2, 1.3, 1.4, 1.5; R&W 2.2, 2.4, 2.5; IU 3.2; KAL 4.2, 4.3, 4.5; LLS 5.1, 5.3, 5.4, 5.5, 5.7 |
| **Unit 2A** | **Leisure**<br>• Talking about what you like doing in your free time<br>• Talking about going shopping<br>• Saying what you did on holiday<br>• Describing past events<br>• Talking about what you did when you were younger | • *gustar* and similar verbs with nouns and verbs<br>• Direct object pronouns (for things/objects)<br>• Revision of the preterite tense (regular and some irregular verbs)<br>• Preterite (some irregular) and imperfect verbs | • Justifying opinions<br>• Adapting previously learnt language in a new context<br>• Responding to open-ended questions<br>• Summarising and recounting what happened<br>• Giving opinions | • Freetime and leisure activities | L&S 1.1, 1.2, 1.4; R&W 2.2, 2.4, 2.5; IU 3.2; KAL 4.1, 4.3, 4.4, 4.5, 4.6; LLS 5.1, 5.4, 5.5 |

| | | | | | |
|---|---|---|---|---|---|
| **Unit 2B** | **Come to Madrid!**<br>• Talking about different means of transport<br>• Recognising some tourist attractions in Madrid<br>• Buying travel tickets<br>• Talking about what you did on a day out in the past<br>• Recognising names of shops and giving directions | • Preposition *a*<br>• Relative pronouns *que* and *lo que*<br>• The immediate future<br>• Questions<br>• The preterite of some common irregular verbs<br>• Simple imperatives and prepositions | • Tackling an unfamiliar text<br>• Transforming level 4 speaking or writing into level 5<br>• Identifying key vocabulary from context<br>• Extending work to achieve a higher level<br>• Sounding Spanish when pronouncing words with *z*, *ce* or *ci* | • Learning about Madrid | L&S 1.1, 1.2, 1.4; R&W 2.2, 2.4, 2.5; IU 3.2; KAL 4.1, 4.4, 4.5, 4.6; LLS 5.1, 5.4, 5.5, 5.8 |
| **Unit 3A** | **Well-being**<br>• Talking about what you have to/ought to do to maintain a healthy lifestyle<br>• Identifying parts of the body and discussing keeping fit<br>• Talking about illnesses and injuries<br>• Discussing which sports you like doing and how you play them<br>• Talking more about sport and sporting accidents | • Question words and frequency words<br>• Reflexives in the past and present tenses<br>• The verb *doler*<br>• Impersonal 'se'<br>• The imperfect and preterite | • Practising checking work and memorising skills<br>• Adapting previously learnt language in a new context<br>• Understanding instructions<br>• Listening for detail<br>• Revising and extending language already covered | • Sports in Spain | L&S 1.1, 1.2, 1.4, 1.5; R&W 2.1, 2.2, 2.4, 2.5; IU 3.1, 3.2; KAL 4.4, 4.5, 4.6; LLS 5.1, 5.2 |
| **Unit 3B** | **My future**<br>• Talking about what you will do in the future<br>• Talking about what job you will, would like to, or hope to do in the future<br>• Talking about how you earn pocket money<br>• Talking about choosing options/subjects<br>• Finding out and describing how somebody got their dream job | • The future tense including irregular verbs<br>• The conditional tense<br>• Using a variety of tenses (past, present, future) | • Differentiating between the future and the immediate future<br>• Understanding what qualities are necessary for different jobs<br>• Thinking of unusual ways to earn pocket money<br>• Giving reasons for your choices<br>• Producing a piece of extended writing | • Options and jobs in Spain | L&S 1.1, 1.2, 1.4, 1.5; R&W 2.2, 2.4, 2.5; IU 3.1, 3.2; KAL 4.1, 4.3, 4.4, 4.5; LLS 5.1, 5.4, 5.8 |
| **Unit 4A** | **My world**<br>• Describing environmental problems and their causes<br>• Talking about helping the environment<br>• Talking about how you look after your world<br>• Talking about your environment at home and what you are and aren't allowed to do<br>• Telling others how to care for the environment | • Opinions<br>• Superlatives<br>• We can/must/have to<br>• The imperative<br>• Negatives<br>• *(no) me permite(n)/ (no) puedo* | • Understanding and using very large numbers<br>• Carrying out and writing up a survey<br>• Making and referring to notes<br>• Reading skills<br>• Summarising and recounting<br>• Speaking and writing for different audiences using *tú* and *usted* | • Caring for the environment from the point of view of Spanish students | L&S 1.1, 1.2, 1.3, 1.4, 1.5; R&W 2.2, 2.4, 2.5; IU 3.1, 3.2; KAL 4.5, 4.6; LLS 5.1, 5.4, 5.5 |
| **Unit 4B** | **Spanish spoken here!**<br>• Giving key facts about a country<br>• Revising describing people<br>• Finding out about some Latin American festivals<br>• Talking about the importance of language learning<br>• Describing people's nationality and personality | • Comparatives and superlatives<br>• Adjectives<br>• Idiomatic uses of *tener*<br>• *soler* + infinitive when talking about the past<br>• *lo* + adjective to express opinions<br>• Adjectival agreement | • Carrying out research on the Internet<br>• Identifying false friends<br>• Pronouncing *ll*, *ñ* and *r/rr* correctly<br>• Using grammar knowledge to eliminate wrong answers in reading tasks<br>• Sounding Spanish when pronouncing cognates | • Spanish-speaking countries and people<br>• Latin American festivals | L&S 1.1, 1.2, 1.3, 1.4, 1.5; R&W 2.1, 2.2, 2.4, 2.5; IU 3.1, 3.2; KAL 4.1, 4.3, 4.4, 4.5; LLS 5.4 |

| *Zoom español 2* Long Term Plan | | | | | | | | | |
|---|---|---|---|---|---|---|---|---|---|
| | Year 8*/ Year 9 objectives | | | | | | | | |
| | Unit 0 | Unit 1A | Unit 1B | Unit 2A | Unit 2B | Unit 3A | Unit 3B | Unit 4A | Unit 4B |
| **Strand 1: Listening and speaking (L&S)** | | | | | | | | | |
| L&S 1.1: Understanding and responding to the spoken word | • | • | • | • | • | • | • | • | • |
| L&S 1.2: Developing capability and confidence in listening | • | • | • | • | • | • | • | • | • |
| L&S 1.3: Being sensitive to the spoken word | • | • | • | | | | | • | • |
| L&S 1.4: Talking together | • | • | • | • | • | • | • | • | • |
| L&S 1.5: Presenting and narrating | • | • | • | | | • | • | • | • |
| **Strand 2: Reading and Writing (R&W)** | | | | | | | | | |
| R&W 2.1: Understanding and responding to the written word | • | • | | | | • | | | • |
| R&W 2.2: Developing capability and confidence in reading | • | • | • | • | • | • | • | • | • |
| R&W 2.3: Being sensitive to the written word | | | | | | | | | |
| R&W 2.4: Adapting and building text | • | • | • | • | • | • | • | • | • |
| R&W 2.5: Writing to create meaning | • | • | • | • | • | • | • | • | • |
| **Strand 3: Intercultural understanding (IU)** | | | | | | | | | |
| IU 3.1: Appreciating cultural diversity | | • | | | | • | • | • | • |
| IU 3.2: Recognising different ways of seeing the world | • | • | • | • | • | • | • | • | • |
| **Strand 4: Knowledge about language (KAL)** | | | | | | | | | |
| KAL 4.1: Letters and sounds | • | • | | • | • | | • | | • |
| KAL 4.2: Words | | | • | | | | | | |
| KAL 4.3: Gender, number and other inflections | • | • | • | • | | | • | | • |
| KAL 4.4: Sentence structure | | • | | • | • | • | • | | • |
| KAL 4.5: Verbs and tenses | • | • | • | • | • | • | • | • | • |
| KAL 4.6: Questions and negatives | | | | • | • | • | | • | |
| **Strand 5: Language learning strategies (LLS)** | | | | | | | | | |
| LLS 5.1: Identifying patterns in the target language | • | • | • | • | • | • | • | • | |
| LLS 5.2: Memorising | | | | | | • | | | |
| LLS 5.3: Using knowledge of English or another language | | • | • | | | | | | |
| LLS 5.4: Working out meaning | • | • | • | • | • | | • | • | • |
| LLS 5.5: Using reference materials | • | • | • | • | • | | | • | |
| LLS 5.6: Reading aloud | | • | | | | | | | |
| LLS 5.7: Planning and preparing | • | | • | | | | | | |
| LLS 5.8: Evaluating and improving | • | • | | | • | | • | | |

* Year 8 objectives start in *Zoom español 1*

# Introduction

## The course

Welcome to ***Zoom español 2***

***Zoom español***

- is a broad-ability Spanish course for 11–14 year olds with a fully-integrated video drama
- is fully flexible for all abilities with opportunities for reinforcement and extension throughout
- delivers the revised Key Stage 3 Programme of Study, PLTS and the Renewed Framework for Languages.

## The components of *Zoom español 2*

### Student Book

The 176-page Student Book consists of nine main units. Two clear routes through the book are suggested, one for students following a two-year course, and one for students following a three-year course. Depending on the route followed, one unit represents either four or six weeks' work.

The Student Book contains the following sections:

#### Unidades 0–4B

There are nine 16-page units set in different contexts. Each unit has been planned to be interesting and motivating, as well as to provide a coherent and systematic approach to language development in terms of grammar, pronunciation and study skills. An outline of the content of each unit is given on pages 4–5 of this book.

Each unit is divided into:

- four core spreads each of which includes activities in all four skills, language learning tips and grammar explanations
- a fifth spread, offering more coverage of the topic areas specifically intended for students following a three-year Key Stage 3
- a grammar and skills spread *(Labolengua)* which is divided into three sections:
  Grammar (focusing on the key grammar points from the core spreads), Skills (promoting language learning strategies), and Pronunciation
- two pages of reinforcement and extension material, one for lower- and one for higher-ability students *(Extra Star* and *Extra Plus)*, which are ideal for independent work – these can be used in class by students who finish other activities quickly or as alternative homework material
- a test page *(Prueba)*, which revises the language and structures of the unit, and can also be used as a quick formative test of all four skills
- a vocabulary list and checklist
- a page of extra reading and homework material *(Leer)*.

#### Leer

***Zoom español 2*** has a nine-page reading section for students to attempt once they are confident with the core language of the unit. These pages are designed to encourage independent reading and help students develop reading strategies. There is one reading page per unit, providing activities suitable for students of all abilities. The material can be used in class by students who finish other activities quickly or for homework.

#### Gramática

The key grammar points taught in each unit are consolidated in a grammar reference section at the back of the Student Book. This section also provides extra practice activities focusing on selected grammar points. Further grammar practice is provided in the Copymasters and Workbooks, and on the *Interactive OxBox CD-ROM.*

#### Glosario

A Spanish–English glossary contains the words in the Student Book for students' reference.

### Teacher Book

Each unit contains the following detailed teaching notes:

- a Unit Overview Grid, providing a summary of the unit: contexts and objectives, language learning, grammar, key language, Renewed Framework objectives and NC levels for each spread
- a Week-by-Week overview, providing details of the two- and three-year routes through each unit
- a Planner section for each core teaching spread for ease of lesson planning, providing cross-references to other course components and including suggestions for starter, plenary and homework activities
- ideas for presenting and practising new language
- detailed notes on all the Student Book material, including answers to all activities
- suggestions for further activities to reinforce and extend the content of the Student Book
- transcripts for all listening material and video clips
- answers and transcripts for the Workbook activities
- answers for the extra practice activities in the *Gramática* section at the end of the Student Book.

### Audio CDs and MP3 files

The audio CD pack provides the listening material to accompany the Student Book (CDs 1, 2, and 3) and Workbooks (CDs 3 and 4). The Workbook audio is also available on the CDs included in each individual Workbook. Track numbers in this Teacher Book are provided for both versions. Sound files for the Student Book are also available in MP3 format on the *Interactive OxBox CD-ROM.* The Copymaster audio is provided on the *Interactive OxBox CD-ROM* and the Assessments audio is provided on the *Assessment OxBox CD-ROM.* All listening material was recorded by native speakers.

## Copymasters

The Copymasters provide opportunities for further practice and extension of the language of the Student Book units. All the Copymasters, together with answers and transcripts, are provided on the *Interactive OxBox CD-ROM*. Each unit has the following Copymasters:

- *Vocabulario:* a list of key vocabulary from the unit, which students can use as a reference or as an aid to learning
- *Ya sé...:* a checklist of the core language of the unit, providing an opportunity for students to review their progress and reflect on areas for improvement
- *Empezar y terminar:* starter and plenary activities
- *Escucha Star* and *Plus:* one page of listening activities suitable for lower-ability students and one page for higher-ability students
- *Habla:* speaking activities
- *Lee y escribe Star* and *Plus:* two pages of reading and writing activities, one page suitable for lower-ability students and one page for higher-ability students
- *Gramática:* consolidation and practice of key grammar points
- *¿Cómo se hace?:* language learning strategies
- *Extra Star* and *Plus:* extra material for students covering ***Zoom español*** in three years.

## Workbooks

Reinforcement and extension activities are provided in the ***Zoom español 2*** Foundation and Higher Workbooks. There is one page to accompany spreads 1–5 of each unit of the Student Book, followed by:

- *Labolengua:* extra grammar practice
- *Técnica:* skills practice and language learning strategies
- *Vocabulario:* a list of key vocabulary from the unit
- *Checklist:* a checklist of the core language of the unit

The Workbooks are designed for students to write in, so are ideal for setting homework. Rubrics are provided in English throughout so that students can work independently.

## OxBox CD-ROMs

The ***Zoom español*** course is accompanied by two CD-ROMs: The ***Zoom español 2*** *Interactive OxBox and the* ***Zoom español 2*** *Assessment OxBox.*

- The *Interactive OxBox* is a CD-ROM of teacher and student-oriented resources which parallel the topic coverage of ***Zoom español 2*** Student Book.
- The *Assessment OxBox* offers a suite of interactive and paper-based tests to accompany the Student Book.

OxBox also contains a "User Management" folder, into which you can import class registers and create user accounts for your students. OxBox provides two separate environments, one for teachers and one for students. Teachers have access to all of the resources; students can complete interactive activities and take tests that you have assigned to them.

OxBox is compatible with all standard Microsoft Office programs so, as well as being able to create new plans and assessments using the OxBox interface, you can also import your own Word or Excel-based lesson plans and materials into OxBox and file them in one centralised location. Many of the resources included in OxBox are themselves fully editable Word and PowerPoint files, permitting you to adapt them to the needs of a particular class or combine them with your own materials as you see fit.

The ***Zoom español 2*** *Interactive OxBox* contains:

**Lesson planning:**

- Course overviews and unit plans
- Lesson plans offering ideas and strategies for delivering the ***Zoom español*** course, and suggestions on how you can combine the different resources available in the ***Zoom español*** Student Book and on OxBox
- The lesson planner provides a simple template in which you can write additional lesson plans which link to resources in OxBox. Using the lesson planner, you can also customise existing plans, tailoring them to different classes by changing the materials used in the lesson.

**Teaching materials:**

- The video clips that are used throughout the ***Zoom español 2*** Student Book
- Audio clips: the audio for the ***Zoom español 2*** Student Book and Copymasters
- Copymasters together with answers and transcripts
- An interactive activity accompanying each unit of the ***Zoom español 2*** Student Book. These consist of a foundation screen (NC levels 1–4) and a higher screen (NC levels 2–5/6) and practise listening, reading and writing. Interactive activities include the following activity types:
  - drag and drop
  - fill the gap
  - linking lines
  - ordering
  - multiple choice
  - sorting (putting things into categories)
- A record and playback activity and a pronunciation activity to practise speaking
- Pelmanism games
- Grammar presentations which are PowerPoint adaptations of the *Labolengua* spread
- An eBook of the ***Zoom español 2*** Student Book.

The ***Zoom español 2*** *Assessment OxBox* contains:

- Formative tests, designed to be completed by students as they progress through the course, helping them to master what they have learned and improve any areas of weakness. There are formative tests in listening, speaking, reading, writing and grammar for each unit of the course, each consisting of foundation and higher level questions. Question types for the listening, reading and grammar are as for the interactive activities above. Students have two chances to answer each question, after which they can see a breakdown of which bits they got right and which they got wrong. Speaking tests are in the form of record and playback activities. Writing tests are provided as Word documents, consisting of one foundation level question and one higher level question per unit.

- Summative tests intended to help you assess students' progress and provide them with a snapshot of the level they have reached at the end of each unit. There is one summative test per unit, consisting of five questions per skill, for listening, reading and grammar. There is also a summative record and playback activity to test speaking for each unit. Summative tests are supplied in interactive form and as Word documents that can be printed out if you don't have access to the ICT suite. Summative writing tests are provided as Word documents, consisting of one foundation level question and one higher level question per unit. In a summative (interactive) assessment, students may only attempt each question once and will not receive any feedback until they see their final result at the end of the test. Once all the members of a class have sat a summative test, the results are aggregated automatically enabling you to identify areas of strength and weaknesses.
- Summative assessment guidance notes including answers, the marks available for each question and a breakdown of the National Curriculum levels that particular overall percentage scores equate to.

### Video

A key feature of ***Zoom español 2*** is a video drama focusing on three teenagers. It is available as part of the *Interactive OxBox* package. The function of the video is threefold:

- it serves to provide an authentic view of life in a Spanish-speaking country
- it introduces three aspirational Spanish-speaking characters, providing students with added motivation for learning Spanish
- it provides examples of key language in use, translating language learning from theory into practice.

There is a video clip for each unit. This is in the form of an episode of the video drama featuring three teenagers and ties in with activities on one or more of the four core spreads.

Each video drama can be used in its entirety to set the scene for the corresponding unit. Later in the unit, excerpts from the video drama will be used again to focus on specific language points.

When using the video drama as a unit starter, try to concentrate initially on visual content rather than on an understanding of the script. This helps to boost students' confidence in their ability to cope with authentic speech: it shows that even without understanding everything that is said, it is still possible to work out quite a lot by focusing on visual information, body language, tone of voice, etc.

Set students other visual challenges: for example, ask them to spot Spanish signs on buildings, city landmarks, etc. – a few suggestions are given at the start of the teaching notes for each unit. Students will enjoy showing how sharp-eyed they are! In later units, challenge them to identify familiar language in the clip before you move on to focus on the new language points.

The videos show Spanish being spoken in a real-life context but are made accessible for all via the activities and support provided in the Student Book and suggested in the teaching notes. This approach enables students of all abilities to experience authentic material at a higher level.

## Course progression

***Zoom español*** is a two-part course, consisting of two Student Books of nine units each. It caters both for schools following a two-year Key Stage 3 and for those following a three-year Key Stage 3 by offering different 'routes' through each unit.

- For the three-year Key Stage 3, we suggest that you cover each unit in its entirety, including core spreads 1–4, the optional spread 5 (which provides more in-depth coverage of the unit themes) and spread 6 (grammar and skills), selecting additional material from the Extra and Leer pages as appropriate. This provides sufficient material for a half-term's teaching per unit. Following this route, two units are covered per term.
- For the two-year Key Stage 3, we suggest that your main focus should be core spreads 1–4 and spread 6 (grammar and skills), but that you may wish to use additional material selectively if time permits. On the core spreads themselves, certain activities are optional, so you may wish to use these selectively too. In the teaching notes, we have used pale grey highlighting to identify core activities on the core spreads, so that it is easy to see what is optional and what is essential. Following this 'accelerated' route, three units are covered per term.

The Week-by-Week overviews, which can be found at the beginning of each unit's teaching notes in this book, give a detailed breakdown of which activities and spreads to cover each week according to the route you are following.

| | **Suggested 2-year pathway** | **Suggested 3-year pathway** |
|---|---|---|
| **1st year** | Book 1 Units 0–1B | Book 1 Units 0–1A |
| | Book 1Units 2A–3A | Book 1 Units 1B–2A |
| | Book 1Units 3B–4B | Book 1 Units 2B–3A |
| **2nd year** | Book 2 Units 0–1B | Book 1 Units 3B–4A |
| | Book 2Units 2A–3A | Book 1 Unit 4B,<br>Book 2 Unit 0 |
| | Book 2Units 3B–4B | Book 2 Units 1A–1B |
| **3rd year** | | Book 2 Units 2A–2B |
| | | Book 2 Units 3A–3B |
| | | Book 2 Units 4A–4B |

## PLTS in Zoom español 2

A key aim of ***Zoom español 2*** is that students should be able to learn in a meaningful way, thinking flexibly, analysing language, problem solving, justifying answers and making predictions based on previous knowledge. The activity types included in ***Zoom español 2*** help to promote thinking skills and creativity. The Planner section at the beginning of each spread lists some of the activities that promote any one of the six personal learning and thinking skills. As a guide, the following features and types of activity in ***Zoom español 2*** help to promote the six PLTS:

- **Independent enquirers**
  - Video drama, Leer section: provide stimulus material prompting students to explore aspects of Spanish lifestyle and culture and to consider different attitudes and perspectives.
- **Creative thinkers**
  - *Think* boxes throughout, *Labolengua*: encourage students to think creatively about language, e.g. by identifying and explaining language patterns, working out meaning and developing language learning strategies.
  - *Challenge* (on spreads 1–5 of each unit) and other open-ended activities: provide opportunities for students to give a creative or personal response to the unit themes.
- **Reflective learners**
  - Spread objectives: clearly state the focus of each spread so that students know what they are about to learn and can review their progress afterwards.
  - NC levels shown for key activities in the Student Book: this helps students to evaluate their progress and set goals. Some of the *Think* boxes encourage sharing of assessment criteria with students, so that they understand what needs to be done in order to achieve a particular NC level.
  - *Prueba* and "I can …" checklist (end of each unit): opportunity for students to review what they've learned and reflect on areas for improvement.
- **Team workers**
  - Opportunities throughout for students to work together in pairs and groups.
- **Self-managers**
  - *Think* boxes, *Labolengua*: encourage students to take responsibility for their own learning.
  - *Glosario* (end-of-unit, end-of-book), *Gramática* (end-of-book): encourage independent use of reference materials.
  - *Prueba* and "I can …" checklist: opportunity for students to review what they've learned and set their own goals for improvement.
  - *Extra Star, Extra Plus, Leer* section: ideal for independent work.
  - Workbooks: designed for self-study.
- **Effective participators**
  - Opportunities throughout for students to engage with issues of interest to young people and to consider different attitudes and perspectives.

## The Renewed MFL Framework

- ***Zoom español*** has been carefully planned to ensure that all Framework objectives are covered in familiar contexts.
- **The Long Term Plan** on page 6 of this book provides an overview of the objectives to be covered in ***Zoom español 2***.
- **The Summary of Unit Contents** grid on page 4 shows the objectives covered in each unit of ***Zoom español 2***.
- **The Unit Overview grids** which can be found at the beginning of the teaching notes for each unit in this book show which objectives are covered in each spread of each unit.
- The **Planner** section at the beginning of each spread includes a list of the objectives covered in that spread.

***Zoom español*** reflects the focus of the Renewed MFL Framework on key areas of teaching and learning. These include:

- Starters – suggestions for starter activities for each core spread are given in the Planner sections in this Teacher Book and are given in the lesson plans on the OxBox Interactive CD-ROM. Additional starter activities are provided on the *Empezar y terminar* Copymasters.
- Setting lesson objectives – The Planner sections provide a clear list of objectives for each spread.
- Modelling – ***Zoom español*** provides clear examples for all activities where appropriate.
- Questioning
- Practice
- Plenaries – suggestions for plenary activities for each core spread are given in the Planner sections in this Teacher Book and are given in the lesson plans on the OxBox Interactive CD-ROM. Additional plenary activities are provided on the *Empezar y terminar* Copymasters.

# 0 Conocer personas nuevas

## Unit Objectives

**Contexts and cultural focus:** meeting new people, going out
**Grammar:** questions, *ser* and *estar* to describe character and mood, *me llevo bien con .../me cae mal ..., conmigo/contigo/con él/ con ella*, etc., the personal *a*
**Language learning:** greeting people formally and informally, being aware of false friends, revising opinions, accepting/refusing politely, responding politely

- *Aim*: To learn how to speak about other people
- Each unit has an associated video which will feature throughout the unit. Below is the transcript of the video for this unit.

**Video clip: Unit 0 (CD 1, track 6)**

**Part 1**

*Elena, Juan and Roberto are hanging out in the old town with a view over Segovia.*

Elena: Hola soy Elena y este es mi primo. ¿Cómo te llamas?
Roberto: Ah sí. Me llamo Roberto.
Elena: ¿Y de dónde eres?
Roberto: Ya lo sabes, soy de Colombia.
Elena: Y vas a estar en Segovia tres meses.
Roberto: Mucho tiempo.
Elena: Pero, te llevas bien conmigo. ¿A que sí?
Roberto: Sí. Me llevo bien contigo. ¡Cuando está de buen humor!
Juan: Y yo soy Juan. Soy el hermano de Elena y claro Roberto es mi primo también.
Elena: ¡No me llevo bien con Juan es muy pesado! Y dice mentiras.
Roberto: Pero a mí, me cae bien porque cuenta muchas chistes.
Juan: ¡Bienvenidos a nuestra familia!

**Part 2**

Roberto: ¿Qué vamos a hacer hoy?
Elena: ¿Cuánto dinero tenemos?
Roberto: Yo tengo diez euros.
Juan: Yo tengo cinco euros.
Elena: Yo tengo diez euros también. Este es el problema, nunca tenemos mucho dinero.
Roberto: Pero, ¿Qué vamos a hacer hoy?
Elena: Me gustaría ir al cine. ¿Te gustaría venir conmigo?
Roberto: Sí, me gustaría. Juan, ¿vienes?
Juan: Depende ¿Qué vamos a ver?
Elena: Me gustaría ver Transformers en 3D.
Roberto: Pero, antes de las 7. A las nueve hay un partido de futbol en la tele que quiero ver.
Elena: Y no podemos gastar más de 25 euros en las tres entradas.
Juan: ¿Transformers en 3D, antes de las siete, y tres entradas por menos de 25 euros?
Roberto: Va a ser difícil.
Elena: Vamos a intentarlo.
Juan: A ver quién gana.

Opción A

*Inside a cinema at the ticket booth*

Employee: Hola buenos días. ¿En qué te puedo ayudar?
Elena: Me gustaría ver Transformers en 3D. ¿A qué hora hay sesiones?
Employee: ¿Para qué día?
Elena: Para hoy.
Employee: Hoy tenemos entradas a las 18.45 y a las 21.30.
Elena: ¿A cuánto son las entradas?
Employee: Hay entradas a 8.50 euros y 9.50 euros para las películas en 3D.
Elena: ¿Y tienen descuento para estudiantes?
Employee: Sí, tenemos entradas a 7 euros para estudiantes menores de 18 años.

Opción B

*Roberto looking at a poster.*

Roberto: A ver, aquí ponen Transformers a las 18.45 y a las 21.30 – ¡qué bien! Pero¿Qué día es hoy? Hoy es miércoles. Podemos ir a la sesión de las 18.45. ¿Cuánto costarán las entradas? Las entradas cuestan 8.50 euros o 9.50 euros. ¿Habrá descuento para jóvenes?

Option C

*Juan outside the theatre looking at the "have your birthday at the cinema" poster.*

Juan: Hola, buenos días. ¿Hay alguna sesión de Transformers hoy?
Employee: Sí, tenemos una sesión que empieza a las 18.45.
Juan: ¿Y es una sesión 3D?
Employee: Por supuesto.
Juan: ¿Y cuánto cuestan las entradas?
Employee: Tenemos entradas a 9 euros con cincuenta y a 7 euros con descuento para jóvenes.
Juan: ¿Y la oferta "cumpleaños"?
Employee: Cuando es tu cumpleaños tienes 4 entradas por 8 euros cada una y el del cumpleaños para gratis, con palomitas y bebidas incluidas.

Resultado

Elena: A ver, queremos ver Transformers en 3D antes de las 7 y queremos gastarnos menos de 25 euros. ¿Roberto?

Roberto: Hay sesión a las 18.45. Hay entradas a 9 euros con cincuenta, pero no sé si hay descuentos para jóvenes. ¿Y tú Elena?

Elena: Sesión a las 18.45 y entradas con descuento para jóvenes a 7 euros cada una. ¿Y tú Juan?

Juan: Sesión a las 18.45 con 4 entradas, palomitas y bebida incluidas y por solo 24 euros.

*Repeat of correct scene with added ending.*

Juan: Hola buenos días. ¿Hay alguna sesión de Transformers hoy?

Employee: Sí, tenemos una sesión que empieza a las 18.45.

Juan: ¿Y es una sesión 3D?

Employee: Por supuesto.

Juan: ¿Y cuánto cuestan las entradas?

Employee: Tenemos entradas a 9.50 euros y a 7 euros con descuento para jóvenes.

Juan: ¿Y la oferta "cumpleaños"?

Employee: Cuando es tu cumpleaños tienes 4 entradas por 8 euros cada una y el del cumpleaños para gratis, con palomitas y bebidas incluidas.

Juan: Pues, hoy es mi cumple.

Employee: Felicidades. Aquí tienes las cuatro entradas.

Juan: Y aquí tiene los 25 euros.

Employee: Toma.

Juan: Muchas gracias.

*Back outside.*

Elena: Pero Juan – hoy no es tu cumpleaños.

Roberto: Además tienes cuatro entradas y somos tres. ¿A quién vas a invitar?

Juan: *On the phone.* Hola Nati, ¿te vienes conmigo al cine esta tarde? Te invito.

**Punto Lengua**

Hola soy Elena y este es mi primo.
Ah sí. Me llamo Roberto.
Y yo soy Juan. Soy el hermano de Elena.
No me llevo bien con Juan, es muy pesado.
Pero a mí, me cae muy bien porque cuenta muchos chistes.

As a starter activity to introduce the unit and familiarise students with the language they will meet, you may find it useful for the class to view the video as a whole. Are there any words or phrases that they have recognised? What do they think it is about? Watch the first part. Explain that you will look at it in more detail later in this unit.

*Synopsis:*
Elena, Juan and their cousin Roberto want to go to the cinema to see a film, but the problem is, they don't have much money and the film needs to start before 7pm. Who can find a suitable film to watch?

**Unit 0 Conocer personas nuevas Overview grid**

| Page reference | Contexts and objectives | Language learning | Grammar | Key language | Framework | AT level |
|---|---|---|---|---|---|---|
| Pages 4–5 **¡Bienvenido!** | • meeting and greeting people; talking about a journey | • greet people formally and informally | • use the imperfect tense; ask questions about someone's journey | *Bienvenido/a; Encantado/a; ¿Qué tal el viaje? soy; Vale; Vamos; era; fatal; largo; incómodo; Había mucho tráfico. el avión; el tren; el barco; el coche; cómodo/ incómodo; rápido; ruidoso; aburrido; de retraso* | L&S 1.1, 1.2, 1.3; R&W 2.4, 2.5; KAL 4.1; LLS 5.4 | 1.3, 2.3, 3.2, 4.3–5 |
| Pages 6–7 **¿Cómo estás?** | • say how you feel | • be aware of 'false friends' | • use *ser* to describe character and *estar* to describe mood | *Soy: pesado/a; generoso/a; divertido/a; simpático/a; testarudo/a; inteligente Estoy: aburrido/a; contento/a; decepcionado/a; furioso/a; ilusionado/a; triste* | L&S 1.1, 1.2, 1.3, 1.4; R&W 2.4, 2.5; KAL 4.3, 4.5; LLS 5.4 | 1.4, 2.2, 3.2, 3.4, 4.3–4 |

| | | | | | | |
|---|---|---|---|---|---|---|
| Pages 8–9 **Me llevo bien con Elena** | • say if you get on with your friends and family | • revise opinions | • *me llevo bien con ... / me cae mal ...* | *llevarse bien/mal con; caer bien/mal; no soporto a ...; (no) me ayuda; (no) me escucha; (no) me habla (mucho); (no) dice mentiras; (no) cuenta chismes; (no) es pesado/a; (no) es estricto/a; siempre está de mal humor; nunca está de mal humor* | L&S 1.2, 1.4; R&W 2.2, 2.4; LLS: 5.1, 5.7 | 1.3, 2.3–4, 3.2–3.4, 4.3–4 |
| Pages 10–11 **¿Vienes conmigo?** | • accept and refuse invitations, buy cinema tickets | • accept and refuse politely | • understand use of the personal *a*, use *conmigo/ contigo* | *¿A qué hora hay sesiones? Hoy hay una sesión a las 21 horas. Tenemos una sesión que empieza a las 21 horas. ¿A cuánto son las entradas? ¿Cuánto cuestan las entradas? Hay entradas a 8.50 euros. Tenemos entradas a 8.50. Las entradas cuestan 8.50 euros. ¿Tienen algún descuento para estudiantes? ¿Vienes? Voy a ...; Me gustaría ir ...; ¿Te gustaría venir? Lo siento, no puedo. ¿Quieres venir conmigo? el rechazo; la excusa; aceptar; rechazar; cortés/cortesa; grosero/a* | L&S 1.1, 1.2, 1.3, 1.4, 1.5; IU 3.2; LLS 5.1 | 1.4, 2.3–4, 3.3, 4.3–4 |
| Pages 12–13 **Excusas, excusas** | • make excuses | • respond politely | • *conmigo, contigo, con él, con ella,* etc. | | L&S 1.1, 1.2, 1.3, 1.4, 1.5; R&W 2.2, 2.4; LLS 5.1, 5.4 | 1.5 , 2.4–5, 3.3, 3.5, 4.4–5 |
| Pages 14–15 **Labolengua** | • review language and grammar from the unit | | | | KAL 4.1, 4.5; LLS 5.1, 5.5, 5.8 | |
| Pages 16–17 **Extra Star Extra Plus** | • differentiated extension/ homework material | • revise and consolidate all vocabulary and grammar covered in the unit | • revise and consolidate all vocabulary and grammar covered in the unit | | R&W 2.2, 2.4; KAL 4.5 | 3.2–4, 4.2–3 |
| Page 18 **Prueba** | • end-of-unit test | | | | L&S 1.1, 1.2, 1.4; R&W 2.2, 2.4; KAL 4.3, 4.5 | 1.3, 2.3, 3.4, 4.3–4 |
| Page 19 **Vocabulario** | • a summary of the key language covered in each core spread of this unit | | | | | |
| Page 148 **Leer 0** | • practice of longer reading texts based on the theme of the unit | | | | R&W 2.1, 2.4 | 3.4 |

**Week-by-week overview**
**(Three-year KS3 Route: assuming six weeks' work or approximately 10–12.5 hours)**
**(Two-year KS3 Route: assuming four weeks' worth or approxmately 6.5-8.5 hours)**

**About Unit 0, *Conocer personas nuevas:*** Students work in the context of meeting and greeting new people. They also talk about how they feel and if they get on with family and friends. They practise buying cinema tickets, accepting and refusing invitations and making excuses. Students use questions to ask about journeys and use *ser* and *estar* to describe character and mood. They also use *me llevo bien con ..., me cae mal ..., conmigo, contigo, con él, con ella,* etc. and look at the use of the personal *a*. The unit also provides tips on language learning techniques.

| Three-Year KS3 Route | | | Two-Year KS3 Route | | |
|---|---|---|---|---|---|
| **Week** | **Resources** | **Objectives** | **Week** | **Resources** | **Objectives** |
| **1** | **0.1 ¡Bienvenido!**<br>**0.6 Labolengua E** (p.15) | meet and greet people; talk about a journey<br>use the imperfect tense; ask questions about someone's journey<br>greet people formally and informally | **1** | **0.1 ¡Bienvenido!** (Omit activities 2, 4 & Challenge)<br>**0.6 Labolengua E** (p.15)<br>**Omit activity 6** | meet and greet people; talk about a journey<br>use the imperfect tense; ask questions about someone's journey<br>greet people formally and informally |
| **2** | **0.2 ¿Cómo estás?**<br>**0.6 Labolengua A, B, C** (p.14) | say how you feel<br>use *ser* to describe character and *estar* to describe mood;<br>be aware of 'false friends' | **2** | **0.2 ¿Cómo estás?** (Omit activities 4, Think & Challenge)<br>**0.6 Labolengua A, B** (p.14) | say how you feel<br>use *ser* to describe character and *estar* to describe mood;<br>be aware of 'false friends' |
| **3** | **0.3 Me llevo bien con Elena**<br>**0.6 Labolengua F** (p.15) | say if you get on with your friends and family<br>*me llevo bien con ... / me cae mal ...*<br>revise opinions | **3** | **0.3 Me llevo bien con Elena** (Omit activities 6 & Challenge)<br>**0.6 Labolengua F** (p.15) | say if you get on with your friends and family<br>*me llevo bien con ... / me cae mal ...*<br>revise opinions |
| **4** | **0.4 ¿Vienes conmigo?**<br>**0.6 Labolengua D** (p.14) | accept and refuse invitations, buy cinema tickets<br>understand use of the personal *a;* use *conmigo/contigo*<br>accept and refuse politely | **4** | **0.4 ¿Vienes conmigo?** (Omit activities 6, Think & Challenge)<br>**0.6 Labolengua D** (p.14)<br>**0.8 Prueba** (p.18)<br>**Vocabulario** (p.19) | accept and refuse invitations<br>buy cinema tickets, understand use of the personal *a*<br>use *conmigo/contigo;* accept and refuse politely<br>Prepare and carry out assessment in all four skills<br>Recapping on vocabulary of the unit |
| **5** | **0.5 Excusas, excusas** | make excuses<br>*conmigo, contigo, con él, con ella* etc.<br>respond politely | | | |
| **6** | **0.7 Extra (Star)** (p.52)<br>**0.7 Extra (Plus)** (p.53)<br>**0.8 Prueba** (p.54)<br>**Vocabulario** (p.55)<br>**Leer** (p.148) | Further reinforcement and extension of the language of the unit.<br>Prepare and carry out assessment in all four skills<br>Recapping on vocabulary of the unit<br>Further reading to explore the language of the unit and cultural themes | | | |

## 0.1 ¡Bienvenido!

páginas 4–5

# Planner

### Objectives
- practise meeting and greeting people; talk about a journey
- use the imperfect tense; ask questions about someone's journey
- greet people formally and informally

### Resources
Student Book, pages 4–5
CD 1, tracks 2–3
Foundation Workbook, page 8
Higher Workbook, page 8
Foundation Workbook audio, CD 3, track 28 (Workbook 8)
Higher Workbook audio, CD 4, track 8
Interactive OxBox, Unit 0
Copymasters 1–8

### Key language
*Bienvenido/a; Encantado/a; ¿Qué tal el viaje? soy; Vale; Vamos; era; fatal; largo; incómodo; Había mucho tráfico. el avión; el tren; el barco; el coche; cómodo/incómodo; rápido; ruidoso; aburrido; de retraso; Estoy mareado/a*

### Grammar
- an introduction to the imperfect tense

### Renewed Framework references
L&S 1.1, 1.2, 1.3; R&W 2.4, 2.5; KAL 4.1; LLS 5.4

### PLTS
Activity 1: Self-managers
Activity 3: Independent enquirers
Activity 4: Effective participators
Activity 5: Reflective learners
Activity 6: Reflective learners
Challenge: Creative thinkers

### Starters
- Go round the class practising greetings. You start: *¡Hola! Soy Señor, Señora, Señorita …*; the student nearest you then continues, *Y yo soy…* and so on until all students have introduced themselves.
- Students play a memory game called *¿Qué tal el viaje?*. You start by asking a student *¿Qué tal el viaje?*. He or she replies, e.g. *El avión era cómodo*. Next ask another student *¿Qué tal el viaje?*. This student must repeat what the first student said and then add a sentence of his/her own, e.g. *El avión era cómodo y el tren era rápido*. And so on until students run out of new ideas.

### Plenaries
- Challenge students to write five sentences on the theme of the spread using the key language. More able students should include connectives and adjectives to make their sentences as interesting as possible.
- Students describe the worst journey ever! They should include as many forms of transport as possible and as many negative adjectives as possible, e.g. *El tren era muy ruidoso, y de retraso, y el barco era muy, muy incómodo. Estoy mareada. El coche era cómodo pero había mucho tráfico, y era aburrido*. Volunteers could read their descriptions to the class who votes for the 'worst' journey.

### Homework/Self-study
Students make up their own conversation based on the conversation in Activity 1. They could practise it with a partner in class.

AT 1.3 | PLTS | L&S1.1, 1.2

**1 Escucha y pon en orden la conversación.**
Students listen and then order the conversation. Give them time to read through the sentences first and to decide what they think the order will be.

**CD 1, track 2** — **página 4, actividad 1**

Elena: ¡Hola! Soy Elena.
Juan: Y yo soy Juan.
Roberto: ¡Encantado! Soy Roberto.
Elena: Bienvenido a Segovia.
Roberto: ¡Gracias!
Juan: ¿Qué tal el viaje?
Roberto: Bien, gracias. El avión era cómodo y el tren era rápido.
Elena: ¡Vamos!
Roberto: ¡Vale!

*Answers:*
*8, 1, 10, 2, 9, 4, 3, 7, 5, 6*

AT 4.3

**2 Escribe la conversación en el orden correcto.**
Students now write the conversation from Activity 1 in the correct order.

*Answers:*
*as in transcript for Activity 1*

AT 3.2 | PLTS | LLS 5.4

**3 Empareja las frases en español con las frases en inglés.**
Students match the Spanish expressions to the English ones.

*Answers:*
***1** d; **2** f ;**3** a; **4** h; **5** g; **6** e; **7** b; **8** c*

AT 2.3 | PLTS | KAL 4.1

**4 Practica la conversación con tu compañero.**
Students practise the conversation from Activity 1 with a partner. Allow them to listen to the script again and mark each other for correct pronunciation.

AT 1.3 | PLTS | LLS 5.4

**5 Escucha. Empareja las conversaciones con los dibujos.**
Students listen and match each conversation to the correct picture. Before they listen to the recording, ask them to study the pictures and to think about vocabulary they may hear for each one.

**CD 1, track 3** **página 5, actividades 5 y 6**

**1**
– ¡Hola, Andrés! ¿Qué tal el viaje?
– Pues, ¡fenomenal! El avión era rápido y cómodo.

**2**
– ¡Hola, Angelita! ¿Qué tal el viaje?
– ¡Fatal! Muy largo, y el barco era muy, muy incómodo. Estoy mareada.

**3**
– ¡Hola, abuela! ¿Qué tal el viaje?
– Muy malo, mi niña, muy malo. El tren era muy ruidoso.

**4**
– ¡Buenas tardes, señor Morales! ¿Qué tal el viaje?
– Pues, así así. El coche era cómodo pero había mucho tráfico, y fue aburrido.

*Answers:*
***1** b; **2** d; **3** a; **4** c*

## Think

This is to be used alongside Activity 5. Ask students how the last person greets the last traveller? Elicit *Buenos tardes*. Next ask students why this is? Discuss the difference between *tú* and *usted* and ask students to think back to previous units and of other instances where they have used *tú* and *usted*. Finally, ask them how they would greet people politely in English to show that you don't necessarily need different words for "you" to show you are being polite.

KAL 4.1

## Think

Draw students' attention to the different pronunciation of **r** and **rr** and work through the examples given.

AT 1.3 | PLTS | L&S 1.1, 1.2

**6 Escucha otra vez. ¿Qué tipo de transporte era? ¿Qué tal el viaje?**
Students listen again to the audio from Activity 5, note down the type of transport mentioned and say how the journey went.

*Answers:*
***1** avión – fenomenal, rápido, cómodo; **2** barco – muy largo, muy incómodo; **3** tren – muy ruidoso; **4** coche – cómodo, mucho tráfico, aburrido*

AT 3.2 | R&W 2.4 | L&S 1.3

**7 ¿Formal o informal? Clasifica las frases.**
Further work on formal and informal language. Students read the sentences and note down whether each one is formal or informal.

*Answers:*
*formal – 2, 3; informal – 1, 4*

KAL 4.1

## Think

Remind students that **n** and **ñ** are two different letters in Spanish. Practise pronouncing these letters to ensure all students understand how they sound different. Ask students to list any words they already know that contain **ñ** (*año, araña, bañarse, campaña, cariñoso, castaño, castañuelas, cumpleaños, español, mañana, niño, otoño, pequeño, piña, señora* are all in *Zoom español 1*).

AT 4.3–4 | R&W 2.4

**8 Escribe y crea un dibujo animado en el aeropuerto o en la estación de tren. Usa las actividades 1 y 6 para ayudarte.**
Students will find a copy of the transcript for Activity 5 helpful at this point. They can do it in cartoon strip form, or use pictures out of a magazine, etc. to illustrate it. It could also be done as a PowerPoint.

PLTS | AT 4.3–5 | R&W 2.4, 2.5

## Challenge

**With your partner, write and act out a scene where you meet someone at an airport or station. How good or bad was the journey?**
Encourage students to go as far as their ability allows in saying what kind of journey they had. It is those who use the imperfect who will obtain a level 5. Remind students that their writing will flow better and sound more interesting if they use words like *muy, un poco, bastante,* etc. The rest of the class could award points for creativity, good acting, unusual Spanish, etc.

## 0.2 ¿Cómo estás? páginas 6–7

# *Planner*

### Objectives
- say how you feel
- use *ser* to describe character and *estar* to describe mood
- be aware of 'false friends'

### Resources
Student Book, pages 6–7
CD 1, track 4
Foundation Workbook, page 9
Higher Workbook, page 9
Foundation Workbook audio, CD 3, track 29 (Workbook 9)
Higher Workbook audio, CD 4, track 9
Interactive OxBox, Unit 0
Copymasters 1–8

### Key language
*Soy: pesado/a; generoso/a; divertido/a; simpático/a; testarudo/a; inteligente*
*Estoy: aburrido/a; contento/a; decepcionado/a; furioso/a; ilusionado/a; triste*

### Renewed Framework references
L&S 1.1, 1.2, 1.3, 1.4; R&W 2.4, 2.5; KAL 4.3, 4.5; LLS 5.4

### PLTS
Activity 1: Independent enquirers
Activity 2: Self-managers
Activity 3: Effective participators
Activity 4: Reflective learners
Activity 5: Reflective learners
Activity 6: Self-managers
Challenge: Creative thinkers

### Starters
- Display the headings *Soy* and *Estar* and, in jumbled order next to these, the rest of the key language. Give students a time limit to categorise each word under *Soy* or *Estar*. Check answers as a class.
- Ask students to give you as many 'moods' and character traits as they can think of. Display this and add any they have missed. Ask a confident volunteer to come to the front and act out one of the words, e.g. *contento/a*. The rest of the class guesses which word he/she is acting out. The student who guesses correctly then has a go at the front.

### Plenaries
- Display the list from Starter Activity 1. Challenge students to write five sentences using this key language, e.g. *De momento, estoy furioso/a*. More able students should extend their sentences to give reasons as well, e.g. *Estoy furioso/a, porque mamá dice que no puedo ir a la discoteca*. Also encourage more able students to use *ser* or *estar* in as many forms as possible, i.e. *estamos, sois*, etc. Compare answers as a class.

### Homework/Self-study
Student Book, p.6, Activity 4
Student Book, p.7, Challenge: students find a photo of their favourite celebrity, a friend or someone in their family to use in the Challenge Activity.

AT 3.2 | AT 4.3 | PLTS | KAL 4.3 | LLS 5.4

**1 Responde a las preguntas.**
Students study the illustration and answer the questions. Draw attention to the adjectival endings and elicit why they are different (agreement – masculine, singular, etc.). Use the Think box alongside this activity to highlight the 'false friend' *decepcionado*. Point out that an easy way to remember this if to think that if you are deceived you are *disappointed*. Students could remember *ilusionado* by thinking of a magician's trick or illusion which can be very exciting! Also look at the Grammar box and draw attention to the agreement of the adjectival endings. Can students remember the rule from Zoom 1 Unit 1B?

*Answers:*
***1*** *triste;* ***2*** *decepcionadas;* ***3*** *ilusionados;* ***4*** *contento;*
***5*** *furiosa;* ***6*** *aburridos*

AT 1.4 | PLTS | L&S 1.1, 1.2, 1.3

**2 Escucha. Escoge la palabra correcta de la actividad 1. ¿Por qué están así?**
Students listen and use the words in the box to explain how each person is feeling. They then note down why each person is feeling this way.

CD 1, track 4 **página 6, actividad 2**

**1**
Roberto: ¿Cómo estás, mamá?
Mamá: Estoy triste, hijo, porque tú estás en España.

**2**
Roberto: ¿Cómo estás, papá?
Papá: Estoy contento, hijo, porque tengo un coche nuevo.

**3**
Roberto: ¿Cómo estáis, abuelos?
Abuela: Estamos ilusionados, porque ¡nos vamos de vacaciones a Méjico!

**4**
Roberto: ¿Cómo estás, Gabriela?
Gabriela: Ahora mismo, estoy furiosa, porque mamá dice que no puedo ir a la discoteca.

**5**
Roberto: ¿Cómo estáis, Ricardo y Rogelio?
Ricardo: En estos momentos, estamos aburridos. Está lloviendo y no podemos jugar al fútbol.

**6**
Roberto: ¿Cómo estáis, María e Isabel?
María y Isabel: Estamos decepcionadas. No podemos ir al cine porque no tenemos bastante dinero.

*Answers:*
***1** mamá – triste – Roberto está en España; **2** papá – contento – nuevo coche; **3** abuelos – ilusionados – van de vacaciones; **4** Gabriela – furiosa – no puede ir a la discoteca; **5** Ricardo y Rogelio – aburridos – no pueden jugar al fútbol; **6** María e Isabel – decepcionadas – no pueden ir al cine*

AT 2.2 | L&S 1.4 | PLTS

**3 Habla con tu compañero. ¿Cómo estás? ¿Quién eres?**
This is a simple guessing game. Less able students can use the photos for support; more able ones can memorise who feels what first, then see if B can remember correctly when A says how 'they' feel.

AT 4.3 | PLTS | KAL 4.3, 4.5

**4 Escribe. ¿Cómo están en este momento? ¿Qué dicen?**
Students use singular and plural forms of the first person of *estar* and make the correct adjectival agreements.

*Answers:*
***1** Estoy contenta. **2** Estamos decepcionadas. **3** Estoy aburrido.*

KAL 4.3

## Think

Students think about adjectival endings and exceptions to the normal rules. The second Think box emphasises the importance of using *ser* and *estar* correctly. Students will do more work on this in Activity 5.

AT 3.4 | PLTS | L&S 1.4

**5 Clasifica los adjetivos en la descripción de la familia de Roberto. ¿Carácter o sentimiento? Busca las palabras que no conoces en un diccionario, o pregunta al profesor o a tu compañero.**
This practises the verbs *ser* and *estar* and when to use each of these. Get students to look for the words they don't know in a dictionary or ask their partner or the teacher. The only new character words are *pesado* and *generoso*.

*Answers:*
***carácter:** simpática, divertido, testarudos, pesada, generosos, inteligentes. **sentimiento:** triste, contento, furiosa, aburridos, ilusionados, decepcionadas*

AT 4.3–4 | PLTS | R&W 2.4 | KAL 4.3

**6 Escribe. Describe a ti mismo. ¿Cómo te llamas? ¿Cómo eres? ¿Cómo estás en este momento?**
This is an open-ended task. Brainstorm some reasons with the class first. Display one of the moods, e.g. *furioso* and elicit possible reasons for being in this mood, e.g. *tengo que hacer mis deberes, no puedo ir al cine,* etc. Encourage students to use language they already know and apply it to this situation rather than try to translate complicated reasons.

AT 4.4 | PLTS | R&W 2.4, 2.5 | KAL 4.3

## Challenge

**Find a photo of your favourite celebrity, a friend or someone in your family. Tell your partner about them, or write a description. Who are they? What are they like? How are they feeling in the picture?**
This activity could either be done as a piece of written work or an oral presentation. More able students could write about more than one person.

## 0.3 Me llevo bien con Elena

páginas 8–9

# *Planner*

### Objectives
- say if you get on with your friends and family
- *me llevo bien con ... / me cae mal ...*
- revise opinions

### Resources
Student Book, pages 8–9
CD 1, track 5
Foundation Workbook, page 10
Higher Workbook, page 10
Foundation Workbook audio, CD 3, track 30 (Workbook 10)
Higher Workbook audio, CD 4, track 10
Interactive OxBox, Unit 0
Copymasters 1–8

### Key language
*llevarse bien/mal con; (no) me llevo bien con...; caer bien/mal; (no) me cae bien...; no soporto a ...; (no) me ayuda; (no) me escucha; (no) me habla (mucho); (no) dice mentiras; (no) cuenta chismes; (no) es pesado/a; (no) es estricto/a; siempre está de mal humor; nunca está de mal humor; en cambio*

### Renewed Framework references
L&S 1.2, 1.4; R&W 2.2, 2.4; LLS: 5.1, 5.7

### PLTS
Activity 1: Independent enquirers
Activity 3: Effective participators
Activity 4: Reflective learners
Activity 6: Effective participators
Challenge: Team workers

### Starters
- Display the headings *me llevo bien con ... porque...* and *no me llevo bien con ... porque ...* and ask students to think of as many reasons as possible to go under each of these headings, e.g. *nunca está de mal humor*, etc.
- Play a class game. A volunteer leaves the class for a few minutes. Explain that when he/she comes back into the classroom, he/she must ask the rest of the class questions to find out which five students don't get on with certain members of their family, e.g. *Te llevas bien con tu familia?*. While the student is absent, allocate sentences about how students get on with members of their family. Most of the students will have positive sentences, e.g. *Me llevo muy bien con mi padre*. Five will have negative sentences, e.g. *Me llevo mal con mi prima porque...* Once the volunteer has found these five students, choose a new volunteer.

### Plenary
- Students make up a family and describe all of the family members saying why they do/don't like each one. Remind them that the family is made up and they can make their work as humorous as they like as long as the language is correct. You may want to display the list from Starter Activity 1 for support. A few volunteers could present their fictional family to the class.

### Homework/Self-study
Activity 3: After completing this activity, students write down who they do and don't get on with.
Gramática: Students make up more sentences using the *llevarse bien/mal con* and *caer bien/mal*.

PLTS | AT 1.3 | AT 3.2 | L&S 1.2

**1 Escucha. ¿Qué dice Elena?**
Before students attempt this activity, look at the vocabulary box as a class. Check that they understand what the new vocabulary means and that they understand how to use the expressions negatively and positively, e.g. *me llevo bien, no me llevo bien, me llevo mal, no me llevo mal*, etc.

**CD 1, track 5** — **página 8, actividades 1 y 2**

**1**
Roberto: A ver, Elena, ¿te llevas bien con tu familia?
Elena: Pues, me llevo muy bien con mi padre porque es divertido.

**2**
Roberto: ¿Y tu madre? ¿Es simpática?
Elena: Sí, es simpática pero no me cae bien porque es demasiado estricta.

**3**
Roberto: ¿Qué tal tu hermano Juan?
Elena: ¡Qué va! ¡No soporto a Juan – es muy pesado!

**4**
Roberto: ¿Y tu abuelo?
Elena: Me llevo bien con mi abuelo porque me ayuda mucho.

**5**
Roberto: ¿Te llevas bien con tu prima Ágata?
Elena: Me cae muy bien Ágata también porque me escucha y es simpática.

**6**
Roberto: ¿Y tu primo Ramón?
Elena: Pues, me llevo bastante bien con Ramón porque es divertido, pero a veces me cuenta mentiras y me cae mal.

*Answers:*
*2, 3, 4*

AT 1.3 | L&S 1.2

**2 Escucha otra vez. Empareja las frases.**
Students listen again and this time match the sentences. More able students could do this from memory and then listen again to check their answers.

*Answers:*
***1** b; **2** a; **3** d; **4** e; **5** f; **6** c*

KAL 4.5 | LLS 5.1

## Gramática
If necessary, remind students how *gustar* works. They practise manipulating these verbs then using names of people they know or celebrities to make it memorable.

AT 2.3–4 | PLTS | L&S 1.4

**3 Habla con tu compañero. ¿Te llevas bien con tu familia?**
Less able students can make simple sentences. Encourage more able ones to extend their responses with connectives, qualifiers, fillers, and reasons.

AT 3.4 | PLTS | R&W 2.2

**4 Elena habla de los jóvenes de su clase del insti. Lee lo que dice.**
Much of the vocabulary in the descriptions comes from *Zoom español 1* so encourage students to pick out all the words and phrases they know before focussing on new vocabulary. This should encourage them that they already know most of it.

AT 3.4 | R&W 2.2

**5 Lee las descripciones otra vez. ¿Quién es?**
Students read the descriptions again and then identify who is being described each time. This activity practises using the third person *le cae bien*, etc.

*Answers:*
***1** Julio; **2** Lucía; **3** Pepe y Pilar; **4** Lucía; **5** Pepe y Pilar; **6** Julio*

AT 2.3–4 | L&S 1.4 | PLTS

**6 Habla con tu compañero. ¿De quién hablas?**
Students use the descriptions from Activities 4 and 5 to describe one of Elena's classmates for their partner to identify. This provides good practice of using the third person forms. Weaker students could pretend to be Elena and just pick out phrases from the text for their partner to identify, e.g. *A – No me cae bien. B – Lucía.*

PLTS | AT 4.3–4 | AT 2.3–4 | R&W 2.4 | LLS 5.7

## Challenge
**Carry out a survey. Ask your friends who they get on with in their family and why. Present some of your findings to the class and write them up.**
This open-ended activity can be as complex or simple as the level of the class allows. Prepare the activity by getting students to draw up a list of questions they are going to ask first, and to think of possible answers, especially for the reasons they do or don't get on with someone. Results can be presented orally *55% de personas en la clase se llevan bien con sus madres* or in written form and illustrated with graphs or quotes as you like.

## 0.4 ¿Vienes conmigo?

páginas 10–11

# Planner

### Objectives

- accept and refuse invitations, buy cinema tickets
- understand use of the personal *a*, use *conmigo/contigo*
- accept and refuse politely

### Resources

Student Book, pages 10–11
CD 1, tracks 6–7
Foundation Workbook, page 11
Higher Workbook, page 11
Foundation Workbook audio, CD 3, track 31 (Workbook 11)
Higher Workbook audio, CD 4, Track 11
Interactive OxBox, Unit 0
Copymasters 1–8

### Video

Video clip, Unit 0

### Key language

*¿A qué hora hay sesiones? Hoy hay una sesión a las 21 horas. Tenemos una sesión que empieza a las 21 horas. ¿Qué precio tienen las entradas? ¿A cuánto son las entradas? ¿Cuánto cuestan las entradas? Hay entradas a 8.50 euros. Tenemos entradas a 8.50. Las entradas cuestan 8.50 euros. ¿Tienen algún descuento para estudiantes? Sí, tenemos entradas a 5 euros para estudiantes. ¿Vienes? Voy a ...; Me gustaría ir ...; ¿Te gustaría venir? Sí, me gustaría mucho. Lo siento, no puedo. ¿Quieres venir conmigo? el rechazo; la excusa; aceptar; rechazar; cortés/cortesa; grosero/a*

### Renewed Framework references

L&S 1.1, 1.2, 1.3, 1.4, 1.5; IU 3.2; LLS 5.1

### PLTS

Activity 2: Independent enquirers
Activity 5: Creative thinkers
Activity 6: Reflective learners
Activity 7: Effective participators
Challenge: Team workers

### Starters

- Split the class into two groups. Display a question, e.g. *¿Te gustaría ir al museo de Segovia conmigo?* One of the groups will go round the students in the other group asking this question. Also display some possible answers, e.g. *Sí, me gustaría mucho.* or *¡Qué horror! Odio los museos, son aburridos.* The students in the other group must reply using one of these answers. Both students then decide if this is polite, semi-polite or rude.

### Plenaries

- Following Activity 7, split students into small groups or pairs and get them to act out the sentences they have written.
- After Activity 3, students work in pairs to practise asking questions in a cinema to find out when the film showings are, how much the tickets cost and if there is a discount for students. You may want to brainstorm possible answers to these questions, or, with more able students, let them make up their own answers.

### Homework/Self-study

Gramática: Students write six more sentences using the personal *a*.
Think: Students list any Spanish words they find beginning with *v* and practise pronouncing them correctly.

AT 1.4 | L&S1.1, 1.2 | IU3.2

**1 Mira el video (primera parte) y completa las frases.**

Students watch the video and complete the sentences. They should listen out for words and phrases that they have met in this unit.

**Video clip: Unit 0 (CD 1, track 6)**

**Part 1**

*Elena, Juan and Roberto are hanging out in the old town with a view over Segovia.*

Elena: Hola soy Elena y este es mi primo. ¿Cómo te llamas?
Roberto: Ah sí. Me llamo Roberto.
Elena: ¿Y de dónde eres?
Roberto: Ya lo sabes, soy de Colombia.
Elena: Y vas a estar en Segovia tres meses.
Roberto: Mucho tiempo.
Elena: Pero, te llevas bien conmigo. ¿A que sí?
Roberto: Sí. Me llevo bien contigo. ¡Cuando está de buen humor!
Juan: Y yo soy Juan. Soy el hermano de Elena y claro Roberto es mi primo también.
Elena: ¡No me llevo bien con Juan es muy pesado! Y dice mentiras.
Roberto: Pero a mí, me cae bien porque cuenta muchas chistes.
Juan: ¡Bienvenidos a nuestra familia!

*Answers:*
***a*** *Elena, buen humor,* ***b*** *Juan, pesado, mentiras,* ***c*** *Juan, chistes*

PLTS | AT 1.4 | L&S 1.1, 1.2 | IU 3.2

**2 Mira el video y contesta a las preguntas en inglés.**
Again, encourage students to listen out for words and phrases that they have met in this unit.

**Video clip: Unit 0 (CD 1, track 6)**

**Part 2**

Roberto: ¿Qué vamos a hacer hoy?
Elena: ¿Cuánto dinero tenemos?
Roberto: Yo tengo diez euros.
Juan: Yo tengo cinco euros.
Elena: Yo tengo diez euros también. Este es el problema, nunca tenemos mucho dinero.
Roberto: Pero, ¿Qué vamos a hacer hoy?
Elena: Me gustaría ir al cine. ¿Te gustaría venir conmigo?
Roberto: Sí, me gustaría. Juan, ¿vienes?
Juan: Depende ¿Qué vamos a ver?
Elena: Me gustaría ver Transformers en 3D.
Roberto: Pero, antes de las 7. A las nueve hay un partido de futbol en la tele que quiero ver.
Elena: Y no podemos gastar más de 25 euros en las tres entradas.
Juan: ¿Transformers en 3D, antes de las siete, y tres entradas por menos de 25 euros?
Roberto: Va a ser difícil.
Elena: Vamos a intentarlo.
Juan: A ver quién gana.

Opción A
*Inside a cinema at the ticket booth*
Employee: Hola buenos días. ¿En qué te puedo ayudar?
Elena: Me gustaría ver Transformers en 3D. ¿A qué hora hay sesiones?
Employee: ¿Para qué día?
Elena: Para hoy.
Employee: Hoy tenemos entradas a las 18.45 y a las 21.30.
Elena: ¿A cuánto son las entradas?
Employee: Hay entradas a 8.50 euros y 9.50 euros para las películas en 3D.
Elena: ¿Y tienen descuento para estudiantes?
Employee: Sí, tenemos entradas a 7 euros para estudiantes menores de 18 años.

Opción B
*Roberto, looking at a poster.*
Roberto: A ver, aquí ponen Transformers a las 18.45 y a las 21.30 – ¡qué bien! Pero ¿Qué día es hoy? Hoy es miércoles. Podemos ir a la sesión de las 18.45. ¿Cuánto costarán las entradas? Las entradas cuestan 8.50 o 9.50 euros. ¿Habrá descuento para jóvenes?

Option C
*Juan outside the theatre looking at the "have your birthday at the cinema" poster.*
Juan: Hola, buenos días. ¿Hay alguna sesión de Transformers hoy?
Employee: Sí, tenemos una sesión que empieza a las 18.45.
Juan: ¿Y es una sesión 3D?
Employee: Por supuesto.
Juan: ¿Y cuánto cuestan las entradas?
Employee: Tenemos entradas a 9.50 euros y a 7 euros con descuento para jóvenes.
Juan: ¿Y la oferta "cumpleaños"?
Employee: Cuando es tu cumpleaños tienes 4 entradas por 8 euros cada una y el del cumpleaños para gratis, con palomitas y bebidas incluidas.

Resultado
Elena: A ver, queremos ver Transformers en 3D antes de las 7 y queremos gastarnos menos de 25 euros. ¿Roberto?
Roberto: Hay sesión a las 18.45. Hay entradas a 9 euros con cincuenta, pero no sé si hay descuentos para jóvenes. ¿Y tú Elena?
Elena: Sesión a las 18.45 y entradas con descuento para jóvenes a 7 euros cada una. ¿Y tú Juan?
Juan: Sesión a las 18.45 con 4 entradas, palomitas y bebida incluidas y por solo 24 euros.

*Repeat of correct scene with added ending.*
Juan: Hola buenos días. ¿Hay alguna sesión de Transformers hoy?
Employee: Sí, tenemos una sesión que empieza a las 18.45.
Juan: ¿Y es una sesión 3D?
Employee: Por supuesto.
Juan: ¿Y cuánto cuestan las entradas?
Employee: Tenemos entradas a 9.50 euros y a 7 euros con descuento para jóvenes.
Juan: ¿Y la oferta "cumpleaños"?
Employee: Cuando es tu cumpleaños tienes 4 entradas por 8 euros cada una y el del cumpleaños para gratis, con palomitas y bebidas incluidas.
Juan: Pues, hoy es mi cumple.
Employee: Felicidades. Aquí tienes las cuatro entradas.
Juan: Y aquí tiene los 25 euros.
Employee: Toma.
Juan: Muchas gracias.

*Back outside.*
Elena: Pero Juan – hoy no es tu cumpleaños.
Roberto: Además tienes cuatro entradas y somos tres. ¿A quién vas a invitar?
Juan: *On the phone.* Hola Nati, ¿te vienes conmigo al cine esta tarde? Te invito.

*Answers:*
***a** Go to the cinema; **b** Don't have a lot of money; **c** 25€;*
***d** before 7 o'clock (Roberto wants to watch a football match at 9 pm)*

AT 3.3 | L&S 1.4

**3 Which of these questions ask about...**
Students categorise the questions under subject a, b,or c.

*Answers:*
***a** when the film showings are: ¿A qué hora hay sesiones? ¿Hay alguna sesión hoy? **b** how much the tickets cost: ¿A cuánto son las entradas? ¿Cuánto cuestan las entradas? ¿Qué precio tienen las entradas? **c** if there is a discount for students: ¿Tienen algún descuento para estudiantes?*

AT 1.4 | L&S1.1, 1.2 | IU 3.2

**4 Mira el video y completa la tabla.**
Students watch the second part of the video again and fill in the table. This will help students to complete Activity 5.

*Answers: **Elena**: a las18.45 horas, 7€ cada una; **Roberto**: a las 18.45 horas, 8.50€ o 9.50€; **Juan**: a las 18:45, 24€ para 4 entradas*

AT 1.4 | L&S 1.1, 1.2 | IU 3.2 | PLTS

**5 Who do you think won? Watch the video again.**
Students watch the video as a whole and note down who won the competition.

*Answer:*
Juan, as he pretends that it is his birthday and gets the special offer!

AT 1.4 | PLTS | L&S 1.3, 1.4, 1.5

**6 Lee y escucha las excusas para rechazar a las invitaciones. ¿Son rechazos corteses o groseros?**
Students listen and look at the picture. The sound of the words will help identify how polite the reply is.

**CD 1, track 7** **página 11, actividad 6**

Elena: ¿Te gustaría ir al museo de Segovia conmigo?
Roberto (A): El museo? ¡Qué horror! Odio los museos, son aburridos.
(B): Lo siento, pero no me gustan mucho los museos.
(C): Muchas gracias, pero no puedo ir contigo al museo. Voy al partido de fútbol con Juan.

*Answers:*
*polite: C; semi-polite: B; rude: A*

## Gramática

Read through the Grammar explanation as a class and look at the examples. Then ask students to come up with some examples of their own. Depending on the level of the class, you may want to display some useful vocabulary.

LLS 5.1

## Think

Students a work in pairs or small groups to practise this.

AT 4.3–4 | PLTS | L&S 1.3, 1.4

**7 Tus amigos te invitan a salir. ¿Cuál es tu respuesta? Puedes ser cortés o grosero.**
Students use what they have learnt in Activity 6 to practise being polite, semi-polite or rude.

AT 2.3–4 | PLTS | L&S1.3, 1.4, 1.5

## Challenge

**Work in groups of three or four. One person is given different invitations by the others, and has to decide to accept or refuse, and how. Act it out to the rest of the class, who will vote for the best group.**
Students could gain marks in different categories, e.g. good use of Spanish, inventive excuses, polite refusal, humour value, etc.

## 0.5 Excusas, excusas

páginas 12–13

# Planner

### Objectives
- make excuses
- *conmigo, contigo, con él, con ella*, etc.
- respond politely

### Resources
Student Book, pages 12–13
CD 1, track 8
Foundation Workbook, page 12
Higher Workbook, page 12
Foundation Workbook audio, CD 3, track 32 (Workbook 12)
Higher workbook audio, CD 4, track 12
Interactive OxBox, Unit 0
Copymasters 1–8

### Renewed Framework references
L&S 1.1, 1.2, 1.3, 1.4, 1.5; R&W 2.2, 2.4; LLS 5.1, 5.4

### PLTS
Activity 2: Reflective learners
Activity 4: Independent enquirers
Activity 5: Team workers
Activity 6: Self-managers
Activity 7: Creative thinkers
Challenge: Creative thinkers

### Starters
- Have a class competition. Students work in groups and come up with as many excuses as they can. They get a point for each correct sentence, two points for each unique one. You could also award points for the most original, funny, silly, etc. excuse.
- Go round the class inviting each student to the cinema/swimming pool/a birthday party, etc. Each student must give an excuse to say that they can't come and why. It is up to them if they refuse politely or not!
- Play a memory game. You start by saying, e.g. *Lo siento, no puedo ir contigo porque tengo muchos deberes.* The student nearest you repeats your excuse and adds one of his/her own, e.g. *Lo siento, no puedo ir contigo porque tengo muchos deberes y no tengo bastante dinero.* And so on.

### Plenaries
- Challenge students to write a sentence in Spanish containing each of the following: with me, with you, with him, with her, with us, with you (plural), with them (female), with them (male), with you (plural polite). Each sentence should be different. You could give them a time limit. When they have finished, compare answers as a class.
- Display the text from Activity 6, but this time with the immediate future verbs blanked out for students to fill in. Depending on the level of the class, you may want to quickly recap how to form the immediate future first. You could make it more difficult by having a time limit.

### Homework/Self-study
Activity 4
Challenge Activity

AT 3.3 | R&W 2.2 | LLS 5.4

**1 Lee la invitación y la respuesta.**
Students read the invitation and the refusal – both the thought bubble and the speech bubble. Encourage them to think back to previous spreads in order to understand what is being said.

AT 1.5 | PLTS | L&S 1.1, 1.2

**2 Escucha las tres conversaciones. Empareja las frases con la conversación correcta.**
Students listen to the three conversations and then match each sentence to the correct one.

**CD 1, track 8** — **página 12, actividades 2 y 3**

**1**

Ana: Hola, Carlos. Luisa y yo vamos a la piscina. ¿Quieres venir con nosotras?

Carlos: (*thinking*) ¡No quiero ir a la piscina con ellas! ¡Qué aburrido! Odio nadar. (*talking*) Lo siento, no puedo ir con vosotras. Tengo muchos deberes.

**2**

Beatriz: Voy a la fiesta del cumpleaños de Diego. ¿Vienes conmigo?

Sara: (*thinking*) No me cae bien Diego. Es muy antipático. No quiero ir con ella. (*talking*) Pues, lo siento mucho, pero no puedo. No tengo bastante dinero para comprar un regalo. No puedo ir contigo.

**3**

Tomás: Buenas tardes, señora. Vamos al restaurante para celebrar el nacimiento de nuestro nieto. ¿Les gustaría venir con nosotros?

Valentina: (*thinking*) ¡Qué horror! ¡Tomás y su familia son muy pesados! No queremos ir con ellos. (*talking*) Pues, muchas gracias Tomás, es usted muy amable, pero no podemos ir con ustedes. Vamos al campo a visitar a mis padres.

*Answers:*
***1:** a, c, e; **2:** d, g, i; **3:** b, f, h*

AT 1.5 | L&S 1.2, 1.3

**3 Escucha otra vez. ¿Cuáles son las excusas, y cuál es la verdad?**
Students listen again and note down what are excuses and what is the truth. Remind them that it isn't just the vocabulary that they should be listening out for, but also the way in which the speakers say things.

*Answers:*
***1** excusa – tiene muchos deberes, verdad – odia nadar;*
***2** excusa – no tiene dinero, verdad – no le cae bien Diego;*
***3** excusa – van a visitar a sus padres, verdad – la familia de Tomás es muy pesado*

AT 3.3 | PLTS

**4 Empareja las excusas con los dibujos.**
This gives students a few more excuses to work with before going on to invent some of their own, and shows them how they already have enough language at their disposal to do so.

*Answers:*
***1** f; **2** c; **3** a; **4** e; **5** b; **6** d*

## Think

Elicit from students that *Voy a visitar a mis abuelos* uses the personal *a*. If students have had difficulty remembering this, encourage them to look back at page 11. You could also quickly go round the class asking students to provide other examples.

AT 2.4–5 | PLTS | L&S 1.4, 1.5

**5 Con tu compañero inventa excusas para rechazar invitaciones. Utiliza las palabras de la casilla.**
The words provided are to start students off thinking how to formulate an excuse, and can be used in a variety of ways depending on the ability of the student, e.g. *Voy a visitar a mi tío, Voy al restaurante con mi tío, Voy al partido de fútbol con mi tío para sus cumpleaños.* Students could act out their excuses in front of the class.

AT 3.5 | PLTS | R&W 2.2

**6 Lee y completa el email con las palabras de la actividad 5.**
Students read the text and then use the words from Activity 5 to fill in the gaps.

*Answers:*
***1** madrastra; **2** cumpleaños; **3** medio-hermano; **4** partido; **5** tío; **6** vacaciones; **7** restaurante; **8** acostarme*

AT 4.4–5 | PLTS | R&W 2.4

**7 Escribe la respuesta de Sofía. ¿Acepta o rechaza la invitación?**
Students can decide whether to accept or reject the invitation to go to the cinema and how to do this.

AT 4.4–5 | R&W 2.4 | PLTS

## Challenge

**Write text messages inviting your friends to go out, and reply to their messages, making excuses. Think up some outrageous excuses if you can.**
If facilities permit, students could email each other the messages rather than writing pretend texts on paper. Can more able students make up an unbelieveable excuse that is actually true?

## 0.6 Labolengua

páginas 14–15

### Planner

**Objectives**
- review language and grammar from the unit

**Resources**
Student Book, pages 14–15
CD 1, track 9
Foundation Workbook, pages 13–14
Higher Workbook, pages 13–14
Interactive OxBox, Unit 0
Copymasters 9–10

**Grammar**
- *Ser* and *estar*

**Renewed Framework references**
KAL 4.1, 4.5; LLS 5.1, 5.5, 5.8

**PLTS**
All activities: Reflective learners/Self-managers
Activity 7: Team workers

**Homework/Self-study**
Activity 4: Students write some more sentences using the personal *a*.

### Comprender – *Ser* and *estar*

#### A *Ser*

KAL 4.5 PLTS **1 Complete the description using the correct part of the verb ser.**
Practice of using *ser* correctly.

*Answers:*
***1** soy; **2** soy; **3** es; **4** es; **5** es; **6** son; **7** somos; **8** son*

#### B Estar

PLTS **2 Find the mistakes in the following sentences. Say what the problems are, and correct them.**
Practice of using *estar* correctly.

*Answers:*
1. *Marcos **es** (character – uses ser) inteligente pero no **está** (mood – uses estar) muy contento.*
2. *Mi casa **está** (location – uses estar) en las afueras de la ciudad. **Es** (description – uses ser) bonita.*
3. ***Somos** (character – uses ser) organizados, y ellos **están** (mood – uses estar) deprimidos.*
4. *Mi tío **es** (profession – uses ser) futbolista, y **está** (mood – uses estar) triste.*

#### C More phrases using estar

PLTS **3 Write a caption for each picture using the phrases.**
Further practice of using *estar*.

*Suggested answers:*
***1** Están casados; **2** Están divorciados; **3** Está vivo;*
***4** Está muerte*

#### D The personal *a*

LLS 5.1 PLTS **4 Should you use the personal *a* in these sentences?**
Practise of using the personal *a*.

*Answers:*
***1** Voy a sacar la basura. **2** Voy a ayudar a mi amigo.*
***3** Quiero a mis padres. **4** Busco el cine.*

### Aprender – Dictionary skills

#### E Using a dictionary

LLS 5.5 PLTS **5 Find these words in a dictionary. What do they mean? What kind of words are they (noun, verb, adjective, adverb)?**
You can choose a different group of words for students to investigate if you wish.

LLS 5.5 PLTS **6 Write sentences using these words to help you remember them.**
Using these words in context will help students to remember what they mean.

### Hablar – Vowel sounds

#### F Sounding Spanish

KAL 4.1 PLTS **7 Practise these words with a partner.**
Practice of pronouncing Spanish vowels correctly.

LLS 5.8 PLTS **8 Now listen. How Spanish did you sound?**
Students check that they have pronounced the vowels from Activity 7 correctly.

CD 1, track 9 — página 15, actividad 8

Europa, inteligente, actividad, café, tenis, fútbol, catedral, elefante, grande, televisión, transporte, vacaciones, supermercado

## 0.7 Extra Star

página 16

### Planner

**Objectives**
- talk about feelings and character
- practise using *ser* and *estar*
- give invitations

**Resources**
Student Book, page 16
Copymaster 11

**Renewed Framework references**
KAL 4.5

**PLTS**
Activity 1: Reflective learners
Activity 3: Self-managers
Activity 4: Effective participators

AT 3.3 | KAL 4.5 | PLTS

**1 ¿Carácter o sentimiento? Elige la palabra correcta.**
Students complete each sentence with the correct form of *ser* or *estar* depending on whether it is character or mood. Look at the Grammar box as a class before students complete this activity.

*Answers:*
***1** es; **2** está; **3** son; **4** están; **5** Somos; **6** Estás*

AT 3.2

**2 Empareja las frases de la actividad 1 con los dibujos.**
Students match the sentences from Activity 1 to the pictures.

*Answers: **1** d; **2** b; **3** e; **4** a; **5** c; **6** f*

AT 3.3 | PLTS

**3 Empareja las dos partes de las frases.**
Students match the sentence halves.

*Answers: **1** c; **2** a; **3** b; **4** d*

AT 4.2–3 | PLTS

**4 Invita a tu amigo/a a estos lugares.**
Students invite a friend to the places shown in the pictures.

## 0.7 Extra Plus

página 17

### Planner

**Objectives**
- say if you get on with someone
- practise using *ser* and *estar*
- respond to invitations

**Resources**
Student Book, page 17
Copymaster 12

**Renewed Framework references**
R&W 2.2, 2.4; KAL 4.5

**PLTS**
Activity 2: Self-managers
Activity 3: Creative thinkers

AT 3.3–4 | KAL 4.5

**1 ¿Ser o estar? Completa las frases con las palabras de la casilla.**
Students complete each sentence with the correct form of *ser* or *estar*.

*Answers:*
***1** estás; **2** sois; **3** Estamos; **4** están; **5** está; **6** son*

AT 3.4 | R&W 2.2 | PLTS

**2 Lee lo que opina Rosario. ¿Son las frases verdaderas o falsas?**
Students read the text and then decide if each of the statements is true or false.

*Answers:*
***1** verdad; **2** falso; **3** falso; **4** verdad; **5** verdad; **6** falso*

AT 4.3 | R&W 2.4 | PLTS

**3 Tus amigos te invitan a salir. Acepta o rechaza las invitaciones.**
Students work in pairs. Partner A invites B out. Partner B decides whether or not to accept. They then swap roles. Will they be polite or rude?

## 0.8 Prueba
página 18

### *Planner*

**Resources**
Student Book, page 18
CD 1, track 10
Assessment OxBox, Unit 0

**Renewed Framework references**
L&S 1.1, 1.2, 1.4; R&W 2.2, 2.4; KAL 4.3, 4.5

**PLTS**
All activities: Reflective learners

### Escuchar

AT 1.3 | L&S 1.1, 1.2 | PLTS

**Listen to the three people. Which is speaking? How were their journeys?**
This activity tests listening skills using the language covered in this unit.

**CD 1, track 10** — **página 18, actividad 1**

**1**
– ¿Qué tal el viaje?
– Bueno, así así. No estoy muy contento. Fue bastante rápido pero el tren no era muy cómodo.

**2**
– ¿Qué tal el viaje?
– ¡Maravilloso! Muy rápido, muy cómodo. ¡Me encanta mi coche!

**3**
– ¿Qué tal el viaje?
– ¡Fatal! ¡Un desastre! ¡El avión tuvo un accidente! ¡Estoy viva de milagro!

*Answers:*
***1** b; **2** a; **3** c*

### Hablar

AT 2.3 | L&S 1.4 | PLTS

**Invite your friend to one of these places. Accept or refuse their invitation.**
This activity tests speaking skills using the language covered in this unit. Students use the prompts to ask and answer the questions.

### Leer

AT 3.4 | R&W 2.2 | PLTS

**Read the description of Ofelia and decide if the sentences are true or false.**
This activity tests reading skills using the language covered in this unit.

*Answers:*
***1** verdad; **2** falso; **3** falso; **4** verdad; **5** verdad; **6** falso*

### Escribir

AT 4.3–4 | R&W 2.4 | KAL 4.3, 4.5 | PLTS

**Describe one of these people. What are they like? How are they feeling?**
This activity tests writing skills using the language covered in this unit.

*Answers: Students' own answers*

## Leer 0

página 148

### Planner

**Resources**
Student Book, page 148

**Renewed Framework references**
R&W 2.1, 2.4

**PLTS**
Activity 1: Reflective learners; Self-managers

AT 3.4 | R&W 2.1, 2.2

**1 Lee los textos y contesta a las preguntas.**

*Answers:*
***1*** *Jacinta;* ***2*** *Jacinta;* ***3*** *Nicolas;* ***4*** *Nicolas;* ***5*** *Nicolas;* ***6*** *Jacinta;* ***7*** *Jacinta;* ***8*** *Nicolas*

**Follow-up**
Students write a description of their own family using the reading texts as a model. It can be as brief or as detailed as their ability allows. You could read some of the descriptions to the class to see if they can guess who wrote them.

## Foundation Workbook

### Página 4 Pronunciation, vowels

AT 1.1 | AT 2.1 | KAL 4.1

**1 Listen and repeat these words.**
Practice of pronouncing Spanish vowels correctly.

**CD 3, track 22 (Workbook 2)** **página 4, actividad 1**
casa, enero, familia, comedor, número, once, doce

KAL 4.1

**2 Listen and repeat these words.**
Practice of pronouncing words with two vowels together.

**CD 3, track 23 (Workbook 3)** **página 4, actividad 2**
siete, viento, abuelo, bueno, nueve, seis, veinte, ciudad, cuidado

AT 1.2 | AT 2.2 | KAL 4.1

**Now practise saying these sentences.**

### Página 5 Pronunciation, consonants

AT 1.2 | AT 2.2 | KAL 4.1

**1 Read these sentences, then listen and check your pronunciation.**
Practice of pronouncing Spanish consonants correctly.

**CD 3, track 24 (Workbook 4)** **página 5, actividad 1**
**a** Me llamo Iñaki, soy de España.
**b** Hablo español y estudio historia.
**c** Quiero ir a La Quebrada.

KAL 4.1

**2 Sort the *c* consonants into hard and soft.**

*Answers:*
***hard:*** *casa, Colombia, café, castillo*
***soft:*** *Barcelona, piscina, baloncesto*

KAL 4.1

**3 Sort the *g* consonants into hard and soft.**

*Answers:*
***hard:*** *tengo, inglés, me gusta*
***soft:*** *colegio, tecnología, inteligente*

LLS 5.8

**4 Listen and check your answers to Activities 2 and 3.**

**CD 3, track 25 (Workbook 5)** **página 5, actividad 4**
**Hard:** casa, Colombia, café, castillo
**Soft:** Barcelona, piscina, baloncesto

**Hard:** tengo, inglés, me gusta
**Soft:** colegio, tecnología, inteligente

## Página 6 Pronunciation, longer and unfamiliar words

KAL 4.1 LLS 5.8 **1 Read these sentences carefully. Even when you think you know a word, still follow the rules.**

KAL 4.1 LLS 5.8 **2 Here are some unfamiliar sentences. Follow the rules to read them with confidence, even if you don't understand it all yet.**

KAL 4.1 LLS 5.8 **3 Read these sentences, then listen and check your pronunciation.**
Practice of pronouncing cognates correctly.

**CD 3, track 26 (Workbook 6)** **página 6, actividad 3**

**a** Fuimos al parque de atracciones. Lo pasamos fatal.
**b** En el centro de la ciudad hay una plaza con un restaurante.
**c** Comimos chile con carne y escuchamos la radio.

KAL 4.1 LLS 5.8 **4 Listen to a Spanish person saying these names. Then try to say them in the same way.**

**CD 3, track 27 (Workbook 7)** **página 6, actividad 4**

**a** David Beckham
**b** Kiera Knightley
**c** Deep Purple
**d** Birmingham
**e** Mozart
**f** Ricky Martín

## Página 7 Pronunciation, rules

KAL 4.1 LLS 5.8 **1 Read these sentences in your head. Make notes on words to watch out for and pronunciation rules to follow.**

KAL 4.1 LLS 5.8 **2 Now read the sentences aloud. Afterwards, note down the words you felt uncomfortable with.**

KAL 4.1 LLS 5.8 **3 Write down the pronunciation rules or hints that would help you to tackle the words you found difficult.**

## Página 8 0.1 ¡Bienvenido!

- Use with Student Book, pages 4–5

AT 4.1 **1 Choose one letter from each box to find the forms of transport in Spanish. Write the word and then write the English.**
If necessary, go through the first one as a class to ensure all students know what to do.

*Answers:*
***a** tren – train; **b** avión – plane; **c** barco – boat; **d** coche – car*

AT 1.3 L&S 1.2 **2 Listen and put this conversation into the correct order.**
This practises meeting and greeting in Spanish.

**CD 3, track 28 (Workbook 8)** **página 8, actividad 2**

– ¡Hola! Soy Ángela.
– ¡Encantado! Soy Beto.
– Bienvenido a España.
– ¡Gracias!
– ¿Qué tal el viaje?
– Bien, gracias. El avión era cómodo.
– ¡Vamos!
– ¡Vale!

*Answers: as in transcript*

AT 4.3 R&W 2.4 **2 Now use the Spanish in Activity 2 to welcome Lionel to Manchester.**
Further practice of meeting and greeting people in Spanish.

## Página 9 0.2 ¿Cómo estás?

- Use with Student Book, pages 6–7

AT 4.1 **1 Unscramble these adjective anagrams.**

*Answers:*
***a** divertido; **b** decepcionado; **c** simpático; **d** contento; **e** generoso; **f** ilusionado; **g** triste; **h** inteligente*

AT 1.2 **2 Listen. Circle the correct verb: *ser* or *estar*.**

**CD 3, track 29 (Workbook 9)** **página 9, actividades 2 y 3**

**a** Soy bastante simpática.
**b** Soy muy inteligente.
**c** Estoy triste.
**d** Estoy contento.
**e** Somos muy generosos.
**f** Estamos decepcionados.
**g** Estoy muy ilusionada.

*Answers: as in transcript*

AT 1.2 **3 Listen again and circle the adjective with the correct ending.**

*Answers: as in transcript*

## Página 10 0.3 Me llevo bien con Elena

- Use with Student Book, pages 8–9

AT 1.2 L&S 1.2 **1 Listen to Julia's game. Who does she think is great?**

CD 3, track 30 (Workbook 10) **página 10, actividades 1 y 2**

Me cae bien
o me cae mal
Es pesado o
¡FENOMENAL!

¡Javi, Javi, eres fenomenal!

*Answer: Javi*

AT 1.2 L&S 1.2 **2 Listen again and copy out Julia's rhyme in the correct order.**

*Answers: as in transcript*

AT 2.2 **2 Now do the rhyme yourself, pointing to each person in turn to find out who you think is great.**
This provides practise of using opinion phrases.

## Página 11 0.4 ¿Vienes conmigo?

- Use with Student Book, pages 10–11

AT 3.2 **1 Tick the question which does not mean the same as the others.**
*Answer: c ¿Tienen algún descuento para estudiantes?*

AT 3.3 **2 Draw lines to match up the questions to the answers.**
*Answers:*
***a** ¿A cuánto son las entradas? Cuestan diez euros. **b** ¿A qué hora hay sesiones? Hay una sesión que empieza a las seis. **c** ¿Tienen algún descuento para estudiantes? Sí, tenemos entradas a ocho euros.*

AT 2.2–3 **3 Listen to the five customers and answer their questions using the information.**
Students listen and then answer each question orally using the information given.

CD 3, track 31 (Workbook 11) **página 11, actividad 3**

1 ¿A cuánto son las entradas?
2 ¿A qué hora hay sesiones?
3 ¿Cuánto cuestan las entradas?
4 ¿Qué precio tienen las entradas?
5 ¿Tienen algún descuento para estudiantes?

## Página 12 0.5 Excusas, excusas

- Use with Student Book, pages 12–13

AT 1.3 L&S 1.1, 1.2 **1 Listen to Raquel, Juan, Beatriz, and Iván talking about where to go. Tick where they suggest going.**
Practise of giving, accepting and refusing invitations.

CD 3, track 32 (Workbook 12) **página 12, actividades 1, 2 y 3**

Raquel: Vamos a la piscina.
Juan: Qué buena idea.
Beatriz: Muy bien, vamos.
Raquel: Iván, ¿quieres venir?
Iván: No. No me gusta nadar. Es aburrido.

Beatriz: Vamos al cine.
Juan: Excelente.
Raquel: Vamos, vamos.
Beatriz: Iván, ¿quieres venir?
Iván: No. No, no me gustan las películas que ponen. Y no tengo dinero.

Iván: Me voy a mi casa.
Beatriz: Excelente.
Juan: Muy buena idea.
Raquel: Bien, bien.
All 3: Adiós, Iván.

Raquel: Entonces, ¿vamos a la piscina o al cine?
Juan: ¿Los dos?
Beatriz: Sí, vamos a la piscina y al cine.
Raquel: Excelente.
Juan: ¡Muy divertido!

*Answers: pool and cinema*

AT 1.3 L&S 1.1, 1.2 **2 Listen again. Tick the excuses Iván gives.**

*Answer: doesn't like swimming, it's boring, doesn't like the films, no money*

AT 1.3 L&S 1.1, 1.2 **3 When Iván goes home, where do the others decide to go?**

*Answers: pool AND cinema*

AT 4.2–3 **4 Draw the story as a cartoon strip and write in the speech bubbles in Spanish. Then act it out in groups of four.**
This is a fun way to ensure that students have really understood the script.

## Página 13 0.6A Labolengua

- Use with Student Book, pages 14–15

KAL 4.5 **1 Cross out all the letters that are in the present tense of the verb *ser*. Use the letters that are left to make a word that can follow *es* ...**
Practice of the present tense of the verb *ser*.

*Answer: azul*

KAL 4.5 **2 Cross out all the letters that are in the present tense of the verb *estar*. Use the letters that are left to make a word that can follow *está* ...**
Practice of the present tense of the verb *ser*.

*Answer: aburrido*

KAL 4.5 **3 Sort these sentences into *ser* and *estar*.**
Practice of differentiating between *ser* and *estar*.

*Answers:*
***Ser:*** *Soy inteligente. Es generoso. Somos ingleses. Son mis primos.*
***Estar:*** *Está en España. Estamos tristes. Está contento. Estoy enfermo.*

### Página 14 0.6B Técnica

- Use with Student Book, pages 14–15

LLS 5.5 **1 James has tried to look up the word 'drink' in a bilingual dictionary. Draw a line to match up each problem with the reason.**

*Answers:*
***1** d; **2** b; **3** e; **4** a; **5** c*

LLS 5.5 **2 What should James do to make sure he finds the correct Spanish word for 'watch' in the following sentence?**
Students should use what they have done in Activity 1 to help them decide what James should (and shouldn't) do.

LLS 5.5 **3 What is the word he needs?**

*Answer: ver* **or** *mirar*

## Higher Workbook

### Página 4 Pronunciation, vowels

AT 1.1 AT 2.1 KAL 4.1 LLS 5.8 **1 Practise saying these words, then listen and check your pronunciation.**
Practice of pronouncing Spanish vowels correctly.

**CD 4, track 2** **página 4, actividad 1**
casa, enero, familia, comedor, número, once, doce

KAL 4.1 LLS 5.8 **2 Look carefully at the order of the vowels in these words. Try saying them, then listen and check your pronunciation.**
Practice of pronouncing words with two vowels together.

**CD 4, track 3** **página 4, actividad 2**
siete, viento, abuelo, bueno, nueve, seis, veinte, ciudad, cuidado

AT 1.2 AT 2.2 KAL 4.1 LLS 5.8 **3 Now practise saying these sentences.**

### Página 5 Pronunciation, consonants

KAL 4.1 LLS 5.8 **1 Read these sentences, then listen and check your pronunciation.**
Practice of pronouncing Spanish consonants correctly.

**CD 4, track 4** **página 5, actividad 1**
**a** Me llamo Iñaki, soy de España.
**b** Hablo español y estudio historia.
**c** Quiero ir a La Quebrada.

KAL 4.1 **2 Sort the *c* and *g* consonants into hard and soft.**

*Answers:*
***hard:*** *casa, Colombia, café, castillo, tengo, inglés, me gusta*
***soft:*** *Barcelona, piscina, baloncesto, colegio, tecnología, inteligente*

**3 Listen and check your answers to Activity 2.**

**CD 4, track 5** **página 5, actividad 3**
**Hard:** casa, Colombia, café, castillo
tengo, inglés, me gusta

**Soft:** Barcelona, piscina, baloncesto
colegio, tecnología, inteligente

## Página 6 Pronunciation, longer and unfamiliar words

KAL 4.1 LLS 5.8 **1 Read these sentences carefully. Even when you think you know a word, still follow the rules.**

KAL 4.1 LLS 5.8 **2 Here are some unfamiliar sentences. Follow the rules to read them with confidence, even if you don't understand it all yet.**

KAL 4.1 LLS 5.8 **3 Read these sentences, then listen and check your pronunciation.**
Practice of pronouncing cognates correctly.

**CD 4, track 6** **página 6, actividad 3**

**a** Fuimos al parque de atracciones. Lo pasamos fatal.
**b** En el centro de la ciudad hay una plaza con un restaurante.
**c** Comimos chile con carne y escuchamos la radio.

KAL 4.1 LLS 5.8 **4 Listen to a Spanish person saying these names. Then try to say them in the same way.**

**CD 4, track 7** **página 6, actividad 4**

**a** David Beckham
**b** Kiera Knightley
**c** Deep Purple
**d** Birmingham
**e** Mozart
**f** Ricky Martín

## Página 7 Pronunciation, rules

KAL 4.1 LLS 5.8 **1 Read this paragraph in your head. Make notes on words to watch out for and pronunciation rules to follow.**

KAL 4.1 LLS 5.8 **2 Now read the paragraph aloud. Afterwards, note down the words you felt uncomfortable with.**

KAL 4.1 LLS 5.8 **3 Write down the pronunciation rules or hints that would help you to tackle the words you found difficult.**

## Página 8 0.1 ¡Bienvenido!

- Use with Student Book, pages 4–5

AT 4.1 **1 Choose one letter from each box to find the forms of transport in Spanish. Write the word and then write the English.**
If necessary, go through the first one as a class to ensure all students know what to do.

*Answers:*
***a** tren – train; **b** avión – plane; **c** barco – boat; **d** coche – car*

AT 1.3 L&S 1.2 **2 Try to put this conversation into the correct order. Then listen and check your answer.**
This practises meeting and greeting in Spanish.

**CD 4, track 8** **página 8, actividad 2**

– ¡Hola! Soy Ángela.
– ¡Encantado! Soy Betc.
– Bienvenido a España.
– ¡Gracias!
– ¿Qué tal el viaje?
– Bien, gracias. El avión era cómodo.
– ¡Vamos!
– ¡Vale!

*Answers: as in transcript*

AT 4.3 R&W 2.4 **2 Now use the Spanish in Activity 2 to welcome Lionel to Manchester.**
Further practice of meeting and greeting people in Spanish.

## Página 9 0.2 ¿Cómo estás?

- Use with Student Book, pages 6–7

AT 3.1 AT 4.1 **1 Unscramble this adjective string.**
Students use their knowledge of Spanish adjectives to unscramble the string.

*Answers:*
***a** divertido; **b** decepcionado; **c** simpático; **d** contento; **e** generoso; **f** ilusionado; **g** triste; **h** inteligente*

KAL 4.5 AT 3.2 AT 1.2 **2 Circle the correct verb: *ser* or *estar*. Listen and check your answers.**

**CD 4, track 9** **página 9, actividades 2 y 3**

**a** Soy bastante simpática.
**b** Soy muy inteligente.
**c** Estoy triste.
**d** Estoy contento.
**e** Somos muy generosos.
**f** Estamos decepcionados.
**g** Estoy muy ilusionada.

*Answers: as in transcript*

AT 1.2 **2 Listen again and circle the adjective with the correct ending.**

*Answers: as in transcript*

## Página 10 0.3 Me llevo bien con Elena

- Use with Student Book, pages 8–9

AT 1.2 L&S 1.2 **1 Listen to Julia's game. Who does she think is great?**

**CD 4, track 10** **página 10, actividades 1 y 2**

Me cae bien
o me cae mal
Es pesado o
¡FENOMENAL!

¡Javi, Javi, eres fenomenal!

*Answer: Javi*

AT 1.2 L&S 1.2 KAL 4.3 **2 Listen again and write out Julia's rhyme.**
This requires an understanding of forming Spanish verbs and adjectives.

*Answers: as in transcript*

AT 2.2 **3 Now do the rhyme yourself, pointing to each person in turn to find out who you think is great.**
This provides practise of using opinion phrases.

## Página 11 0.4 ¿Vienes conmigo?

- Use with Student Book, pages 10–11

AT 3.2 **1 Use two different colours to underline the questions and group them together by meaning. Which is the odd one out?**

*Answer: e ¿Tienen algún descuento para estudiantes?*

AT 4.2–3 **2 Write possible answers to these questions.**
Students should think back to the Student Book spread for ideas for answers.

*Example answers:*
***a** Cuestan diez euros. **b** Empieza a las seis. **c** Sí, tenemos entradas a ocho euros.*

AT 1.2–3, 2.2–3 **3 Listen to the customers and answer their questions using the information below.**
Students listen and then answer each question orally using the information given.

**CD 4, track 11** **página 11, actividad 3**

**1**
¿A qué hora hay sesiones hoy?
¿A cuánto son las entradas para la sesión de las cinco?
¿Tienen algún descuento para estudiantes?

**2**
¿A qué hora empieza la película?
¿Cuánto cuestan las entradas?
¿Tienen algún descuento para estudiantes?

## Página 12 0.5 Excusas, excusas

- Use with Student Book, pages 12–13

AT 1.3 L&S 1.1, 1.2 **1 Listen to Raquel, Juan, Beatriz and Iván talking about where to go. Where do they suggest going?**
Practice of giving, accepting and refusing invitations.

**CD 4, track 12** **página 12, actividades 1, 2 y 3**

Raquel: Vamos a la piscina.
Juan: Qué buena idea.
Beatriz: Muy bien, vamos.
Raquel: Iván, ¿quieres venir?
Iván: No. No me gusta nadar. Es aburrido.

Beatriz: Vamos al cine.
Juan: Excelente.
Raquel: Vamos, vamos.
Beatriz: Iván, ¿quieres venir?
Iván: No. No, no me gustan las películas que ponen. Y no tengo dinero.

Iván: Me voy a mi casa.
Beatriz: Excelente.
Juan: Muy buena idea.
Raquel: Bien, bien.
All 3: Adiós, Iván.

Raquel: Entonces, ¿vamos a la piscina o al cine?
Juan: ¿Los dos?
Beatriz: Sí, vamos a la piscina y al cine.
Raquel: Excelente.
Juan: Muy divertido.

*Answers: pool and cinema*

AT 1.3 L&S 1.1, 1.2 **2 Listen again. What excuses does Iván give?**

*Answers: doesn't like swimming; it's boring; doesn't like the films; no money*

AT 1.3 L&S 1.1, 1.2 **3 When Iván goes home, where do the others decide to go?**

*Answers: pool AND cinema*

AT 4.3 **4 Draw the story as a cartoon strip and write in the speech bubbles in Spanish. Then act it out in groups of four.**
This is a fun way to ensure that students have really understood the script.

## Página 13 0.6A Labolengua

- Use with Student Book, pages 14–15

KAL 4.5 **1 Cross out all the letters that are used in the present tense of the verb *ser*. Use the letters that are left to make a word that can follow *es* ...**

*Answer: azul*

KAL 4.5 **2 Cross out all the letters that are in the present tense of the verb *estar*. Use the letters that are left to complete a word that can follow *está* ...**

*Answer: aburrido*

KAL 4.5 **3 Sort these words according to whether they are used with *ser* or *estar*. Write them next to a suitable person of the verb to make sensible sentences.**
Practice of differentiating between *ser* and *estar*.

*Answers:*
***Ser:*** *Soy inteligente. Mi hermano es generoso. Somos ingleses. Son mis primos.*
***Estar:*** *Estoy en España. Mi hermano está contento. Raquel está enferma. Estamos tristes.*

## Página 14 0.6B Técnica

- Use with Student Book, pages 14–15

LLS 5.5 **1 James has tried to look up the word 'drink' in a bilingual dictionary. Explain what he has probably done wrong in each of these cases.**

*Suggested answers:*
***a*** *He is looking for an English word in the Spanish half of the dictionary.*
***b*** *He is looking at the phonetic pronunciation.*
***c*** *He needs to decide if he wants a verb or a noun.*
***d*** *The dictionary is telling him it's a verb.*
***e*** *The dictionary is telling him it's a noun.*

LLS 5.5 **2 What should James do to make sure he finds the correct Spanish word for 'watch' in the following sentence?**
Students should use what they have done in Activity 1 to help them decide what James should (and shouldn't) do.

LLS 5.5 **3 What is the word he needs?**

*Answer: ver* **or** *mirar*

# 1A Hospedarse en España

## Unit Objectives

**Contexts and cultural focus:** daily life in Spain
**Grammar:** *soler;* frequency adverbs; the present continuous; the present tense of radical-changing verbs; quantities and large numbers; revision of the present tense including *hay* and no *hay*
**Language learning:** adapting previously learnt language; using a dictionary; memorising verb patterns; expressing opinions

- *Aim*: To learn about daily life in Spain
- Each unit has an associated video which will feature throughout the unit. Below is the transcript of the video for this unit.

### Video clip: Unit 1A (CD 1, tracks 18 and 21)

**Part 1**

*Elena, Roberto and Juan are eating some empanadas.*

Elena: ¿Te gusta la comida española, Roberto?
Roberto: Sí, pero ¿por qué se come tan tarde? La comida es a las dos o a las 3 y no cenamos hasta las 9 o aún más tarde.
Juan: Es verdad, pero ¿a qué hora se come en Colombia?
Roberto: En Colombia, comemos a las 12.30 o a la una y cenamos a las 6.30 o a las 7.
Juan: Aquí la merienda es a las 6.
Roberto: Me encantan las empanadas.
Juan: Aquí los llamamos empanadillas
Roberto: Mi madre hace unas empanadas exquisitas.
Elena: Ah, no las de mi madre son las mejores.
Roberto: Las de mi madre están más ricas.
Elena: Ah no, las de *mi* madre.
Roberto: Ah que no.
Elena: Ah que sí.
Juan: Basta. Es fácil, mañana vais a preparar unas empanadillas, y como la madre de Roberto no está, vosotros las vais a preparar.
Elena: Vale. Ya verás, Roberto.
Roberto: De acuerdo.

**Part 2**

*The following day in the kitchen.*

Juan: Preparados, listos, ¡ya!
Roberto: Para la masa: Harina de maíz – un paquete – sí. Un poco de sal. Dame la sal, Elena.
Elena: La necesito yo.
Roberto: Sólo necesito un poquito.
Elena: Vale, aquí la tienes.
Roberto: Aceite vegetal – unas cucharadas y un poquito de azúcar.
Elena: ¿Azúcar? ¿Vas a echar azúcar en las empanadas?
Roberto: Es la receta de mi madre.
Elena: Bueno, en la receta de mi madre no hay azúcar. Hay harina de trigo, agua, sal y un huevo.
Roberto: ¿Y para el picadillo?
Elena; ¿Quieres decir para el relleno, no? Para el relleno, pues tengo una cebolla, una lata de atún, una lata de tomates, un poco de perejil, un huevo cocido y un pimiento.
Roberto: Y el picadillo colombiano necesita: carne molida, aceitunas, alcaparras y uvas pasas.
Elena: ¿Y uvas pasas? ¡Qué raro!
Juan: ¡Venga vamos!, tengo hambre.
Roberto: Primero, tengo que hacer la masa. Se amasa la harina con otros ingredientes. Dos cucharadas de aceite, una pizca de sal, y una pizca de azúcar, un poco de agua.
Elena: Caliento el agua, sal, la harina de trigo, y después añado el huevo. Sí.
Juan: Veinte minutos.
Roberto: Con un rodillo se aplasta sobre una mesa cubierta de harina.
Juan: Quince minutos.
Juan: Diez minutos.
Elena: Se fríe la cebolla, se añade el atún, y los tomates y los otros ingredientes.
Roberto: Se añade las aceitunas, y las acaparras, las uvas pasas, la carne molida.
Juan: Cinco minutos.
Roberto: Y luego se fríen en aceite.
Juan: Dos minutos.
Roberto: Pero espera un poco.
Juan: Un minuto.
Elena: Espera.
Juan: Tiempo.

*At the table*

Juan: Estas son las empanadas de Roberto. Muy sabrosas, un poco dulce con las pasas pero me gusta la carne.
Elena: ¿Y las mías?
Juan: Son muy crujientes. Y me gusta el atún.
Roberto: ¿Pero quién gana?
Juan: Bueno tengo que probar otra.
Elena: ¿Quién gana Juan?
Juan: Tengo que probar otra. Y vosotros, ¿qué opináis?

**Punto Lengua**

En Colombia, comemos a las 12.30 o a la una y cenamos a las 6.30 o a las 7.
Aquí la merienda es a las 6.
Me encantan las empanadas.
Son muy crujientes y me gusta el atún.

As a starter activity to introduce the unit and familiarise students with the language they will meet, you may find it useful for the class to view the video as a whole. Are there any words or phrases that they have recognised? What do they think it is about? Get students to write down any food items, opinions and times that they have recognised. Explain that you will look at it in more detail later in this unit.

*Synopsis:*
Elena and Roberto both think that their version of 'empanadas' are the best. There is only one way to decide once and for all – a cook-off! Who will be able to produce the best 'empanadas' – Roberto with his Colombian version, or Elena with her Spanish ones. Juan will be the judge...

| Unit 1A Hospedarse en España Overview grid | | | | | | |
|---|---|---|---|---|---|---|
| **Page reference** | **Contexts and objectives** | **Language learning** | **Grammar** | **Key language** | **Framework** | **AT level** |
| Pages 20–21 **Primeras impresiones** | • discuss differences in daily routines | • adapt previously learnt language to revise the present tense | • use the verb *soler;* frequency adverbs | *soler; a pie; cerca (de); lejos (de); en el invierno; en el verano; el instituto; el colegio; comer; la cantina; levantarse; acostarse; vivir; volver; una ciudad; histórico/a; las montañas; en el quinto piso; a orillas del mar* | L&S 1.1, 1.2, 1.4; IU 3.1, 3.2; KAL 4.3, 4.4, 4.5; LLS 5.3, 5.4 | 1.3–4, 2.4, 3.3–4, 4.3–4 |
| Pages 22–23 **Faenas caseras** | • say what you do and have to do to help at home | • hints on how to use a dictionary to look up verbs | • use the present continuous | *sacar la basura; poner la mesa; escribir la lista de la compra; recoger el dormitorio; pasear al perro; hacer la cama; ¿Qué estás haciendo? está durmiendo; está leyendo; tener que; deber; jugar; dormir; pasar la aspiradora; limpiar; cocinar* | L&S 1.1, 1.2, 1.4; KAL 4.3, 4.5; LLS 5.1, 5.4, 5.5 | 1.2, 1.4, 3.2–3, 4.2–4 |
| Pages 24–25 **¡Buen provecho!** | • revise mealtimes and say what you prefer to eat | • practise memorising verb patterns | • use the present tense of radical-changing verbs | *el desayuno; desayunar; el almuerzo; almorzar; la merienda; merendar; la cena; cenar; la comida; un bocadillo; el jamón; el tomate; una mazorca; una piña; el arroz; la carne; una tortilla; la ensalada; los cereales; las tostadas; el café; sabroso/a; delicioso/a; soso/a; salado/a; picante; dulce; crujiente* | L&S 1.1, 1.2, 1.4, 1.5; R&W 2.4; IU: 3.1, 3.2; KAL 4.5; LLS 5.8 | 1.3–4, 2.3–4, 3.1, 3.3, 4.4 |

| Unit 1A Hospedarse en España Overview grid | | | | | | |
|---|---|---|---|---|---|---|
| **Page reference** | **Contexts and objectives** | **Language learning** | **Grammar** | **Key language** | **Framework** | **AT level** |
| Pages 26–27 **A cocinar algo típico** | • discuss recipes, ingredients and local dishes | • reading a Spanish recipe | • use quantities and large numbers | *un kilo de; medio kilo de; 100 gramos de; medio litro de; una lata de; un paquete de; una bolsa de; cien; quinientos/as; setecientos/as; novecientos/as; el aceite de oliva; un huevo; la harina (de trigo); la harina de maíz; una cebolla; el atún; el perejil; la sal; el azúcar; el agua; la carne molida; las aceitunas; las alcaparras; las uvas pasas; un pimiento; la masa; el relleno/el piquillo* | L&S 1.1, 1.2; R&W 2.1, 2.2, 2.5; IU 3.1, 3.2; LLS 5.3, 5.4, 5.5 | 1.3–4, 3.4, 4.4 |
| Pages 28–29 **La vida regional** | • talk about life in different regions and countries | • give opinions and descriptions | • revise the present tense including *hay* and *no hay* | | L&S 1.1, 1.2, 1.3; R&W 2.2, 2.4, 2.5; IU 3.1, 3.2; KAL 4.3 | 1.3–4, 2.2–3, 3.1, 3.4, 4.2–4 |
| Pages 30–31 **Labolengua** | • review language and grammar from the unit | | | | KAL 4.1, 4.5; LLS 5.1, 5.6 | |
| Pages 32–33 **Extra Star Extra Plus** | • differentiated extension/ homework material | • revise and consolidate all vocabulary and grammar covered in the unit | • revise and consolidate all vocabulary and grammar covered in the unit | | R&W 2.4; IU 3.1, 3.2; KAL 4.3, 4.5 | 3.2–4, 4.1–4 |
| Page 34 **Prueba** | • end-of-unit test | | | | L&S 1.1, 1.2, 1.4; R&W 2.2, 2.4; KAL 4.3, 4.5 | 1.4, 2.3–4, 3.4, 4.3–4 |
| Page 35 **Vocabulario** | • a summary of the key language covered in each core spread of this unit | | | | | |
| Page 149 **Leer 1A** | • practice of longer reading texts based on the theme of the unit | | | | R&W 2.1, 2.2 | 3.4–5 |

# 1A Hospedarse en España

| **Week-by-week overview**<br>**(Three-year KS3 Route: assuming six weeks' work or approximately 10–12.5 hours)**<br>**(Two-year KS3 Route: assuming four weeks' worth or approxmately 6.5-8.5 hours)** |
|---|
| **About Unit 1A, *Hospedarse en España:*** Students work in the context of day-to-day life in Spain. They discuss differences in daily routines and talk about how they help at home. They revise mealtimes and say what they like to eat. They discuss recipes, ingredients and local dishes. Students use the verb *soler* as well as frequency adverbs and the present continuous. They also use the present tense of radical-changing verbs, quantities and large numbers and revise the present tense. The unit also provides tips on language learning techniques. |

| **Three-Year KS3 Route** | | | **Two-Year KS3 Route** | | |
|---|---|---|---|---|---|
| **Week** | **Resources** | **Objectives** | **Week** | **Resources** | **Objectives** |
| **1** | **1A.1 Primeras impresiones**<br>**1A.6 Labolengua A & C** (p.30) | discuss differences in daily routines<br>use the verb soler; frequency adverbs adapt previously learnt language to revise the present tense | **1** | **1A.1 Primeras impresiones**<br>(Omit activities 7, 8 & Challenge)<br>**1A.6 Labolengua A & C** (p.30) | discuss differences in daily routines<br>use the verb *soler*; frequency adverbs adapt previously learnt language to revise the present tense |
| **2** | **1A.2 Faenas caseras**<br>**1A.6 Labolengua D & F**(p.31) | say what you do and have to do to help at home<br>use the present continuous<br>hints on how to use a dictionary to look up verbs | **2** | **1A.2 Faenas caseras**<br>(Omit activities 5 & Challenge)<br>**1A.6 Labolengua D & F** (p.31) | say what you do and have to do to help at home<br>use the present continuous<br>use a dictionary to look up verbs |
| **3** | **1A.3 ¡Buen provecho!**<br>**1A.6 Labolengua B** (p.30) | revise mealtimes and say what you prefer to eat<br>use the present tense of radical-changing verbs<br>practise memorising verb patterns | **3** | **1A.3 ¡Buen provecho!**<br>(Omit activities 5, Think & Challenge)<br>**1A.6 Labolengua B** (p.30) | revise mealtimes and say what you prefer to eat<br>revise the present tense of radical-changing verbs<br>practise memorising verb patterns |
| **4** | **1A.4 A cocinar algo típico** | discuss recipes, ingredients and local dishes<br>use quantities and large numbers<br>read a Spanish recipe | **4** | **1A.4 A cocinar algo típico**<br>(Omit activities 4, 8 & Challenge)<br>**1A.8 Prueba** (p.34)<br>**Vocabulario** (p.35) | discuss recipes, ingredients and local dishes<br>use quantities and large numbers<br>read a Spanish recipe<br>Prepare and carry out assessment in all four skills<br>Recapping on vocabulary of the unit |
| **5** | **0.5 La vida regional** | talk about life in different regions and countries<br>revise the present tense including *hay* and *no hay*<br>give opinions and descriptions | | | |
| **6** | **1A.7 Extra (Star)** (p.32)<br>**1A.7 Extra (Plus)** (p.33)<br>**1A.8 Prueba** (p.34)<br>**Vocabulario** (p.35)<br>**Leer** (p.149) | Further reinforcement and extension of the language of the unit.<br>Prepare and carry out assessment in all four skills<br>Recapping on vocabulary of the unit<br>Further reading to explore the language of the unit and cultural themes | | | |

## 1A.1 Primeras impresiones

páginas 20–21

# Planner

### Objectives
- discuss differences in daily routines
- use the verb *soler*; frequency adverbs
- adapt previously learnt language to revise the present tense

### Resources
Student Book, pages 20–21
CD 1, tracks 11–13
Foundation Workbook, page 16
Higher Workbook, page 16
Interactive OxBox, Unit 1A
Copymasters 14–21

### Key language
*soler; a pie; cerca (de); lejos (de); hace calor; hace frío; en el invierno; en el verano; el instituto; el colegio; comer; la cantina; levantarse; acostarse; vivir; volver; una ciudad; histórico/a; las montañas; en el quinto piso; a orillas del mar; en cambio; de costumbre; normalmente; por lo general*

### Renewed Framework references
L&S 1.1, 1.2; IU 3.1, 3.2; KAL 4.3, 4.4, 4.5; LLS 5.3, 5.4

### PLTS
Activity 2: Creative thinkers
Gramática: Reflective learners
Activity 7: Reflective learners
Challenge: Reflective learners

### Starters
- Before starting work on this spread, display the key language and ask students to write the English for as many of the words as they can. They will already be familiar with much of this vocabulary from previous spreads. Go through the answers as a class. This serves to show students that language is recycled from topic to topic. If there are any words that they don't know, leave these and explain that you will come back to them at the end of the spread when they should be able to fill in the English.
- Quickly revise times with students before they start Activity 6. Split the class into two teams. Display two outlines of analogue clocks. A member of each team comes to the front. Call out a time in Spanish. The first one to draw the correct time onto the clock gets a point for their team. Another member of each team comes to the front, and so on. Alternatively, display a time, either on an outline of a clock or in digital form. The first team to give you the correct time in Spanish gets a point.

### Plenaries
- Once students have completed Activity 8, ask them to close their books. Split the class into pairs or small groups. Give them a time limit to note down all the differences they can remember between Spain and Colombia. It is up to you whether they do this in English or Spanish. Compare answers as a class. Which group has remembered the most?
- Following the Challenge Activity, students work with a partner. They compare the differences to what they usually do, e.g. *Me levanto a las seis pero aquí tú te levantas a las siete.* etc. Depending on the level of the class, you may find it useful to display the transcript from Activity 8 for support.

### Homework/Self-study
Activity 7: Students continue to practise using the verb *soler* + infinitive by writing five sentences saying what they usually do.

AT 3.3 | LLS 5.4

**1 Lee y empareja las frases con los dibujos.**
Students read the sentences and then match them to the pictures.

*Answers:*
***1** e; **2** b; **3** d; **4** a; **5** c; **6** f*

AT 3.3 | PLTS

**2 Lee las frases otra vez. ¿Puedes advinar quién habla? ¿Roberto o Elena?**
Students read the sentences again and guess whether it is Roberto or Elena who is speaking.

AT 1.3 | LLS 5.4

**3 Escucha la conversación entre Roberto y Elena y verifica.**
Students listen to check their answers to Activity 2.

**CD 1, track 11** — **página 20, actividad 3**

Elena: Aquí en Segovia suelo al insti ir a pie porque todo queda bastante cerca. ¿Cómo vas tú al insti, Roberto?

Roberto: Bueno, suelo ir en el autobús escolar porque el colegio queda lejos del centro de Cartagena.
Elena: En tu **colegio** tienes que llevar uniforme, ¿verdad?
Roberto: Pues sí, llevamos uniforme. No vamos al **insti** como tú en vaqueros y camiseta.
Elena: ¿Y siempre hace mucho calor en Cartagena?
Roberto: Sí, suele hacer mucho calor en Cartagena todo el año.
Elena: No como aquí en Segovia. Aquí suele hacer frío en invierno y bastante calor en verano.

*Answers:*
***1** Elena; **2** Roberto; **3** Roberto; **4** Elena; **5** Roberto **6** Elena*

IU 3.1

## Think

Elicit from students that the two words for school mentioned in the recording are *insti* and *colegio*. Point out that in Spain they tend to use the word *insti* for secondary school whereas in Colombia they still use the word *colegio*.

PLTS

## Gramática

Look at the examples that cover all of the different persons. Do students remember any of the phrases using *soler* + infinitive from Activities 1, 2 and 3? Ask for examples of other radical-changing verbs and elicit from students that the two persons which are the same as in regular present tense verbs are the *nosotros* and *vosotros* forms. There is more on this in Labolengua section, B.

AT 1.4, 3.4
L&S 1.2

**4 Escucha y lee la conversación entre Roberto y su madre.**
Students listen to and read the conversation between Roberto and his mother.

**CD 1, track 12** **página 21, actividad 4**

- ¡Hola, hijo! ¿Qué tal te va en casa de tus tíos?
- Bueno … pues, la vida es bastante diferente.
- ¿A qué hora sueles levantarte para ir al colegio?
- Normalmente me levanto temprano a las seis y media.
- ¿Qué hora es ahora en España?
- Es la una de la tarde aquí pero son las siete de la mañana en Cartagena, ¿verdad?
- Así es; hay seis horas de diferencia. ¿Qué sueles hacer los sábados?
- Elena, Juan y yo solemos ir al cine a las cuatro porque mis tíos suelen trabajar.
- ¿Y los domingos?
- Solemos comer en familia, una comida grande a las tres de la tarde.

AT 3.4
L&S 1.2

**5 Lee otra vez y anota el orden de los relojes.**
Students read the conversation from Activity 5 again. They could also listen again if you wish. They then put the clocks into the correct order.

*Answers:*
*d, b, e, c, a*

AT 1.4
L&S 1.1, 1.2
IU 3.2

**6 Escucha otra conversación entre Roberto y Elena. Anota las diferencias. Copia y completa las fichas.**
Students listen and fill in the files.

**CD 1, track 13** **página 21, actividad 6**

Elena: La vida aquí en Segovia es bastante diferente, ¿verdad?
Roberto: Claro. En Cartagena me levanto a las seis pero aquí tú te levantas a las siete.
Elena: Vale, y tú no comes pan con la comida pero mi familia suele comer mucho pan.
Roberto: Y yo llevo uniforme pero tú no llevas uniforme – ¡qué suerte!
Elena: Tú vives en un apartamento, pero nosotros vivimos en una casa.
Roberto: Sí, y tu vives en una casa en el campo pero yo vivo en un apartamento que está en el quinto piso.
Elena: Bueno, bueno y tú sueles volver a casa a las dos de la tarde pero yo vuelvo a las cinco después de las clases.
Roberto: Es verdad, y durante la semana normalmente me acuesto a las diez y media, ¡pero tú siempre te acuestas muy tarde a la medianoche!
Elena: Bueno, ya ves que hay muchas diferencias entre nosotros o mejor dicho entre tu vida y la mía.

*Answers:*
***Roberto:*** *seis, pan, uniforme, un apartamento, dos, diez y media*
***Elena:*** *siete, pan, uniforme, una casa, cinco, medianoche*

AT 4.3 | PLTS

**7 Escribe cinco frases sobre lo que suele hacer Juan en un día típico. Usa los verbos y las frases de abajo para ayudarte.**
Students practise using *soler* + infinitive. They should use the words from the box to help them. Volunteers could read their sentences out to the class.

AT 2.4

**8 Elige la ficha de Roberto o la ficha de Elena. Lee la ficha a tu compañero.**
Practice of talking about different daily routines.

PLTS | AT 4.3–4 | KAL4.4, 4.5

**Challenge**
**Write six sentences in Spanish about what you usually do during the day. Include the time and write two sentences each for the morning, the afternoon and the evening.**
Encourage students to draw upon the vocabulary they have learnt in the unit so far. Remind them that they don't have to tell the truth, but should try to make their sentences as interesting and varied as possible. Can they include any negatives? Volunteers could read their sentences out to the class.

## 1A.2 Faenas caseras

páginas 22–23

# *Planner*

### Objectives
- say what you do and have to do to help at home
- use the present continuous
- hints on how to use a dictionary to look up verbs

### Resources
Student Book, pages 22–23
CD 1, tracks 14–15
Foundation Workbook, page 17
Higher Workbook, page 17
Foundation Workbook audio, CD 3, track 33 (Workbook 13)
Higher Workbook audio, CD 4, track 13
Interactive OxBox, Unit 1A
Copymasters 14–21

### Key language
*sacar la basura; poner la mesa; escribir la lista de la compra; recoger el dormitorio; pasear al perro; hacer la cama; ¿Qué estás haciendo? está durmiendo; está leyendo; tener que; deber; jugar; dormir; tocar la guitarra; la revista; pasar la aspiradora; limpiar; quitar el polvo; cocinar; fregar los platos; beber*

### Renewed Framework references
L&S 1.1, 1.2, 1.4; KAL 4.3, 4.5; LLS 5.1, 5.4, 5.5

### PLTS
Activity 1: Reflective learners
Gramática: Self-managers; Independent enquirers; Reflective learners
Activity 3: Reflective learners
Activity 5: Effective participators
Challenge: Team workers; Effective participators

### Starters
- Play a variation of 'Simon Says' to reinforce the key language. Explain that if you call out a statement beginning with *tener que*, or *deber* then students should mime this activity, e.g. If you say *Tengo que recoger mis libros.* students mime tidying away books, or if you call out *Debo hacer mi cama.* students mime making a bed. However, if you call out a statement that doesn't begin with *tener que*, or *deber* then students should not mime the activity, e.g. if you say *Estoy paseando el perro.* they should just stand still. You can call out statements in any person you wish.
- To remind students how to use *tener que* and *deber* before they attempt Activity 6, read the second Grammar box on page 23 of the Student Book and then go round the class quickly asking each student to give you one household chore that they have to or must do. With less able classes, display some useful key language for support.

## Plenaries

- Following Activity 3, ask students to write a present continuous sentence in each person. Compare answers as a class.
- Following Activity 7, ask students to write their own set of instructions for a visitor or a sibling. They can make this as humorous as they wish. Volunteers could read their instructions to the class and points could be awarded for the funniest, silliest, most sensible, etc.

## Homework/Self-study

After working through the Grammar box (Student Book, page 22), students write their own sentences using the present continuous.
Students write out the sentence they produced in Starter Activity 1 and add at least four more.

AT 3.2 | PLTS | LLS 5.4

**1 Empareja los dibujos con la frase adecuada.**
Students match each sentence to the appropriate picture. Encourage them to concentrate on any words with which they are already familiar and use these to work out the meaning of the sentence.

*Answers:*
***1** d; **2** b; **3** f; **4** c; **5** a; **6** e*

AT 1.2 | L&S 1.2

**2 Escucha e indica quién es.**
Students listen and refer back to the sentences in Activity 1 to say who each bit of audio is referring to.

**CD 1, track 14** — **página 22, actividad 2**

1 Bueno, mírame; estoy poniendo la mesa.
2 Y yo, yo estoy haciendo mi cama.
3 Vale, y yo estoy paseando al perro.
4 ¿Ves? Estoy recogiendo mi dormitorio.
5 Uf – yo estoy sacando la basura.
6 Bueno, bueno, yo estoy escribiendo la lista de la compra.

*Answers:*
***1** Isa; **2** Toni; **3** Merche; **4** Pablo; **5** Sebas; **6** Luchi*

PLTS | KAL 4.5

### Gramática

This Grammar box is to be used alongside Activities 1 and 2. Elicit from students that the English equivalent of the Spanish *-ando* and *-iendo* is *–ing* (doing, singing, etc.). Allow students to use the information given to come up with their own rules about how to form the present continuous. Compare ideas as a class and then check with the information on page 31 of the Student Book. Explain also that there will be exceptions to this rule and that students will have to learn these.

AT 2.2 | L&S 1.4 | KAL 4.3, 4.5 | PLTS

**3 Mira los ejemplos de la actividad 1. Pregunta y contesta con tu compañero.**
Students take turns to ask and answer the questions. The examples from Activity 1 use *está* with the present continuous form. Remind students that they will have to put the sentences into the first person. Refer them to the Think box to show that it isn't just the verb that they will need to change.

AT 4.2–3 | PLTS | LLS 5.1, 5.5

**4 ¿Qué está haciendo el robomop? Escribe ocho frases.**
Students should try to write as many sentences as they can and only use a dictionary when they are sure they don't know the word/verb.

AT 2.2 | PLTS | L&S 1.4

**5 La persona A hace la mímica. La persona B adivina lo que está haciendo.**
This is a fun way for students to practise using the present continuous. You could turn it into a class game where a student mimes an action at the front and the class guesses what he/she is doing.

AT 4.3 | KAL 4.5 | LLS 5.1, 5.5

**6 Mira los dibujos de la actividad 1 y escribe lo que tienes que o debes hacer.**
Work through the Grammar box with the class before they attempt this activity to remind them how to use *tener que* + the infinitive and *deber* + the infinitive correctly. Students then write sentences based on the pictures in Activity 1.

AT 3.3 | KAL 4.5

**7 Lee las instrucciones de Juan para Roberto. Completa el texto con uno de los verbos de la casilla.**
Explain to students that Roberto has to share a room with Elena's younger brother Juan. Juan has left some instructions for him, but there are gaps in these. Students complete the text with the correct verbs.

*Answers:*
***1** recoger; **2** hacer; **3** limpiar; **4** tocar; **5** leer; **6** comer*

AT 1.4 | L&S 1.1, 1.2

**8 Escucha. Anota todos los verbos.**
Student listen and list all the verbs they hear.

**CD 1, track 15** **página 23, actividades 8 y 9**

Elena: Oye, Roberto, yo estoy recogiendo mi dormitorio y tú, ¿qué estás haciendo?
Roberto: Pues en este momento, nada.
Elena: Debes ayudarme a limpiar la casa.
Roberto: ¿Qué dices? ¿Cómo? ¿¡Limpiar la casa!? ¿Yo?
Elena: Claro. Tienes que hacer tu cama y pasar la aspiradora y …
Roberto: Bueno, bueno, recojo mis cosas todas las mañanas y paso la aspiradora y siempre hago mi cama, así que ¿de qué hablas?
Elena: Vale, pero yo debo fregar los platos y poner la mesa y quitar el polvo y cocinar y …
Roberto: ¡Basta ya! Estoy leyendo mi revista favorita – ¡por favor!

*Answers:*
*estoy recogiendo; estás haciendo; ayudarme; limpiar; dices; tienes; hacer; pasar; recojo; paso; hago; debo; fregar; poner; quitar; cocinar; estoy leyendo*

AT 1.4 | L&S 1.1, 1.2

**9 Escucha otra vez. ¿Quién ayuda más en casa, Roberto o Elena? Escribe dos listas.**
Students listen to Roberto and Elena and write a list for each saying what they do to help around the house. Who does the most?

*Answers:*
*Roberto says he tidies up, vacuums and makes his bed. Elena says she tidies her room, washes the dishes, lays the table, dusts and cooks. So she does more than Roberto.*

AT 2.3–4, 4.3–4 | PLTS

**Challenge**

**Quiz: ¿Qué haces o tienes que hacer para ayudar en casa?**
Depending on the level of the class and the time available, either make this a quick survey done orally or ask students to prepare a written survey which is then presented graphically with statistics.

## 1A.3 ¡Buen provecho!

páginas 24–25

### Planner

#### Objectives
- revise mealtimes and say what you prefer to eat
- revise the present tense of radical-changing verbs
- practise memorising verb patterns

#### Resources
Student Book, pages 24–25
CD 1, tracks 16–17
Foundation Workbook, page 18
Higher Workbook, page 18
Interactive OxBox, Unit 1A
Copymasters 14–21

#### Video
Video clip, Unit 1A

#### Key language
*el desayuno; desayunar; el almuerzo; almorzar; la merienda; merendar; la cena; cenar; la comida; un bocadillo; el jamón; el tomate; una mazorca; una piña; el arroz; la carne; una tortilla; la ensalada; los cereales; las tostadas; el café; sabroso/a; delicioso/a; soso/a; salado/a; picante; dulce; crujiente*

#### Renewed Framework references
L&S 1.1, 1.2, 1.4, 1.5; R&W 2.4; IU: 3.1, 3.2; KAL 4.5; LLS 5.8

#### PLTS
Activity 1: Reflective learners
Gramática: Independent enquirers
Challenge: Self-managers; Effective participators; Creative thinkers; Team workers

## Starters

- Before beginning work on this spread, explain to students that you are going to look at Spanish mealtimes and foods. Split them into groups and ask them to list as much food vocabulary as they can. Compare answers as a class. Look back at Unit 3A (pages 88 and 89) of *Zoom español 1* which details Spanish meals, times they are eaten and what is generally eaten. Is there any vocabulary that students have forgotten?
- Play a memory game to reinforce food vocabulary. Start with a statement, e.g. *Me gusta comer la ensalada.* A student continues, *Me gusta comer la ensalada y el arroz* and so on until someone forgets one of the food ítems.
- To prepare students for Activity 6, brainstorm adjectives that could be used to describe food, e.g. *soso/a, picante, dulce,* etc.

## Plenaries

- Students compare their homework on the times they eat their meals. Do most students tend to eat at the same time?
- Following Activity 6, students work in groups to present the results of the survey graphically.
- Students work in groups to produce a dialogue similar to that in Activity 7.

## Homework/Self-study

After looking at the second Think box as a class, ask students to write an account of what they eat in a day: what time do they eat their meals and where – at school, at home, etc.?

AT 3.1 | PLTS | IU 3.1

**1 Mira los dibujos y decide para qué comida son.**

This activity provides very basic revision and reuses only vocabulary that students have already met in Unit 3A of *Zoom español 1*. Starter Activity 1 provides a quick recap of Spanish meals, what they consist of, times they are eaten, etc.

*Answers:*
***a** el desayuno, el almuerzo, la merienda, la cena; **b** el almuerzo or la cena; **c** el desayuno, el almuerzo or la cena; **d** el almuerzo or la cena; **e** el desayuno, la cena, or el almuerzo; **f** el almuerzo or la cena; **g** el desayuno; **h** el desayuno, el almuerzo, la merienda or la cena*

AT 1.3-4

**2 Escucha y verifica**

Students listen and check their answers for Activity 1.

**CD 1, track 16** **página 24, actividades 2 y 3**

Roberto: ¿A qué hora sueles despertarte, Elena?
Elena: Me despierto temprano sobre las seis y media y tomo el desayuno a las siete – algo ligero como cereales o tostadas. ¿Y tú?
Roberto: No suelo desayunar mucho – tal vez un café con leche porque tengo que salir temprano para ir al cole.
Elena: Yo siempre voy a la casa de mi abuela a las dos en punto para almorzar.
Roberto: Yo tengo la costumbre de irme a casa y comer con mi hermana a eso de la una de la tarde. Normalmente almorzamos bien – sopa con mazorca, arroz con carne y piña, me encanta la piña.
Elena: Cuando llego a casa sobre las cinco, meriendo un bocadillo de jamón y tomate que me gusta mucho.
Roberto: Nosotros no merendamos porque almorzamos bien y cenamos en casa pasadas las siete.
Elena: Aquí esperamos hasta las nueve para cenar con toda la familia. ¡No creo que pueda comer tan temprano! Entre semana cenamos tortilla y ensalada.
Roberto: ¡Por eso siempre tengo hambre! Me encanta comer delante de la tele cuando mi madre no está en casa.

AT 1.3–4, 3.3

**3 Lee las frases de abajo y escucha. ¿Quién dice lo siguiente – Roberto o Elena?**

Students listen again and this time note down who says each of the sentences listed.

*Answers:*
***Roberto:** 2, 4, 6; **Elena:** 1, 3, 5, 7, 8*

## Think

This is a good opportunity to look at time phrases again.

AT 4.4 | R&W 2.4

**4 ¿Qué diferencias hay entre Roberto y Elena? Escribe cuatro frases.**

Answers will be students' own conclusions – a combination of facts from the sentences 1–8 and the recording. It may help some students if you display the transcript so that they can begin to match what they hear with what they read.

PLTS | KAL 4.5

## Gramática

Elicit from students that the 1, 2, 3, 6 pattern comes from the fact that it is the first, second and third person singular and the third person plural where the stem changes.
Give students chance to conjugate the verbs listed before checking answers as a class:
*preferir (ie): prefiero, prefieres, prefiere, preferimos, preferís, prefieren*
*querer (ie): quiero, quieres, quiere, queremos, queréis, quieren*
*comenzar (ie): comienzo, comienzas, comienza, comenzamos; comenzáis; comienzan*
Point out to students that although the stems of these three verbs change in the same way, the endings differ. They should be able tell you that this is because *preferir (ie)* is an –ir verb, *querer (ie)* is an –er verb and *comenzar (ie)* is an –ar verb.

AT 2.3

**5 Sondeo en clase.**
Students carry out a class survey to find out who eats what for each meal.

AT 1.4 | L&S 1.1, 1.2

**6 Escucha. ¿Qué prefieren comer? ¿A qué hora? ¿Qué opinan? Copia y completa la tabla.**
Students listen and note down what each speaker likes eating and when.

**CD 1, track 17** — **página 25, actividad 6**

| | |
|---|---|
| Teacher: | Hola, clase. Vamos a ver lo que soléis comer en cada comida y cuál es el plato más popular. A ver, vamos a comenzar contigo, Teresa. |
| Teresa: | Bueno, prefiero no desayunar demasiado – un zumo de naranja me basta. Pero al mediodía me encanta comer pizza porque es muy rica y sabrosa. Ahora tú, Miguel. |
| Miguel: | Siempre tengo hambre así que desayuno mucho. Me gusta preparar huevos con tostadas – ¡dos o tres! Me encantan, son deliciosos. A ver, Merche, ¿tú qué comes? |
| Merche: | Prefiero comer algo exótico y picante, sobre todo si salimos los sábados por la noche con mis padres. Nos encanta la comida mejicana; chili con carne, por ejemplo. Es una cena rica. ¿Verdad, Sebas? ¿Tú qué dices? |
| Sebas: | Pues no puedo comer platos picantes. Prefiero la comida más sosa y más normal como el arroz blanco. Para mí es delicioso. También me gusta el pollo asado si está crujiente y bien tostado. |

*Answers:*
***Teresa:** zumo de naranja; el desayuno; –*
*pizza; el almuerzo/medodía; sabrosa*
***Miguel:** huevos sobre tostadas; el desayuno; deliciosos*
***Merche:** la comida mejicana; la cena; rica*
***Sebas:** arroz blanco, pollo asado; el almuerzo/la cena; delicioso*

IU 3.1, 3.2 | AT 1.4

**7 Mira la primera parte del video y contesta a las preguntas en inglés.**
Students watch the first part of the video and answer the questions in English.

**Video clip: Unit 1A (CD 1, track 18)**

**Part 1**
*Elena, Roberto and Juan are eating some empanadas.*

| | |
|---|---|
| Elena: | ¿Te gusta la comida española, Roberto? |
| Roberto: | Sí, pero ¿por qué se come tan tarde? La comida es a las 2 o a las 3 y no cenamos hasta las 9 o aún más tarde. |
| Juan: | Es verdad, pero ¿a qué hora se come en Colombia? |
| Roberto: | En Colombia, comemos a las 12.30 o a la una y cenamos a las 6.30 o a las 7. |
| Juan: | Aquí la merienda es a las 6. |
| Roberto: | Me encantan las empanadas. |
| Juan: | Aquí los llamamos empanadillas |
| Roberto: | Mi madre hace unas empanadas exquisitas. |
| Elena: | Ah, no las de mi madre son las mejores. |
| Roberto: | Las de mi madre están más ricas. |
| Elena: | Ah no, las de **mi** madre. |
| Roberto: | Ah que no. |
| Elena: | Ah que sí. |
| Juan: | Basta. Es fácil, mañana vais a preparar unas empanadillas, y como la madre de Roberto no está, vosotros las vais a preparar. |
| Elena: | Vale. Ya verás, Roberto. |
| Roberto: | De acuerdo. |

*Answers:*
***a** lunch, dinner, tea/a snack; **b** the times they eat in Spain – he finds that they eat late; **c** his mother's are delicious*

AT 2.4 | L&S 1.4

**8 Lee el diálogo, luego practícala.**
Students work in pairs to practise the dialogue. Volunteers could perform the dialogue in front of the class.

## Challenge

PLTS | AT 2.4 | AT 4.4 | L&S 1.5 | R&W 2.4 | LLS 5.8

**Write an imaginary dialogue at the meal table. Offer, accept, refuse and say why you don't like different foods. Then practise your dialogue with a partner. Use the dialogue in Activity 8 to help you.**
If possible, allow students to record their dialogues so that they can assess their own and their partner's pronunciation.

## 1A.4 A cocinar algo típico

páginas 26–27

### Planner

**Objectives**
- discuss recipes, ingredients and local dishes
- use quantities and large numbers
- read a Spanish recipe

**Resources**
Student Book, pages 26–27
CD 1, tracks 19–21
Foundation Workbook, page 19
Higher Workbook, page 19
Foundation Workbook audio, CD 3, track 34 (Workbook 14)
Higher Workbook audio, CD 4, track 14
Interactive OxBox, Unit 1A
Copymasters 14–21

**Video**
Video clip, Unit 1A

**Key language**
*un kilo de; medio kilo de; 100 gramos de; medio litro de; una lata de; un paquete de; una bolsa de; cien; quinientos/as; setecientos/as; novecientos/as; el aceite de oliva; un huevo; la harina (de trigo); la harina de maíz; una cebolla; el atún; el perejil; la sal; el azúcar; el agua; la carne molida; las aceitunas; las alcaparras; las uvas pasas; un pimiento; la masa; el relleno/el piquillo*

**Renewed Framework references**
L&S 1.1, 1.2; R&W 2.1, 2.2, 2.5; IU 3.1, 3.2; LLS 5.3, 5.4, 5.5

**PLTS**
Gramática: Self-managers
Challenge: Creative thinkers; Independent enquirers; Self-managers

**Starters**
- To prepare students for this spread have a quick-fire quantities quiz. Call out a variety of quantities, e.g. *medio litro de* – to begin with go quite slowly. Students note down what you have called out. Check answers as a class. Do this again but speed up. Continue in this way, getting quicker each time.

**Plenaries**
- Following Activity 4, have a memory quiz. Split the class into small groups. Give them a time limit to write down as much as they can remember about Colombian *empanadas:* ingredients, quantities, etc. When the time is up, compare and check answers. The group that has remembered the most correct information wins.
- Display the verbs from Activity 4 and challenge students to use each one in a sentence on the theme of the spread.

**Homework/Self-study**
Gramática: Students write sentences containing the high numbers they have practised.

AT 1.3 | L&S1.1, 1.2

**1 Escucha y anota lo que compra Elena.**
Students listen to Elena and note down what she buys.

**CD 1, track 19** — **página 26, actividades 1 y 2**

Elena:
A ver, a ver, tengo que comprar una botella de aceite de oliva – medio litro es suficiente, creo.

Necesito unos huevos – dos huevos son suficientes pero voy a comprar media docena por si acaso.

Claro, tengo que comprar un paquete de harina de trigo… sólo la venden en paquetes de un kilo – bueno, un kilo de harina de trigo.

A ver, ¿qué más? Ay, claro, el atún: ¿una o dos latas de atún? Con una lata grande de 250 gramos es suficiente y una lata de tomates de cuatrocientos gramos.

Eso es todo. Ay no, qué tonta, necesito comprar cebollas y perejil. Medio kilo de cebollas y una bolsa pequeña de perejil. Ya estamos – listos para cocinar las empanadas.

*Answers:*
***1*** *a bottle of olive oil – half a litre;* ***2*** *eggs – half a dozen;* ***3*** *flour (wheat) one kilo bag;* ***4*** *tin of tuna – large 250 grams;* ***5*** *tin of tomatoes – 400 grams;* ***6*** *onions – half a kilo;* ***7*** *parsley – a small bag*

AT 1.3 | L&S1.1, 1.2

**2 Escucha otra vez y anota las cantidades de cada ingrediente.**
Students listen to the recording from Activity 1 again and this time note down the quantities mentioned.

*Answers: see answers for Activity 1*

PLTS **Gramática**
Students have heard some high numbers in the recording for Activities 1 and 2. Students practise these with a partner.

AT 1.4 L&S 1.1, 1.2 **3 Escucha el mensaje de Roberto y escoge la palabra(s) adecuada(s).**
Students listen to Roberto's answerphone message and choose the correct word to complete the sentence each time.

**CD 1, track 20** **página 26, actividad 3**

Mamá, es urgente: tienes que decirme cómo se preparan las empanadas. Mañana voy a cocinar con Elena. Ella dice que las empanadas españolas son las mejores, y yo insisto que las colombianas son superiores pero la verdad es que no tengo la menor idea de cómo se preparan. Escríbeme urgentemente y explícame primero qué ingredientes tengo que comprar y también tienes que indicarme paso a paso cómo voy a prepararlas. Gracias, vale - espero tu email pronto pero muy pronto.

*Answers:*
***1** ayuda; **2** cocinar; **3** preparar; **4** ingredientes; **5** se cocinan*

AT 3.4 R&W 2.2 **4 Lee el email de la madre de Roberto y empareja los dibujos con las instrucciones. Usa un diccionario.**
Students read the e-mail and match the instructions to the pictures. They can use a dictionary for support.

*Answers:*
***1** f; **2** d; **3** a; **4** b; **5** g; **6** e; **7** c*

AT 3.4 R&W 2.2 **5 Lee las instrucciones otra vez. Empareja los verbos subrayados con las palabras inglesas abajo.**
Students read the instructions again and then translate the words into Spanish.

*Answers:*
***cut**– cortar; **fill** – rellenar; **fry** – freír; **mix** – mezclar; **flatten/ roll out** – aplastar; **put into** – poner; **take out** – sacar; **open up** – abrir*

AT 1.4 **6 Anota todas los ingredientes mencionados en el video.**
Student watch the second part of the video and note down all ingredients mentioned.

*Answers:*
*maíz, sal, aceite vegetal, cucharados, azúcar, agua, un huevo, atún, tomates, perejil, carne, molida, aceitunas, alcaparras, uvas pasas, cebolla*

AT 1.4 **7 Mira el video y contesta a las preguntas en inglés.**
Students watch the second part of the video and then answer the questions. Explain that they will have met much of the vocabulary in this spread and that they won't need to understand every word.

**Video script: Unit 1A (CD 1, track 21)**

**Part 2**
*The following day in the kitchen.*

Juan: Preparados, listos, ¡ya!
Roberto: Para la masa:
Harina de maíz – un paquete – sí.
Un poco de sal. Dame la sal, Elena.
Elena: La necesito yo.
Roberto: Sólo necesito un poquito.
Elena: Vale, aquí la tienes.
Roberto: Aceite vegetal – unas cucharadas y un poquito de azúcar.
Elena: ¿Azúcar? ¿Vas a echar azúcar en las empanadas?
Roberto: Es la receta de mi madre.
Elena: Bueno, en la receta de mi madre no hay azúcar. Hay harina de trigo, agua, sal y un huevo.
Roberto: ¿Y para el picadillo?
Elena; ¿Quieres decir para el relleno, no? Para el relleno, pues tengo una cebolla, una lata de atún, una lata de tomates, un poco de perejil, un huevo cocido y un pimiento.
Roberto: Y el picadillo colombiano necesita: carne molida, aceitunas, alcaparras y uvas pasas.
Elena: ¿Y uvas pasas? ¡Qué raro!
Juan: ¡Venga vamos!, tengo hambre.
Roberto: Primero, tengo que hacer la masa. Se amasa la harina con otros ingredientes. Dos cucharadas de aceite, una pizca de sal, y una pizca de azúcar, un poco de agua.
Elena: Caliento el agua, sal, la harina de trigo, y después añado el huevo. Sí.
Juan: Veinte minutos.
Roberto: Con un rodillo se aplasta sobre una mesa cubierta de harina.
Juan: Quince minutos.
Juan: Diez minutos.
Elena: Se fríe la cebolla, se añade el atún, y los tomates y los otros ingredientes.
Roberto: Se añade las aceitunas, y las acaparras, las uvas pasas, la carne molida.
Juan: Cinco minutos.
Roberto: Y luego se fríen en aceite.
Juan: Dos minutos.
Roberto: Pero espera un poco.
Juan: Un minuto.
Elena: Espera
Juan: Tiempo.

*At the table*

| | |
|---|---|
| Juan: | Estas son las empanadas de Roberto. Muy sabrosas, un poco dulce con las pasas pero me gusta la carne. |
| Elena: | ¿Y las mías? |
| Juan: | Son muy crujientes. Y me gusta el atún. |
| Roberto: | ¿Pero quién gana? |
| Juan: | Bueno tengo que probar otra. |
| Elena: | ¿Quién gana Juan? |
| Juan: | Tengo que probar otra. Y vosotros, ¿qué opináis? |

*Answers:*
***a** tuna; **b** Juan likes Roberto's – even though the raisins make them a bit sweet he likes the meat; he also likes Elena's as they are very crunchy and he likes the tuna*

**8 Who do you think makes the best empanadas?**
*Answer: Students' own opinions*

AT 4.4 | PLTS | R&W 2.5 | LLS5.5

## Challenge

**Write a brief description of your favourite regional or family dish. Write a list of ingredients and explain how to cook it in five easy steps. Say why you like it. Use a dictionary to help you.**
Remind students of the words for opinions and encourage them to use a dictionary if they want to add more ideas of their own.

# 1A.5 La vida regional

páginas 28–29

## *Planner*

### Objectives

- talk about life in different regions and countries
- revise the present tense including *hay* and *no hay*
- give opinions and descriptions

### Resources

Student Book, pages 28–29
CD 1, tracks 22–23
Foundation Workbook, page 20
Higher Workbook, page 20
Interactive OxBox, Unit 1A
Copymasters 14–21

### Renewed Framework references

L&S 1.1, 1.2, 1.3; R&W 2.2, 2.4, 2.5; IU 3.1, 3.2; KAL 4.3

### PLTS

Activity 1: Reflective learners
Activity 5: Self-managers
Activity 7: Reflective learners
Activity 9: Self-managers
Challenge: Creative thinkers; Effective participators; Self-managers

### Starters

- Activity 1 is an exact revision of page 72 in the *Zoom español 1* Student Book and is ideal to recap regions vocabulary.
- Ask students to give you as many adjectives as they can which describe places you live, e.g. *bonito, aburrida*, etc. Elicit from students that adjectives must agree with the noun they are describing.

### Plenaries

- Following Activities 8 and 9, students write their own gapped letter with artwork prompts for a partner to complete. The letter should say where they live, what time they get up and what they have for breakfast. They can make it as simple or complicated as they wish.
- Students describe the worst town or village they can think of. What is there (or isn't there), where is it, etc.? Volunteers read their description to the class who votes for the 'worst' town or village.

### Homework/Self-study

Activity 5, page 28
Activity 6, page 28
Activity 9, page 29

PLTS | AT 3.1

**1 Empareja las fotos con la palabra adecuada.**
This is an ideal Starter Activity to start students off on the comparing process.

*Answers:*
***1** d; **2** c; **3** a; **4** b; **5** e; **6** f*

AT 1.3 | L&S 1.1, 1.2

**2 Escucha y anota dónde viven.**
Students listen and note down where each person lives. You may find it useful to quickly revise compass points before they start listening.

**CD 1, track 22** — **página 28, actividades 2 y 3**

**1** ¡Hola! Me llamo Ana y vivo en el campo en el norte de España. Mi pueblo es bonito y muy tranquilo.
**2** ¡Saludos desde el sur de España! Soy Isidoro y vivo en una aldea bastante pequeña. Está en las montañas y la vida aquí es bastante aburrida.
**3** Buenas – me llamo Pedro y soy de Valladolid en el oeste de España. Es una ciudad bastante industrial y ruidosa. No está muy lejos de Madrid, la capital.
**4** ¡Hola! Soy Maite y vivo en Palamós en el noreste de España. Es un pueblo grande en la Costa Brava. Me encanta porque está a orillas del mar.

*Answers:*
***Ana:*** *campo, norte;* ***Isidoro:*** *aldea, sur;* ***Pedro:*** *ciudad, oeste;* ***Maite:*** *pueblo, noreste*

AT 1.3 | L&S 1.2, 1.3

**3 Escucha otra vez y añade una descripción de la casilla.**
Students listen again and note down adjectives used to describe where each person lives.

*Answers:*
***Ana:*** *bonito y tranquilo;* ***Isidoro:*** *pequeña y aburrida;* ***Pedro:*** *industrial y ruidosa;* ***Maite:*** *grande, a orillas del mar*

AT 2.3

**4 Habla con tu compañero.**
Students work with a partner to ask and answer questions about the recording.

AT 4.2–3 | PLTS | KAL 4.3

**5 Escribe una frase para cada persona.**
Students now use what they have done in Activities 2 and 3 to write their own sentences about where each of the speakers lives. Remind them to pay attention to adjectival agreement. Students will also need to change the verbs to the third person singular.

*Possible answers:*
1. *Ana vive en el campo en un pueblo bonito.*
2. *Isidoro vive en una aldea bastante pequeña en las montañas.*
3. *Pedro es de Valladolid en el oeste de España. Es una ciudad bastante industrial y ruidosa.*
4. *Maite y vivo en Palamós en el noreste de España en un pueblo grande.*

AT 3.4 | R&W 2.2

**6 Lee. ¿Verdad, mentira o no se menciona?**
Students read the e-mail and note down whether each statement is true (v), false (m) or not mentioned (nm).

*Answers:* ***1*** *m;* ***2*** *v;* ***3*** *nm;* ***4*** *nm;* ***5*** *m;* ***6*** *v*

AT 1.3 | PLTS | L&S1.2

**7 Escucha y anota los lugares mencionados.**
Again, students will already be familiar with this language, but this activity will help them to make comparisons and discuss differences in where they live using the present tense only.

**CD 1, track 23** — **página 29, actividades 7 y 8**

1. Hola, me llamo Lidia. En mi ciudad hay mucho que hacer porque hay varios restaurantes, un cine, un bonito parque y un supermercado grande. Pero no hay una discoteca, ¡qué lástima!
2. Bueno, yo me llamo Enrique y vivo en un pueblo pequeño así que no hay mucho de interés. Tenemos un banco, un colegio y un parque pequeño y menos mal que tenemos una estación de tren. Pero no hay un cine.
3. Soy Guadalupe – Lupe – y vivo en una ciudad enorme. Hay mucho pero mucho que ver y que hacer aquí. Hay parques, cines, supermercados, una catedral y museos y un hospital muy moderno. Claro, hay una estación de tren, varios colegios, bancos y por supuesto muchos restaurantes. ¡Hay de todo!
4. Y yo soy Pablo. Mi ciudad está en las montañas cerca de Madrid. No hay mucho que hacer aquí pero me encanta. Tenemos un instituto y un banco, un parque grande y un pequeño supermercado. No hay una estación de tren.

*Answers:*
***1*** *h, g, j, b, k* ***2*** *i, f, j, e, g* ***3*** *j, g, b, a, c, d, e, f, i, h;* ***4*** *f, i, j, b, e*

AT 1.4 | L&S 1.1, 1.2

**8 Escucha otra vez y anota lo que *no* hay en la ciudad.**
This activity can be extended by asking more able students to make comparisons between each town and region.

AT 3.4 | PLTS

**9 Copia y completa la carta ilustrada. Usa el vocabulario de la casilla para ayudarte.**
Students use the artwork prompts and vocabulary box to complete the letter.

*Answers:*
*sur; montañas; mar; las seis; me ducho; uniforme; deporte; zumo de naranja; cereales; tostadas; yogur; peinarme; lavarme los dientes*

AT 3.4 | R&W 2.2

**10 Lee la carta otra vez y contesta a las preguntas.**
Students read the letter again and, this time, answer the questions in English.

*Answers:*
***1*** *He's in the south of Spain in Gaucín.* ***2*** *in the mountains, not far from the sea, very pretty, isolated;* ***3*** *six o'clock;* ***4*** *He does a lot of sport.* ***5*** *orange juice, cereal, toast or yoghurt;* ***6*** *combs his hair and brushes his teeth*

AT 4.4 | R&W 2.4, 2.5 | IU 3.1, 3.2 | PLTS

## Challenge

**Write an extract for a brochure to attract visitors to the area where you live. Describe the region and explain what there is and isn't. You can also include details such as typical regional dishes. Use the present tense.**
This task can be as simple or detailed as you wish depending on the level of students. It may help some students to be given a writing template and other students may like to desk top publish their work to make it more attractive.

## 1A.6 Labolengua

páginas 30–31

### Planner

**Objectives**

- review language and grammar from the unit

**Resources**

Student Book, pages 30–31
CD 1, track 24
Foundation Workbook, pages 21–22
Higher Workbook, pages 21–22
Interactive OxBox, Unit 1A
Copymasters 22–23

**Grammar**

- The present tense of verbs (revision)

**Renewed Framework references**

KAL 4.1, 4.5; LLS 5.1, 5.6

**PLTS**

All activities: Reflective learners/Self-managers
Activity 5: Independent enquirers

**Homework/Self-study**

Activity 1: Students use each of the verbs in a sentence on the theme of the spread. Encourage more able students to use more than one person.
Activity 5, page 30

### Comprender – The present tense of verbs (revision)

#### A Regular verbs

KAL 4.5 | LLS 5.1 | PLTS

**1 Write out these verbs on to learning cards with the English on one side and the Spanish on the other.**
Practice of conjugating regular verbs in Spanish.

*Answers:*
***cantar:*** *canto, cantas, canta, cantamos, cantáis, cantan*
***aprender:*** *aprendo, aprendes, aprende, aprendemos, aprendéis, aprenden*
***escribir:*** *escribo, escribes, escribe, escribimos, escribís, escriben*

#### B Radical-changing verbs

PLTS | KAL 4.5 | LLS 5.1

**2 Copy these sentences and write the correct form of the verb.**
Practice of conjugating radical-changing verbs.

*Answers:*
***1*** *prefiere;* ***2*** *quiere;* ***3*** *prefieren;* ***4*** *podemos;* ***5*** *juega*

#### C Reflexive verbs

PLTS | KAL 4.5 | LLS 5.1

**3 Complete the sentences with the correct form of the verb.**
Practise of using reflexive verbs in the present tense.

*Answers:*
***1*** *se despierta;* ***2*** *se levanta;* ***3*** *te acuestas;* ***4*** *me lavo;* ***5*** *nos vestimos*

#### D Present continuous

KAL 4.5 | LLS 5.1 | PLTS

**4 Add the verb endings.**
Practise of using the present continuous.

*Answers:*
*estoy comiendo; estás escribiendo; está cenando; estamos recogiendo; estáis durmiendo; están leyendo*

#### E Irregular verbs

KAL 4.5 | LLS 5.1 | PLTS

**5 Write out learning cards for irregular verbs with the Spanish on one side and the English on the other. *Estar* is done. Check the others on page 162.**
Encourage students to write out and learn as many irregular verbs as they can.

### Aprender – Dictionary work

#### F Checking verbs

LLS 5.6 | KAL 4.5 | PLTS

**6 See if you can recognise these verbs and think about their infinitive form. Then look them up in a dictionary and write down how they are set out.**
Practice of using a dictionary correctly.

*Answers:*
*beben – beber; comiendo – comer; vivimos – vivir; habláis – hablar*

LLS 5.6 KAL 4.5 PLTS

**7 Analyse these radical-changing verbs and think about how they would be set out in a dictionary. Then check them.**
It is less obvious to students which verbs they need to look up here. Encourage them to refer back to section B on page 30 for support if they need to.

*quiero – querer (ie); pueden – poder (ue); prefieres – preferir (ie); jugamos – jugar (ue)*

LLS 5.6 KAL 4.5 PLTS

**8 Don't forget that some verbs are both reflexive and radical-changing. How are these verbs set out in a dictionary?**
Further practice of looking up verbs in a dictionary.

*Answers:*
*me acuesto – acostarse; se visten – vestirse; te despiertas – despertarse*

LLS 5.6 KAL 4.5 PLTS

**9 If you have learnt the irregular verbs by heart then you should be able to recognise these words. Which verbs do they belong to?**
This reinforces the importance of learning irregular verbs by heart.

*Answers:*
*hacemos–hacer; tengo – tener; estáis – estar; son – ser; voy – ir*

### Hablar – Pronunciation

### G The sound of the letters c and z

KAL 4.1 PLTS

**10 Listen and repeat these examples. Make up a rule to rememeber how to pronounce the sounds *ca, co, cu* then *ce* and *ci*.**
Practice of pronouncing the letters c and z correctly.

**CD 1, track 24** **página 31, actividad 10**

**Spain:** Cartagena; centro; ciudad; Colombia; Cuba
**Latin America:** Cartagena; centro; ciudad; Colombia; Cuba
**Spain:** En el centro de la ciudad de Cartagena en Colombia comen arroz con coco pero en Cuba comen cerdo.
**Latin America:** En el centro de la ciudad de Cartagena en Colombia comen arroz con coco pero en Cuba comen cerdo.

## 1A.7 Extra Star

página 32

## *Planner*

### Objectives
- talk about chores and meals
- revise the present tense
- extending your sentences

### Resources
Student Book, page 32
Copymaster 24

### Renewed Framework references
R&W 2.4; IU 3.1, 3.2

### PLTS
Activity 1: Reflective learners
Activity 2: Effective participators
Activity 4: Creative thinkers

AT 3.2 AT 4.2 PLTS

**1 Empareja la acción con un dibujo adecuado.**
Practice of reflexive verbs. Students match the actions to the correct picture.

*Answers:*
***1** d; **2** f; **3** a; **4** b; **5** e; **6** c*

IU 3.1, 3.2 AT 3.2

**2 Lee. ¿Es para el desayuno, el almuerzo, la merienda o la cena?**
Students read the sentences and decide for which meal you would eat the food mentioned.

*Answers:*
***1** el desayuno; **2** la merienda; **3** el almuerzo; **4** la cena*

PLTS

**3 Escoge una hora adecuada para cada comida.**
Students write down a suitable time for each meal. Draw students' attention to the Think box before they begin writing. This could lead to a class discussion or a survey on daily routine.

AT 4.3–4 PLTS R&W 2.4

**4 Escribe ocho frases sobre lo que haces cada día y a qué hora.**
Students could either write a realistic account of a typical day for them, or could pretend to be a famous person and write about a typical day in the life of that person. Either way, they should include the structures and vocabulary they have met in this unit.

## 1A.7 Extra Plus — página 33

### Planner

**Objectives**
- talk about daily routine at weekends and after school
- use the present tense from memory
- check and correct work using a dictionary

**Resources**
Student Book, page 33
Copymaster 25

**Renewed Framework references**
R&W 2.4; KAL 4.3, 4.5

**PLTS**
Activity 1: Reflective learners
Activity 2: Reflective learners; Self-managers; Creative thinkers

KAL 4.3, 4.5 | AT 3.3–4 | PLTS

**1 Copia y completa el texto con los verbos correctos de la casilla.**
Before students start, refer them to the Think box.

*Answers:*
***1** ayudar; **2** limpiando; **3** recogiendo; **4** escuchando; **5** salir; **6** solemos; **7** estar; **8** comemos; **9** es; **10** me acuesto*

AT 4.4 | R&W 2.4 | PLTS

**2 Prepara un párrafo breve. Escribe por lo menos diez frases. Usa un diccionario para ayudarte.**
This brings together the language and grammar that students have met in this spread.

AT 3.4

**3 Lee los textos de María y Sofía y contesta a las preguntas.**
Students read the text and then answer the questions.

*Answers:*
***1** She wants to go to the town centre this afternoon, after school. **2** Sofía; **3** She has to do her homework and help her mum around the house. **4** She asks her to say that she is going to her house to eat with her. **5** cooking; **6** She isn't going to lie to her mum as she relies on her and would punish her; **7** She is going to go alone. **8** in the school yard*

## 1A.8 Prueba — página 34

**Resources**
Student Book, page 34
CD 1, track 25
Assessment OxBox, Unit 1A

**Renewed Framework references**
L&S 1.1, 1.2, 1.4; R&W 2.2, 2.4; KAL 4.3, 4.5

**PLTS**
All activities: Reflective learners

## Escuchar

AT 1.4 | L&S 1.1, 1.2 | PLTS

**Read sentences 1–8 and then listen and decide which five are true.**
This activity tests listening skills using the language covered in this unit.

**CD 1, track 25** **página 34, actividad 1**

Hola, me llamo Gabriela y soy la hermana de Roberto que está en Segovia con mi prima Elena. Ahora estoy estudiando en Cartagena y tengo clases todos los días incluso los sábados pero no me importa porque me gusta mi colegio y mis profesores.
Me encanta ayudar a mi madre en casa y siempre tengo que fregar los platos y preparar la cena porque ella llega tarde. Prefiero los platos típicos de Colombia porque la comida de España es bastante rica en aceite de oliva y eso no me gusta mucho. Mis amigas van bastante al cine y a comer pizza pero no me gusta acompañarlas. Prefiero quedarme en casa con mi madre viendo la tele y siempre me acuesto temprano a eso de las diez y media.

*Answers: 1, 3, 4, 5, 8*

## Hablar

AT 2.3–4 | L&S 1.4 | PLTS

**Answer the questions using the illustrations to help you.**
This activity tests speaking skills using the language covered in this unit.

## Leer

AT 3.4 | R&W 2.2 | PLTS

**Read Gabriela's email and answer the questions.**
This activity tests reading skills using the language covered in this unit.

*Answers:*
***1*** *Cartagena;* ***2*** *A typically Colombian recipe;* ***3*** *tasty and delicious;* ***4*** *their mum prepares her favourite dish every Sunday as Roberto, who doesn't like it, isn't there;* ***5*** *she has to help wash up afterwards;* ***6*** *(any three of) gets up early, takes the school bus, goes to lesson, goes home at about 2.30pm, does her homework, listens to her MP3 player;* ***7*** *her lessons;* ***8*** *You need fresh fish.* ***9*** *Segovia, where Roberto is staying, is far from the sea.* ***10*** *To call at 9pm Spanish time so that they can talk more.*

## Escribir

AT 4.3–4 | R&W 2.4 | KAL 4.3, 4.5 | PLTS

**Write a paragraph about your daily life.**
This activity tests writing skills using the language covered in this unit.

*Answers: Students' own answers*

# Leer 1A

página 149

**Resources**
Student Book, page 149

**Renewed Framework references**
R&W 2.1, 2.2

**PLTS**
Activity 3: Self-managers; Independent enquirers

AT 3.4 | R&W 2.1, 2.2

**1 Lee los textos. Busca seis palabras que son similares a palabras inglesas.**
Students find cognates in the text and make a note of these.

AT 3.5 | R&W 2.1. 2.2

**2 Contesta a las preguntas.**
Students note down to which city each of the phrases is referring.

*Answers:*
***1*** *Cartegena;* ***2*** *Segovia;* ***3*** *Cartegena;* ***4*** *Segovia;* ***5*** *Cartegena*

AT 3.5 R&W 2.1, 2.2 PLTS **3 What have the two cities got in common?**
Students note down any similarities between Segovia and Cartagena.

### Follow-up

Students research another Spanish-speaking city and note down some information about it – in Spanish or in English according to their ability. If there is time, the class could produce a display with information about a variety of Spanish-speaking cities.

## Foundation Workbook

### Página 16 1A.1 Primeras impresiones

- Use with Student Book, pages 20–21

AT 3.2 **1 Find this sentence in the word snake grid. The snake can go up, down or across, but not diagonally.**
Practice of daily routine vocabulary.

AT 3.2 **2 Find the sentence in this word snake grid.**
Practice of daily routine vocabulary.

*Answer:*
*Por lo general suelo levantarme a las seis.*

AT 4.2 **3 Now create your own daily routine word snake sentence in Spanish for a friend to do.**
Students should refer back to the Student Book, pages 20 and 21 if necessary to recap on daily routine vocabulary.

### Página 17 1A.2 Faenas caseras

- Use with Student Book, pages 22–23

AT 3.2 **1 Read this list of jobs and tick the ones you have to do.**
As an extension activity, you could collate all students' answers and students could present the information in the form of a graph labelled in Spanish.

AT 1.2 L&S 1.1, 1.2 **2 Now listen and tick the jobs Paco has to do.**

**CD 3, track 33 (Workbook 13)** **página 17, actividades 2 y 3**

Tengo que sacar la basura.
No tengo que pasear al perro.
Suelo cocinar.
No tengo que fregar los platos.
Tengo que hacer mi cama.
No hago las compras.
No suelo pasar la aspiradora.

*Answers: Paco does a, c and e*

AT 1.2 L&S 1.1, 1.2 **3 Listen again and when Paco says what he has to do, you can agree or disagree by saying what you do/don't do.**

### Página 18 1A.3 ¡Buen provecho!

- Use with Student Book, pages 24–25

AT 3.3 R&W 2.1, 2.2 **1 Read what Celia says and complete the tables with the relevant information.**

*Answers:*

| *Meal* | *Time* | *What?* |
|---|---|---|
| *Breakfast* | *8.00* | *juice, tea, toast, butter* |
| *Snack* | *11.00* | *sandwich, water* |
| *Lunch* | *2.30* | *pasta or rice with meat or fish* |
| *Dinner* | *10.00ish* | *meat with potatoes, pasta or rice* |

AT 4.2–3 R&W 2.4 **2 Complete these sentences to write about your own meals and mealtimes.**
Volunteers could read their work out to the class.

### Página 19 1A.4 A cocinar algo típico

- Use with Student Book, pages 26–27

AT 1.2 L&S 1.1, 1.2 **1 Listen and complete the shopping lists in English.**

**CD 3, track 34 (Workbook 14)** **página 19, actividad 1**

1 Un paquete de harina, media docena de huevos, un litro de leche, un paquete de azúcar, dos limones
2 Una barra de pan, doscientos gramos de jamón, quinientos gramos de queso, mantequilla y una ensalada

*Answers – including quantities:*
***1** packet of flour, half dozen eggs, litre of milk, packet of sugar, two lemons.*
***2** loaf of bread, 200g ham, 500g cheese, butter, a salad.*

**2 What do you think the people in Activity 1 might be making?**
Students should write the name of the dishes in Spanish.

*Answers:*
***1*** *pancakes;* ***2*** *sandwiches*

AT 4.1–2 **3 Write shopping lists in Spanish for ingredients to make two of the following.**
You may want to discuss this as a class in English first. Alternatively, you could ask students to find out which ingredients they would need for each of the items before listing these in Spanish. The most important thing is to practise the Spanish vocabulary.

## Página 20 1A.5 La vida regional

- Use with Student Book, pages 28–29

AT 3.1 **1 Cross out either the first or the second letter in every box to make a correct sentence. There are two possible answers in each case.**
If necessary, do the first one as a class to ensure that students understand what to do.

*Answers:*
***a*** *un pueblo or una aldea;* ***b*** *el campo or la costa;* ***c*** *ruidoso or pequeño;* ***d*** *no me gusta or me encanta;* ***e*** *cerca or lejos*

AT 4.2 **2 Complete these sentences with information about where you live.**
Students can refer back to pages 28 and 29 of the Student Book as well as using the words on the page for support.

## Página 21 1A.6A Labolengua

- Use with Student Book, pages 30–31

KAL 4.5 **1 Put the verbs below into the correct column of the grid. Some may need to go in more than one column. Look at the examples.**

*Answers:*

| -ar verbs | -er verbs | -ir verbs | radical changers | reflexives |
|---|---|---|---|---|
| *jugar (ue)* | *comer* | *vivir* | *jugar (ue)* | *llamarse* |
| *llamarse* | *beber* | *preferir (ie)* | *preferir (ie)* | *despertarse (ie)* |
| *despertarse (ie)* | | | *despertarse (ie)* | *lavarse* |
| *lavarse* | | | | *levantarse* |
| *levantarse* | | | | |

KAL 4.5 **2 Draw a line to match each of these verbs to its infinitive.**

*Answers:*
***a*** *jugar;* ***b*** *vivir;* ***c*** *llamarse;* ***d*** *preferir;* ***e*** *despertarse;* ***f*** *beber*

KAL 4.5 **3 Put these verbs into the first person of the present tense ('I').**

*Answers:*
***a*** *vivo;* ***b*** *prefiero;* ***c*** *juego;* ***d*** *me despierto;* ***e*** *bebo;* ***f*** *me levanto*

## Página 22 1A.6B Técnica

- Use with Student Book, pages 30–31

KAL 4.5 **1 Which of these are infinitives? Take the first letter of all the infinitives and rearrange these letters to make them into the infinitive of another verb.**

*Answer:*
***infinitives:*** *comer, alojarse, acostarse, negar, tener, reír*
***new infinitive:*** *cantar*

LLS 5.5 **2 Fill in the grid to explain why these verbs are not in the dictionary.**

*Answer:*

| *Word* | *It means* | *You have to look up:* |
|---|---|---|
| *voy* | *I'm going* | *ir – to go* |
| *nado* | *I swim* | *nadar – to swim* |
| *comiendo* | *eating* | *comer – to eat* |
| *bailamos* | *we dance* | *bailar – to dance* |

LLS 5.5 **3 Use a dictionary to translate the underlined verbs into English. What jobs do you think these people do?**

*Answer:*
***a*** *I rest, I work; any nocturnal job* ***b*** *I know, driving; taxi driver or bus driver*

## Higher Workbook

### Página 16 1A.1 Primeras impresiones

- Use with Student Book, pages 20–21

AT 3.2 **1 Find this sentence in the word snake grid. The snake can go up, down or across, but not diagonally.**
Practice of daily routine vocabulary.

AT 3.2 **2 Find the sentences in this word snake grid.**
Practice of daily routine vocabulary.

*Answer:*
*Por lo general suelo levantarme a las seis y media y voy al instituto.*

AT 4.2 **3 Now create your own daily routine word snake sentence in Spanish for a friend to do.**
Students should refer back to the Student Book, pages 20 and 21 if necessary to recap on daily routine vocabulary.

### Página 17 1A.2 Faenas caseras

- Use with Student Book, pages 22–23

AT 3.2 **1 Read this list of jobs and tick the ones you have to do.**
As an extension activity, you could collate all students' answers and students could present the information in the form of a graph labelled in Spanish.

AT 1.4 L&S 1.1, 1.2 **2 Now listen and tick the jobs Paco has to do.**

**CD 4, track 13** **página 17, actividades 2 y 3**

En mi casa, hago muchas tareas. Por ejemplo, tengo que sacar la basura todos los días.
No tengo que pasear al perro, porque no tenemos perro.
Los fines de semana suelo cocinar porque estoy en casa y no tengo que estudiar.
Mi madre suele fregar los platos, y además tenemos lavaplatos.
Tengo que hacer mi cama y recoger mi dormitorio.
Mis padres suelen hacer las compras – yo no hago eso.
No tenemos aspiradora – no tenemos moquetas en casa.

*Answers: Paco does a, c and e*

AT 1.4 L&S 1.1, 1.2 **3 Listen again and when Paco says what he has to do, you can agree or disagree by saying what you do/don't do.**

### Página 18 1A.3 ¡Buen provecho!

- Use with Student Book, pages 24–25

AT 3.4 R&W 2.1, 2.2 **1 Read what Celia says about her meals and mealtimes and complete this table with the relevant information.**

*Answer:*

| *Meal* | *Time* | *What?* | *Extra information* |
|---|---|---|---|
| *Breakfast* | *8.00* | *juice, tea, toast, butter* | *quickly off to school* |
| *Snack* | *11.00* | *sandwich, water* | |
| *Lunch* | *2.30* | *pasta or rice with meat or fish* | *at home* |
| *Tea* | *5.00* | *bread or cake* | *for little brother* |
| *Dinner* | *10.00ish* | *meat with potatoes, pasta or rice* | *watch TV and talk* |

AT 4.3–4 R&W 2.4, 2.5 **2 Use what Celia has written to write about your own meals and mealtimes.**
Volunteers could read their work out to the class.

### Página 19 1A.4 A cocinar algo típico

- Use with Student Book, pages 26–27

AT 1.2 L&S 1.2 **1 Listen and write the shopping lists in English.**

**CD 4, track 14** **página 19, actividad 1**

1 Un paquete de harina, media docena de huevos, un litro de leche, un paquete de azúcar, dos limones
2 Una barra de pan, doscientos gramos de jamón, quinientos gramos de queso, mantequilla y una ensalada

*Answers – including quantities:*
***1** packet of flour, half dozen eggs, litre of milk, packet of sugar, two lemons.*
***2** Loaf of bread, 200g ham, 500g cheese, butter, a salad*

**2 What do think the people in Activity 1 might be making?**
Students should write the names of the dishes in Spanish.

*Answers:*
***1** pancakes; **2** sandwiches*

AT 4.1–2 **3 Write shopping lists in Spanish for ingredients to make two of the following.**

You may want to discuss this as a class in English first. Alternatively, you could ask students to find out which ingredients they would need for each of the items before listing these in Spanish. The most important thing is to practise the Spanish vocabulary.

## Página 20 1A.5 La vida regional

- Use with Student Book, pages 28–29

AT 3.1 **1 Cross out one letter in each box to make a correct sentence. There are two possible answers in each case.**

If necessary, do the first one as a class to ensure that students understand what to do.

*Answers:*
***a** un pueblo* or *una aldea;* ***b** el campo* or *la costa;* ***c** ruidoso* or *pequeño;* ***d** no me gusta* or *me encanta;* ***e** cerca* or *lejos*

AT 4.2–3 **2 Complete these sentences with information on where you live.**

Students can refer back to pages 28 and 29 of the Student Book, if necessary.

## Página 21 1A.6A Labolengua

- Use with Student Book, pages 30–31

KAL 4.5 **1 Draw a line to match each verb to its infinitive.**

*Answers:*
***a** jugar;* ***b** vivir;* ***c** llamarse;* ***d** preferir;* ***e** despertarse;* ***f** beber*

KAL 4.5 **2 Put the verbs into the correct column of the grid. Some may need to go in more than one column.**

*Answers:*

| ***-ar verbs*** | ***-er verbs*** | ***-ir verbs*** | ***radical changers*** | ***reflexives*** |
|---|---|---|---|---|
| *juega* | *como* | *vive* | *juega* | *se llaman* |
| *se llaman* | *bebemos* | *prefiere* | *prefiere* | *se despiertan* |
| *se despiertan* | | | *se despiertan* | *me lavo* |
| *me lavo* | | | | *me levanto* |
| *me levanto* | | | | |

KAL 4.5 **3 Write these verbs in the correct form in Spanish.**

*Answers:*
***a** viven;* ***b** prefiere;* ***c** juega;* ***d** juega;* ***e** me despierto;* ***f** bebemos;* ***g** se levantan*

## Página 22 1A.6B Técnica

- Use with Student Book, pages 30–31

KAL 4.5 **1 Which of these are infinitives? Take the first letter of all the infinitives and rearrange these letters to make them into the infinitive of another verb.**

*Answers:*
***infinitives:*** *comer, alojarse, acostarse, negar, tener, reír*
***other infinitive:*** *cantar*

LLS 5.5 **2 Explain why these verbs are not in the dictionary and what word you would have to look for instead.**

*Answer:*
***a** 'Voy' means 'I'm going'. You have to look up 'ir' (to go).*
***b** 'Nado' means 'I swim'. You have to look up 'nadar' (to swim).*
***c** 'Comiendo' means 'eating'. You have to look up 'comer' (to eat).*
***d** 'Bailamos' means 'we dance'. You have to look up 'bailar' (to dance).*

LLS 5.5 **3 Use a dictionary to translate the underlined verbs into English. What jobs do you think these people do?**

*Answer:*
***a** I rest, I work; any nocturnal job;* ***b** I know, driving; taxi driver or bus driver*

# 1B La moda

## Unit Objectives

**Contexts and cultural focus:** fashion and clothes
**Grammar:** opinion; the imperfect tense; demonstrative adjectives; comparatives and superlatives; singular and plural verb forms (revision)
**Language learning:** transferring previous knowledge to new situations; using cognates; working out the meaning of new vocabulary; understanding Spanish clothes sizes; revising numbers; making choices; evaluating options; understanding and producing descriptions

- *Aim:* To learn how to speak about fashion and clothes shopping in Spanish.
- Each unit has an associated video which will feature throughout the unit. Below is the transcript of the video for this unit.

**Video clip: Unit 1B (CD 1, track 29)**

**Part 1**

*In the street*

Juan: ¿Qué vamos a hacer hoy?
Elena: Necesito comprar ropa nueva para el verano.
Juan: Pero tienes mucha ropa. Tienes faldas, mini-faldas, pantalones, camisetas, vestidos...
Roberto: Y zapatos, tienes de todo: tacón alto, tacón bajo, sandalias, botas, playeras...
Elena: Pero no tengo nada estiloso.
Roberto: A mí también me gustaría comprar algo nuevo.
Juan: Pero si no tenéis dinero...
Elena: Sí, tengo los 100 euros de mi cumpleaños.
Roberto: Y yo tengo 100 euros de mis padres.
Elena: ¡Vamos de compras entonces!
Juan: ¿Y yo?
Elena: Tú puedes decidir quién compra el mejor conjunto.
Juan: Siempre tan competitivos.

**Part 2**

*In a clothes shop*

Juan: Tienen 15 minutos para elegir un conjunto cada uno por menos de 100 euros. Podéis elegir el mejor conmigo.
Elena: Me gustan estos shorts.
Juan: Son muy cortos.
Roberto: Me gustan estas bermudas.
Juan: ¿Estas? Son muy largas.
Elena: Me gusta esta chaqueta.
Juan: ¿Esa? No me gusta nada.
Roberto: Este sombrero es guay.
Juan: Me gusta más éste que aquél.
Elena: Quiero probarme este vestido, este pañuelo y esta chaqueta.
Assistant: ¿Qué talla usas?
Elena: La 36.
Assistant: Si es la 36.
Elena: Y quiero probarme esas sandalias.
Assistant: ¿Qué número calzas?
Elena: El 38.
Assistant: Aquí tienes.
Elena: Gracias.
Roberto: Quería probarme estas bermudas, esta camiseta y esta gorra.
Assistant: ¿Qué talla usas?
Roberto: Una "M" creo.
Assistant: Sí, esta es tu talla.
Roberto: Y también quería probarme estas playeras.
Assistant: ¿Qué número usas?
Roberto: Un 45.
Assistant: Aquí tienes. Los probadores están a la derecha.
Roberto: Gracias.
Assistant: De nada.

Juan: Aquí tenemos a Elena con un vestido largo estilo Hippy. Las flores están muy de moda este año. Elena lleva el vestido con una chaqueta rosa y unas sandalias beis, y también lleva un pañuelo azul. Roberto lleva unas bermudas de verano, una camiseta de color azul marino y unas playeras blancas, y una gorra verde y negro.
Roberto: ¿Cuánto cuesta tu conjunto, Elena?
Elena: Cuesta 80.50 euros, porque hay rebajas. ¿Y el tuyo?
Roberto: El mío cuesta 75.80 euros. Más barato que el tuyo.
Elena: ¿Cuál os gusta más?¿El mío?
Roberto: ¿O el mío?
Elena: Juan, ¿cuál te gusta más? ¿Juan? ¿Dónde estás?
Juan: Me gusta más *mi* nueva ropa, unos vaqueros y una camiseta súper guay.

**Punto Lengua**

Me gusta más éste que aquél.
¿Qué número calzas?
¿Qué talla usas?
¿Qué número usas?

As a starter activity to introduce the unit and familiarise students with the language they will meet, you may find it useful for the class to view the video as a whole. Are there any words or phrases that they have recognised? What do they think it is about? View Part 1 again a couple of times, as this sets the scene. Students can write down any items of clothing or prices they recognise. Explain that you will look at it in more detail later in this unit.

*Synopsis:*

Elena, Juan and Roberto are talking about clothes and Elena says that she needs to buy some new summer clothes. She has 100 euros from her birthday to spend.

Roberto also has 100 euros from his mother to spend. They decide to compete and see who can buy the best outfit for 100 euros! Part 2 of the video shows the teenagers in a clothes shop choosing and trying on clothes.

**Unit 1B La moda Overview grid**

| Page reference | Contexts and objectives | Language learning | Grammar | Key language | Framework | AT level |
|---|---|---|---|---|---|---|
| Pages 36–37 **¿Qué opinas de la moda?** | • talk about clothes and give your opinion on them | • transfer previous knowledge to new situations; use cognates | • give your opinion: review of singular and plural | *un abrigo; un anorak; una blusa; unas botas; unas botas de goma; una bufanda; unos calcetines; una camisa; una camiseta; una chaqueta; un cinturón; un jersey; un paraguas; un pijama; una rebeca; unas sandalias; unos shorts; un sombrero; un traje; un vestido; unas zapatillas; una manga; llevar; bonito/a; cómodo/a; feo/a; incómodo* | L&S 1.2, 1.4; R&W 2.4; KAL 4.2, 4.3, 4.5; LLS 5.3, 5.4 | 1.3, 2.1, 2.3, 3.1, 4.1, 4.3–4 |
| Pages 38–39 **Mi estilo** | • discuss different styles and eras of fashion | • work out the meaning of new vocabulary | • use the imperfect tense to say 'used to' | *los años sesenta/ setenta; un chaleco; un corsé; las medias; los pantalones de campana; el siglo diecinueve; el siglo dieciseis; cónico/a; corto/a; elegante; formal* | L&S 1.1, 1.2, 1.4, 1.5; R&W 2.2, 2.4; KAL 4.3, 4.5; LLS 5.4 | 1.5, 2.3–5, 3.2–5, 4.3–5 |
| Pages 40–41 **¿Me queda bien?** | • try on clothes, talk about sizes and how well clothes fit | • understand Spanish clothes sizes, revise numbers | • use demonstrative adjectives | *¿Qué talla usas?; ¿Qué número calzas?; ajustado/a; al fondo; holgado/a; largo/a; los probadores; quedar bien; Quiero probarme* | L&S 1.1, 1.2, 1.3, 1.4, 1.5; R&W 2.4; IU 3.2; KAL 4.2, 4.3; LLS: 5.4, 5.7 | 1.3–4, 2.3–4, 3.1, 4.3 |
| Pages 42–43 **¿Dónde comprar?** | • discuss different types of shops | • make choices, evaluate options | • use comparatives and superlatives | *los grandes almacenes; la boutique; el centro comercial; el mercado; la tienda de una cadena; la tienda de mano; anticuado/a; barato/a; caro/a; está demoda; una ganga; regatear; tener suerte* | L&S 1.1, 1.2, 1.4; R&W 2.2, 2.4; LLS 5.1, 5.4, 5.5, 5.7 | 1.4, 3.3–4, 4.3–4 |

| | | | | | | |
|---|---|---|---|---|---|---|
| Pages 44–45<br>**La ropa especializada** | • describe clothes for different activities and occasions | • understand and produce descriptions | • revise singular and plural verb forms | *un bastón (de senderismo/de esquí); una chaqueta acolchada; de colores muy vivos; los disfraces; un forro polar; un macuto; una malla; los pantalones impermeables; la tela sintética; un traje de nieve; un traje neopreno; las zapatillas de ballet; los zapatos neoprenos; algún tipo; entrenar* | L&S 1.1, 1.2, 1.4, 1.5;<br>R&W 2.2, 2.4, 2.5;<br>IU 3.2;<br>KAL 4.3, 4.5;<br>LLS 5.4, 5.5 | 1.4 , 2.4, 3.4, 4.4 |
| Pages 46–47<br>**Labolengua** | • review language and grammar from the unit | | | | L&S 1.1, 1.2, 1.4, 1.5;<br>R&W 2.2, 2.4, 2.5; IU 3.2;<br>KAL 4.3, 4.5;<br>LLS 5.4, 5.5 | |
| Pages 48–49<br>**Extra Star**<br>**Extra Plus** | • differentiated extension/ homework material | • revise and consolidate all vocabulary and grammar covered in the unit | • revise and consolidate all vocabulary and grammar covered in the unit | | R&W 2.4;<br>KAL 4.3, 4.5;<br>LLS 5.1, 5.4 | 3.3, 4.2–4 |
| Page 50<br>**Prueba** | • end-of-unit test | | | | L&S 1.1, 1.2, 1.4;<br>R&W 2.2, 2.4;<br>KAL 4.3, 4.5;<br>LLS 5.4 | 1.3–4, 2.3–4, 3.4, 4.4 |
| Page 51<br>**Vocabulario** | • a summary of the key language covered in each core spread of this unit | | | | | |
| Page 150<br>**Leer 1B** | • practice of longer reading texts based on the theme of the unit | | | | 2.1, 2.4, 2.5, 5.4 | 3.4 |

**Week-by-week overview**
**(Three-year KS3 Route: assuming six weeks' work or approximately 10–12.5 hours)**
**(Two-year KS3 Route: assuming four weeks' worth or approxmately 6.5–8.5 hours)**

**About Unit 1B, *La moda*:** Students work in the context of describing clothes and talking about shopping for clothes. They give their opinion on different types of clothes and discuss different styles and eras of fashion. They also practise buying clothes, saying what size they are and how well clothes fit, they discuss different types of shops and they describe clothes for different activities and occasions. Students revise giving their opinion, they learn how to use the imperfect tense to say *used to*, use demonstrative adjectives, use comparatives and superlatives and revise singular and plural verb forms. The unit also provides tips on language learning techniques.

| Three-Year KS3 Route | | | Two-Year KS3 Route | | |
|---|---|---|---|---|---|
| **Week** | **Resources** | **Objectives** | **Week** | **Resources** | **Objectives** |
| 1 | **1B.1 ¿Qué opinas de la moda?**<br>**1B.6 Labolengua C** (p.47) | talk about clothes and give your opinion on them<br>transfer previous knowledge to new situations; use cognates<br>give your opinion: review of singular and plural | 1 | **1B.1 ¿Qué opinas de la moda?** (Omit activities 4, 5 & Challenge)<br>**1B.6 Labolengua C** (p.47) | talk about clothes and give your opinion on them<br>transfer previous knowledge to new situations; use cognates<br>give your opinion: review of singular and plural |
| 2 | **1B.2 Mi estilo**<br>**1B.6 Labolengua A** (p.46) | discuss different styles and eras of fashion<br>work out the meaning of new vocabulary use the imperfect tense to say 'used to' | 2 | **1B.2 Mi estilo** (Omit activities 3, 7 & Challenge)<br>**1B.6 Labolengua A** (p.46) | discuss different styles and eras of fashion<br>work out the meaning of new vocabulary use the imperfect tense to say *used to* |
| 3 | **1B.3 ¿Me queda bien?**<br>**1B.6 Labolengua D** (p.47) | try on clothes, talk about sizes and how well clothes fit<br>understand Spanish clothes sizes, revise numbers use demonstrative adjectives | 3 | **1B.3 ¿Me quedabien?** (Omit activities 1, 7, 10 & Challenge)<br>**1B.6 Labolengua D** (p.47) | try on clothes, talk about sizes and how well clothes fit<br>understand Spanish clothes sizes, revise numbers use demonstrative adjectives |
| 4 | **1B.4 ¿Dónde comprar?**<br>**1B.6 Labolengua B** (p.46) | discuss different types of shops<br>make choices, evaluate options<br>use comparatives and superlatives | 4 | **1B.4 ¿Dónde comprar?** (Omit the Challenge activity)<br>**1B.6 Labolengua B** (p.46)<br>**1B.8 Prueba** (p.50)<br>**Vocabulario** (p.51) | discuss different types of shops<br>make choices, evaluate options<br>use comparatives and superlatives<br>Prepare and carry out assessment in all four skills<br>Recapping on vocabulary of the unit |
| 5 | **1B.5 La ropa especializada** | describe clothes for different activities and occasions<br>understand and produce descriptions<br>revise singular and plural verb forms | | | |
| 6 | **1B.7 Extra (Star)** (p.48)<br>**1B.7 Extra (Plus)** (p.49)<br>**1B.8 Prueba** (p.50)<br>**Vocabulario** (p.51)<br>**Leer** (p.150) | Further reinforcement and extension of the language of the unit.<br>Prepare and carry out assessment in all four skills<br>Recapping on vocabulary of the unit<br>Further reading to explore the language of the unit and cultural themes | | | |

## 1B.1 ¿Qué opinas de la moda? páginas 36–37

# *Planner*

### Objectives
- talk about clothes and give your opinion on them
- give your opinion: review of singular and plural
- transfer previous knowledge to new situations; use cognates

### Resources
Student Book, pages 36–37
CD 1, track 26
Foundation Workbook, page 24
Higher Workbook, page 24
Foundation Workbook audio, CD 3, track 35 (Workbook 15)
Higher Workbook audio, CD 4, track 15
Interactive OxBox, Unit 1B
Copymasters 27–34

### Key language
*un abrigo; un anorak; una blusa; unos calcetines; una camisa; unas botas; unas botas de goma; una bufanda; una manga; una camiseta; una chaqueta; un cinturón; un jersey; un paraguas; un pijama; una rebeca; unas sandalias; unos pantalones cortos; un sombrero; un traje; un vestido; unas zapatillas; llevar; bonito/a; cómodo/a; feo/a; incómodo*

### Grammar
- give your opinion: singular and plural (review)

### Renewed Framework references
L&S 1.2, 1.4; R&W 2.4; KAL 4.2, 4.3, 4.5; LLS 5.3, 5.4

### PLTS
Activities 1 and 2: Reflective learners
Activity 4: Effective participators
Activity 5: Independent enquirers

### Starters
- Have a class competition. Split the class into small groups and give each group two minutes to write down as many items of clothes in Spanish as they can. When the time is up, compare lists. Award each group a point for each item and two points if no other group has listed a particular item. The group with the most points wins. With less able classes, provide groups with a list of items of clothing in Spanish and a list in English and give them a time limit to match them up.
- Go round the class giving each student an item of clothing, e.g. *los vaqueros azules*. The student must give an opinion, e.g. *Me gustan mucho*. Remind students that adjectives should agree with the subject. It may be useful to display a list of possible opinions/adjectives first.

### Plenaries
- Challenge students to write out the different present tense verb endings in Spanish. Compare answers.
- Play a class game. Split the class into two teams. Ask a student from each team to come to the front and describe an outfit to their team who must draw it. The team who produces the most accurate drawing wins. Continue with another student.

### Homework/Self-study
Following on from the Think Activity, students make a list of any cognates they come across in the spread. They can add to this list as the course progresses.
Students write sentences using *me gusta* and *me interesa*.

AT 2.1 | PLTS | KAL 4.2 | LLS 5.3, 5.4

**1 Trabaja con un compañero. ¿Recuerdas las palabras en español para la ropa?**
Students work with a partner to practise clothes vocabulary in Spanish. They name the items of clothing in Spanish.

AT 3.1 | AT 4.1 | PLTS | LLS 5.4

**2 Escribe dos listas de palabras. ¿Son positivas o negativas?**
Students study the wordsnake and write a list of positive and negative words. For less able students, photocopy the graphic so pupils can separate the words by cutting them up. More able students can use each opinion phrase in a (preferably silly) sentence to help them remember it, e.g. *¡El elefante es sensacional!*.

*Answers:*
***positivo:*** *bonito; cómodo; me encanta; formal; me flipa; genial; me gusta; qué guay; me chifla; me mola; precioso; sensacional*
***negativo:*** *qué asco; qué horror; fatal; feo; formal; incómodo; no me gusta; ridículo*

AT 1.3 | L&S 1.2

**3 Mira la ropa de arriba y escucha. ¿Qué opinan?**
Students listen and note down the opinions about the clothes items. Pause after each item for weaker students. More able ones can tackle two or three chunks at once.

**CD 1, track 26** **página 36, actividad 3**

1 Pues, a mí me gustan bastante los vaqueros azules. Son muy cómodos, ¿no?
2 Mm… prefiero la blusa blanca con mangas cortas – es muy elegante.
3 ¡Zapatos amarillos! ¡Qué horror! ¡No me gustan nada!
4 La falda gris es bastante elegante pero es fea. No me gusta mucho.
5 – Me encantan los calcetines rojos. ¡Son muy divertidos!
– ¡Ay, no! Son feos.
6 – ¡Qué asco! ¡Un jersey marrón! Es muy feo.
– Estoy de acuerdo contigo. ¡Es horrible!
7 – Zapatillas negras – qué raro. No son muy bonitas.
– Y los pantalones verdes son bastante ridículos también.
8 – Mm, la camisa negra es genial.
– Pero el jersey rosa es mejor – ¡me mola!

*Answers: as in transcript.*

AT 2.3 | PLTS | L&S 1.4

**4 Habla con tu compañero. ¿Qué opinas de la ropa?**
Start this activity off by asking students directly, *Te gustan los pantalones verdes?*, etc. Students continue in pairs or small groups once they understand what to do. For more realism, distribute magazines, and ask students to choose a picture and say if they like it or not and why.

KAL 4.3

### Gramática
Ensure that students understand that in Spanish, adjectives change to agree with the noun they are describing, according to whether it is singular or plural.

AT 3.4 | PLTS | LLS 5.4

**5 Lee las descripciones e identifica la ropa. Anota las palabras de opiniones.**
Students read the descriptions and identify the clothes mentioned and note down any opinion words given.

*Answers:* ***1*** *d, me flipan;* ***2*** *a, me parece muy formal;* ***3*** *e, ridículo, me encanta, es genial*

PLTS | KAL 4.2 | LLS 5.3, 5.4

### Think
Students use their knowledge of Spanish to work out the meanings of the words in the *Vocabulario* section on page 51. Explain to them that words that look very similar in two different languages are called cognates and ask them to make a note of any cognates from Activity 5.

AT 4.3

**6 Completa la descripción del dibujo c. Usa el vocabulario de las actividades 2 y 5.**
Students look at picture c and then complete the description of what the girl is wearing. Remind them to pay attention to adjective endings.

*Answers:* ***1*** *jersey;* ***2*** *rosa;* ***3*** *genial or guay;* ***4*** *botas;* ***5*** *preciosas;* ***6*** *blanco*

KAL 4.5

### Gramática
This Grammar box is to be used in association with Activities 5 and 6. Can students remember any other verbs they have learnt and how the endings change according to the person?

*Answers: llevo; llevamos*

AT 4.4 | R&W 2.4

**7 Escribe una descripción para el dibujo b.**
Students write a description of the clothes in illustration b. Remind them to refer back to the vocabulary in the spread and to include opinion words.

PLTS | AT 4.4 | R&W 2.4 | KAL 4.3

### Challenge
**Produce your own page for a fashion magazine. Draw your model or use ready-made pictures. Label it and write about it.**
This open-ended writing activity can be as simple or as complex as you like. The finished pages could be compiled into a class fashion magazine and compared with that of a parallel class, or displayed. It could be part of cross-curricular work with the Art Department or even the Textiles Department.

## 1B.2 Mi estilo

páginas 38–39

# Planner

### Objectives
- discuss different styles and eras of fashion
- use the imperfect tense to say 'used to'
- work out the meaning of new vocabulary

### Resources
Student Book, pages 38–39
CD 1, track 27
Foundation Workbook, page 25
Higher Workbook, page 25
Foundation Workbook audio, CD 3, track 36 (Workbook 16)
Higher Workbook audio, CD 4, track 16
Interactive OxBox, Unit 1B
Copymasters 27–34

### Key language
*los años sesenta/setenta; un chaleco; un corsé; las medias; los pantalones de campana; el siglo diecinueve; el siglo dieciseis; cónico/a; corto/a; elegante; formal*

### Grammar
- use the imperfect tense to say *used to*

### Renewed Framework references
L&S 1.1, 1.2, 1.4, 1.5; R&W 2.2, 2.4; KAL 4.3, 4.5; LLS 5.4

### PLTS
Activity 2: Reflective learners
Activity 5: Independent enquirers
Activity 7: Self-managers
Think: Independent enquirers

### Starters
- Display the key language from the spread and give students a time limit to work out the English for each of the terms listed. Check answers as a class. With less able classes, you may prefer to display the English translation in jumbled order next to the list of key language.
- Display the heading, **ser** – *to be* and explain to students that they will have one minute to write out this verb in the imperfect tense. When the time is up, check answers as a class. Then go round the class asking each student to give you a sentence using a form of *ser* in the imperfect tense.

### Plenaries
- Play a memory game using clothes vocabulary and *llevar* in the imperfect tense. You start with a sentence, e.g. *Llevaba pantalones grises.* Students continue in turn with each one repeating what has already been said and adding a new sentence of their own, e.g. *Llevaba pantalones grises y un traje blanco.* etc. Remind students that they don't have to tell the truth – they could say they used to wear a corset, for example!
- Choose a volunteer to come to the front of the class and describe clothes from a certain era. The rest of the class must guess which era they are referring to. The person who guesses correctly then has a go at describing clothes from a different era, and so on.

### Homework/Self-study
Activity 2: Students list all the words they definitely know, and those they think they can guess.
Activity 6: Students write a few sentences about a fashion era of their choice. They should also give their opinion of the clothes they mention. Provide less able students with gapped sentences and adjectives/opinion words to choose from.
Challenge: Students find an old garment or a picture of one from a past fashion era to use for the Challenge Activity.

AT 3.2

**1 Identifica la fecha de la casilla.**
Students look at the illustrations and match each one to its era. Although this may look complicated to the students, the initial activity is a simple revision of some numbers. The only new word is *siglo* which most students should be able to work out from context with some prompting.

*Answers: **a** el siglo dieciséis; **b** los años sesenta; **c** el siglo diecinueve; **d** los años setenta*

AT 3.5 | PLTS | R&W 2.2 | KAL 4.5 | LLS 5.4

**2 Empareja las descripciones y los dibujos.**
Do some work on the Grammar box before proceeding to this activity. Get students to say in Spanish 'I wear (something)', then elicit in English *used to wear* by giving them a sentence like 'I wear jeans but when I was little I ... dungarees', and explain that this activity is all about what people used to wear. The text might look quite dense, but once students start unpicking it, there is not much that is new or not understandable from context.

*Answers: **1** b; **2** a; **3** d; **4** c*

KAL 4.5

## Gramática

Read through the Grammar box as a class and work through some examples using 'to wear' in the imperfect tense. Display some sentences using this verb in the present tense and ask students to put them into the imperfect. Check answers as a class. Once you feel students are familiar with this verb in the imperfect, move onto Activity 2.

AT 2.3–5 | L&S 1.4

**3 Habla con tu compañero.**
Students work with a partner asking and answering questions to practise using the imperfect tense with *llevar*.

AT 3.3 | KAL 4.5

**4 Completa las frases con la parte correcta de *llevar*.**
Further practice of the verb *llevar*. Students complete the sentences with the correct form of the verb *llevar*.

*Answers: **1** llevaba; **2** llevábamos; **3** llevabais; **4** llevabas*

AT 3.4 | PLTS | L&S 1.4

**5 Trabaja con tu compañero. Identifica las palabras en español de la actividad 2.**
Students work with a partner to work out the Spanish for the English words listed. They then give their opinion on each item of clothing using the opinion words from spread 1.

*Answers:*
***corset***– *un corsé;* ***conical*** – *cónico/a;* ***flared trousers*** – *los pantalones de campana;* ***miniskirt*** – *una minifalda*

AT 1.5 | L&S 1.1, 1.2 | LLS 5.4

**6 Mira los dibujos de la activated 1 y escucha a los estudiantes. ¿Qué estilo describen? ¿Qué opinan?**
Following on from previous activities, students listen to Spanish students describe styles of clothing and note down which fashion era they are describing and the opinions that they give.

**CD 1, track 27** — **página 39, actividad 6**

1 Me parece un estilo muy romántico y elegante pero el vestido de la mujer era muy incómodo. Un corsé – ¡qué horror!
2 Me flipa el estilo hippy. Es muy divertido. Sobre todo me encanta la camisa de muchos colores. ¡Los pantalones de campana son enormes!
3 Me encanta ese estilo. ¡Además las minifaldas están todavía de moda! Parece bastante moderno.
4 Pues, el vestido de la mujer es muy bonito, pero parece incómodo. Una falda cónica – es muy extraña. En mi opinión, las medias del hombre eran bastante ridículas.

*Answers: **1** el siglo diecinueve – romántico, elegante, incómodo; **2** los años setenta – divertido; **3** los años sesenta – moderno; **4** el siglo dieciseis – bonito, incómodo, extraño, ridículo*

AT 3.5 | PLTS | R&W 2.2 | LLS 5.4

**7 Mira las fotos y completa el párrafo con las palabras de la derecha.**
This is another opportunity for students to use different techniques to work out vocabulary.

*Answers:*
***1** llevaba; **2** vestidos; **3** minifaldas; **4** un traje blanco; **5** pantalones de campana; **6** un chaleco; **7** una camisa elegante; **8** camisetas muy grandes*

LLS 5.4 | PLTS

**Think**
This encourages students to think of strategies they could use to work out the meaning of new words and to become independent learners.

AT 4.3–5 | R&W 2.4

**8 Mira las fotos otra vez. ¿Qué opinan?**
Students give their opinions of the clothes in the photos.

AT 4.5 | L&S 1.5 | R&W 2.4 | KAL 4.3

**Challenge**
**Find a picture of a fashion from a previous time or bring in an old item of clothing. Prepare a few sentences and then describe it to the rest of the class. Don't forget to give your opinion. Use at least two tenses.**
This could be set as a homework activity, or be used as an opportunity for students to give a brief presentation to the class on their chosen garment. Introduce humour in by getting students to describe outrageous garments. Also encourage debate by getting one student to say what they like about a garment (it doesn't have to be true!) and another to disagree.

## 1B.3 ¿Me queda bien?

páginas 40–41

### *Planner*

**Objectives**
- try on clothes, talk about sizes and how well clothes fit
- use demonstrative adjectives
- understand Spanish clothes sizes, revise numbers

**Video**
Video clip, Unit 1B

**Resources**
Student Book, pages 40–41
CD 1, tracks 28–29
Foundation Workbook, page 26
Higher Workbook, page 26
Foundation Workbook audio, CD 3, tracks 37–38 (Workbook 17–18)
Higher Workbook audio, CD 4, tracks 17–18
Interactive OxBox, Unit 1B
Copymasters 27–34

**Video**
Video clip, Unit 1B

**Key language**
*¿Qué talla usas?; ¿Qué número calzas?; ajustado/a; al fondo; holgado/a; largo/a; Quiero probarme; los probadores; quedar bien*

**Grammar**
- use demonstrative adjectives

**Renewed Framework references**
L&S 1.1, 1.2, 1.3, 1.4, 1.5; R&W 2.4; IU 3.2; KAL 4.2, 4.3; LLS: 5.4, 5.7

**PLTS**
Activity 3: Reflective learners
Activity 4: Team workers
Activity 5: Team workers
Challenge: Team workers; Reflective learners

**Starters**
- Split the class into small groups and challenge them to list as many items of clothing and opinion words as they can in Spanish in the time given. When the time is up, compare lists. The team with the most correct words listed wins.
- Use classroom items to practise demonstrative adjectives. Hold up a pen and elicit from students either *este* or *ese bolígrafo*. Move the pen further away and elicit *aquel bolígrafo*. Do the same with other classroom items or items of clothing if possible.

**Plenaries**
- Challenge students to write sentences containing the demonstrative adjectives in their singular, plural, masculine and feminine forms. Compare sentences as a class to ensure that students have fully understood how to use these correctly.
- Students write a short role play in a clothes shop along the lines of that in the Challenge Activity, but starring celebrities (Spanish-speaking if possible) of their choice, e.g. Rafael Nadal, Fernando Alonso, etc.

**Homework/Self-study**
Gramática: Students write more sentences using the expression *Me queda bien*.

AT 1.3 L&S 1.2 **1 Escucha y decide. ¿Este, ese o aquel?**
Students listen to the recording and note down if *esta*, *ese* or *auquel* is used each time. Before listening, ask students what they understand from the picture. Draw attention to *este*, *ese* and *aquel*, and ask what they think the three words could mean.

**CD 1, track 28** **página 40, actividad 1**

1 Ese jersey azul marino y blanco con rayas es muy elegante.
2 No me gusta aquella rebeca. Marrón – ¡qué color más feo!
3 Estos pantalones negros son muy elegantes.
4 Me encantan esas botas, están muy de moda.
5 Quiero comprar esta bufanda. Me encantan los colores.
6 ¡Mira aquel pijama blanco con flores! ¡Es muy bonito!
7 Aquellos guantes azules parecen muy cómodos.
8 Quiero probarme esta minifalda rosa. ¡Es genial!

*Answers: as in audio script*

**2 Escoge la palabra correcta.**
Students choose the correct word to complete the sentence each time. Look at the Grammar box before doing this activity. Practise some examples using familiar words, maybe classroom objects or items of clothing. Get students to demonstrate they understand by placing objects around the classroom e.g. *Este lápiz es negro. Ese lápiz es rojo, pero aquel lápiz es verde.*

*Answers:* ***1*** *esta;* ***2*** *ese;* ***3*** *aquel;* ***4*** *esos*

AT 4.3 PLTS **3 Completa las frases.**
Students use what they have learnt in the previous activity and the Grammar box to complete the sentences.

*Answers:* ***1*** *aquellas;* ***2*** *estos;* ***3*** *este;* ***4*** *aquella*

## Gramática

Use this Grammar box on Demonstrative adjectives with Activities 1, 2 and 3 of this spread.

AT 2.3 PLTS L&S 1.4 **4 Juega con tu compañero o en grupo. ¿Qué quieres?**
Students play a game to practise demonstrative adjectives using either pencil case items or cards with items of clothing written or drawn on them, and a symbol to indicate *this*, *that*, or *that one over there*. Students turn over a card with an item of clothing and a symbol on it; if they can give the correct sentence for, e.g. *aquellos pantalones*, they keep the card. The game can be extended as far as you want by making them add in colour and pattern, and turning it into an opinion sentence, e.g. *Me encantan aquellos pantalones verdes con flores.*

AT 2.3 L&S 1.4 PLTS **5 Pregunta a tus compañeros. ¿Qué talla usas? ¿Qué número calzas? Elige una talla imaginaria.**
This can be a partner or small group activity. Make sure students have grasped the different questions. *¿Qué número calzas?* refers to shoes only.

AT 3.1 KAL 4.2 LLS 5.4 **6 ¿Cómo se dicen en inglés las palabras subrayadas?**
Using the illustrations to help them, students work with a partner to try and work out what the underlined words are in English.

*Answers:* ***1*** *baggy;* ***2*** *tight;* ***3*** *long;* ***4*** *short*

KAL 4.3 **Gramática**
Read through the Grammar explanation as a class. To ensure that students have understood how to use the expression *me queda bien*, display a few other singular and plural items of clothing and ask them to write sentences using this expression with the items of clothing listed.

AT 4.3 **7 Escribe una frase para cada dibujo de arriba.**
Students write a brief sentence for each picture from Activity 6, saying if the item suits the wearer or not.

AT 1.4 **8 Mira el video y contesta a las preguntas.**
Students watch the video and then answer the questions. Play the video as many times as necessary.

### Video script: Unit 1B (CD 1, track 29)

**Part 1**

*In the street*

Juan: ¿Qué vamos a hacer hoy?
Elena: Necesito comprar ropa nueva para el verano.
Juan: Pero tienes mucha ropa. Tienes faldas, mini-faldas, pantalones, camisetas, vestidos…
Roberto: Y zapatos, tienes de todo: tacón alto, tacón bajo, sandalias, botas, playeras…
Elena: Pero no tengo nada estiloso.
Roberto: A mí también me gustaría comprar algo nuevo.
Juan: Pero si no tenéis dinero…
Elena: Sí, tengo los 100 euros de mi cumpleaños.
Roberto: Y yo tengo 100 euros de mis padres.
Elena: ¡Vamos de compras entonces!
Juan: ¿Y yo?
Elena: Tú puedes decidir quién compra el mejor conjunto.
Juan: Siempre tan competitivos.

**Part 2**

*In a clothes shop*

Juan: Tienen 15 minutos para elegir un conjunto cada uno por menos de 100 euros. Podéis elegir el mejor conmigo.
Elena: Me gustan estos shorts.
Juan: Son muy cortos.
Roberto: Me gustan estas bermudas.
Juan: ¿Estas? Son muy largas.
Elena: Me gusta esta chaqueta.
Juan: ¿Esa? No me gusta nada.
Roberto: Este sombrero es guay.
Juan: Me gusta más éste que aquél.
Elena: Quiero probarme este vestido, este pañuelo y esta chaqueta.
Assistant: ¿Qué talla usas?
Elena: La 36.
Assistant: Si es la 36.
Elena: Y quiero probarme esas sandalias.
Assistant: ¿Qué número calzas?
Elena: El 38.
Assistant: Aquí tienes.
Elena: Gracias.
Roberto: Quería probarme estas bermudas, esta camiseta y esta gorra.
Assistant: ¿Qué talla usas?
Roberto: Una "M" creo.
Assistant: Sí, esta es tu talla.
Roberto: Y también quería probarme estas playeras.
Assistant: ¿Qué número usas?
Roberto: Un 45.
Assistant: Aquí tienes. Los probadores están a la derecha.
Roberto: Gracias.
Assistant: De nada.
Juan: Aquí tenemos a Elena con un vestido largo estilo hippy. Las flores están muy de moda este año. Elena lleva el vestido con una chaqueta rosa y unas sandalias beis, y también lleva un pañuelo azul.
Roberto lleva unas bermudas de verano, una camiseta de color azul marino y unas playeras blancas, y una gorra verde y negra.
Roberto: ¿Cuánto cuesta tu conjunto, Elena?
Elena: Cuesta 80.50 euros, porque hay rebajas. ¿Y el tuyo?
Roberto: El mío cuesta 75.80. Más barato que el tuyo.
Elena: ¿Cuál os gusta más?¿El mío?
Roberto: ¿O el mío?
Elena: Juan, ¿cuál te gusta más? ¿Juan? ¿Dónde estás?
Juan: Me gusta más *mi* nueva ropa, unos vaqueros y una camiseta súper guay.

*Answers:*
***a*** *They are shopping for clothes.* ***b*** *una falda – skirt, unos shorts – shorts; una chaqueta – jacket, sombrero – hat, un vestido – dress, un cinturón – belt, unas chanclas – flip-flops, una camiseta – a T-shirt, una gorra – a cap, unas playeras – canvas shoes, unos vaqueros – jeans, unas bermudas – bermuda shorts;* ***c*** *Elena: 36 (S)/38, Roberto: M/45*

AT1.4 **9 Mira el video otra vez. Completa la conversación.**

*Answers:*
***1*** *estas;* ***2*** *esta;* ***3*** *esta;* ***4*** *talla;* ***5*** *estas;* ***6*** *número*

AT1.4 **10 Whose outfit is best and why?**

*Answer: Students' own opinion*

PLTS AT 2.4 L&S 1.5 LLS 5.7

### Challenge

**With a friend or a small group, prepare and perform a role play in a clothes shop.**
Ideally, this should be a full-blown drama scene, but if time and resources do not allow, it can be done as a written dialogue or play script, an illustrated comic script, or for the most able, a written diary entry.

## 1B.4 ¿Dónde comprar?

páginas 42–43

# Planner

### Objectives
- discuss different types of shops
- use comparatives and superlatives
- make choices, evaluate options

### Resources
Student Book, pages 42–43
CD 1, track 30
Foundation Workbook, page 27
Higher Workbook, page 27
Interactive OxBox, Unit 1B
Copymasters 27–34

### Key language
*los grandes almacenes; la boutique; el centro comercial; el mercado; la tienda de una cadena; la tienda de segunda mano; anticuado/a; barato/a; caro/a; una ganga; regatear; tener suerte*

### Grammar
- use comparatives and superlatives

### Renewed Framework references
L&S 1.1, 1.2, 1.4; R&W 2.2, 2.4; LLS 5.1, 5.4, 5.5, 5.7

### PLTS
Activity 4: Reflective learners
Challenge: Effective participators

### Starters
- Display the photographs of shops form page 42 of the Student Book. Ask volunteers to tell you the Spanish for each of the shops and display this. Also ensure that students know what these terms mean in English. Next, make a statement, e.g. *Es más caro que el centro comercial pero es menos caro que las boutiques de ropa.* and ask the class which shop you could be describing. Point out that in some cases more than one answer could be correct.

### Plenaries
- Students write a paragraph about the shops in their town, or a fictional town if they prefer, and compare these using comparatives and superlatives and the vocabulary from the spread. Depending on the level of the class, you might find it useful to display the key language from the spread as well as comparatives and superlatives that they could use in their descriptions.
- Following on from Plenary Activity 1, students prepare a short talk saying which is their favourite type of shop and why. Again, you could display the key language and other useful vocabulary. Confident volunteers could present their talk to the class who could say if they agree or disagree.

### Homework/Self-study
Activity 3: If students have done this as a speaking activity, ask them to write it out.
Activity 4: Students write five sentences of their own on the subject of the spread using the comparatives and superlatives they have just met.

AT 3.4 | R&W 2.2 | LLS 5.4, 5.5

**1 Empareja las descripciones y las fotos.**
Students match the descriptions to the illustrations. Check that students understand what the different photos represent. *Boutique* should be self-explanatory and *mercado* and *centro comercial* fairly easy to guess at. Maybe take a vote as to what the words mean, then get them to check; or get each group to write down what they think they mean and give points for correct answers. Students can tackle the Reading activity independently using a dictionary or a glossary. For students requiring more support, read through the text asking them to call out when they reach a word they don't know. Alternatively, ask questions such as 'Which paragraph mentions designer clothing?' using cognates, near-cognates and known vocabulary to help students work out the texts before they match them to the pictures.

*Answers:* ***a** 3;* ***b** 4;* ***c** 1;* ***d** 2;* ***e** 5;* ***f** 6*

### Gramática
Explain to students that they will need these terms for Activity 2. Work through some examples before students attempt the activity.

AT 3.3 | LLS 5.1

**2 Trabaja con tu compañero. ¿Qué tienda es la más barata?**
Students read through the statements with their partner and decide which shop is the cheapest in each case.

*Answers:* ***1** el mercado;* ***2** la tienda de segunda mano;* ***3** los grandes almacenes;* ***4** el centro comercial*

AT 4.3 | L&S 1.4

**3 Describe la ropa de los dibujos.**
Students work with a partner to describe the clothes in the pictures. This can be done as a speaking or written activity.

AT 1.4 | PLTS | L&S 1.1, 1.2

**4 Escucha las conversaciones. ¿Qué deciden?**
Before doing the listening activity, spend some time looking at the picture and the Grammar box, and explaining the comparative and superlative. Ask for predictions as to which shop type will be the cheapest, etc.; students can then see if the recording matches their expectations. Discuss what might be meant by environmentally friendly, and ask students what type of vocabulary they might have to listen out for. Use can be made of the script afterwards especially for filler words (you know, really, um, etc.) which are all useful when students are doing speaking activities and role plays.

**CD 1, track 30** **página 43, actividad 4**

**1**
Ana: Ay, los precios de los grandes almacenes. Son muy caros, ¿sabes?
Alfredo: Estoy de acuerdo. Son más caros que los del centro comercial.
Ana: Verdad. Pero son menos caros que los de las boutiques de ropa de diseñador.
Alfredo: Tienes razón. Las boutiques son las tiendas más caras.

**2**
Ricardo: Las cadenas de tiendas tienen precios muy razonables, ¿no te parece?
Alfredo: Es verdad, pero el mercado es más barato que las cadenas.
Ricardo: ¡El mercado! Bueno, si hablamos del mercado, entonces las tiendas de segunda mano son las más baratas. ¿Te gusta esa ropa?
Alfredo: Bueno, no, pero sí que es barata...

**3**
Ana: En mi opinión las cadenas de tiendas como Zara están muy de moda.
Marta: Es verdad. Y los grandes almacenes están menos de moda – ahí la ropa es un poco anticuada para mi gusto.
Ana: Estoy de acuerdo. Pero creo que la ropa en las boutiques es la que está más de moda. Pero es muy cara: ¡Qué lástima!

**4**
Alfredo: No me gusta comprar ropa en el mercado. En mi opinión no hay mucha variedad.
Ricardo ¿De veras? Yo creo que hay bastante variedad, aunque es cierto que hay más variedad en las cadenas de tiendas.
Alfredo: Mm, sí... pero es siempre el mismo estilo. En el centro comercial hay mucha variedad de tiendas, y hay más variedad de ropa, ¿no te parece?

**5**
Ana: Me encanta la ropa muy original, pero no hay mucha en el centro comercial.
Marta: Tienes razón. Hay más ropa original en las boutiques, ¿no?
Ana: Pues, sí, pero ¡es muy cara!
Marta: Es verdad, sobre todo en las boutiques de ropa de diseñador. Bueno, ¿te gusta comprar ropa en el mercado? Es bastante barata, y en mi opinión ahí es donde venden la ropa más original.
Ana: ¡El mercado! Bueno, no sé...

**6**
Alfredo: Sabes, me encanta ir al centro comercial con mis amigos, pero no es muy ecológico comprar ropa allí. Hay que ir en coche.
Ricardo: Bueno, pues entonces puedes ir al mercado en el metro. ¡Es más ecológico!
Alfredo: Sí, y la ropa es barata, pero quizás está hecha por gente sin dinero en países pobres...
Ricardo: Ya, ya... pues entonces están las tiendas de segunda mano. El reciclaje es lo más ecológico, ¿no es verdad?

*Answers:*
***1** las boutiques; **2** las tiendas de segunda mano;*
***3** las boutiques; **4** el centro comercial; **5** el mercado;*
***6** las tiendas de segunda mano*

AT 4.4 | PLTS | R&W 2.4 | LLS 5.7

## Challenge

**Compare different places for buying clothes in your town for a Spanish visitor. Take photos and write a short description of each one.**
This could be a fairly simple homework assignment, a big presentation by small groups to the whole class, or even information sent to a partner school in Spain, inviting a response about what they think about the shops in *their* town.

# 1B.5 La ropa especializada

páginas 44–45

## Planner

### Objectives
- describe clothes for different activities and occasions
- revise singular and plural verb forms
- understand and produce descriptions

### Resources
Student Book, pages 44–45
CD 1, tracks 31–32
Foundation Workbook, page 28
Higher Workbook, page 28
Interactive OxBox, Unit 1B
Copymasters 27–34

### Renewed Framework references
L&S 1.1, 1.2, 1.4, 1.5; R&W 2.2, 2.4, 2.5; IU 3.2; KAL 4.3, 4.5; LLS 5.4, 5.5

### PLTS
Activity 1: Self-managers
Activity 4: Reflective learners
Activity 5: Effective participators
Challenge: Creative thinkers

### Starters
- Display the titles: *Los deportes acuáticos; El esquí; El baile; El fútbol; Los carnavales; El senderismo*. Challenge students to list as many items of clothing they can under each heading. Depending on the level of the class you may or may not wish to display some items of clothing for students to sort into the correct category. Check answers as a class.
- Play a memory game using key language from the spread. Start with a sentence such as: *Me gusta llevar ropa de esquí porque abriga mucho y es muy cómoda.* The next student must repeat this and add a garment and reason of their own, e.g. *Me gusta llevar ropa de esquí porque abriga mucho y es muy cómoda y me gusta llevar un tutú porque…* Less able classes can just mention types of clothing, rather than adding reasons as well.

### Plenaries
- Following on from Activity 5, play a Consequences type game. Students work in pairs; student A writes down what they would like to wear, e.g. *Me gusta llevar...*; on the back of the same paper, student B writes why (without knowing what the first person wrote), e.g. ... *porque es....* Each pair then reads out to the class what they have written. The class decides if it makes any sense or not. Points could be awarded if the two halves work together, or for humour value!

### Homework/Self-study
Gramática: Students write five sentences using the verb *llevar*. Encourage them to use this verb in both its singular and plural form. Provide less able classes with gapped sentences to fill in the correct form of the verb.

Challenge: Following on from the Challenge Activity, students design another outfit, this time for their favourite celebrity, a fictional character, or on a theme, e.g. aliens, pirates, cowboys, etc.

AT 3.4 | PLTS | R&W 2.2 | IU 3.2 | LLS 5.4

**1 Empareja las fotos con las descripciones.**
There should be enough clues for students match the descriptions to the illustrations fairly easily. This can be done individually, or in small groups with points awarded for each correct guess. Spend a little time discussing any activity they are not very sure of. Explain about carnival in Spain and the huge variety of costumes that can be seen.

*Answers:*
***1** Los carnavales; **2** El senderismo; **3** Los deportes acuáticos; **4** El esquí; **5** El fútbol; **6** El baile*

AT 1.4

**2 Escucha. Verifica tus respuestas.**
Students listen and check their answers to Activity 1.

**CD 1, track 31** — **página 45, actividad 2**

**La ropa especializada**

**Los deportes acuáticos.**
Esta gente lleva un traje de neopreno, y muchas veces zapatos de neopreno. Es muy cómodo y protege del agua fría.

**El esquí.**
Para este deporte de invierno se necesitan pantalones de esquí y una chaqueta acolchada, o para los niños un traje de nieve. La gente también lleva botas de esquí y bastones. Normalmente lleva gafas de sol.

**El baile.**
Hay muchos tipos de baile – el ballet, el jazz, el hip hop, el bollywood, la danza folklórica etc. Normalmente la gente lleva algún tipo de malla y zapatillas de ballet cuando entrenan. Para el ballet las chicas muchas veces llevan un tutú.

**El fútbol.**
Para este deporte se necesita una camiseta especial en el color del equipo con un número y el nombre del jugador en la espalda, unos pantalones cortos y botas. La tela sintética es muy importante para la ropa de deporte hoy en día.

**Los carnavales.**
Todo el mundo lleva disfraces de colores muy vivos, y baila en la calle toda la noche con mucha música.

**El senderismo.**
La gente que practica este deporte lleva ropa que abriga mucho, como un forro polar, pantalones impermeables, y botas de senderismo. Normalmente lleva una mochila y a veces también usan bastones para caminar.

**AT 3.4** **LLS 5.4, 5.5**

**3 Busca la expresión en español para las palabras y frases.**
Students write the Spanish for the English words and phrases. Some of the more difficult phrases can be found out by using vocabulary the students already know. Ask them which text they would look at to find specific words, e.g. it is unlikely they would find the word for ballet shoes in the text about watersports!

*Answers:*
***ballet shoes** – las zapatillas de ballet; **colourful** – de colores muy vivos; **fleece** – un forro polar; **padded jacket** – una chaqueta acolchada; **rucksack** – un macuto; **snow suit** – un traje de nieve; **waterproof trousers** – los pantalones imermeables; **wetsuit** – el traje neopreno; **poles**– bastones; **synthetic**– sintética*

**KAL 4.3, 4.5**

## Think

This Think box is to be used in association with Activities 1 and 2. Elicit from students that *abriga mucho* comes from *un abrigo*, a coat. Remind students that with a plural item, such as *los pantalones*, the verb must be used in its plural form, i.e. *Los pantalones abrigan mucho*. Go on to look at the second expression, *se necesita* and look at the example sentence with students. Ask them to provide you with additional examples. If necessary, display items of clothing. Ensure that they understand that *se necesita* can be used with any person.

**AT 1.4** **PLTS** **L&S 1.1, 1.2**

**4 Escucha: ¿Dónde está? ¿Qué hace? ¿Qué ropa se menciona? Anota en inglés.**
Students listen and note in English where each speaker is and what they are doing. The background will provide a clue, but encourage students also to listen out for specific words. More able students can write their notes in Spanish.

**CD 1, track 32** **página 45, actividad 4**

1 Estoy con mi equipo. Llevo una camiseta negra y amarilla con el número cinco en la espalda, unos pantalones cortos negros, y unas zapatillas.

2 Estoy en el teatro, y llevo un tutú blanco y rosa, con medias blancas y zapatillas rosas.

3 Estoy con mis amigos y ¡lo pasamos bomba! Hace bastante frío en el agua, así que llevo un traje y unos zapatos de neopreno. ¡Qué bien!

4 Estoy con mi familia de vacaciones en las montañas. Llevo unos pantalones de esquí y una chaqueta acolchada. Hace frío en la nieve pero también hace sol, así que llevo gafas de sol. ¡Me encanta este deporte!

5 ¡Qué estupendo es esto! ¡Todo el mundo está aquí! ¡Vamos a bailar toda la noche! ¡Llevo un disfraz fántastico – soy un gato blanco y negro!

6 Esta montaña es muy alta. Me gusta mucho hacer este deporte porque se practica al aire libre. Llevo un forro polar, unos pantalones impermeables, y, claro, unas botas. Tengo una mochila bastante grande y bastones. ¡Voy a caminar muchos kilómetros!

*Answers:*
***1** playing football; **2** dancing in a ballet; **3** doing watersports; **4** skiing; **5** at a carnival; **6** out hillwalking*

**KAL 4.3, 4.5**

## Gramática

Elicit from the class what the verb 'to wear' is in Spanish. Remind them that the verb ending changes according the person. Work through a few examples and then ask them to provide some of their own. Finally ask them to translate the two sentences.

*Answers:*
*El equipo lleva. Los miembros del equipo llevan.*

**AT 2.4** **PLTS** **L&S 1.4**

**5 Habla con tu compañero: ¿qué describes?**
Students work with a partner. They take it in turns to describe one of the clothes-types from the beginning of the spread using the vocabulary that they have learnt. For less able groups, model some examples, emphasising language such as *lleva, se necesita, normalmente, también*.

**AT 4.4** **R&W 2.4** **KAL 4.3, 4.5**

**6 Escribe. ¿Qué te gusta llevar? ¿Cuando? ¿Por qué?**
The idea here is to reuse the language in written form before embarking on the open-ended challenge. The paragraph can be as brief or long as your students' abilities allow.

**AT 4.4** **L&S 1.5** **R&W 2.4, 2.5** **KAL 4.3, 4.5** **PLTS**

## Challenge

**Design an outfit for a special event or your favourite activity. What items do you need? What colours? Are any particular materials necessary? Is it comfortable / practical / beautiful? Present your design.**
This open-ended activity can stretch the most able as far as you want. It can be hand-drawn and presented on paper, or students could use the computer, producing a PowerPoint presentation, for example, to present to the whole class.

## 1B.6 Labolengua

páginas 46–47

### Planner

**Objectives**
- review language and grammar from the unit

**Resources**
Student Book, pages 46–47
CD 1, track 33
Foundation Workbook, pages 29–30
Higher Workbook, pages 29–30
Foundation Workbook audio, CD 3, track 39 (Workbook 19)
Higher Workbook audio, CD 4, track 19
Interactive OxBox, Unit 1B
Copymasters 35–36

**Grammar**
- The imperfect tense, comparatives and superlatives

**Renewed Framework references**
L&S 1.2; KAL 4.3, 4.5; LLS 5.1, 5.4

**PLTS**
All activities: Reflective learners/Self-managers
Activity 9: Effective participators

**Homework/Self-study**
Activity 1: Students make up their own examples of what they used to do to practise using the imperfect and become familiar with it.
Activity 8: Students use the phrases in sentences of their own.
Activity 9: Students make a note of useful all-purpose words that they could use to get their message across.

### Comprender – the imperfect tense, comparatives and superlatives

### A The imperfect tense – 'used to'

KAL 4.3, 4.5 | PLTS

**1 Complete these sentences with the correct part of the verb.**
Practice of using the imperfect tense correctly.

*Answers:* ***1*** *llevaba;* ***2*** *íbamos;* ***3*** *parecían;* ***4*** *era*

### B Comparatives and superlatives – cheap, cheaper, cheapest!

KAL 4.3 | LLS 5.1 | PLTS

**2 Complete these sentences.**
Practice of using comparatives and superlatives.

*Answers:* ***1*** *El jersey marrón es lo más feo.* ***2*** *Los pantalones amarillos son los más ridículos.*

### Aprender – learning to listen

### C Listening to long texts

L&S 1.2 | PLTS

**3 Listen to this conversation between six friends. Don't try to take any notes, just sit back, maybe close your eyes if it helps you concentrate, and listen. What do you think they are talking about?**

The aim of this activity is to raise students' confidence in listening to longer and more difficult extracts. For that reason, for most classes, it would be better to play the whole conversation. For less able groups, play it in smaller chunks.

**CD 1, track 33** — **página 47, actividades 3–7**

Belén: Me encanta ir de compras a las cadenas de tiendas como Zara o Mango. La ropa es joven y está muy de moda.
Conchi: Mm, sí, pero en mi opinión, las boutiques pequeñas están aún más de moda.
Belén: Vale, pero las boutiques también son muy caras, ¿verdad?
Pedro: No es cierto. Fui con mi madre al Corte Inglés, unos grandes almacenes, y ella dice que la ropa de allí es más cara que la de las boutiques.
Raúl: ¡Qué va! Las boutiques de moda de diseñador son las más caras.
Felicidad: Tienes razón. Menos mal que las tiendas del centro comercial son bastante baratas.
Guillermo: Sí, pero el mercado es todavía más barato que el centro comercial.
Conchi: Pero la ropa de allí no está muy de moda. Y no hay mucha variedad.
Belén: Para mí, el centro comercial tiene más variedad que el mercado.

| | |
|---|---|
| Felicidad: | Sí, claro, pero las cadenas de tiendas como Zara tienen la mayor variedad – cambian de ropa cada semana. |
| Guillermo: | ¿Sabéis cuáles son las más baratas? Las tiendas de segunda mano. |
| Pedro: | ¡Las tiendas de segunda mano! ¡Qué horror! Ropa anticuada, nada de variedad ... |
| Guillermo: | Pero sí que son las más baratas, y también tienen ropa muy original. |
| Felicidad: | Hay ropa más original en las boutiques. |
| Conchi: | No estoy segura. Creo que la ropa más original es la del mercado. |
| Guillermo: | De todas formas, las tiendas de segunda mano son las más ecológicas. Son más ecológicas que los grandes almacenes, y que los centros comerciales ... |
| Raúl: | Vale, vale. Las tiendas de segunda mano son las más ecológicas. ¡De acuerdo! |

L&S 1.2 LLS 5.4 PLTS

**4 This time, before you listen, write down the names of any shops you heard. Listen again. Were you right? Do you need to change anything?**
Students should try to think shop types and shop names that they might hear.

*Answers: chain stores: Zara, Mango; boutiques; department store: Corte Inglés; charity shops*

L&S 1.2 LLS 5.4 PLTS

**5 Listen again. This time, near the bottom of your page, write down any opinions you hear, either during or after listening. Compare what you have written with someone else. Did they hear anything different?**
If students have an automatic tendency to write while listening, get them to experiment with just listening and writing after, and vice versa, to see what works best for them.

L&S 1.2 PLTS

**6 Listen again. Can you match any of your opinions to the shops?**
Students listen again and try to match the opinions from Activity 5 to the shops mentioned.

L&S 1.2 PLTS

**7 Last job. Listen again. Underline any opinions expressed by a boy. Circle any opinions expressed by a girl.**
Decide what level of detail you want your students to listen out for.

*Answers:*
***las cadenas de tiendas:*** *ropa joven, muy de moda, la más variedad, son las más caras*

***los boutiques (de moda diseñador):*** *más de moda (que la tienda de cadena), muy caros, más ropa original que la tienda de caridad*

***los grandes almacenes:*** *más caros que los boutiques*

***el centro comercial:*** *bastante baratas, tiene más variedad (que el mercado)*

***el mercado:*** *más barato que el centro comercial, no es muy de moda, no tiene mucha variedad, hay la más ropa original*

***la tienda de caridad:*** *la más barata, ropa anticuada, nada de variedad,tiene ropa muy original, muy ecológico, más ecológico que el almacén, más ecológico que el centro comercial, la más ecológico*

**Why is listening so hard? Is it easier to 'listen' to a video? Why?**
Elicit from students that with videos you have lots of visual clues as well.

## Hablar – speaking in real situations
## D Speaking Spanish in shops

PLTS

**8 Can you remember how to say: thank you, I would like, I'm interested in?**
This requires students to think back to earlier in the unit.

*Answers: gracias; Quiero ...; Me interesa…*

PLTS

**9 Without looking anything up, how would you ask for...?**
Accept anything that gets the message across reasonably correctly. This encourags students to use the language they DO know. Allow them to collaborate in pairs to produce their answers. They certainly won't know all the vocabulary so will have to rely on words they know, and the demonstrative adjectives learnt in this chapter. Ask them what other all-purpose words would be useful to them. They should come up with things like *there, the other one, up there, down there, on the left*, etc.

## 1B.7 Extra Star

página 48

### Planner

**Objectives**

- practise describing clothes
- use the impersonal expression *me queda bien*
- give an opinion on whether something suits you

**Resources**

Student Book, page 48
Copymaster 37

**Renewed Framework references**

KAL 4.3, 4.5; LLS 5.1, 5.4

**PLTS**

Activity 3: Reflective learners

AT 3.3 | KAL 5.4

**1 Empareja las frases con las dibujos.**
Students match the phrases to the pictures.

*Answers:* ***1** c, **2** a, **3** b, **4** d*

AT 4.2

**2 ¿Me queda bien? Completa las frases.**
Before attempting this activity, read through the Grammar box as a class to remind students of the impersonal expression, *me queda bien*.

*Answers: **1** La camiseta **me queda bien**. **2** La bufanda **no me queda bien**. **3** Los zapátos **no me quedan bien**. **4** Los vaqueros **me quedan bien**.*

AT 4.2–3 | KAL 4.3, 4.5 | LLS 5.1 | PLTS

**3 Escribe frases para los dibujos. ¿Qué opinas?**
Students study the pictures and then using the vocabulary from the unit, write sentences giving their opinion of each item of clothing.

*Possible answers:*
***1** Me gustan los zápatos. ¡Qué guay! **2** Me gusta la bufanda, es muy cómodo. **3** No me gustan los vaqueros, son demasiado largos. **4** No me gusta la camiseta – es muy feo.*

AT 4.3 | KAL 4.3, 4.5 | LLS 5.1

**4 Escribe más frases. ¿Te queda bien?**
Following on from Activity 3, students write some more sentences about the clothes in the pictures, saying if each item suits them or not.

*Suggested answers:*
***1** Me quedan bien los zapátos. **2** Me queda bien la bufanda. **3** No me quedan bien los vaqueros. **4** No me queda bien la camiseta.*

## 1B.7 Extra Plus

página 49

### Planner

**Objectives**

- practise saying what suits you and others
- use the impersonal expression *me / te / le queda bien*
- give opinions politely

**Resources**

Student Book, page 49
Copymaster 38

**Renewed Framework references**

R&W 2.4; KAL 4.3, 4.5; LLS 5.1, 5.4

AT 3.3 | KAL 4.3, 4.5

**1 Completa las frases y emparéjalas con los dibujos.**
Students complete the sentences with the correct word and then match them to the pictures. Once students have completed this activity, refer them to the Grammar box to ensure that they remember what *me queda bien*, *te queda bien* and *le queda bien* mean and how to use these expressions correctly.

*Answers: **1** c en la onda; **2** a elegante; **3** d grande; **4** b precioso*

AT 3.3 | LLS 5.4

**2 Empareja las dos partes de las frases.**
Students match the sentence halves.

*Answers:* ***1** c, **2** d, **3** a, **4** b*

AT 4.3–4 | KAL 4.3, 4.5 | LLS 5.1

**3 Escribe una descripción para cada dibujo. ¿Le queda bien?**
Students write a sentence for each picture, saying if the item is too big/small, etc, and if it suits the wearer.

AT 4.3–4 | R&W 2.4 | KAL 4.3, 4.5 | LLS 5.1

**4 Busca una foto de una persona famosa. Describe su ropa. ¿Qué opinas?**
Ask students to find a picture of a celebrity, or provide some for them to use. Explain that they are going to describe their clothes and give their opinion on what they are wearing.

## 1B.8 Prueba

página 50

### Planner

**Resources**
Student Book, page 50
CD 1, track 34
Assessment OxBox, Unit 1B

**Renewed Framework references**
L&S 1.1, 1.2, 1.4; R&W 2.2, 2.4; KAL 4.3, 4.5; LLS 5.4

**PLTS**
All activities: Reflective learners
Hablar: Creative thinkers
Escribir: Creative thinkers

### Escuchar

AT 1.3–4 | L&S 1.1, 1.2 | PLTS

**Listen to the two conversations in the shop and answer the questions.**
This activity tests listening skills using the language covered in this unit.

**CD 1, track 34** **página 50, actividad 1**

**1**
Señora: Buenos días. Quiero probarme una camisa.
Dependiente: Muy bien. ¿Qué talla usa?
Señora: Pues, mediana.
Dependiente: Vale. Tenemos en verde o azul. ¿Qué prefiere?
Señora: Mm... Creo que prefiero esa camisa azul.
Dependiente: Muy bien. Los probadores están a la derecha ...

**2**
Señor: Buenas tardes. Busco un traje de baño.
Dependiente: ¿Un traje de baño? Muy bien, señor. ¿De talla grande o mediana?
Señor: De talla grande.
Dependiente: Muy bien. Tenemos ese en rojo y este en negro en talla grande.
Señor: En negro, claro. ¡De color rojo! ¡Qué feo ...!

*Answers:*
***1 a*** *a shirt;* ***b*** *medium;* ***c*** *blue;* ***d*** *far – that one*
***2 a*** *swimming costume;* ***b*** *large;* ***c*** *black;* ***d*** *near – this*

### Hablar

AT 2.3–4 | L&S 1.4 | PLTS

**Have a conversation with a friend. One plays the shop assistant, and one the customer.**
This activity tests speaking skills using the language covered in this unit. Students use the prompts to ask and answer the questions.

### Leer

AT 3.4 | R&W 2.2 | LLS 5.4 | PLTS

**Read the descriptions and match them to the pictures.**
This activity tests reading skills using the language covered in this unit.

*Answers:* ***1*** *c;* ***2*** *a;* ***3*** *b*

### Escribir

AT 4.4 | R&W 2.4 | KAL 4.3, 4.5 | PLTS

**Write a description of this boy's style and clothes. Do you think they suit him?**
This activity tests writing skills using the language covered in this unit.

*Answers: Students' own answers*

## 1B Leer

página 150

**Resources**
Student Book, page 150

**Renewed Framework references**
R&W 2.1, 2.4, 2.5, LLS 5.4

**PLTS**
Activity 3: Creative thinkers; Reflective learners

AT 3.4 | R&W 2.1, 2.2

**1 Contesta a las preguntas.**
Students read the text and answer the questions.

*Answers:*
***1*** *new sports kit;* ***2*** *people to design the kit;* ***3*** *free tickets for them and a friend to watch their team, for a whole year;* ***4*** *football team, dance team, canoeing team, tennis team, skiing team*

AT 3.4 | R&W 2.1, 2.2

**2 ¿Verdad o mentira?**
Students answer true (verdad) or false (mentira).

*Answers:*
***1*** *mentira (son azul y rojo);* ***2*** *mentira;* ***3*** *mentira;* ***4*** *verdad;* ***5*** *verdad*

AT 4.4 | PLTS

**3 Escribe y diseña.**
Students design new kit for one of the teams and then write a description of the style of clothing they have designed in Spanish.

### Follow-up

Students choose one of their local/favourite sporting teams and write a description of their kit in Spanish.

## Foundation Workbook

### Página 24 1B.1 ¿Qué opinas de la moda?

- Use with Student Book, pages 36–37

AT 3.1 **1 Unscramble the Spanish and the English for these clothes words by choosing the correct letter from each box.**

*Answers:*
***a** falda – skirt; **b** pantalón – trousers; **c** botas – boots; **d** paraguas – umbrella; **e** un jersey – a sweater*

AT 1.3 L&S 1.2 **2 Listen to Muriel talking about Iñaki's clothes. Draw lines from the words to the picture to show what she says about his outfit.**
Practice of understanding opinions about clothes.

**CD 3, track 35 (Workbook 15)** **página 24, actividades 2 y 3**

Me gustan los pantalones cortos.
No me gusta la camiseta con el logotipo.
El anorak es feo.
Las botas con puntos son bonitas.
Me encanta el paraguas.

*Answers: as per transcript*

AT 1.3 L&S 1.1 **3 Now pick the words <u>you</u> think apply to each bit of his outfit. Listen again and reply to Muriel, agreeing or disagreeing with her.**
Practice of giving opinions about clothes.

### Página 25 1B.2 Mi estilo

- Use with Student Book, pages 38–39

AT 3.3, 1.3 R&W 2.1, 2.2 L&S 1.2 **1 Read about the different shirts David Beckham has worn for different teams. Try to match up each shirt with the correct team. Then listen and find out the real answers.**

**CD 3, track 36 (Workbook 16)** **página 25, actividad 1**

**1**
Cuando jugaba con el Preston North End, llevaba una camiseta blanca con un logotipo azul y amarillo.

**2**
Con el Manchester United, llevaba una camiseta roja con un logotipo amarillo. Llevaba el número diez o el número siete.

**3**
Con el Real Madrid llevaba el número veintitrés y una camiseta blanca con un logotipo azul.

**4**
Cuando jugaba con el LA Galaxy, llevaba una camiseta blanca y amarilla y llevaba el número veintitrés.

**5**
Con el AC Milán, llevaba una camiseta rayada, roja y negra, con el número treinta y dos.

**6**
Y con el equipo nacional de Inglaterra, llevaba una camiseta blanca o roja, con el número siete o el diecisiete.

*Answers:*
***1** f; **2** a; **3** c; **4** b; **5** e; **6** d*

AT 2.2–3 L&S 1.5 **2 Research the career of one of these famous people. Explain to partner what they used to wear.**
This provides good practise of describing clothes.
If possible, students could also give their opinion on the different kit each one of the famous people wore.

*Answers:*
*Michael Owen is a footballer who has had a succession of different clubs (although there is a rugby player of the same name). Michelle Wie is a golfer. Mia Hamm was a female footballer. Michael Jordan was a basketball player.*

### Página 26 1B.3 ¿Me queda bien?

- Use with Student Book, pages 40–41

AT 3.2 **1 Draw lines to match up the questions to the answers.**

*Answers: **a** Una camiseta. **b** Verde. **c** Mediana. **d** Sí. **e** Te queda guay.*

AT 1.3 L&S 1.2 **2 Listen and check your answers to Activity 1.**

CD 3, track 37 (Workbook 17) **página 26, actividad 2**

- ¿Qué deseas?
- Quiero comprar una camiseta.
- ¿De qué color?
- Una camiseta verde.
- ¿Qué talla usas?
- Mediana.
- Tengo esa y esta.
- Quiero probarme esa.
- Sí, los probadores están a la derecha.
- ¿Me queda bien?
- Te queda guay.

AT 1.3, 2.2-3 | L&S 1.1, 1.5

**3 Listen and give your own answers to the questions.**

Students should try to use as much of the vocabulary from the Student Book spread as possible.

CD 3, track 38 (Workbook 18) **página 26, actividad 3**

¿Qué deseas?
¿De qué color?
¿Qué talla usas?
¿Te gusta?

## Página 27 1B.4 ¿Dónde comprar?

- Use with Student Book, pages 42–43

AT 3.1

**1 One of these words is NOT in the wordsearch. Which is it?**

*Answer: mercado*

AT 4.1

**2 Create your own clothes shopping wordsearch puzzle in Spanish for a friend to do. You will find some useful words on page 31.**
Students can also refer back to pages 42 and 43 in the Student Book for some useful vocabulary.

## Página 28 1B.5 La ropa especializada

- Use with Student Book, pages 44–45

AT 3.2

**1 Roll dice to see what the model is wearing on each part of the body. Draw it on.**

A fun way to practise clothes vocabulary. Students could also colour in the items of clothing in order to make their description in Activity 2 more interesting.

AT 2.2-3 | L&S 1.5

**2 Describe your picture to a friend.**
Remind students to mention colours and, if possible, give opinions. They should refer back to pages 44 and 45 of the Student Book for support if necessary.

## Página 29 1B.6A Labolengua

- Use with Student Book, pages 46–47

KAL 4.2, 4.4

**1 The letters have fallen out of each column into a heap. Put them back into the column they fell from to make this sentence.**

*Answer: Llevaba ropa de deporte pero hoy llevo ropa elegante.*

KAL 4.2, 4.4

**2 Make your own fallen sentence puzzle in Spanish about what you used to wear. Then swap puzzles with a friend.**

## Página 30 1B.6B Técnica

- Use with Student Book, pages 46–47

LLS 5.8

**1 Match up the problems with what you think would be the best advice.**

*Answers: **1** a and f; **2** f; **3** d and c; **4** c and d; **5** e; **6** b and c; **7** a and e; **8** b and c; **9** g and h*

LLS 5.8

**2 Pick out two areas you need to work on and set yourself some targets/strategies.**

AT 1.4 | L&S 1.1,1.2

**3 Listen and answer the questions.**

CD 3, track 39 (Workbook 19) **página 30, actividad 3**

Bueno, si hablamos de compras, entonces a mí me encantan los centros comerciales. Voy cada sábado con mis amigos y paseamos viendo lo que hay en los escaparates. A veces entramos pero como no tenemos mucho dinero no vale la pena. ¿Quién quiere ver cosas que no puede comprar? Tiendas de aparatos, sí, entramos porque podemos jugar y ver las novedades, por ejemplo la Applestore, pero ropa, no. Yo compro mi ropa en el supermercado, o más bien mi madre me la compra.

*Answers: **b** shopping; **c** shopping centres; **d** he can't afford the clothes in the shops there and buys clothes at the supermarket; **e** shops that sell appliances, such as the Apple store; **f** his mum*

**4 Describe how you did, how you felt, and what strategies you tried in Activity 3.**

## Higher Workbook

### Página 24 1B.1 ¿Qué opinas de la moda?

- Use with Student Book, pages 36–37

AT 3.1

**1 Work out these clothes words. Each box has a letter from the English word, one from the Spanish, and a random letter.**
Go through the first one as a class to ensure that students understand what to do.

*Answers:* ***a*** *falda – skirt;* ***b*** *pantalón – trousers;* ***c*** *botas – boots;* ***d*** *paraguas – umbrella;* ***e*** *un jersey – a sweater*

AT 1.3
L&S 1.2

**2 Listen to Muriel talking about Iñaki's clothes. Label his outfit with her opinions.**

Practice of understanding opinions about clothes.

**CD 4, track 15** **página 24, actividades 2 y 3**

Me gustan los pantalones cortos, con las flores.
No me gusta la camiseta con el logotipo.
El anorak es feo y ridículo.
Las botas de goma con puntos son bonitas.
Me encanta el paraguas, es como el arco iris.

*Answers: as per transcript*

AT 1.3
L&S 1.1

**3 Now pick the words you think apply to each bit of his outfit. Listen again and reply to Muriel, agreeing or disagreeing with her.**
Practice of giving opinions about clothes.

### Página 25 1B.2 Mi estilo

- Use with Student Book, pages 38–39

AT 3.3
AT 1.4
R&W 2.1–2.2
L&S 1.1

**1 Read about the different shirts David Beckham has worn for different teams. Try to match up each shirt with the correct team. Then listen and find out the real answers.**

**CD 4, track 16** **página 25, actividad 1**

Muchos asocian a David Beckham con el color rojo, ya que llevaba una camiseta roja con el Manchester United.

Pero en la mayoría de sus clubes, llevaba otro color: el blanco. Cuando jugaba con el Preston, llevaba una camiseta blanca con un logotipo azul y amarillo.

Con el Real Madrid y con el LA Galaxy, llevaba una camiseta también blanca, con el número veintitrés. La diferencia era el logotipo – azul en el Madrid y de color amarillo con Los Ángeles.

Con el equipo nacional de Inglaterra llevaba los colores: el blanco o el rojo, y llevaba el número siete o el diecisiete.

También con el Manchester llevaba el número siete, aunque al principio llevaba el número diez.

El AC Milán era diferente: una camiseta rayada, roja y negra. Y llevaba el número treinta y dos.

*Answers:* ***1****f;* ***2****a;* ***3****c;* ***4****b;* ***5****e;* ***6****d*

AT 2.2–4
L&S 1.5

**2 Research the career of one of these famous people. Explain to a partner what they used to wear.**
This provides good practise of describing clothes. Students could also give their opinion on the different kit each one of the famous people wore.

*Answers:*
*Michael Owen is a footballer who has had a succession of different clubs (although there is a rugby player of the same name). Michelle Wie is a golfer. Mia Hamm was a female footballer. Michael Jordan was a basketball player.*

### Página 26 1B.3 ¿Me queda bien?

- Use with Student Book, pages 40–41

AT 3.3

**1 Put this conversation into a logical order.**

*Answers: a, j, b, d, e, c, h, g, k, i, f*

AT 1.3
L&S 1.2

**2 Listen and check your answers to Activity 1.**

**CD 4, track 17** — **página 26, actividad 2**

- ¿Qué deseas?
- Quiero comprar una camiseta.
- ¿De qué color?
- Una camiseta verde.
- ¿Qué talla usas?
- Mediana.
- Tengo esa y esta.
- Quiero probarme esa.
- Sí, los probadores están a la derecha.
- ¿Me queda bien?
- Te queda guay.

AT 2.2–4 | L&S 1.1–1.5

**3 Listen and give your own answers to the questions.**

Students should try to use as much of the vocabulary from the Student Book spread as possible.

**CD 4, track 18** — **página 26, actividad 3**

¿Qué deseas?
¿De qué color?
¿Qué talla usas?
¿Te gusta?

## Página 27 1B.4 ¿Dónde comprar?

- Use with Student Book, pages 42–43

AT 3.1

**1 Find these words in Spanish in the wordsearch. There is an extra word to find. What is it? Also, one of the words in the list is NOT in the wordsearch? Which one?**

*Answers: mercado; precio*

AT 4.1

**2 Create your own clothes shopping wordsearch puzzle in Spanish for a friend to do. You will find some useful words on page 31.**
Students can also refer back to pages 42 and 43 in the Student Book for some useful vocabulary.

## Página 28 1B.5 La ropa especializada

- Use with Student Book, pages 44–45

AT 3.2

**1 Roll dice to see what the model is wearing on each part of the body. Draw it on.**
A fun way to practise clothes vocabulary. Students could also colour in the items of clothing in order to make their description in Activity 2 more interesting.

AT 2.3 | L&S 1.5

**2 Describe your picture to a friend.**
Remind students to mention colours and give opinions. They should refer back to pages 44 and 45 of the Student Book for support if necessary.

## Página 29 1B.6A Labolengua

- Use with Student Book, pages 46–47

KAL 4.2, 4.4

**1 The letters have fallen out of each column into a heap. Put them back in the column they fell from to make a sentence about what you <u>used to wear</u> and what you <u>wear today</u>.**

*Answer: Llevaba ropa de deporte pero hoy llevo ropa elegante.*

KAL 4.2, 4.4

**2 Now make your own fallen sentence puzzle in Spanish about what you used to wear. Then swap puzzles with a friend.**

## Página 30 1B.6B Técnica

- Use with Student Book, pages 46–47

LLS 5.8

**1 Suggest some advice for each of these frustrations.**

*Possible answers:*
*Concentrate on what you do understand.*
*Use the questions to help you focus on detail.*
*Listen once to locate the answers, then listen again.*
*Make quick notes and write your full answers later.*
*Build your confidence by doing lots of listening.*
*Make a sensible guess, then listen again for more clues.*
*Revise the pronunciation/spelling rules.*
*Try writing down tricky words – reading can be easier than listening.*

LLS 5.8

**2 Pick out two areas you need to work on and set yourself some targets/strategies.**

AT 1.4 | L&S 1.1,1.2

**3 Listen and answer the questions.**

**CD 4, track 19** — **página 30, actividad 3**

Bueno, si hablamos de compras, entonces a mí me encantan los centros comerciales. Voy cada sábado con mis amigos y paseamos viendo lo que hay en los escaparates. A veces entramos pero como no tenemos mucho dinero no vale la pena. ¿Quién quiere ver cosas que no puede comprar? Tiendas de aparatos, sí, entramos porque podemos jugar y ver las novedades, por ejemplo la Applestore, pero ropa, no. Yo compro mi ropa en el supermercado, o más bien mi madre me la compra.

*Answers:*
***b** shopping; **c** shopping centres; **d** he can't afford the clothes so there is no point; he buys clothes from the supermarket.*
***e** shops that sell appliances, such as the Apple store; **f** his mum*

**3 Describe how you did, how you felt, and what strategies you tried in Activity 3.**

# 2A El ocio

## Unit Objectives

**Contexts and cultural focus:** freetime and leisure activities
**Grammar:** *gustar* and similar verbs with nouns and verbs; direct object pronouns (for things/objects); revision of the preterite tense (regular and some irregular verbs); preterite (some irregular) and imperfect verbs
**Language learning:** justifying opinions; adapting previously learnt language in a new context; responding to open-ended questions; summarising and recounting what happened; giving opinions

- *Aim*: To learn how to speak about freetime and leisure activities.
- Each unit has an associated video which will feature throughout the unit. Below is the transcript of the video for this unit.

**Video clip: Unit 2A (CD 1, track 44)**

**Part 1**

*Elena, Roberto and Juan walking down a path in the woods on their way to the Pino a Pino*

Roberto: ¿Juan, qué hacemos aquí?
Juan: Es una sorpresa.
Elena: ¡Es algo sensacional!
Juan: Lo vas a pasar fenomenal.
Elena: Yo el año pasado vine y me lo pasé bomba.
Roberto: ¿Pero chicos, qué es?
Juan: ¿Te gustan las películas de Tarzan?
Roberto: ¡Claro que sí!
Juan: Pues sí, vamos a hacer como Tarzan en el Pino a Pino.
Roberto: ¿Y vamos a ver quién gana?
Juan: Sí, pero esta vez es más complicado.
Elena: ¿Cómo?
Juan: Esta vez, el último tiene que contar lo que hacía durante el recorrido y cómo le fue.
Roberto: ¿Tienes buena memoria Juan? ¡Porque voy a ganar yo!

**Part 2**

*Training session*

Juan: Primero hay que hacer la formación.
Instructor: Agarra aquí por favor. Agarra aquí por favor. Gírate un poquito. Agarra aquí. Son los más importantes porque nos permiten estar siempre enganchados a los objetos que sean de color rojo. Lo primero que tengo que hacer es engancharme con ambos mosquetones. Nos vamos a encontrar con este formato un juego que se llama Salto de Tarzan. Es un juego relativamente físico porque tenemos que aguantar nuestro peso con la fuerza de los brazos.

*At the sign post with the different courses.*

Roberto: ¿Vamos a hacer el "desafío"?
Ernesto: Mejor hacemos aventurero ya que Juan tiene sólo 15 años.
Roberto: Va ser aún más fácil ganar para mí.

*They climb up on to the first section of ropes.*

Juan: Primero vamos a subir por este árbol y después a pasar por el túnel.
Roberto: Yo primero.
Elena: ¡Me encanta! Me siento como un mono en los árboles. ¡Venga chicos! ¿Y ahora, cómo llego allí?
Roberto: Muy aburrido. Es demasiado fácil.
Juan: Ahora vamos a saltar por la tirolina. ¿Cómo paro?
Roberto: No lo soporto es peligroso.
Roberto: ¡Lo odio!
Juan: ¡He ganado!
Elena: ¡Venga Roberto!
Juan: Este último es fantástico.
Elena: Es súper rápido.
Roberto: Lo odio.

Juan: ¿Quién ganó, Roberto?
Roberto: Tú, Juan.
Elena: Y ¿Quién quedó segundo?
Roberto: Tú, Elena.
Juan: Y ¿Quién terminó el último?
Roberto: Yo. Yo terminé el último.
Elena: Ahora nos tienes que contar todo lo que pasó.
Roberto: De acuerdo. Primero hicimos la formación, fue muy interesante, pero cuando subimos a los arboles me fue fatal. Nada más subir a los arboles tuve un ataque de vértigo, Elena y Juan lo hacían sin miedo. Saltaban de un árbol a otro como monos, pero a mí me temblaban las piernas. Caminé de un árbol a otro atado con una cuerda. Salté con un arnés de una plataforma a otra y lo hice mal. ¡Me quedé allí suspendido en el aire! ¡Lo pasé mal pero supermal! Terminé el último. ¡Qué vergüenza!
Elena: No pasa nada.

**Punto Lengua**

Yo, el año pasado vine y me lo pasé bomba.
Esta vez, el último tiene que contar lo que hacía durante el recorrido y cómo le fue.
Elena y Juan lo hacían sin miedo.
¡Lo pasé mal pero supermal!

As a starter activity to introduce the unit and familiarise students with the language they will meet, first play Part 1 a couple of times. Do students understand what this is about? As this sets the scene, understanding this will help students with the second part. The class can then view the video as a whole. Are there any words or phrases that they have recognised? What do they think it is about? Explain that you will look at it in more detail later in this unit.

*Synopsis:*
Roberto thinks that Elena and Juan's surprise activity will be boring and far too easy for him, but is in for a shock when he discovers how difficult it really is ...

**Unit 2A El ocio Overview grid**

| Page reference | Contexts and objectives | Language learning | Grammar | Key language | Framework | AT level |
|---|---|---|---|---|---|---|
| Pages 52–53 **Mi tiempo libre** | • talk about what you like doing in your free time; talk about music you like/don't like | • justify opinions | • use *gustar* and similar verbs with nouns and verbs | *la canción; los pasatiempos; me aburre; me apasiona; me encanta; me fastidia; me interesa; aburrido/a; creativo/a; divertido/a; emocionante; estrepitoso/a; fatal; genial; ruidoso/a; descargar; leer revistas; pintar; salir con amigos* | L&S 1.1, 1.2, 1.4; R&W 2.2, 2.4, 2.5; KAL 4.1, 4.3, 4.5; LLS 5.4 | 1.3–4, 2.3, 3.3–4, 4.3–5 |
| Pages 54–55 **De compras** | • talk about going shopping | • adapt previously learnt language in a new context | • use direct object pronouns (for things/ objects) | *la carnicería; la charcutería; la frutería; la pescadería; la tienda de comestibles; el aceite de oliva; las aceitunas; los caramelos; un helado; el jamón; la leche; una lechuga; los limones; las manzanas; las patatas fritas; el pescado; el pollo; las sardinas; las truchas; ¿Qué falta?; un regalo; la planta baja; el sótano* | L&S 1.1, 1.2, 1.4; KAL 4.3, 4.4; LLS 5.4, 5.5 | 1.3–4, 2.3–4, 3.1, 4.4 |
| Pages 56–57 **De vacaciones** | • say what you did on holiday and what it was like | • respond to open-ended questions, e.g. *¿Adónde fuiste?* | • revise the preterite tense (regular and some irregular verbs) | *¿Adónde fuiste? ¿Qué tal lo pasaste? acostarse; alojarse en; comer; ir de camping; ir (fui); salir; ser (fui); tener (tuve); empezó a llover; lo pasé/ pasamos bomba; anoche; anteayer; ayer; el sábado pasado; el avión; desastroso/a; increíble; una feria; el parque de atracciones; un viaje* | L&S 1.2, 1.4; R&W 2.2, 2.4, 2.5; KAL 4.1, 4.5; LLS: 5.4 | 1.3–5, 2.4–5, 3.3, 3.5, 4.4–5 |

| Unit 2A El ocio Overview grid | | | | | | |
|---|---|---|---|---|---|---|
| **Page reference** | **Contexts and objectives** | **Language learning** | **Grammar** | **Key language** | **Framework** | **AT level** |
| Pages 58–59<br>**¡Lo pasamos bomba!** | • describe past events | • summarise and recount what happened | • use a mix of preterite (some irregular) and imperfect verbs | *¿Cuánto tiempo? ¿Qué tiempo hizo? estar (estuve); ganar; ser (fui); tener (tuve); fatal; madrileño/a; la corrida (de toros); los fuegos artificiales; un regalo; un traje típico* | L&S 1.2, 1.4; R&W 2.2, 2.5; IU3.2; KAL 4.5, 4.6 | 1.5, 2.5, 3.5, 4.5–6 |
| Pages 60–61<br>**Cuando era joven …** | • talk about what you did when you were younger | • adapt previously learnt language and give opinions | • use a mix of preterite and imperfect tenses | | L&S 1.2, 1.4; R&W 2.2, 2.4, 2.5; KAL 4.3, 4.4, 4.5 | 1.5, 2.5, 3.5, 4.5–6 |
| Pages 62–63<br>**Labolengua** | • review language and grammar from the unit | | | | L&S 1.4; KAL 4.3, 4.4, 4.5, 4.6; LLS 5.1 | |
| Pages 64–65<br>**Extra Star**<br>**Extra Plus** | • differentiated extension/ homework material | • revise and consolidate all vocabulary and grammar covered in the unit | • revise and consolidate all vocabulary and grammar covered in the unit | | R&W 2.2, 2.4; KAL 4.3, 4.5; LLS 5.1 | 3.3–5, 4.3–5 |
| Page 66<br>**Prueba** | • end-of-unit test | | | | L&S 1.1, 1.2, 1.4; R&W 2.2, 2.4; KAL 4.3, 4.5; LLS 5.4 | 1.5, 2.5, 3.5, 4.5–6 |
| Page 67<br>**Vocabulario** | • a summary of the key language covered in each core spread of this unit | | | | | |
| Page 151<br>**Leer 2A** | • practice of longer reading texts based on the theme of the unit | | | | R&W 2.1, 2.2, 2.4; KAL 4.6 | 3.5, 4.4–5 |

**Week-by-week overview**
**(Three-year KS3 Route: assuming six weeks' work or approximately 10–12.5 hours)**
**(Two-year KS3 Route: assuming four weeks' worth or approxmately 6.5–8.5 hours)**

**About Unit 2A, *El ocio:*** Students work in the context of freetime and leisure activities. They talk about what they like doing in their free time, going shopping and what they did on holiday. They describe past events and talk about what they did when they were young. Students use *gustar* and similar verbs with nouns and verbs as well as direct object pronouns (for things and people). They revise the preterite tense (regular and some irregular verbs) and use a mix of preterite (some irregular) and imperfect verbs. The unit also provides tips on language learning techniques.

| Three-Year KS3 Route | | | Two-Year KS3 Route | | |
|---|---|---|---|---|---|
| **Week** | **Resources** | **Objectives** | **Week** | **Resources** | **Objectives** |
| 1 | **2A.1 Mi tiempo libre**<br>**2A.6 Labolengua**<br>**E** (p.63) | talk about what you like doing in your free time and music you like/don't like<br>justify opinions<br>use *gustar* and similar verbs with nouns and verbs | 1 | **2A.1 Mi tiempo libre**<br>(Omit activities 3, Think & Challenge)<br>**2A.6 Labolengua**<br>**E** (p.63) | talk about what you like doing in your free time and music you like/ don't like<br>justify opinions<br>use *gustar* and similar verbs with nouns and verbs |
| 2 | **2A.2 De compras**<br>**2A.6 Labolengua**<br>**A** (p.62) | talk about going shopping<br>adapt previously learnt language in a new context<br>use direct object pronouns (for things/objects) | 2 | **2A.2 De compras**<br>(Omit activities 1, Think, 6, 7 & Challenge)<br>**2A.6 Labolengua**<br>**A (Omit activity 2)**<br>(p.62) | talk about going shopping<br>adapt previously learnt language in a new context<br>use direct object pronouns (for things/ objects) |
| 3 | **2A.3 De vacaciones**<br>**2A.6 Labolengua**<br>**B** (p.62) **and D** (p.63) | say what you did on holiday and what it was like<br>respond to open-ended questions, e.g. *¿Adónde fuiste?*<br>revise the preterite tense (regular and some irregular verbs) | 3 | **2A.3 De vacaciones**<br>(Omit activities Gramática & Challenge)<br>**2A.6 Labolengua B**<br>(p.62) **and D** (p.63) | say what you did on holiday and what it was like<br>respond to open-ended questions, e.g. *¿Adónde fuiste?*<br>revise the preterite tense (regular and some irregular verbs) |
| 4 | **2A.4 ¡Lo pasamos bomba!**<br>**2A.6 Labolengua**<br>**C** (p.63) | describe past events<br>summarise and recount what happened<br>use a mix of preterite (some irregular) and imperfect verbs | 4 | **2A.4 ¡Lo pasamos bomba!**<br>(Omit activities 2 & Challenge)<br>**2A.6 Labolengua C**<br>(Omit activity 6)<br>(p.63)<br>**2A.8 Prueba** (p.66)<br>**Vocabulario** (p.67) | describe past events<br>summarise and recount what happened<br>use a mix of preterite (some irregular) and imperfect verbs<br>Prepare and carry out assessment in all four skills<br>Recapping on vocabulary of the unit |

| Three-Year KS3 Route | | | Two-Year KS3 Route | | |
|---|---|---|---|---|---|
| **Week** | **Resources** | **Objectives** | **Week** | **Resources** | **Objectives** |
| **5** | **2A.5 Cuando era joven …** | talk about what you did when you were younger<br>adapt previously learnt language and give opinions<br>use a mix of preterite and imperfect tenses | | | |
| **6** | **2A.7 Extra (Star)** (p.64)<br>**2A.7 Extra (Plus)** (p.65)<br>**2A.8 Prueba** (p.66)<br>**Vocabulario** (p.67)<br>**Leer** (p.151) | Further reinforcement and extension of the language of the unit.<br>Prepare and carry out assessment in all four skills<br>Recapping on vocabulary of the unit<br>Further reading to explore the language of the unit and cultural themes | | | |

## 2A.1 Mi tiempo libre

páginas 52–53

# Planner

### Objectives
- talk about what you like doing in your free time; talk about music you like/don't like
- use *gustar* and similar verbs with nouns and verbs
- justify opinions

### Resources
Student Book, pages 52–53
CD 1, tracks 35–37
Foundation Workbook, page 32
Higher Workbook, page 32
Interactive OxBox, Unit 2A
Copymasters 40–47

### Key language
*la canción; los pasatiempos; me aburre; me apasiona; me encanta; me fastidia; me interesa; aburrido/a; creativo/a; divertido/a; emocionante; estrepitoso/a; fatal; genial; ruidoso/a; descargar; leer revistas; pintar; salir con amigos*

### Renewed Framework references
L&S 1.1, 1.2, 1.4; R&W 2.2, 2.4, 2.5; KAL 4.1, 4.3, 4.5; LLS 5.4

### PLTS
Gramática: Reflective learners
Activity 3: Effective participators
Activity 4: Reflective learners; Creative thinkers
Gramática: Self-managers; Creative thinkers
Think: Reflective learners

### Starters
- In preparation for the work students will do in this spread, ask them to write out the verbs *gustar, preferir, poder* and *querer* from memory. What can they tell you about each of these verbs, i.e. regular, radical-changing, irregular, etc.? Check answers as a class and then ask students to write a sentence for each of the verbs. With less able classes, display some examples.
- Go round the class asking students to say a sentence using either the present continuous or the imperfect tense. They will already be familiar with these tenses, but with less able classes, work through a few examples first.

### Plenaries
- Following Activity 2, students work in pairs to give their opinion of the activities mentioned. First, brainstorm opinion words and display these for support. Remind students that adjectives must agree with the noun they are describing. Compare answers as a class.
- Carry out a class survey. students ask and answer the questions: *¿Qué tipo de música prefieres ahora? ¿Por qué?* and *¿Quién era tu músico preferido cuando tenías diez años?*
- Students work in small groups to write and act out a conversation about what they like and don't like doing. Encourage each member of the group to choose a different activity and for there to be some disagreement over what is interesting/boring/exciting, etc. Remind students that they don't have to tell the truth – it is more importance to use as wide a variety of Spanish as possible.

### Homework/Self-study
Gramática: Students write a sentence for each of the verbs listed in the Grammar box.
Present findings in pie charts.

AT 1.3
L&S 1.1, 1.2

**1 Escucha y anota los pasatiempos.**
Students listen and note down which of the leisure activities illustrated are mentioned each time.

**CD 1, track 35** **página 52, actividades 1 y 2**

**1**
¿Qué hago en mi tiempo libre? Bueno, pues me encanta salir con mis amigos y …ummm … jugar con videojuegos y … ¡también ver la tele! Es muy divertido. Sí, eso es todo.
**2**
Vale, y a mí me apasiona el cine. Es emocionante. También me gusta salir con mis amigos porque son interesantes y divertidos.
**3**
Bueno, a mí me aburre el cine pero sí me interesa mucho leer; puedo pasar horas leyendo – libros, revistas, novelas, comics. Me parece fenomenal.
**4**
Pues yo prefiero el arte. Me encanta pintar y dibujar. Es creativo y emocionante.
**5**
Para mí el arte es aburrido. Lo que me apasiona son los videojuegos. Me encanta competir y los últimos videojuegos son increíbles. Y claro también me mola hablar con mis amigos en Internet – ¡está guay!

*Answers:*
***1** a, c, g; **2** b, a; **3** e; **4** f; **5** c, d*

AT 1.3 | L&S 1.1, 1.2

**2 Escucha otra vez e indica la opinión.**
Students listen again and note down the opinions given each time.

*Answers:*
***1** divertido; **2** emocionante, interesantes, geniales; **3** fenomenal; **4** creativo, emocionante; **5** aburrido, guay*

PLTS

## Gramática

Students will already be familiar with the verb *gustan* but this is a chance to reinforce what they already know. To check understanding of the other verbs listed, go round the class asking students to give you a sentence using any one of these verbs. With less able classes, display an example sentence for support.

AT 2.3 | L&S 1.4 | PLTS

**3 Pregunta y contesta usando expresiones diferentes.**
Students work with a partner and take it in turns to ask and answer questions about what they like doing in their free time.

AT 4.3 | PLTS | R&W 2.4, 2.5

**4 Escribe cinco frases sobre lo que te gusta o no te gusta hacer. Justifica tu opinión.**
Students use the grammar and vocabulary from Activities 1, 2 and 3 to write sentences about what they like and don't like doing. Remind students that by incorporating expressions from the Grammar box and justifying their opinions, they will improve the level of their Spanish.

AT 3.4 | LLS 5.4

**5 Lee el mensaje de Ana Luisa y contesta a las preguntas.**
Students read the message and answer the questions, either with short phrases or in full sentences.

*Answers:*
***1** escuchando música/saliendo con amigos/haciendo sudoku; **2** al cine; **3** el deporte; **4** va a hacer sus deberes y va a ver la tele*

AT 1.4 | AT 3.4 | KAL 4.1

**6 Escucha y lee.**
Students listen and read the speech bubbles. Through listening to and then imitating the pronunciation they will begin to understand the vocabulary better than if they only read a text. It helps them to think more about the language used than if they simply match words visually.

**CD 1, track 36** — **página 53, actividad 6**

Roberto: A mí me apasiona la música. Paso horas escuchando el MP3 y descargando música del Internet. Prefiero la música con un ritmo fuerte porque me encanta tocar los tambores tradicionales de Colombia. También toco la batería en un grupo de rock. Ahora me mola la fusión de música típica española con los ritmos de rock y de salsa. ¿A ti, te gusta la música?

Elena: Claro que me gusta pero prefiero la música suave y lírica. Paso horas tocando la guitarra e inventando mis propias canciones. Cuando era pequeña siempre cantaba cancioncillas infantiles. Me encantan las baladas antiguas; me parecen muy agradables. No me gusta la música estrepitosa como el grunge; está fatal y es muy ruidosa.

AT 3.4 | R&W 2.2

**7 Lee los textos otra vez. ¿Verdad, mentira o no se menciona?**
Students read the text again and note down whether each of the statements is true (v), false (m), or not mentioned (nm).

*Answers:*
***1** v; **2** m; **3** nm; **4** m; **5** nm; **6** v*

AT 1.3 | L&S 1.2

**8 Escucha y anota el tipo de música y la opinión.**
Students listen and note down the type of music mentioned and the opinion given each time.

**CD 1, track 37** — **página 53, actividad 8**

¿Qué tipo de música prefieres?

1. Prefiero la música rock porque tiene ritmo y es divertida. En cambio, el heavy metal es ruidoso y no tiene sentido en mi opinión.
2. A mí me apasiona la música clásica porque es emocionante.
3. Pues a mí me encantan las canciones de los años sesenta porque son suaves. Odio la música grunge porque es ruidosa y estrepitosa.
4. Sí, tienes razón, me parece nulo y fatal. A mi lo que realmente me flipa es la salsa, es una música genial.
5. Para mí la música ska es sensacional y creativa. Me mola mucho.

*Answers:*
***1** la música rock – rítmica, divertida; el metal – ruidoso, nulo; **2** la música clásica – emocionante; **3** las canciones de los años sesenta – suaves; la música grunge – ruidosa, estrepitosa; **4** la música grunge – nulo, fatal; la salsa – genial; **5** la música ska – sensacional, creativa*

PLTS | KAL 4.5

### Gramática

Work through the Grammar box as a class. Encourage students to be as creative as possible when writing their three sentences. They don't have to tell the truth, but should try to use a wide variety of vocabulary and structures in order to show off their Spanish!

PLTS | LLS 5.4

### Think

Students should remember meeting terms such as *los años setenta/noventa in* unit 1B when talking about clothes and styles! This is another example of the same language being recycled and used in different contexts.

PLTS | AT 4.4–5 | R&W 2.4, 2.5 | KAL 4.3, 4.5

### Challenge

**Write a reply to Ana Luisa's message (Activity 5). Make sure you answer all the questions and include as much detail as possible about your hobbies, what you do in your free time and what kind of music you like. Make sure you give your opinion as well.**

Encourage students to be as creative as they can and to draw upon what they have learnt in the spread. Draw their attention to the Think box. Explain that using more than one tense makes their writing more interesting and will also gain them higher marks.

## 2A.2 De compras

páginas 54–55

### *Planner*

#### Objectives

- talk about going shopping
- use direct object pronouns (for things/objects)
- adapt previously learnt language in a new context

#### Resources

Student Book, pages 54–55
CD 1, tracks 38–40
Foundation Workbook, page 33
Higher Workbook, page 33
Interactive OxBox, Unit 2A
Copymasters 40–47

#### Key language

*la carnicería; la charcutería; la frutería; la pescadería; la tienda de comestibles; el aceite de oliva; las aceitunas; los caramelos; un helado; el jamón; la leche; una lechuga; los limones; las manzanas; las patatas fritas; el pescado; el pollo; las sardinas; las truchas; ¿Qué falta?; un regalo; la planta baja; el sótano*

#### Renewed Framework references

L&S 1.1, 1.2, 1.4; KAL 4.3, 4.4; LLS 5.4, 5.5

#### PLTS

Activity 1: Reflective learners
Activity 2: Independent enquirers
Activity 3: Reflective learners
Activity 4: Team workers
Activity 5: Creative thinkers
Activity 6: Reflective learners; Independent enquirers

#### Starters

- Quickly revise the shopping vocabulary that students already know. They have already covered shopping for souvenirs in *Zoom español 1* and shopping for clothes in Unit 1B of *Zoom español 2*. Display all of the words and expressions that they can remember. Explain that much of this language will be recycled in this unit.
- This spread also revises *este,ese* and *aquel* from Unit 1B of *Zoom español 2*. Challenge students to write a sentence using *este, ese* and *aquel*. Compare answers as a class.

#### Plenaries

- Split the class into small groups and play a class game. Give the groups a time limit to write a shopping list, including as many items as they can. They should include articles where possible. When the time is up, compare answers as a class. Groups score one point for each correct item and two points if they have included any items that no other group has listed.
- Following on from the *Gramática* Activity, display a list of food items from this spread and others if you wish and ask students to write which pronoun they would use to replace each item. Depending on the level of the class, ask students to use the pronouns in simple sentences, e.g. ***los** tomates, aquí **los** tienes.*

#### Homework/Self-study

Activity 7, page 55
Challenge: Students write out their conversation.

PLTS
AT 3.1

**1 Empareja las compras con la palabra adecuada.de la casilla**
Students will have met most of this vocabulary Unit 1A so should start with matching the items they already know.

*Answers:*
***a** manzanas; **b** pescado; **c** aceite de oliva; **d** patatas fritas*
***e** pollo; **f** aceitunas; **g** chorizo; **h** limones*

AT 1.3
PLTS
L&S1.2
LLS 5.4

**2 Escucha la conversación e indica en qué tienda están.**
Students listen and note down at which shop you can buy each item from Activity 1. Before students listen, draw their attention to the names of shop 1, *la frutería,* shop 2, *la carnicería* and shop 4, *la pescadería*. What words that they already know are in the names of these shops? Explain that using existing knowledge to work out the meaning of new words in this way is a useful skill.

**CD 1, track 38** **página 54, actividades 2 y 3**

**1**
- Buenos días. ¿Qué quiere usted?
- Quiero un kilo de manzanas, por favor.
- Vale, pero ¿cuáles prefiere? Tengo éstas rojas o ésas verdes.
- ¿Aquéllas amarillas a cuánto son?
- Son a 2 euros el kilo. ¿Algo más?
- No, gracias, eso es todo.

**2**
- ¡Hola! ¿Qué desea usted?
- A ver, quiero pescado. ¿Qué me recomienda usted?
- Pues, creo que estas sardinas son mejores que las truchas – ¡están más frescas!
- Vale, entonces póngame medio kilo, por favor.
- ¿Eso es todo?
- Sí, de momento eso es todo, gracias.

**3**
- ¡Hola! Buenos días. ¿Me puedes dar una botella de aceite de oliva? Aquélla que es de primera clase.
- Vale. ¿Algo más?
- Pues sí. Quiero 250 gramos de aceitunas. Estas verdes de aquí, no aquéllas negras. Ah sí y necesito chorizo, a ver, a ver… este chorizo de aquí parece delicioso.
- Así es. Está muy sabroso.
- Ya está. Eso es todo, gracias

**4**
- Mamá, quiero pollo esta noche para la cena.
- Vale, hijo. Voy a comprar un pollo entero y vamos a ponerlo al horno.
- Rico, mami, me parece rico.

*Answers:*
***1** en la frutería; **2** en la pescadería; **3** en la charcutería* or *la tienda de comestibles; **4** en la carnicería*

AT 1.3
L&S 1.2
PLTS

**3 Escucha otra vez y anota lo que compra cada persona.**
Students listen again and this time note down what each person buys. This activity revises work done in Unit 1A of the *Zoom español* 2 Student Book.

*Answers:*
***1** un kilo de manzanas amarillas; **2** pescado/sardinas – medio kilo; **3** una botella de aceite de oliva; 250 gramos de aceitunas verdes y chorizo; **4** pollo*

## Think

Have a revision session on quantities and high numbers from page 26 (Unit 1A) and how to say *this, these, that* and *those* from page 44 (Unit 1B). Starter Activity 2 revises *this, these* and *those.*

PLTS
KAL 4.3, 4.4

## Gramática

Read through the Grammar box as a class and look at the examples. At this stage, keep things simple; students are only expected to understand how to substitute the noun. Where to place pronouns will be introduced at a later stage. To check that students have understood which pronoun to use when, give them a few minutes to note down which pronoun they would use to replace the following words: *un pimiento; unas aceitunas; el azúcar; una pizza; unos chocolates*

*Answers: lo; las; lo; la; los*

AT 2.3–4
PLTS

**4 Practica los diálogos. Usa los dibujos para ayudarte.**
Students use the artwork prompts to practise the dialogues.

AT 2.4
PLTS
L&S 1.4
LLS 5.5

**5 Inventa otros diálogos usando los dibujos de la actividad 1.**
Students invent their own dialogues, similar to those in Activity 4, using the food items from Activity 1. They could also look back at page 90 of *Zoom español 1* Student Book or to the Vocabulary section on page 67 to find more food vocabulary. Encourage them also to look up words for their favourite food in a dictionary.

AT 4.4

**6 Escribe tus diáloges de la actividad 5.**
Students write out their conversations from Activity 5.

PLTS
LLS 5.4

**7 Lee la lista de la compra.**
Students read the shopping list and think about how many of these words they already know. They should think back to pages 128–129 of the *Zoom español 1* Student Book which covered shopping for souvenirs and to page 26 of the *Zoom español 2* Student Book which looked at quantities.

AT 1.4
L&S 1.2

**8 Escucha y escribe lo que falta de la lista.**
Students listen to the speaker checking the shopping and note down what is missing.

**CD 1, track 39** **página 55, actividad 8**

Bueno, vamos a ver las compras. Tenemos un paquete de galletas… bien. Dos latas de maíz – un momento, quiero tres latas de maíz. Seis botellas de limonada – perfecto. Ahora dos paquetes de café – y es colombiano – bien… Cien gramos de jamón – qué bien, me gusta el jamón. Y finalmente una botella de leche. A ver, ¿qué falta? Claro, falta el azúcar y ¿qué otra cosa? ¡Caramba! Faltan las patatas fritas. Quiero una bolsa grande.

*Answer: una lata de maíz, el azúcar y las patatas fritas*

AT 1.4
L&S 1.1, 1.2

**9 Escucha la discusión y contesta a las preguntas.**
Students listen to the discussion and then answer the questions.

**CD 1, track 40** **página 55, actividad 9**

- Bueno, Juan, ¿estás listo o no? ¡Tienes que acompañarme!
- ¿Por qué? ¿Adónde vamos?
- Tenemos que comprar un regalo para Roberto.
- ¿Por qué?
- Porque pronto cumple años y quiero darle una sorpresa.
- ¿Por qué? ¿Cuántos años va a cumplir?
- Va a cumplir diecisiete y creo que debemos comprarle un buen regalo, así que tenemos que ir al Corte Inglés porque es mejor.
- No lo creo; es más fácil ir a la tienda de deportes del centro – hay menos gente.
- Sí, pero es más práctico ir a una sola tienda donde hay más selección.
- Depende de lo que pienses comprar.
- Vale; voy a comprarle una camiseta verde. ¿Y tú?
- ¿Yo? No sé. No tengo dinero y no pensaba…
- Juan, vas a venir conmigo al Corte Inglés y vas a comprar un regalo para tu primo.¿Me oyes?
- Vale, pero sólo si vamos a comer unos helados después…

*Answers:*
***1** They need to buy Roberto a 17th Birthday present and are arguing over the best place to go and buy it. **2** to the big department store,* el Corte Inglés*; **3** It is more practical to go to just one shop where there is a good selection of products; **4** a green T-shirt; **5** eat ice-cream*

AT 2.3
L&S 1.4

### Challenge

**With a partner play a shopping game. You are in a large department store. Write out a shopping list of ten items either from memory or with the help of a dictionary. Then ask your partner where each item is to be found in the store.**
Before students begin, look at the Think box and how the ordinal numbers (first, second, third, etc.) correspond to the numbers they have learnt. Elicit from them that *Planta baja* is the ground floor and *Sótano* is the basement.

## 2A.3 De vacaciones

páginas 56–57

## *Planner*

### Objectives

- say what you did on holiday and what it was like
- revise the preterite tense (regular and some irregular verbs)
- respond to open-ended questions, e.g. *¿Adónde fuiste?*

### Resources

Student Book, pages 56–57
CD 1, tracks 41–42
Foundation Workbook, page 34
Higher Workbook, page 34
Foundation Workbook audio, CD 3, track 40 (Workbook 20)
Higher Workbook audio, CD 4, tracks 20–21
Interactive OxBox, Unit 2A
Copymasters 40–47

## Key language

*¿Adónde fuiste? ¿Qué tal lo pasaste? acostarse; alojarse en; comer; ir de camping; ir (fui); salir; empezó a llover; lo pasé/pasamos bomba; anoche; anteayer; ayer; el sábado pasado; el avión; desastroso/a; increíble; una feria; el parque de atracciones; un viaje*

## Renewed Framework references

L&S 1.4; R&W 2.2, 2.4, 2.5; KAL 4.1, 4.5; LLS: 5.4

## PLTS

Gramática: Reflective learners
Activity 3: Reflective learners
Activity 4: Team workers
Challenge: Reflective learners; Creative thinkers; Self-managers

## Starters

- Before asking students to carry out Activity 1, display sentences 1–6 and ask them to point to/circle/underline words or phrases which help to indicate the past tense. Can they work out what *anteayer* and *anoche* mean? Elicit from students that these words contain the words *ayer* and *noche*. They should then find it easier to work out that *anteayer* means 'the day before yesterday' and *anoche* means last night.
- Revise the vocabulary from pages 122–127 of Unit 4A, *Zoom español 1* Student Book which covered similar holiday vocabulary. Display the headings: 'When', 'Weather' and 'Activities'. Depending on the level of the class, either provide students with vocabulary to categorise under these headings, or challenge them to write as many words and phrases as possible themselves. They should come up with vocabulary such as: *el verano pasasdo; el invierno pasado; el año pasado; hace dos años; el pasado junio; la Navidades pasadas; hizo sol; hizo calor; hizo frío; hizo viento; hizo buen tiempo; hizo mal tiempo; estuvo nublado; hubo tormenta; hubo niebla; llovió; hice vela; tomé el sol; me bañé en el mar; comimos comida típica; nos relajamos; saqué muchas fotos; salí de compras; compré recuerdos; escribí unas postales*
- Display the headings: *–ar*, *–er* and *–ir* and give students a time limit of your choosing to write down the regular preterite endings for each of these verb types. When time is up, check answers as a class.

## Plenaries

- Following Activities 2 and 3, students work in pairs and use the photos to ask and answer questions about holiday activities, e.g.
  **A** *Foto a: ¿Adónde fuiste el verano pasado?*
  **B** *Fui a hacer camping con mi colegio.*
- Students read out what they have written for the Challenge Activity to a partner. Their partner listens carefully to see if he/she can spot any mistakes. He/She then asks them questions about their holiday using the questions they have practised in Activity 6. Students could use their story as a prompt to begin with, before seeing how many answers they can give from memory.

## Homework/Self-study

Students write out the verbs *comer, viajar, salir* and *hacer* in the preterite tense. They then use each of these verbs in a sentence in the preterite tense (they can choose which person to use each time). More able students could write a sentence for more than one person.

AT 3.3
LLS 5.4

**1 Empareja las frases con las fotos.**
Students match the sentences to the photos. Encourage them to look for words that they already know. If there are any they are unsure of they should leave them until last.

*Answers:* ***1*** *c;* ***2*** *e;* ***3*** *b;* ***4*** *a;* ***5*** *f;* ***6*** *d*

AT 1.3

**2 Escucha y anota el orden de las frases de la actividad 1.**
Students listen and put the sentences into the correct order. **Note:** the recorded sentences are worded slightly differently from what is written in Activity 1. This will encourage students to think carefully about the sentences.

**CD 1, track 41** **página 56, actividad 2**

- Ayer fui de compras.
- Anoche fueron a la disco.
- Fuimos en coche a la playa la semana pasada.
- ¿Fuisteis al parque de atracciones anteayer?
- Fui de camping con el insitituto el verano pasado.
- El sábado pasado Juan fue a la feria.

*Answers:*
*1; 5; 3; 6; 4; 2*

PLTS
KAL 4.5

## Gramática

Students have already met the preterite tense or simple past tense on page 122 of the *Zoom español 1* Student Book. They will also have looked at the endings. This activity serves as revision. Students match each part of the verb *ir* to the English and then translate the sentences in Activity 1.

*Answers:*

**1** *Yesterday you went shopping at the new shopping centre, didn't you?*
**2** *Juan went to the fair last Saturday.*
**3** *Last week we went to the beach by car/drove to the beach.*
**4** *Last Summer I went camping with my school.*
**5** *Last night we all went to the disco.*
**6** *Did you go to the theme park the day before yesterday?*

AT 1.4–5
PLTS

**3 Empareja las preguntas con las respuestas. Luego escucha y verifica. Añade la persona.**
Students match the questions and answers. These are all verbs students should be familiar with by now. Check that they can relate the preterite form to the infinitive form, e.g. *comiste* from verb *comer* so that they understand how to look up verbs in a dictionary. Encourage them to refer back to the *Labolengua* section of unit 1A.

**CD 1, track 42** — **página 56, actividad 3 y página 57, actividad 5**

– María, ¿adónde fuiste de vacaciones?
– Fui a Mallorca y lo pasé bomba. Fui con mis amigos y comimos helados de pistacho. Fue muy divertido.
– Y tú, Tomás, ¿fuiste también?
– No, con María, no. Fui a Los Picos de Europa con mi familia y lo pasé fatal. Fuimos de camping y todo fue un desastre.
– Enrique, supongo que tú también lo pasaste mal.
– No, señor, yo no. Fui en avión a Londres y aunque salí a las seis de la mañana lo pasé bien y todo fue muy interesante. Me puse muy contento.
– ¡Me alegro! Y tú, Lola, ¿qué hiciste?
– Pues, fui con mi padre a Madrid. Fui a muchos museos, pero todas eran muy aburridos. Lo mejor es que fuimos en taxi a todas partes, así que no estaba nunca cansada al final del día.
– Fernando, tú fuiste a Segovia, ¿verdad? ¿Viste algo de interés?
– Sí, mucho, y lo que más me gustó fue el famoso acueducto – es increíble – pero lo pasé mal porque perdí mi cámara con todas mis fotos.
– Lo siento mucho. Y tú, Catalina, ¿te quedaste en casa?
– Desafortunadamente. Llegué tarde al aeropuerto y perdí el avión. ¡Qué desastre! Fue un fracaso total.

*Answers:*
**1** *a Enrique;* **2** *e Fernando* **3** *c María;* **4** *d Tomás;* **5** *b Lola;*

AT 2.4–5
L&S 1.4
PLTS

**4 Practica el diálogo. Luego inventa otros diálogos (ver la actividad 3).**
Look at the Grammar explanation with students before they start this activity. Ensure that they understand how to conjugate the verb *hacer* in the preterite tense. Encourage students to think about the different questions. For example, when they are asked *¿Adónde fuiste?* they need to answer with a place, to answer the question *¿Qué tal lo pasaste?* they should give an opinion and to respond to the question *¿Qué hiciste?* it is up to them to provide all the information. Previous activities should provide ideas of how to respond.

AT 1.4–5
L&S 1.2

**5 Escucha otra vez y completa una tabla así.**
Students listen again to the recording from Activity 3 on page 56 and complete the table.

*Answers:*
*María, Mallorca, ☺; Tomás, Los Picos de Europa, ☹; Enrique, Londres, ☺; Lola, Madrid, ☹ y ☺; Fernando, Segovia, ☺ y ☹; Catalina, en casa, ☹*

AT 3.5
R&W 2.2

**6 Lee la tarjeta postal y empareja las traducciones 1–6 con las palabras en negrita.**
Students read the postcard, paying particular attention to the expressions in bold text. Once they are familiar with the text, they find the Spanish equivalent for the English expressions 1–6.

*Answers:*
**1** *empezó a llover;* **2** *donde nos alojamos;* **3** *temprano;* **4** *un día mejor;* **5** *un viaje desastroso;* **6** *todo resultó ser*

KAL 4.1

## Think

This encourages students to think about how sounds in Spanish work.

AT 3.5

**7 Contesta a las preguntas en inglés.**
Following on from Activity 6, students answer more detailed questions about the text in English.

*Answers:*
**1** *The plane left late and the journey was horrible.* **2** *It was too small;* **3** *It turned out to be very boring and then it started to rain.* **4** *They went to a restaurant.* **5** *nothing*

AT 4-4.5

**8 Ahora escribe un breve párrafo en español sobre el viaje de Ana María**

AT 4.5 R&W 2.4, 2.5 PLTS

**Challenge**

**Write no more than 100 words on what you did during your last holidays. It can be a true account or an imaginary one. Use the verbs from the lists on these pages to help you. Make sure you include some opinions.**

Encourage students to draw upon the vocabulary and grammar they have met in this spread and to be as creative as possible. The length of this work should vary from student to student depending on their ability.

## 2A.4 ¡Lo pasamos bomba!

páginas 58–59

# *Planner*

### Objectives

- describe past events
- use a mix of preterite (some irregular) and imperfect verbs
- summarise and recount what happened

### Resources

Student Book, pages 58–59
CD 1, tracks 43–44
Foundation Workbook, page 35
Higher Workbook, page 35
Interactive OxBox, Unit 2A
Copymasters 40–47

### Video

Video clip, Unit 2A

### Key language

*¿Cuánto tiempo? ¿Qué tiempo hizo? estar (estuve); ganar; ser (fui); tener (tuve); fatal; madrileño/a; la corrida (de toros); los fuegos artificiales; un regalo; un traje típico*

### Renewed Framework references

L&S 1.2, 1.4; R&W 2.2, 2.5; IU 3.2; KAL 4.5, 4.6

### PLTS

Gramática: Reflective learners
Activity 2: Team workers
Activity 9: Creative thinkers; Reflective learners
Challenge: Independent enquirers; Creative thinkers

### Starters

- Quickly revise regular verbs in the preterite again. Go round the class and ask each student to give you a sentence on the topic of this unit in the preterite tense. With less able classes, display a model sentence for support.
- Students work with a partner to ask and answer questions about a past holiday. It doesn't have to be a real holiday; they can make it up if they want to. Encourage students to be as creative as possible, i.e. they could describe a disastrous holiday where everything went wrong, or a dream holiday, etc. Volunteers could act out their conversation in front of the class.

### Plenaries

- Students share what they have found out about the festival of Isidro. Compile an ultimate class factfile in Spanish.
- Following on from the *Gramática* Activity on page 59, students write at least one sentence using the imperfect and preterite tenses. More able students should write more sentences in each tense, using as many forms as possible. Compare sentences as a class.
- Students imagine they took part in photo B from Activity 3 and write an account of what happened. Display model sentences for less able students. You may also want to display more idiomatic phrases for students of a higher ability, e.g. *Hace una semana....*

### Homework/Self-study

Activity 1: After completing this activity, students find out more about the festival of Isidro. Depending on the level of the class, they record any information in either Spanish or in English.
Gramática, page 58
Following on from Activity 2, students write sentences to say what Roberto did. This begins the process of recounting an event in the past. Remind students in class that they will need to write in the third person and if necessary go through an example to start them off.

AT 3.5 R&W 2.2

**1 Empareja las preguntas con las respuestas.**
Students match the questions and the answers. Before they do this, ask the class if anyone has heard of the festival of San Isidro in Madrid. If not, explain to students that San Isidro was born on 15th May and was a humble 12th century farmworker who became Madrid's patron saint. The capital celebrates with a bullfight every day from the 8th–15th May, concerts, fireworks and many other events.

*Answers:* ***1** d; **2** f; **3** b; **4** h; **5** a; **6** g; **7** e; **8** c*

PLTS

## Gramática

Look at the examples of irregular verbs in the preterite tense as a class. For homework, ask students to write out and learn these three verbs. Depending on the level of the class, students could also write a sentence containing each of the verbs in a person of their choice, or more than one person per verb if they wish.

AT 2.5 L&S 1.4 PLTS

**2 Con tu compañero, practica las preguntas y respuestas (actividad 1).**
It is important for students to practise these questions and answers to familiarise themselves with the text and then to be able to transfer the sentences from the first person to third for the suggested homework task (see above). It is also important for students to recognise the verb and its infinitive so they can check out meanings in a dictionary.

AT 1.5 L&S 1.2 IU 3.2

**3 Escucha. ¿Qué imagen se describe?**
Students listen and decide which of the images is being described.

**CD 1, track 43** **página 58, actividades 3 y 4**

El año pasado fuimos a la fiesta mayor de Sitges, un pueblo al sur de Barcelona. Estuvimos allí cinco días del 22 al 26 de agosto. Hizo mucho calor y había muchos turistas. Comimos pescado frito en la playa y bebimos bastante sangría. Nos alojamos en un pequeño hotel cerca de la iglesia. Por la tarde vimos las procesiones de los gigantes y cabezudos. La última noche hicimos una fiesta y vimos unos fuegos artificiales maravillosos. ¡Lo pasamos fenomenal!

*Answer: photo c*

AT 1.5 L&S 1.2 IU 3.2

**4 Escucha otra vez y pon las frases en el orden correcto.**
Students listen again and put the sentences into the correct order.

*Answers: 4; 7; 2; 5; 3; 1; 8, 6*

AT 3.5 KAL 4.6

**5 Empareja las preguntas con las respuestas (actividad 4).**
Students match the questions to the statements in Activity 4. This provides good practice of different question forms and also encourages students to recognise the same verb in the second person singular and first person plural.

*Answers:* ***a** 7; **b** 3; **c** 5; **d** 8; **e** 1, 6; **f** 4; **g** 2*

KAL 4.5

## Gramática

Look at the example as a class. Elicit from students that *lo que hacía* is an example of the imperfect tense and *cómo le fue*, an example of the preterite tense. Look at the English translation to help them understand why each tense has been used. To ensure that they understand this, ask them to complete the sentence.

*Answers: imperfect tense; preterite*

AT 1.5 IU 3.2

**6 Mira el video y contesta a las preguntas.**
Students watch the video clip for Unit 2A and answer the questions.

**Video clip (CD 1, track 44)**

**Part 1**

*Elena, Roberto and Juan walking down a path in the woods on their way to the Pino a Pino*

Roberto: ¿Juan, qué hacemos aquí?
Juan: Es una sorpresa.
Elena: ¡Es algo sensacional!
Juan: Lo vas a pasar fenomenal.
Elena: Yo el año pasado vine y me lo pasé bomba.
Roberto: ¿Pero chicos, qué es?
Juan: ¿Te gustan las películas de Tarzan?
Roberto: ¡Claro que sí!
Juan: Pues sí, vamos a hacer como Tarzan en el Pino a Pino.
Roberto: ¿Y vamos a ver quién gana?
Juan: Sí, pero esta vez es más complicado.
Elena: ¿Cómo?
Juan: Esta vez, el último tiene que contar lo que hacía durante el recorrido y cómo le fue.
Roberto: ¿Tienes buena memoria Juan? ¡Porque voy a ganar yo!

**Part 2**

*Training session*

Juan: Primero hay que hacer la formación.

Instructor: Agarra aquí por favor. Agarra aquí por favor. Gírate un poquito. Agarra aquí. Son los más importantes porque nos permiten estar siempre enganchados a los objetos que sean de color rojo. Lo primero que tengo que hacer es engancharme con ambos mosquetones. Nos vamos a encontrar con este formato un juego que se llama Salto de Tarzan. Es un juego relativamente físico porque tenemos que aguantar nuestro peso con la fuerza de los brazos.

*At the sign post with the different courses.*

Roberto: ¿Vamos a hacer el "desafío"?

Ernesto: Mejor hacemos aventurero ya que Juan tiene sólo 15 años.

Roberto: Va ser aún más fácil ganar para mí.

*They climb up on to the first section of ropes.*

Juan: Primero vamos a subir por este árbol y después a pasar por el túnel.

Roberto: Yo primero.

Elena: ¡Me encanta! Me siento como un mono en los árboles. ¡Venga chicos! ¿Y ahora, cómo llego allí?

Roberto: Muy aburrido. Es demasiado fácil.

Juan: Ahora vamos a saltar por la tirolina. ¿Cómo paro?

Roberto: No lo soporto es peligroso.

Roberto: ¡Lo odio!

Juan: ¡He ganado!

Elena: ¡Venga Roberto!

Juan: Este último es fantástico.

Elena: Es súper rápido.

Roberto: Lo odio.

Juan: ¿Quién ganó, Roberto?

Roberto: Tú, Juan.

Elena: Y ¿Quién quedó segundo?

Roberto: Tú, Elena.

Juan: Y ¿Quién terminó el último?

Roberto: Yo. Yo terminé el último.

Elena: Ahora nos tienes que contar todo lo que pasó.

Roberto: De acuerdo. Primero hicimos la formación, fue muy interesante, pero cuando subimos a los arboles me fue fatal. Nada más subir a los arboles tuve un ataque de vértigo, Elena y Juan lo hacían sin miedo. Saltaban de un árbol a otro como monos, pero a mí me temblaban las piernas. Caminé de un árbol a otro atado con una cuerda. Salté con un arnés de una plataforma a otra y lo hice mal. ¡Me quedé allí suspendido en el aire! ¡Lo pasé mal pero supermal! Terminé el último. ¡Qué vergüenza!

Elena: No pasa nada.

*Answers:*

***a** opinion words: sensacional; fenomenal; me lo pasé bomba; es aburrido; es demasiado fácil; es divertido; es fantástico; fatal; **b** the loser must recount what he/she did on the course and how it went*

AT 1.4–5

**7 Watch the second part of the video (as many times as you need to) and note down when a preterite tense is used and when an imperfect tense is used.**

*Answers:*

***preterite:** ganó; quedó; terminó; terminé; pasó; hicimos; fue; subimos; fue; tuve; caminé; salté; hice; quedé; pasé; terminé*

***imperfect:** hacían; saltaban; temblaban*

AT 1.4–5

**8 Lee y completa el texto con un verbo adecuado de la casilla.**

Students complete the text.

*Answers:*

***1** hicimos; **2** Fue; **3** subimos; **4** fue; **5** tuve; **6** hacían; **7** saltaban; **8** temblaban; **9** Caminé; **10** Salté; **11** hice; **12** quedé; **13** Terminé*

AT 4.5 | PLTS | R&W 2.5

**9 Escribe sobre una aventura (como el "pino a pino"). Usa el texto de Roberto para ayudarte.**

Students draw upon Roberto's account in Activity 6 to write about their own made up adventure.

AT 4.5–6 | PLTS | R&W 2.5 | KAL 4.5

## Challenge

**Write no more than 100 words about an event you went to last year. Try to use both the preterite and the imperfect tenses. For help on the imperfect tense, look back at page 46. To achieve level 6 you would need to say what you are going to do next year as well.**

Depending on the level of independence/ability of students, you may want to provide support by displaying a list of verbs or even a writing template to for them to complete.

## 2A.5 Cuando era joven ...

páginas 60–61

# *Planner*

### Objectives

- talk about what you did when you were younger
- use a mix of preterite and imperfect tenses
- adapt previously learnt language and give opinions

### Resources

Student Book, pages 60–61
CD 1, tracks 45–46
Foundation Workbook, page 36
Higher Workbook, page 36
Interactive OxBox, Unit 2A
Copymasters 40–47

### Renewed Framework references

L&S 1.2, 1.4; R&W 2.2, 2.4, 2.5; KAL 4.3, 4.4, 4.5

### PLTS

Activity 3: Reflective learners; Self-managers
Activity 6: Independent enquirers; Creative thinkers
Activity 7: Reflective learners; Self-managers
Activity 8: Team workers; Creative thinkers
Challenge: Creative thinkers; Self-managers; Reflective learners

### Starters

- Students write the rule for when to use the imperfect tense and when to use the preterite. Compare these as a class and ensure that all students understand when to use each of these tenses by asking each student to give you a sentence in either the imperfect or preterite tense on the theme of the spread.
- Play a memory game to practise using the imperfect tense. Start by saying, e.g. *Cuando tenía diez años iba con mi madre a hacer las compras*. The student nearest to you continues, *Cuando tenía diez años iba con mi madre a hacer las compras y…* and so on around the class.

### Plenaries

- Discuss answers to Activity 6 as a class. Do most students have a positive or negative impression of Juan's visit? Why?
- Following Activity 8, students write similar interview questions for their favourite celebrity. They then work with a partner who answers as the celebrity in question. Volunteers could act out their interview in front of the class.

### Homework/Self-study

Activity 3, page 60
Challenge Activity, page 61

AT 3.5 | R&W 2.2

**1 Empareja las frases con los dibujos.**
Before students start to match up the sentences and pictures, elicit from them that these sentences are in the imperfect tense because they are describing what used to happen. There will be some unfamiliar words so encourage them to use the vocabulary they do know and cognates to match up the sentences and pictures.

*Answers:* ***1** c; **2** a; **3** f; **4** b; **5** e; **6** d*

AT 1.5 | L&S 1.2

**2 Escucha y anota quién ...**
Following on from Activity 1, students listen and note down which student does which activity. This provides the opportunity to hear how the words they have read in Activity 1 are pronounced in Spanish.

**CD 1, track 45** **página 60, actividad 2**

Teacher: A ver, ¿quién recuerda lo que hacía cuando era pequeño? Isabel, ¿tú qué hacías?
Isabel: Pues me encantaba hacer castillos de arena en la playa cuando iba de vacaciones a la Costa Brava con mis padres.
Teacher: ¿Y tú, Pablo?
Pablo: A mí me encantaba pintar. Pintaba con los dedos y me fascinaban todos los colores, sobre todo los colores vivos.
Teacher: A ver, Sofía. ¿Qué te gustaba hacer?
Sofía: Bueno, entre otras cosas me gustaba nadar. Aprendí a nadar cuando tenía cuatro años.
Teacher: ¡Qué bien! ¿Y tú, Javier?
Javier: Lo que más me gustaba era jugar con mi muñeco de acción. Lo adoraba. ¡Ay, qué bonito!
Teacher: Y Ricardo, ¿tú jugabas también?
Ricardo: Claro que jugaba pero lo que más me gustaba era ir al parque a jugar en los columpios y los toboganes.
Teacher: Magnífico. ¿Y tú, Ana María?
Ana María: Yo profe, yo no hacía mucho porque me encantaba ver *Barrio Sésamo*. Veía programas infantiles.

*Answers:*
***1** Pablo; **2** Sofía; **3** Ana María; **4** Isabel; **5** Javier; **6** Ricardo*

PLTS | KAL 4.5 | AT 4.5

**3 Escribe lo que hacía cada persona.**
Students use their answers from Activity 2 to write sentences saying what each person used to do. This provides further practice of using the imperfect tense and is an ideal homework activity.

AT 3.5 | KAL 4.4, 4.5

**4 Copia y completa el texto con las palabras de la casilla.**
Practice of using the preterite and imperfect tense in sentences.

*Answers:*
***1** tenía; **2** me encantaban; **3** iba; **4** íbamos; **5** había; **6** compró; **7** puso; **8** tuve; **9** decidí; **10** comí; **11** llegamos; **12** quedaba*

AT 1.5 | R&W 2.2

**5 Escucha y verifica.**
Students listen to check their answers to Activity 4.

**CD 1, track 46** **página 60, actividad 5**

Cuando tenía diez años me encantaban los sábados porque siempre iba con mi madre a hacer las compras. Primero íbamos al mercado donde había cantidad de fruta y verdura. Un día mi madre compró unas uvas deliciosas y las puso en la bolsa. Una hora más tarde tuve hambre y decidí comer unas uvas. Poco a poco las comí todas y cuando llegamos a casa ya no quedaba ni una. ¡Por supuesto, mi madre se enfadó conmigo!

AT 3.5 | PLTS

**6 Lee el blog de Juan. ¿Tiene una opinión positiva o negativa de su visita?**
Students read Juan's blog and then note down whether he gives a positive or negative opinion of his visit.

AT 3.5 | KAL 4.5 | PLTS

**7 Haz una lista de todos los verbos en el blog. Decide si están en el tiempo pretérito o en imperfecto. Traduce las frases al inglés.**
This is an ideal homework activity. Depending on the level of the class, you may want to go through a few examples first.

*Answers:*
*Cuando **tenía** diez años (imp)* – when I was ten years old; *me **encantaban** los sábados (imp)* – I used to like Saturdays; *iba con mi madre (imp)* – I would go with my mother; ***íbamos** al mercado (imp)* – we would go to the market; *donde **había** cantidades de frutas y verduras (imp)* – there they had a lot of fruit and vegetables; *mi madre **compró** unas uvas deliciosas (pret)* – my mother bought some delicious grapes; *las **puso** en la bolsa (pret)* – she put them in the bag; ***tenía** hambre (imp)* – I was feeling hungry; ***decidí** comer unas uvas (pret)* – I decided to eat a few grapes; *las **comí** todas (prêt)* – I ate all of them; *cuando **llegamos** a casa (pret)* – when we got back home; *ya no **quedaba** ni una (imp)* – there were none left; *mi madre **estaba** bastante enfadada conmigo (imp)* – my mother was quite annoyed with me

AT 2.5 | PLTS | L&S 1.4

**8 Imagina que vas a entrevistarle a Juan. Prepara una lista de preguntas. Pregunta y contesta con tu compañero.**
This will require students using the second person singular. Students should refer back to Activities 4 and 5 for support.

AT 4.5–6 | R&W 2.4, 2.5 | KAL 4.3, 4.5 | PLTS

## Challenge

**Write a blog of no more than 100 words about an imaginary or real visit you made to somewhere special when you were younger. Set the scene and describe when it was, where you went, what you did and what it was like.**
Remind students that to write at a higher level, they should try to include the past, present and future tense. They should also include useful expressions from the spread and give opinions. Encourage students to be as creative as possible.

# 2A.6 Labolengua

páginas 62–63

## Planner

### Objectives
- review language and grammar from the unit

### Resources
Student Book, pages 62–63
CD 1, track 47
Foundation Workbook, pages 37–38
Higher Workbook, pages 37–38
Interactive OxBox, Unit 2A
Copymasters 48–49

### Grammar
- Direct object pronouns, preterite tense

### Renewed Framework references
L&S 1.4; KAL 4.3, 4.4, 4.5, 4.6; LLS 5.1

### PLTS
All activities: Reflective learners/Self-managers
Activities 5 and 6: Creative thinkers

### Homework/Self-study
Activity 2: Students make up dialogues of their own using as many different direct object pronouns as they can. Students could then work in pairs to act out their dialogues.
Activity 3, page 62
Activity 6, page 63
Following on from Activity 7, students write five sentences, some questions and some statements, ready to read out to a partner in class decides if each sentenceis a question or a statement.

## Comprender – direct object pronouns, preterite tense

### A Direct object pronouns

KAL 4.3, 4.4 | PLTS

**1 Answer these questions. Use direct object pronouns.**
Practice of using direct object pronouns correctly.

*Answers:*
*1 Sí, las compré. 2 Sí, voy a comprarlos. 3 No, no estoy limpiándolo. 4 No, no la veo.*

PLTS | KAL 4.3, 4.4

**2 Completa y practica los diálogos.**
Further practice of direct object pronouns.

*Answers:*
*1 las; las; 2 los; 3 ponerla*

### B Preterite tense

KAL 4.3 | LLS 5.1 | PLTS

**3 Write out the verbs *viajar*, *comer*, and *salir* on learning cards with the Spanish on one side and the English on the other. Learn them by heart.**
Before students write out the irregular preterites, point out that some verbs change their spelling in the *yo* (first person singular) form, e.g.

g → gu *llegar: llegué, llegaste, llegó*, etc.

c → z *hacer: hice, hiciste, hizo*, etc.

KAL 4.5

**4 Complete these sentences with the preterite of the verb in brackets.**
Futher practice of the preterite.

*Answers:*
*1 fuimos; 2 toqué; 3 volvieron; 4 hizo; 5 jugó, jugué*

## Aprender – recounting events and answering questions

### C Recounting and summarising a past event

KAL4.5 | PLTS

**5 Read these examples and write down the verb and the tense used. Think about why each tense has been used.**
This provides useful practice of recognising the imperfect and preterite tense and also understanding when each of these tenses should be used.

*Answers:*
*1 preterite (action that began and ended in the past);*
*2 hacía – imperfect (went on over a longer period); llovió, hizo – preterite (action that began and ended in the past);*
*3 tenía – imperfect (went on over a longer period); iba – imperfect (what used to happen); 4 se puso – preterite (action that began and ended in the past); hacía (went on over a longer period); 5 salimos – preterite (action that began and ended in the past); queríamos – imperfect (went on over a longer period)*

### D Responding to open-ended questions

KAL 4.5 PLTS **6 Now think back to last summer and write five sentences about what you did.**
Further practice of using the imperfect and the preterite tense. Provide less able students with some model sentences.

### Hablar – pronunciation

### E Intonation in questions

KAL 4.6 **7 Listen. What difference can you hear in the way each of these sentences is spoken?**
This requires students listen carefully so that they recognise which are statements and which are questions.

**CD 1, track 47** **página 63, actividad 7**

**a** Mañana vas a ir con tus amigos al cine.
**b** ¿Mañana vas a ir con tus amigos al cine?
**c** Estás comiendo un bocadillo de jamón.
**d** ¿Estás comiendo un bocadillo de jamón?

*Answers:*
***a** statement; **b** question; **c** statement; **d** question*

## 2A.7 Extra Star

página 64

### *Planner*

**Objectives**
- read and write more about hobbies and past events
- use the preterite, imperfect and present tenses
- write a few simple opinions in the past

**Resources**
Student Book, page 64
Copymaster 50

**Renewed Framework references**
R&W 2.2; KAL 4.3, 4.5; LLS 5.1

**PLTS**
Activity 2: Reflective learners
Activity 4: Creative thinkers

AT 3.3 **1 Empareja las preguntas con las respuestas. Mira los dibujos.**
Students match the questions to the answers, using the illustrations to help them.

*Answers:*
***1** f; **2** c; **3** e; **4** a; **5** d; **6** g; **7** b*

AT 4.4–5 PLTS **2 Contesta a las preguntas de la actividad 1. Escribe sobre tus últimas vacaciones.**
Students prepare written answers to the questions in Activity 1 for themselves, saying where they went and what they did last holiday. If students prefer, they can answer about a fantasy holiday.

AT 3.3–4 R&W 2.2 **3 Lee el anuncio e identifica a la persona: Xavi o Maite**
Students read the advert and identify the person it is describing.

*Answer: Maite*

AT 4.3–4 KAL 4.3, 4.5 LLS 5.1 PLTS **4 Escribe un anuncio similar. Usa las palabras de la actividad 3 para ayudarte.**
Following on from Activity 3, students write a similar advert for themselves. Encourage them to be as creative as possible.

## 2A.7 Extra Plus

página 65

### Planner

**Objectives**
- read and understand an account in the past
- use past, present and immediate future tenses
- respond to a variety of questions

**Resources**
Student Book, page 65
Copymaster 51

**Renewed Framework references**
R&W 2.2, 2.4; KAL 4.5

**PLTS**
Activity 2: Reflective learners; Creative thinkers
Activity 3: Reflective learners; Creative thinkers

AT 3.5 | R&W 2.2 | KAL 4.5

**1 Lee el texto y contesta a las preguntas.**
Students read the text and answer the questions.

*Answers:*
***1*** *Trata de Enrique Iglesias;* ***2*** *Cumple años/su cumpleaños es el 8 de mayo;* ***3*** *Sus padres se divorciaron;* ***4*** *Se fue a Miami;* ***5*** *Porque se fue a vivir con su padre;* ***6*** *Administración de Empresas;* ***7*** *Porque le gustaba la música;* ***8*** *Decidió grabar un disco;* ***9*** *Vendió medio millón de copias de su primer disco;* ***10*** *es actor y modelo y productor*

AT 4.5 | PLTS | R&W 2.4 | KAL 4.5

**2 Escribe un párrafo sobre unas vacaciones verdaderas o imaginarias. Contesta a las preguntas.**
Remind students about when to use the preterite and when to use the imperfect tense. They should also try to include other tenses as well if possible such as the present and immediate future.

AT 4.5 | PLTS | R&W 2.4 | KAL 4.5

**3 Ahora escribe lo que vas a hacer durante el próximo verano. Basa tus ideas en la actividad 2.**
Encourage students to be as creative as possible.

## 2A.8 Prueba

página 66

**Resources**
Student Book, page 66
CD 1, track 48
Assessment OxBox, Unit 2A

**Renewed Framework references**
L&S 1.1, 1.2, 1.4; R&W 2.2, 2.4; KAL 4.3, 4.5; LLS 5.4

**PLTS**
All activities: Reflective learners

### Escuchar

AT 1.5 | L&S 1.1, 1.2 | PLTS

**Listen and answer the questions with a single word or a short phrase.**
This activity tests listening skills using the language covered in this unit. The National Curriculum level will vary depending on how much detail students give in their answers.

**CD 1, track 48** — **página 66, actividad 1**

– ¿Sabes, Gabi? El otro día fui con Elena y Juan a Ávila. Fuimos con un grupo del colegio en un autocar de lujo. Es una ciudad con una muralla medieval alrededor, lo mismo que Cartagena. Hacía mucho calor así que todos llevábamos pantalones cortos y camisetas.

- Y ¿qué había en Ávila de interés aparte de las piedras antiguas de las murallas?
- Bueno, no mucho excepto muchos conventos e iglesias. Fue allí donde nació Santa Teresa de Ávila.
- ¿Qué más hicisteis?
- Lo más interesante fue que fuimos a la Sierra de Gredos y vimos los Toros de Guisando, unas estatuas antiguas. Llegamos muy tarde a casa sobre las diez de la noche porque había mucho tráfico. Tenía un hambre feroz así que comí dos bocadillos de jamón y me acosté en seguida. Estuve contento todo el viaje porque, por lo menos fue un día que no tuvimos que ir al colegio.

*Answers:*
***1*** *(Fue) a Avila;* ***2*** *Un grupo (del colegio);* ***3*** *En un autocar (de lujo);* ***4*** *(hacía) mucho calor;* ***5*** *(llevaba) shorts y camiseta;* ***6*** *iglesia;* ***7*** *Los Toros de Guisando;* ***8*** *a las diez (de la noche);* ***9*** *comió dos bocadillos de jamón;* ***10*** *contento*

### Hablar

AT 2.5 | L&S 1.4 | PLTS

**Imagine you went on a similar school trip. Prepare notes and recount what you did. Use the questions in Activity 1 to help you.**
This activity tests speaking skills using the language covered in this unit. It can be done in pairs or as a presentation.

### Leer

AT 3.5 | R&W 2.2 | LLS 5.4 | PLTS

**Read the text and write ten facts about Santi's shopping trip in English.**
This activity tests reading skills using the language covered in this unit.

*Possible answers:*
***1*** *shopping for a birthday present;* ***2*** *went with younger brother Miguelito;* ***3*** *went to Corte Inglés;* ***4*** *went first to book department;* ***5*** *they didn't have the one they wanted;* ***6*** *decided to buy him a tie;* ***7*** *didn't have the colour they wanted;* ***8*** *went to music department;* ***9*** *on third floor;* ***10*** *spent two hours there listening to CDs;* ***11*** *Miguelito disappeared;* ***12*** *looked everywhere for him;* ***13*** *found him at last – fast asleep listening to his MP3 player.*

### Escribir

AT 3.5–6 | R&W 2.2 | LLS 5.4 | PLTS

**Write no more than 100 words about what you did one weekend in the past. Use the questions in Activity 1 and the bullet points below to help you. Remember that to achieve a level 5 you must use two different tenses.**
This activity tests writing skills using the language covered in this unit.

*Answers: Students' own answers*

## Leer 2A

página 151

**Resources**
Student Book, page 151

**Renewed Framework references**
R&W 2.1, 2.2, 2.4; KAL 4.6

**PLTS**
Activity 3: Reflective learners; Self-managers
Activity 4: Reflective learners; Creative thinkers
Activity 5: Reflective learners; Creative thinkers; Independent enquirers

AT 3.5 | R&W 2.1, 2.2

**1 Read Roberto's account and find ...**

*Answers:*
***1*** *(any 5 of) fui; pasamos; llegamos; fuimos; hizo; comimos; bebimos; quedamos;* ***2*** *había; importaba;* ***3*** *(any 4 of) procesiones increíbles; trajes típicos; animales fabulosos; bailes folklóricos; alegres; fenomenales*

AT 3.5 | R&W 2.1, 2.2

**2 Busca las frases en español.**
Students find the Spanish for the English phrases listed.

*Answers:*
***1*** *los más famosos y las mejores;* ***2*** *lo más importante es divertirse;* ***3*** *había miles de personas;* ***4*** *por la noche;* ***5*** *el festival religioso de la Cuaresma.*

AT 3.5 R&W 2.1, 2.2 PLTS

**3 Contesta a las preguntas.**
Students read through the text again and answer the questions.

*Answers:*
***1** north coast of Colombia/Barranquilla; **2** folk dances; devil's costumes; animal masks; processions; **3** four days – Saturday to Tuesday; **4** very hot; **5** watched the processions; ate empanadas; listened to music groups and danced; **6** at three in the morning.*

AT 4.4–5 R&W 2.4 KAL 4.6 PLTS

**4 Escribe cinco preguntas sobre el texto. Contesta a las preguntas de tu compañero.**
Students write their own questions on the reading text. They then swap questions with a partner and answer his/her questions.

AT 4.5 R&W 2.4 KAL 4.6 PLTS

**5 Escribe sobre una fiesta similar.**
Students use some of the information from their work in Activity 4 to produce a poster, advertising a festival.

### Follow-up

Students use some of the information from their work in Activity 5 to produce a poster, advertising a festival. You could display the posters in the classroom.

## Foundation Workbook

### Página 32 2A.1 Mi tiempo libre

- Use with Student Book, pages 52–53

AT 3.2 AT 4.2

**1 Roll dice to make sentences about your free time. Decide if they are sensible or nonsense.**
Students could do this orally or write out the sentences.

**2 Write down the most sensible or true sentence you can make using the grid.**

AT 2.3–4

**3 Use the grid to keep talking for one minute.**

### Página 33 2A.2 De compras

- Use with Student Book, pages 54–55

AT 3.1–2

**1 There is a hidden message in this wordsearch. When you have found all the words in Spanish, read the letters that are NOT used to find a hidden message (in the top six rows of the grid).**

*Answers:*
***Message:** Me gusta ir de compras pero prefiero ir al cine.*

AT 4.1–2

**2 Make your own Spanish shops wordsearch with a hidden message for a friend to do. Use the words for things you find in different shops or the different departments of a big store.**
Students should refer back to pages 54 and 55 of the Student Book for support if necessary.

### Página 34 2A.3 De vacaciones

- Use with Student Book, pages 56–57

AT 3.2

**1 Choose the best word(s) to start the answer to each of these questions? Draw lines to match them up.**

*Answers: **a** Fui a …; **b** Salí a las …; **c** Vi …; **d** Viajé …; **e** Comí …; **f** Lo pasé …; **g** Me alojé*

AT 1.3 KAL 4.6 LLS 5.8

**2 Listen and check your answers to Activity 1.**

**CD 3, track 40 (Workbook 20)** **página 34, actividad 2**

A: ¿Adónde fuiste de vacaciones?
B: Fui a Málaga.
A: ¿A qué hora saliste?
B: Salí a las once de la mañana.
A: ¿Qué viste de interés?
B: Vi muchos monumentos históricos.
A: ¿Cómo viajaste?
B: Viajé en avión.
A: ¿Qué comiste?
B: Comí arroz, pan, pasta, carne.
A: ¿Qué tal lo pasaste?
B: Lo pasé muy bien.
A: ¿Dónde te alojaste?
B: Me alojé en un hotel.

AT 4.3 KAL 4.6 **3 Give your own answers to the questions, using the starters you chose in Activity 1.**
Students should refer back to pages 56 and 57 of the Student Book for support if necessary.

## Página 35 2A.4 ¡Lo pasamos bomba!

- Use with Student Book, pages 58–59

AT 3.4 **1 Try out each of the strategies on this reading text. Evaluate each one.**

AT 3.4 **2 Answer these questions about the text in Activity 1.**

*Answers:*
***a*** *Valencia in Spain;* ***b*** *Las Fallas;* ***c*** *la Mascleta;* ***d*** *statues;* ***e*** *on the last night;* ***f*** *brother;* ***g*** *dad*

## Página 36 2A.5 Cuando era joven...

- Use with Student Book, pages 60–61

AT 3.1–2 **1 Sort out your Spanish toolkit.**

*Answers:*
***opinions:*** *me encanta, me apasiona, me interesa, prefiero*
***connectives:*** *y, pero, porque, por ejemplo, así que*
***future:*** *voy a, el año próximo*
***preterite:*** *fui, comí, viajé, el año pasado*

KAL 4.4, 4.5 LLS 5.8 AT 4.4–5 **2 Use your toolkit to improve this piece of repetitive, simplistic Spanish. Add connectives, a variety of opinions, a range of tenses and extra details.**
Volunteers could read their finished piece of work in class. Does each student's text sound very different now?

## Página 37 2A.6A Labolengua

- Use with Student Book, pages 62–63

**1 Each line has a sentence about holidays in the past. Unscramble the sentences and write them correctly in the boxes. Then put the numbered letters into the correct place at the bottom to reveal a secret message.**

*Answer: Me gustan las vacaciones.*

**2 Make your own Spanish holidays puzzle with a secret message for a friend to do.**

## Página 38 2A.6B Técnica

- Use with Student Book, pages 62–63

KAL 4.5 **1 Sort the verbs below the table into imperfect and preterite.**

*Answers:*
**Imperfect:** *comía; hablaba; llevaba; estaba*
**Preterite:** *fui; vi; viajé; salí; compré*

KAL 4.5 **2 Use your understanding of verbs to circle the correct translation of each sentence.**

*Answers:*
***a*** *I used to go . . .;* ***b*** *I went . . .;* ***c*** *I ate . . .;* ***d*** *I used to stay . . .;* ***e*** *I travelled . . .*

**3 Draw lines to match up what was happening with what you think happened next.**
Suggested answers for this are given below. Do students have the same?

*Suggested answers:*
***a*** *. . . y vi me hermano.* ***b*** *. . . y compré una camiseta.* ***c*** *. . . y fui a Madrid.* ***d*** *. . . y vi la película Kindergarten Cop.*

# Higher Workbook

## Página 32 2A.1 Mi tiempo libre

- Use with Student Book, pages 52–53

AT 3.2–3 **1 Roll dice to make sentences about your free time. Decide if they are sensible or nonsense.**
Students could do this orally or write out the sentences.

AT 4.2–3 **2 Write down the most sensible or true sentence you can make using the grid.**

AT 2.3–4 **3 Use the grid to keep talking for one minute.**

## Página 33 2A.2 De compras

- Use with Student Book, pages 54–55

AT 3.1–2 **1 There are six sorts of food shop in this wordsearch. When you have found all the words in Spanish, read the letters that are NOT used to find a hidden message (in the top six rows of the grid).**

*Answers:*
***Message:*** *Me gusta ir de compras pero prefiero ir al cine.*

AT 4.1–2 **2 Make your own wordsearch with a hidden message for a friend to do. Use the Spanish words for things you would find in a shop, or the departments of a big store.**
Students should refer back to pages 54 and 55 of the Student Book for support if necessary.

## Página 34 2A.3 De vacaciones

- Use with Student Book, pages 56–57

AT 3.2 **1 What would be the best word(s) to start the answer to each of these questions? Write in the start of the answer.**

*Answers:*
***a*** *Fui a …;* ***b*** *Salí a las …;* ***c*** *Vi …;* ***d*** *Viajé …;* ***e*** *Comí …;* ***f*** *Lo pasé …;* ***g*** *Me alojé …*

AT 1.3 KAL 4.6 LLS 5.8 **2 Listen and check your answers to Activity 1.**

**CD 4, track 20** **página 34, actividades 2 y 3**

A: ¿Adónde fuiste de vacaciones?
B: Fui a Málaga.
A: ¿A qué hora saliste?
B: Salí a las once de la mañana.
A: ¿Qué viste de interés?
B: Vi muchos monumentos históricos.
A: ¿Cómo viajaste?
B: Viajé en avión.
A: ¿Qué comiste?
B: Comí arroz, pan, pasta, carne.
A: ¿Qué tal lo pasaste?
B: Lo pasé muy bien.
A: ¿Dónde te alojaste?
B: Me alojé en un hotel.

AT 1.3 L&S 1.1 KAL 4.6 **3 Listen again and complete the rest of the sentences with what you hear.**
*Answers: as in transcript*

AT 4.3–4 KAL 4.6 **4 Listen and give your own answers, using the starters you chose in Activity 1.**
Students should refer back to pages 56 and 57 of the Student Book for support if necessary.

**CD 4, track 21** **página 34, actividad 4**

¿Adónde fuiste?
¿A qué hora saliste?
¿Qué viste de interés?
¿Cómo viajaste?
¿Qué comiste?
¿Qué tal lo pasaste?
¿Dónde te alojaste?

## Página 35 2A.4 ¡Lo pasamos bomba!

- Use with Student Book, pages 58–59

**1 Look at the reading strategies. Put them into the order you would apply them.**

*Suggested answers:*
*Use all the clues in pictures and titles.*
*Spot words that stand out: numbers, names.*
*Spot punctuation clues: questions, exclamations, speech, lists.*
*Read through quickly picking out words you know.*
*Build up your understanding in stages.*
*Read through carefully, pronouncing each word in your head or out loud.*
*Pay attention to the ending of words.*
*Understand the role of unknown words in a sentence: verbs, nouns, connectives, adjectives?*
*Pick words to look up in a dictionary.*
*Look at the questions to see if they guide you through.*
*Use everything you have worked out, to extract as much information as possible.*

AT 3.4 **2 Use the strategies to tackle this text. Evaluate each one.**

AT 3.4 **3 Answer these questions about the text in Activity 2.**

*Answers:*
***a** In March last year; **b** Las Fallas; **c** noisy and incredible; **d** paper and card; **e** they were burned; **f** eating; **g** sleeping*

## Página 36 2A.5 Cuando era joven …

- Use with Student Book, pages 60–61

AT 3.2–3 **1 Sort out your Spanish toolkit.**

*Answers:*
***opinions:** me encanta; me apasiona; me interesa; prefiero*
***connectives:** y; pero; porque; por ejemplo; así que*
***verb + infinitive:** quiero; puedo; tengo que; suelo; voy a*
***future:** voy a; el año próximo*
***preterite:** fui; comí; viajé; el año pasado*
***imperfect:** iba; me alojaba; viajaba; comía*

KAL 4.5 LLS 5.8 AT 4.4–5 **2 Use your toolkit to improve this piece of repetitive, simplistic Spanish. Add connectives, a variety of opinions, a range of tenses and extra details.**
Volunteers could read their finished piece of work in class. Does each student's text sound very different now?

## Página 37 2A.6A Labolengua

- Use with Student Book, pages 62–63

**1 Each line has a sentence about holidays in the past. Unscramble the sentences and write them correctly in the boxes. Take the letters in circles and rearrange them to find the secret message.**

*Answer: Me gustan las vacaciones.*

**2 Make your own Spanish holidays puzzle with a secret message for a friend to do.**
Students should refer back to pages 62 and 63 of the Student Book for ideas.

## Página 38 2A.6B Técnica

- Use with Student Book, pages 62–63

KAL 4.5 **1 Sort the verbs below into imperfect and preterite.**

*Answers:*
***Imperfect:** comía; hablaba; llevaba; estaba*
***Preterite:** fui; vi; viajé; salí; compré*

KAL 4.5 **2 Translate these sentences into English. Decide whether to use 'I used to' or the simple past.**

*Answers:*
***a** I used to go on holiday to France. **b** I went to spain last year. **c** I ate in the hotel restaurant. **d** I used to stay in a hotel. **e** I travelled by plane.*

**3 Draw lines to match up what <u>was</u> happening with what you think happened next.**
Suggested answers for this are given below. Do students have the same?

*Suggested answers:*
***a** …y vi me hermano. **b** …y compré una camiseta. **c** …y fui a Madrid. **d** …y vi la película* Kindergarten Cop.

# 2B ¡Ven a Madrid!

## Unit Objectives

**Contexts and cultural focus:** learning about Madrid
**Grammar:** Preposition *a*; Relative pronouns *que* and *lo que*; the immediate future; questions; the preterite of some common irregular verbs; simple imperatives and prepositions
**Language learning:** tackling an unfamiliar text; transforming level 4 speaking or writing into level 5; identifying key vocabulary from context; extending work to achieve a higher level; sounding Spanish when pronouncing words with *z*, *ce* or *ci*

- *Aim:* To learn about the city of Madrid and its tourist attractions.
- Each unit has an associated video which will feature throughout the unit. Below is the transcript of the video for this unit.

**Video clip: Unit 2B (CD 2, track 6)**

**Part 1**

*Elena and Roberto have just arrived from Segovia at Chamartin Station*

Elena: *To camera*. Hoy estamos en Madrid. Esta es la estación de Chamartín. Es muy moderna.
Roberto: Pero no vinimos a Madrid a ver una estación de trenes.
Elena: No, pero es muy interesante. ¿Qué vamos a hacer hoy?
Roberto: Voy a visitar el museo de El Prado.
Elena: Yo prefiero el arte moderno, voy a visitar el museo de Reina Sofía.
Roberto: También voy a visitar el Palacio Real.
Elena: ¡Qué aburrido! Solo te interesa la historia. Yo voy a ir a la Puerta del Sol.
Roberto: No es verdad. También voy a visitar el estadio del Real Madrid, El Santiago Bernabéu.
Elena: ¡Fútbol! No me interesa para nada. Yo voy a ir a Gran Vía a ver las tiendas.
Roberto: Bueno ¡yo no quiero ir de tiendas!
Elena: ¿Qué vamos a hacer entonces?
Roberto: Vamos a jugar, por supuesto. Vamos a visitar Madrid y sacar fotos y comprar entradas en cada lugar.
Elena: Y la persona que visite más lugares gana.

*Standing as if to go off for a race.*

Roberto: En sus marcas, ¡ya!

**Part 2**

Elena: Yo voy a ir en Metro y en bus porque Madrid tiene uno de los mejores Metros del mundo.
Roberto: Pero yo soy más original, voy a hacer un tour por Madrid en monopatín.
Roberto: Este es el Palacio Real, fue construido en 1892.
Elena: Esta es la Puerta del Sol, es donde viene la gente a celebrar el fin de año.
Roberto: Esto es la Plaza Mayor, en el siglo XV era la plaza de mercado.
Elena: Este es el Oso y el Madroño, símbolo de Madrid.

*Back at home*

Elena: ¡A ver, quién ha ganado!
Roberto: Seguro que fui yo.
Elena: ¿Por qué?
Roberto: Porque hice un tour súperrápido en monopatín y visité todos los monumentos importantes en dos horas.
Elena: ¿Monopatín?
Roberto: Mira.
Elena: ¡Hala, qué guay! ¿Y qué viste?
Roberto: Vi el Palacio Real y la Catedral de la Almudena. Y también la Plaza Mayor y el Templo de Debot.
Elena: El Templo de Debot, nunca he ido. ¿Es interesante?
Roberto: Sí, es egipcio pero como a ti no te gusta la Historia….
Elena: Bueno, yo fui a la Puerta del Sol, y a la Gran Vía.
Roberto: ¿Y qué te compraste?
Elena: ¡Nada para ti!
Roberto: Yo fui a Santiago Bernabéu.
Elena: ¿Y jugaste al futbol?
Roberto: ¿Visitaste al museo Reina Sofía?
Elena: Sí, mira la foto.
Roberto: Yo fui al Museo del Prado.
Elena: Entonces ¿Quién ha ganado?
Roberto: ¡No lo sé! Tenemos tantas fotos, tickets y folletos…
Elena: *To camera*. Decidid vosotros. ¿Quién ha visitado más lugares?
Roberto: Demasiado fácil. También tenéis que contarnos algo de cada lugar.
Elena: Suerte.

**Punto Lengua**

Vamos a visitar Madrid y sacar fotos y comprar entradas en cada lugar.
¿Y qué viste?
Bueno, yo fui a la Puerta del Sol, y a la Gran Vía.
Yo fui a Santiago Bernabéu.

As a starter activity to introduce the unit and familiarise students with the language they will meet, view the video as a whole. Are there any words or phrases that they have recognised from this single viewing? What do they think it is about?
Play Part 1 again a couple of times, as this sets the scene. Do students recognise any of the places mentioned? What places does each person visit? This starts students thinking about the video and will help them understand the second part when you return to look at it in more detail later in this unit.

*Synopsis:*
As usual, Roberto and Elena are competing, this time over who can see the most and the most interesting sites in Madrid. This video sees Roberto and Elena setting off on different forms of transport to sight-see in Madrid. They are both interested in different things, so who will visit the most places?

| Unit 2B ¡Ven a Madrid! Overview grid | | | | | | |
|---|---|---|---|---|---|---|
| **Page reference** | **Contexts and objectives** | **Language learning** | **Grammar** | **Key language** | **Framework** | **AT level** |
| Pages 68–69 **¿Vamos en bici?** | • talk about different means of transport | • tackle an unfamiliar text | • use *a* (preposition) and *que* (relative pronoun) | *en avión; en barco; en bici; en coche; en metro; en tranvía; a pie; es barato; es caro; es gratis; es cómodo; está cerca; está lejos; es rápido* | L&S 1.1, 1.2, 1.4; R&W 2.2; KAL 4.4 | 1.3–4, 2.3, 3.5, 4.3–4 |
| Pages 70–71 **Planes para mañana** | • recognise some tourist attractions in Madrid | • transform level 4 speaking or writing into level 5 | • use the immediate future to talk about plans | *el museo; el palacio; el parque de atracciones; la plaza; la puerta; alquilar; comer; ir; jugar; salir; viajar* | L&S 1.2, 1.4; R&W 2.4; KAL 4.5; LLS 5.4 | 1.3–4, 2.4–5, 3.4–5, 4.5 |
| Pages 72–73 **Billetes de viaje** | • buy travel tickets | • identify key vocabulary from context | • ask questions | *un billete; de ida; de ida y vuelta; clase preferente; clase turista; ¿A qué hora sale? el andén; ¿A qué hora llega? un abono* | L&S 1.2, 1.4; R&W 2.2, 2.4, 2.5; LLS 5.4 | 1.4, 2.3–4, 3.4, 4.3–4 |
| Pages 74–75 **¿Qué hiciste?** | • talk about what you did on a day out in the past | • extend your work to achieve a higher level | • use the preterite of common irregular verbs; adverbs | *fui en el teleférico; hice ciclismo; vi leones; pude tocar un delfín; di un paseo; tuve miedo; fue fabuloso; primero; después; luego; más tarde; antes de; después de; hizo calor; hizo frío; llovió; hizo sol; hizo viento; hizo buen tiempo; lo pasé bomba; lo pasé fenomenal; me encantó; me gustó mucho; fue divertido; fue emocionante; fue un desastre* | L&S 1.2, 1.4; R&W 2.4, 2.5; IU 3.2; KAL 4.4, 4.5, 4.6; LLS 5.4, 5.5 | 1.6, 2.4–5, 3.6, 4.4–6 |
| Pages 76–77 **¿Dónde está?** | • recognise names of shops and give directions | • sound Spanish when pronouncing words with *z*, *ce* or *ci* | • use simple imperatives and prepositions | | L&S 1.1, 1.2, 1.4; R&W 2.4; LLS 5.8 | 1.3, 2.3, 3.2–3, 4.3–4 |
| Pages 78–79 **Labolengua** | • review language and grammar from the unit | | | | R&W 2.4; KAL 4.1, 4.4, 4.5; LLS 5.1, 5.8 | 4.4–6 |

| | | | | | | |
|---|---|---|---|---|---|---|
| Pages 80–81<br>**Extra Star**<br>**Extra Plus** | • differentiated extension/ homework material | • revise and consolidate all vocabulary and grammar covered in the unit | • revise and consolidate all vocabulary and grammar covered in the unit | | KAL 4.2, 4.4 | 3.1, 3.3–4, 4.2–5 |
| Page 82<br>**Prueba** | • end-of-unit test | | | | L&S 1.1, 1.2, 1.4;<br>R&W 2.2, 2.4;<br>LLS 5.4 | 1.4–5,<br>2.4–5,<br>3.4–5,<br>4.4–5 |
| Page 83<br>**Vocabulario** | • a summary of the key language covered in each core spread of this unit | | | | | |
| Page 152<br>**Leer 2B** | • practice of longer reading texts based on the theme of the unit | | | | LLS 5.4 | 3.3 |

# 2B ¡Ven a Madrid!

| **Week-by-week overview**<br>**(Three-year KS3 Route: assuming six weeks' work or approximately 10–12.5 hours)**<br>**(Two-year KS3 Route: assuming four weeks' worth or approxmately 6.5-8.5 hours)** |
|---|
| **About Unit 2B, *¡Ven a Madrid!*:** Students work in the context of tourist attractions in Madrid. They talk about different means of transport and learn about different tourist attractions in Madrid. They practise buying travel tickets and talk about what they did on a day out in the past. They learn the names of shops and give directions. Students use *a* and *que* as well as the immediate future. They ask questions, use the preterite of some common irregular verbs and simple imperatives and prepositions. The unit also provides tips on language learning techniques. |

| **Three-Year KS3 Route** | | | **Two-Year KS3 Route** | | |
|---|---|---|---|---|---|
| **Week** | **Resources** | **Objectives** | **Week** | **Resources** | **Objectives** |
| 1 | **2B.1 ¿Vamos en bici?** | talk about different means of transport<br>tackle an unfamiliar text<br>use *a* (preposition) and *que* (relative pronoun) | 1 | **2B.1 ¿Vamos en bici?**<br>(Omit the Challenge activity) | talk about different means of transport<br>tackle an unfamiliar text<br>use *a* (preposition) and *que* (relative pronoun) |
| 2 | **2B.2 Planes para mañana**<br>**2B.6 Labolengua B** (p.78) | recognise some tourist attractions in Madrid<br>transform level 4 speaking or writing into level 5<br>use the immediate future to talk about plans | 2 | **2B.2 Planes para mañana**<br>(Omit activities 1 & Challenge)<br>**2B.6 Labolengua B** (p.78) | recognise some tourist attractions in Madrid<br>transform level 4 speaking or writing into level 5<br>use the immediate future to talk about plans |
| 3 | **2B.3 Billetes de viaje** | buy travel tickets<br>identify key vocabulary from context<br>ask questions | 3 | **2B.3 Billetes de viaje**<br>(Omit Challenge) | buy travel tickets<br>identify key vocabulary from context ask questions |
| 4 | **2B.4 ¿Qué hiciste?**<br>**2B.6 Labolengua A** (p.78) **and C** (p.79) | talk about what you did on a day out in the past<br>extend your work to achieve a higher level<br>use the preterite of common irregular verbs; adverbs | 4 | **2B.4 ¿Qué hiciste?**<br>(Omit Gramática (p.75) & Challenge)<br>**2B.6 Labolengua A** (p.78) **and C** (p.79)<br>**2B.8 Prueba** (p.82)<br>**Vocabulario** (p.83) | talk about what you did on a day out in the past<br>extend your work to achieve a higher level<br>use the preterite of common irregular verbs; adverbs<br>Prepare and carry out assessment in all four skills<br>Recapping on vocabulary of the unit |
| 5 | **2B.5 ¿Dónde está?**<br>**2B.6 Labolengua D** (p.79) | recognise names of shops and give directions sound Spanish when pronouncing words with *z*, *ce* or *ci*<br>use simple imperatives and prepositions | | | |
| 6 | **2B.7 Extra (Star)** (p.80)<br>**2B.7 Extra (Plus)** (p.81)<br>**2B.8 Prueba** (p.82)<br>**Vocabulario** (p.83)<br>**Leer** (p.152) | Further reinforcement and extension of the language of the unit. Prepare and carry out assessment in all four skills<br>Recapping on vocabulary of the unit Further reading to explore the language of the unit and cultural themes | | | |

## 2B.1 ¿Vamos en bici? páginas 68–69

# Planner

### Objectives
- talk about different means of transport
- use *a* (preposition) and *que* (relative pronoun)
- tackle an unfamiliar text

### Resources
Student Book, pages 68–69
CD 2, track 2
Foundation Workbook, page 40
Higher Workbook, page 40
Foundation Workbook audio, CD 3, track 41 (Workbook 21)
Higher Workbook audio, CD 4, track 22
Interactive OxBox, Unit 2B
Copymasters 53–60

### Key language
*en avión; en barco; en bici; en coche; en metro; en tranvía; a pie; es barato; es caro; es gratis; es cómodo; está cerca; está lejos; es rápido*

### Renewed Framework references
L&S 1.1, 1.2, 1.4; R&W 2.2; KAL 4.4

### PLTS
Gramática: Reflective learners
Activity 6: Team workers; Effective participators
Challenge: Team workers; Effective participators

### Starters
- Display the key language and ask students to allocate each means of transport an adjective, e.g. *avión – rápido*. Discuss the answers as a class. Have students allocated the same adjectives for each means of transport?
- Go round the class asking each student what his/her preferred means of transport is and why, e.g. *Me gusta el avión porque es rápido*. More able students can mention different destinations and when they use this transport, e.g. *Los sábados voy al supermercado en coche porque está lejos.*

### Plenaries
- Once students have completed Activities 1 and 2, test their memories. Firstly, ask them which means of transport were mentioned. Next, ask them how each of these means of transport was described. Finally, ask them to write down any other information they remember. Listen to the recording again to see how much they have remembered correctly.
- Students use the grid from Activity 6 to write some more similar sentences on the topic of means of transport.

### Homework/Self-study
Activity 4, page 69
Gramática (1): Students write a sentence for each of the forms of 'to the'.

AT 1.3
L&S 1.1, 1.2

**1 Escucha. ¿En qué orden se mencionan?**
Before students start listening, give them a moment to study the photos. What kind of vocabulary are they expecting to hear for each one? Students then listen and note down the order in which the forms of transport are mentioned.

**CD 2, track 2** **página 68, actividades 1 y 2**

1 La mejor manera de viajar por Madrid es en metro porque es una manera flexible y barata de moverse por la ciudad y ver sus atracciones turísticas.
2 Madrid tiene una red excelente de autobuses que atraviesan la ciudad de día y de noche.
3 Los turistas y los madrileños también tienen la opción de utilizar los trenes de cercanías que son modernos y no son caros.
4 También puedes visitar la ciudad utilizando los cientos de taxis que hay. Los taxis son fáciles de identificar porque son blancos con una raya roja.
5 Por algunas partes de Madrid también se puede viajar en tranvía que es muy accesible y está bien conectado con la red de trenes y con el metro.
6 Si te gusta estar al aire libre, tienes tiempo y te gusta hacer ejercicio, puedes ver la ciudad andando. Es lo más barato.

*Answers:*
***1** c; **2** f; **3** a; **4** e; **5** b; **6** d*

AT 1.3–4 | L&S 1.1, 1.2

**2 Escucha otra vez. Toma notas en inglés sobre la información adicional.**
Students listen again and note down as much additional information as possible. Before they do this, look at the vocabulary box as a class. Do they know what these adjectives mean? Can any students already tell you any extra information?

AT 4.3 | KAL 4.4

**3 Escribe cinco frases. ¿Cómo vas a los lugares de abajo? ¿Por qué?**
Students use the words in the box as a starting point to write their sentences. Compare answers as a class. Has anyone come up with a sentence that no one else has?

PLTS

## Gramática
Read through the Grammar box as a class. To check that students have remembered how to say 'to the', go round the class asking each of them to give you a sentence containing *al*, *a la*, *a los* or *a las*. If necessary, display a list of places with their genders for support.

AT 3.5 | R&W 2.2

**4 Lee el email. Identifica las cuatro frases correctas.**
Give students time to read the e-mail. Before they identify the correct sentences, look at the Think box.

*Answers:*
*2, 4, 5, 6*

## Gramática
Read through the grammar explanation. To practise using these relative pronouns, ask students to write a sentence using each of these for themselves. They should use the example sentences as models, e.g. *Mi madre, que es...* or *Lo que me gustó más fue el cine*. Go round the class asking each student to read out one of their sentences.

AT 3.5 | R&W 2.2

**5 ¿Cómo se dice en español ...? Elige una frase de color rojo.**
This shows students how relative pronouns are used within a text. Advise them to begin with the expressions they already know and then to move on to the rest which they should be able to work out from the context.

*Answers:*
***1** que es una ciudad bonita; **2** que contiene descripciones; **3** lo que significa que; **4** lo que más me gustó*

AT 2.3 | L&S1.4 | KAL 4.4 | PLTS

**6 Hablar en equipo. ¡Preparados, listos, ya!**
Turn this into a fun class quiz with each team competing to win. Teams take it in turn to produce a sentence. They score a point for each block of the sentence that is correct and an extra point if they produce a whole sentence that is correct and makes sense. The team with the most points at the end wins.

AT 4.4 | L&S1.4 | KAL 4.4 | PLTS

## Challenge
**Using the grid in Activity 6, write down the places where you go and how you get there for each day of the week.**

When students have finished, they can share answers as a class.

## 2B.2 Planes para mañana

páginas 70–71

# Planner

### Objectives
- recognise some tourist attractions in Madrid
- use the immediate future to talk about plans
- transform level 4 speaking or writing into level 5

### Resources
Student Book, pages 70–71
CD 2, track 3
Foundation Workbook, page 41
Higher Workbook, page 41
Foundation Workbook audio, CD 3, track 42 (Workbook 22)
Higher Workbook audio, CD 4, track 23
Interactive OxBox, Unit 2B
Copymasters 53–60

### Key language
*el estadio; el museo; el palacio; el parque de atracciones; la plaza; la puerta; alquilar; comer; ir; jugar; salir; viajar*

### Renewed Framework references
L&S 1.2, 1.4; R&W 2.4; KAL 4.5; LLS 5.4

### PLTS
Gramática: Reflective learners
Activity 4: Reflective learners
Activity 7: Team workers; Effective participators
Challenge: Creative thinkers

### Starters
- Display the key language and give students a time limit to write the English translation for each word. These are all words they should already have come across. Once the time is up, check answers as a class and explain that this language will crop up in this spread in the context of tourist attractions in Madrid.
- Play a memory game using tourist attractions in Madrid. Start by saying, e.g. *Voy a ir al Museo del Prado porque me interesa el arte.*The student nearest to you continues, e.g. *Voy a ir al Museo del Prado porque me interesa el arte y voy a hacer un tour autoguiado del Parque del Retiro.* Continue in this way around the class.

### Plenaries
- Following Activities 2 and 3, students pretend that they are going to Madrid and write down which of the tourist attractions they will visit and why. They can write about more than one if they wish. Compare answers as a class.
- Activity 7: Snakes and ladders game to practise freetime activities vocabulary and tourist attractions in Madrid.

### Homework/Self-study
Following Activity 4, page 71, students write five sentences in the immediate future tense. More able students should produce more complex sentences, e.g. saying when they are going to do what they are going to do and why.

AT 3.4 | LLS 5.4

**1 Lee las descripciones. ¿Qué foto es?**
Students read the descriptions and match them to the photos. Remind them that they don't need to understand every word in order to work out which photo goes with which description.

*Answers:*
***1** d, **2** b, **3** f, **4** a, **5** e, **6** c*

LLS 5.4

**Think**
Thinking about how recognising just a couple of words in a description of this kind can help them understand the gist of the text should help students become more confident in reading and working out meaning.

AT 1.3–4 | L&S1.2 | LLS 5.4

**2 Escucha. ¿Qué sitio les recomiendas?**
Students listen and note down which attraction they would recommend for each speaker.

**CD 2, track 3** **página 70, actividades 2 y 3**

1 Soy una persona muy creativa y me encantan la pintura y la escultura. Me gusta mucho el arte en general.
2 Soy un fanático del fútbol. Nunca me pierdo ningún partido de mi equipo favorito.
3 Me gusta la naturaleza y estar al aire libre. Me gustan los lugares tranquilos y me gusta pasear.
4 Me interesa la arquitectura y siento curiosidad por las Monarquías y la política.

5 Me gustaría asistir a una corrida de toros para comprender por qué son tan populares. Aún asi, no sé si me van a gustar porque pienso que son crueles.
6 No me interesan los museos, prefiero mezclarme con la gente y visitar lugares animados.

*Answers:*
***1** el Museo del Prado; **2** Estadio Santiago Bernabéu; **3** el Parque del Retiro; **4** el Museo del Prado; **5** la Plaza de Toros de las Ventas; **6** la Puerta del Sol*

AT 1.3–4 | L&S 1.2 | PLTS

**3 Escucha otra vez. ¿Qué palabras te ayudaron a encontrar las respuestas de la actividad 2?**
Students listen again and this time note down any words that helped them answer the questions in Activity 2.

PLTS | KAL 4.5

## Gramática
Read through this Grammar box with students before they attempt Activity 4. To ensure that students are confident with forming the immediate future, work through some more examples, e.g. *Voy a comer en un restaurante. Vamos a comprar regalos para la familia.* etc

PLTS | KAL 4.5 | AT 3.5 | AT 4.5

**4 Copia los párrafos y escribe los verbos (que están en la casilla). ¿Qué van a hacer? ¿Cuándo?**
Following their work on the immediate future, students complete the paragraphs with the correct form of the immediate future tense. They use the words in the box.

*Answers:*
*Voy a ir; voy a comer; voy a alquilar; voy a hacer; voy a salir; voy a volver*

*Vamos a ir; vamos a ir; vamos a comprar; vamos a visitarla; vamos a ver*

AT 3.5 | LLS 5.4

**5 Lee las frases. ¿Verdad o mentira?**
Students read the paragraphs from Activity 4 and decide whether the sentences are true (*verdadero*) or false (*mentira*).

*Answers:*
***1** verdad; **2** mentira; **3** mentira; **4** verdad; **5** mentira; **6** verdad*

PLTS | AT 2.4–5 | L&S 1.4

**6 Estás en Madrid. Habla con tu compañero. ¿Adónde vas a ir? ¿Por qué?**
This is a fun way for students to practise freetime activity vocabulary and to use Madrid attractions in their sentences.

AT 4.5 | R&W 2.4 | PLTS

## Challenge
**Imagine you are spending a week in Madrid. Write about your plans. Aim to produce a level 5 piece.**
Remind students that they will need to use more than one tense in order to obtain a level 5.

## 2B.3 Billetes de viaje

páginas 72–73

# *Planner*

### Objectives
- buy travel tickets
- ask questions
- identify key vocabulary from context

### Resources
Student Book, pages 72–73
CD 2, track 4–5
Foundation Workbook, page 42
Higher Workbook, page 42
Foundation Workbook audio, CD 3, track 43 (Workbook 23)
Higher Workbook audio, CD 4, track 24
Interactive OxBox, Unit 2B
Copymasters 53–60

### Key language
*un billete; de ida; de ida y vuelta; clase preferente; clase turista; ¿A qué hora sale? el andén; ¿A qué hora llega? un abono*

### Renewed Framework references
L&S 1.2, 1.4; R&W 2.2, 2.4, 2.5; LLS 5.4

### PLTS
Activity 3: Team workers; Effective participators
Challenge: Self-managers; Independent enquirers

### Starters
- Display the English question words, 'What?', 'When?', 'How much/many?', 'How?', 'Who?', 'Where?', 'Where to?' and 'Why?' and ask students to write down the Spanish for all of these: *¿Qué?, ¿Cuándo?, ¿Cuánto/a/s?, ¿Cómo?, ¿Quién?, ¿Dónde?, ¿Adónde?, ¿Porqué?,* remembering to use Spanish question marks. Students could then work in pairs to ask each other questions in Spanish using these words.
- To check that students are confident with the key language from this spread, have a quick quiz. Call out a word or question in English and ask students to note down the Spanish, e.g. ticket, single, return, payment, 1st class, What time does it get there?, etc. Check answers as a class – students should include the article in front of any nouns.

### Plenaries
- Once students have completed Activity 4, page 73, have a class quiz on the Madrid underground network. Ask them questions in Spanish about the text that they read. How much can they remember? The team that answers the most questions correctly wins.
- Students work in pairs to act out their conversations from the Challenge Activity.

### Homework/Self-study
Gramática, page 72
Activity 5, page 73

AT 3.4 | LLS 5.4

**1 Lee la conversación. ¿Cómo se dice en español?**
Students read the conversation and write the Spanish for the words listed. Remind students to use cognates and context to help them find the correct translations.

*Answers:*
***1** un billete; **2** de ida; **3** de ida y vuelta; **4** clase preferente; **5** clase turista; **6** ¿A qué hora sale el próximo?; **7** el andén; **8** ¿A qué hora llega?*

### Gramática
Read through the Grammar box as a class. To get students in the habit of using Spanish-style question marks, ask them to write down eight questions, one for each of the question words listed, on any topic you have covered so far.

AT 1.4 | L&S 1.2

**2 Escucha y rellena la tabla.**
Students listen fill in the table.

**CD 2, track 4** — **página 72, actividad 2**

**1**
- Hola, ¿qué desea?
- Un billete a Albacete, clase preferente, por favor.
- ¿De ida y vuelta?
- Sí, ida y vuelta, por favor.
- Aquí tiene. Sale a las dieciocho horas dieciocho del andén 4.
- ¿A qué hora llega?
- Llega a las veintiuna seis.
- ¿Cuánto es?
- Son 56 euros con 75.
- Aquí tiene, gracias. Adiós.
- Adiós.

2
- Buenos días. ¿Qué desea?
- Un billete a Ciudad Real, por favor.
- ¿De ida o de ida y vuelta?
- Sólo ida.
- ¿De qué clase lo quiere?
- Clase turista. ¿A qué hora sale el próximo?
- Sale a las quince treinta y cinco.
- ¿De qué andén?
- Andén 11.
- ¿A qué hora llega?
- A las diecisiete veinticinco.
- Vale, gracias. ¿Cuánto es?
- 9 euros con 15.
- Aquí tiene, gracias. Adiós.
- Adiós.

3
- Hola, quiero un billete de ida y vuelta a Barcelona para mañana.
- Muy bien. ¿Qué clase desea?
- Clase preferente. ¿A qué hora sale?
- Sale a las 22:50 y llega a las 08:12 del día siguiente.
- ¿De qué andén va a salir?
- Normalmente sale del andén número 3.
- Gracias. ¿Cuánto es?
- Son 52 euros con 10.
- Aquí tiene.

4
- Hola, ¿qué desea?
- Un billete para Málaga, por favor.
- ¿De ida y vuelta?
- Sí, ida y vuelta.
- ¿Clase preferente?
- No gracias, clase turista. ¡El AVE es muy caro! ¿A qué hora sale el próximo?
- Ahora mismo ha salido uno, el próximo es a las 11:35 del andén número 6.
- ¿A qué hora llega?
- Llega a las 14:07.
- ¿Cuánto es?
- Son 80 euros con 40.
- Aquí tiene, gracias. Adiós.
- Adiós.

*Answers:*
***1** Albacete; ida y vuelta; preferente; 18:18; 21:06; 4; 56,75; **2** Ciudad Real; ida; turista; 15:35; 17:25; 11; 9,15; **3** Barcelona; ida y vuelta; preferente; 22:50; 8:12 al día siguiente; 3; 52,10; **4** Málaga; ida y vuelta; turista; 11:35; 14:07; 6; 80,40*

AT 2.3–4 | L&S 1.4 | PLTS

**3 Practica la conversación de la actividad 1 con tu compañero. Cambia los elementos subrayados.**

Students practise the conversation from Activity 1 with a partner, using the information in the table to change the underlined text each time. After they have done it once, they swap roles and do it again. Volunteers could perform in front of the class.

AT 3.4 | R&W 2.2 | PLTS

**4 Lee y contesta a las preguntas.**

Students read the text and then answer the questions.

*Answers:*
***1** 293; **2** 13; **3** 1€; **4** 10 journeys over the whole of the network; **5** 02:00; **6** until the age of four*

AT 4.4

**5 Copia y completa la conversación con las palabras de la casilla.**

Students copy and complete the conversation with the words from the box.

*Answers:*
*billete; euro; línea; tres; cambiar; parada; dirección*

AT 1.4 | L&S 1.2

**6 Escucha y verifica.**

Students listen and check their answers.

**CD 2, track 5** **página 73, actividad 6**

- Un billete sencillo a Las Ventas, por favor.
- Aquí tiene, es un euro.
- ¿Qué línea es?
- Es la línea tres, dirección a Moncloa.
- ¿Tengo que cambiar?
- Sí, tiene que cambiar en la próxima parada y coger la línea dos con dirección a Las Rosas.
- Gracias.
- Adiós.

PLTS | AT 4.3–4 | R&W 2.4, 2.5

## Challenge

**Your friend who doesn't speak Spanish has asked you to buy him a first class 7-day return ticket for next Thursday morning from Madrid to Bilbao. Write out the conversation you would have at the ticket office. Check your times and prices at www.renfe.es.**

Encourage students to draw upon the vocabulary and grammar they have met in this spread.

## 2B.4 ¿Qué hiciste?

páginas 74–75

# Planner

### Objectives
- talk about what you did on a day out in the past
- use the preterite of common irregular verbs; adverbs
- extend your work to achieve a higher level

### Resources
Student Book, pages 74–75
CD 2, track 6
Foundation Workbook, page 43
Higher Workbook, page 43
Foundation Workbook audio, CD 3, track 44 (Workbook 24)
Higher Workbook audio, CD 4, track 25
Interactive OxBox, Unit 2B
Copymasters 53–60

### Video
Video clip, Unit 2B

### Key language
*fui en el teleférico; hice ciclismo; vi leones; pude tocar un delfín; di un paseo; tuve miedo; fue fabuloso; primero; después; luego; más tarde; antes de; después de; hizo calor; hizo frío; llovió; hizo sol; hizo viento; hizo buen tiempo; lo pasé bomba; lo pasé fenomenal; me encantó; me gustó mucho; fue divertido; fue emocionante; fue un desastre*

### Renewed Framework references
L&S 1.2, 1.4; R&W 2.4, 2.5; IU 3.2; KAL 4.4, 4.5, 4.6; LLS 5.4, 5.5

### PLTS
Activity 2: Independent enquirers; Reflective learners
Activity 4; Creative thinkers; Reflective learners
Activity 6: Creative thinkers
Challenge: Self-managers; Creative thinkers

### Starters
- Activity 2, page 74. You could turn this into a vocab quiz. Display or read out the words in jumbled order and give students a time limit of your choice to write down the English for these terms. Once they have written down all of the words/phrases, ask them to categorise them into four categories. Check answers as a class.
- In preparation for Activity 6, give students a time limit to write down:
  - as many Spanish adverbs as they can
  - as many Spanish connectives as they can
  - as many opinions as they can.

  Compare answers as a class and make a list of adverbs, connectives and opinions. Keep the list and check it again after completing Activity 6. Is there anything you can add to the list?

### Plenaries
- Activity 5, page 75. Following the discussion in pairs or small groups, have a whole class discussion. Display some useful phrases to help students, e.g. *En mi opinion...*
- Display a basic sentence, e.g. *Fui a Madrid.* and ask students to build on this to create a more sophisticated sentence, e.g. *Ayer fui a Madrid con...: primero...* Compare answers as a class.
- Students read out their presentations from the Challenge Activity to the class. The class listens and then votes for what they consider to be the best/most exciting/most unusual, etc. day out.

### Homework/Self-study
Gramática, page 74
Activity 3, page 74

AT 3.2–3 | LLS 5.4

**1 Empareja los dibujos con las frases.**
Students match the pictures to the sentences. Remind students to look first at vocabulary they do know and to use cognates to help them.

*Answers:*
***1*** *a;* ***2*** *d;* ***3*** *f;* ***4*** *g;* ***5*** *h;* ***6*** *c;* ***7*** *b;* ***8*** *e*

PLTS

### Gramática
Students do further work on the preterite tense, this time focusing on irregular verbs. To ensure that they are confident using this tense, ask them to write the meaning of each of the verbs in Activity 1 and then match them to their infinitive.

*Answers:*
***1*** *I went in a cable car. (ir);* ***2*** *I went cycling. (hacer);* ***3*** *I saw lions at the zoo. (ver);* ***4*** *I was able to touch a dolphin at the aquarium (poder);* ***5*** *I ate on the* Paseo de la Gastronomía. *(comer);* ***6*** *I took a walk by the lake. (dar);* ***7*** *I was frightened at the heme park. (tener);* ***8*** *It was fantastic. (ser)*
comer *is regular*

L&S 1.4 | LLS 5.5 | PLTS

**2 Lee las frases. Busca las palabras que no conozcas en un diccionario.**
Students read the words and phrases. Elicit from them that these are in the preterite tense. They look up any words they don't know in a dictionary. This will require students knowing the infinitive of verbs in the preterite. They should, however, already be familiar with many of these words and so this is more of a revision exercise.

AT 3.3

KAL 4.6

**3 Elige una pregunta (1–4) para cada sección (A–D).**
Students look at the four questions and match each of them to one of the sections, A, B, C, or D from Activity 2. Encourage students to think about other sections that could help them to produce a piece of extended writing.

*Answers:*
***1** B; **2** A; **3** D; **4** C*

PLTS

AT 4.4–5

**4 Describe tu día en Casa de Campo, o otro parque de atracciones. Usa las frases A–D.**
Encourage students to make their description as interesting as possible, using interesting adjectives and adverbs.

AT 1.6

L&S 1.2

IU 3.2

LLS 5.4

**5 Mira el video. ¿Es Roberto o Elena?**
Students watch the video clip for Unit 2B. Allow them to watch it as many times as necessary. Depending on the level of the class, you may choose to break it in smaller sections, pausing it to ensure they understand the plot. Students then read the statements and note down whether each one refers to Roberto or Elena.

**Video clip: Unit 2B (CD 2, track 6)**

**Part 1**
*Elena and Roberto have just arrived from Segovia at Chamartín Station*

Elena: *To camera*. Hoy estamos en Madrid. Esta es la estación de Chamartín. Es muy moderna.
Roberto: Pero no vinimos a Madrid a ver una estación de trenes.
Elena: No, pero es muy interesante. ¿Qué vamos a hacer hoy?
Roberto: Hoy voy a visitar el museo de El Prado.
Elena: Yo prefiero el arte moderno, voy a visitar el museo de Reina Sofía.
Roberto: También voy a visitar el Palacio Real.
Elena: ¡Qué aburrido! Solo te interesa la historia. Yo voy a ir a la Puerta del Sol.
Roberto: No es verdad. También voy a visitar el estadio del Real Madrid, el Santiago Bernabéu.
Elena: ¡Fútbol! No me interesa para nada. Yo voy a ir a Gran Vía a ver las tiendas.
Roberto: Bueno ¡yo no quiero ir de tiendas!
Elena: ¿Qué vamos a hacer entonces?
Roberto: Vamos a jugar, por supuesto. Vamos a visitar Madrid y sacar fotos y comprar entradas en cada lugar.
Elena: Y la persona que visite más lugares gana.
*Standing as if to go off for a race.*
Roberto: En sus marcas, ¡ya!

**Part 2**
Elena: Yo voy a ir en Metro y en bus porque Madrid tiene uno de los mejores Metros del mundo.
Roberto: Pero yo soy más original, voy a hacer un tour por Madrid en monopatín.
Roberto: Este es el Palacio Real, fue construido en 1892.
Elena: Esta es la Puerta del Sol, es donde viene la gente a celebrar el fin de año.
Roberto: Esto es la Plaza Mayor, en el siglo XV era la plaza de mercado.
Elena: Este es el Oso y el Madroño, símbolo de Madrid.

*Back at home*
Elena: ¡A ver, quién ha ganado!
Roberto: Seguro que fui yo.
Elena: ¿Por qué?
Roberto: Porque hice un tour súperrápido en monopatín y visité todos los monumentos importantes en dos horas.
Elena: ¿Monopatín?
Roberto: Mira.
Elena: ¡Hala, qué guay! ¿Y qué viste?
Roberto: Vi el Palacio Real y la Catedral de la Almudena. Y también la Plaza Mayor y el Templo de Debot.
Elena: El Templo de Debot, nunca he ido. ¿Es interesante?
Roberto: Sí, es egipcio pero como a ti no te gusta la historia….
Elena: Bueno, yo fui a la Puerta del Sol, y a Gran Vía.
Roberto: ¿Y qué te compraste?
Elena: ¡Nada para ti!
Roberto: Yo fui a Santiago Bernabéu.
Elena: ¿Y jugaste al futbol?
Roberto: ¿Visitaste al museo Reina Sofía?
Elena: Sí, mira la foto.
Roberto: Yo fui al Museo del Prado.
Elena: Entonces ¿Quién ha ganado?
Roberto: ¡No lo sé! Tenemos tantas fotos, tickets y folletos…
Elena: *To camera*. Decidid vosotros. ¿Quién ha visitado más lugares?
Roberto: Demasiado fácil. También tenéis que contarnos algo de cada lugar.
Elena: Suerte.

*Answers:*
***a** Roberto; **b** Roberto; **c** Roberto; **d** Elena; **e** Elena; **f** Roberto; **g** Elena; **h** Roberto*

AT 2.4–5

PLTS

**6 In your opinion, who had the best day out in Madrid? Why?**
Students work in pairs or small groups to discuss which of the characters, Roberto or Elena, they think spent the best day in Madrid. Encourage some disagreement and remind students that they should justify their opinion. Once students have discussed this in pairs or small groups, you could have a whole class discussion.

KAL 4.5

AT 3.6

**7 Lee el email e identifica:**
Analysing how tenses and other grammatical structures are used in context should help students in improving the level of their own written work. Elicit from students that including these elements in their own oral or written responses will ensure that they obtain a level 6 or above!

*Answers:*
***2 present tense verbs:*** *(any 2 of) sabes, me gusta, veo, es, quiero, soy;* ***2 past tense verbs:*** *(any 2 of) fui, hice, fue, visitamos, me gustó, visité, me encantó, hiciste;* ***2 future tense verbs:*** *(any 2 of) voy a ir, vamos a hacer…, voy a echar de menos;* ***2 adverbs that tell us how:*** *(any 2 of) rápidamente, tranquilamente, apresuradamente, lentamente;* ***2 adverbs that tell us when:*** *(any 2 of) normalmente, primero; durante; después; por la tarde, cuando;* ***2 connectives:*** *(any 2 of) como, sin embargo, porque, y, aunque, pero;* ***2 opinions:*** *¡Fue muy guay!, me gustó muchísimo, es muy impresionante;* ***2 reasons:*** *…porque quiero ver muchas cosas antes de volver, porque es muy impresionante, porque soy un fan del Real Madrid*

### Gramática
Remind students that while the majority of Spanish adverbs end in *–mente*, there are exceptions to this rule so they need to look out for these. Once they have listed all of the adverbs from Roberto's e-mail (they will already have found most of these in Activity 6), challenge students to use at least three of them in sentences of their own. Compare answers as a class.

AT 4.5–6

PLTS

R&W 2.4, 2.5

KAL 4.4, 4.5

### Challenge
**Prepare a presentation about an imaginary recent day out. Be as creative as possible. Use Activities 2 and 6 for ideas and structures.**
How much students write will depend largely on their ability, but encourage more able students to include as many of the elements from Activity 6 as possible. To achieve level 6, students must use the past, present and future tenses.

## 2B.5 ¿Dónde está?

páginas 76–77

# Planner

### Objectives
- recognise names of shops and give directions
- use simple imperatives and prepositions
- sound Spanish when pronouncing words with *z*, *ce* or *ci*

### Resources
Student Book, pages 76–77
CD 2, tracks 7–8
Foundation Workbook, page 44
Higher Workbook, page 44
Foundation Workbook audio, CD 3, track 45 (Workbook 25)
Higher Workbook audio, CD 4, track 26
Interactive OxBox, Unit 2B
Copymasters 53–60

### Renewed Framework references
L&S 1.1, 1.2, 1.4; R&W 2.4; LLS 5.8

### PLTS
Activity 3: Effective participators
Activity 4: Reflective learners
Activity 5: Reflective learners
Challenge: Self-managers; Reflective learners

### Starters
- Practise prepositions by playing a class game. Ask students to stand up behind their chairs. Explain to them that you will call out prepositions and they must position themselves accordingly, e.g. if you call out *al lado de* they should stand next to the desk or chair; if you call *delante de*, they stand in front of the desk or chair and so on. Start slowly and gradually get faster. Once students have got the hang of it, explain the last person to stand in the correct place will be out.
- Practise saying 'of the/from the'. Display the prepositions you practised in Starter Activity 1 and the shops featured in this spread. Go round the class asking each student in turn to choose a preposition and a shop and to put them together, e.g. *al lado*

*de* and *panadería* would become *al lado de la panadería* and so on.

## Plenaries

- Display a simple hand-drawn map, i.e. one main road with smaller roads branching off it at right-angles, with the names of shops placed in various positions: straight on, over the bridge, on the first road on the left, etc. Call out directions, e.g. *Tuerce a la izquierda y después a la derecha, luego sigue todo recto y va a estar en frente*. Students follow the directions and tell you where they have ended up on the map, e.g. *delante de los grandes almacenes*. Give the roads names, as this provides another way to refer to them, e.g. *Está a la izquierda después de la calle XXX*.
- Challenge students to write five sentences in the imperative, using regular *-ar*, *-er* and *-ir* verbs. Compare answers as a class.

## Homework/Self-study

Activity 5, page 77

AT 3.2–3

**1 Lee. ¿Verdad o mentira?**
Students have already met these prepositions so this activity serves to refresh their memories. They won't be familiar with all of the shop/stall names, however, so this is an ideal opportunity to introduce them to these.

*Answers:*
***1** mentira; **2** mentira; **3** mentira; **4** verdad; **5** verdad; **6** verdad*

AT 1.3 | L&S1.1, 1.2

**2 Escucha. ¿Qué tienda es?**
Students listen and note down which shop is being referred to each time.

**CD 2, track 7** — **página 76, actividad 2**

1. Está al lado de la carnicería, detrás de la cervecería.
2. Está al lado de la floristería, debajo del hotel.
3. Está enfrente de la frutería, al lado de la tienda de electrodomésticos.
4. Está detrás de la panadería, al lado de la frutería.
5. Está entre el supermercado y la carnicería.
6. Está al lado de la frutería, detrás de la tienda de ropa.

*Answers:*
***1** la pescadería; **2** la cervecería; **3** la tienda de ropa; **4** el supermercado; **5** la fruteria; **6** la carnicería*

AT 2.3 | PLTS | L&S1.4

**3 Mira el barrio La Latina. ¿Dónde están las tiendas donde comprar estos artículos?**
Practice of prepositions and the names of shops.

PLTS | AT 3.2

**4 Empareja 1–6 con a–f.**

*Answers:*
***1** d; **2** e; **3** a; **4** c; **5** b; **6** f*

## Gramática

Read through the grammar explanation as a class. Work through the examples given and to ensure that students have understood, ask them to fill in the table for other regular *-ar*, *-er* and *-ir* verbs.

PLTS | AT 3.3

**5 Lee y mira el mapa. ¿Adónde van?**
Students will already be familiar with giving and understanding directions.

*Answers:*
***1** la peluquería; **2** la tienda de ropa; **3** el restaurante; **4** el metro*

LLS 5.8

## Think

Students practise pronouncing the words listed. If possible, they should record themselves and then listen back to check their pronunciation. How Spanish do they sound?

**CD 2, track 8** — **página 77, Think**

izquierda, zagal, zamparse, Cecilia, cencerro, cizaña, cincel, zodíaco, zorro, zueco, zumbado, azucena.

AT 4.3–4 | R&W 2.4 | PLTS

## Challenge

**Don Quijote needs to do the following errands in Madrid. With a partner, prepare a list of directions he should follow.**
Students use the map of Barrio de Salamanca to give the directions. They should use the sentences in Activity 5 to help them.

## 2B.6 Labolengua

páginas 78–79

### *Planner*

**Objectives**
- review language and grammar from the unit

**Resources**
Student Book, pages 78–79
CD 2, track 9
Foundation Workbook, pages 45–46
Higher Workbook, pages 45–46
Interactive OxBox, Unit 2B
Copymasters 61–62

**Grammar**
- The preterite tense, adverbs

**Renewed Framework references**
R&W 2.4; KAL 4.1, 4.4, 4.5; LLS 5.1, 5.8

**PLTS**
All activities: Reflective learners/Self-managers
Activity 3: Creative thinkers

**Homework/Self-study**
Activity 3, page 79

### Comprender – the preterite tense and adverbs
### A The preterite tense of irregular verbs

KAL 4.5 | PLTS

**1 Complete the sentences with the preterite tense of the verb in brackets. Not all the verbs are irregular.**
Practice of conjugating verbs in the preterite tense.

*Answers:*
***1** fui, comí; **2** hizo, llamó, pudo; **3** estuvieron, hicieron, fue, pasaron; **4** di, fui, compré*

### B Adverbs

LLS 5.1 | PLTS

**2 Work out how to say these adverbs in Spanish. Look up the adjectives if necessary.**
Practice of forming adverbs in Spanish.

*Answers:*
*politely – polite – cortés – cortés – cortésmente*
*frequently – frequent – frecuente – frecuentemente*
*calmly – calm – tranquilo – tranquila – tranquilamente*
*sadly – sad – triste – tristemente*

### Aprender – improving your work
### C Climbing levels

AT 4.4–6 | R&W 2.4 | KAL4.4, 4.5 | LLS 5.8 | PLTS

**3 Imagine last weekend you went to a theme park. You are asked ... *¿Qué hiciste el fin de semana?* Start with a simple answer and use section C to help you build on it.**
Students use the advice given to produce a higher level piece of writing.

### Hablar – pronunciation
### D Words spelt the same as English

PLTS | KAL 4.1

**4 Practise pronouncing these 20 words out loud.**
Practice of pronouncing cognates correctly

PLTS

**5 Listen to the recording and check your pronunciation is accurate.**
Students check that they have pronounced the words from Activity 2 correctly.

**CD 2, track 9** — **página 79, actividad 5**

aeropuerto, autobús, dialecto, edificio, esencial, fascinar, gigante, ideal, injusto, horrendo, justicia, nacional, necesario, ocurrir, paciencia, recientemente, seducir, tragedia, urgencia, velocidad

## 2B.7 Extra Star

página 80

# Planner

### Objectives
- revise travel and getting around
- practise the preterite of the verb *ir*
- use common sense and cognates to rewrite a conversation

### Resources
Student Book, page 80
Copymaster 63

### Renewed Framework references
KAL 4.2

### PLTS
Activity 1: Reflective learners
Activity 4: Independent enquirers, Creative thinkers

AT 3.1 | PLTS | KAL 4.2

**1 Busca el intruso. ¿Por qué es intruso?**
Students revise the vocabulary they have met so far by choosing the odd one out each time.

*Answers:*
***1** museo – all others are means of transport; **2** plaza – all others are verbs; **3** estadio – all others are adjectives; **4** 20€ – others are train journey vocabulary*

AT 4.2–3

**2 ¿Adónde fuiste? ¿Cómo fuiste? Escribe las frases.**
Students use the prompts to write sentences saying where they went and how they got there.

*Answers:*
***1** Fui al Estadio Santiago. Fui a pie. **2** Fui al Museo del Prado. Fui en metro. **3** Fui Bernabéu a la Casa de Campo. Fui en teleférico. **4** Fui a la Plaza de Toros. Fui en autobús. **5** Fui al Parque Warner Bros. Fui en tren.*

AT 3.3–4

**3 Ordena la conversación.**
Students reorder the sentences so that the conversation makes sense.

*Answers:*
*f, j, e, a, b, d, h, i, k, l, m, c, g*

AT 4.2–4 | PLTS

**5 Investiga una de las principales atracciones de Madrid. Crea un poster con información para los visitantes.**
Students research one of Madrid's main attractions and create an information poster containing key information visitors may like to know. The information can be as simple or detailed as students' ability allows.

## 2B.7 Extra Plus

página 81

### *Planner*

**Objectives**

- buy travel tickets
- enhance sentences with adverbs
- invent conversations and role play

**Resources**

Student Book, page 81
Copymaster 64

**Renewed Framework references**

KAL 4.4

**PLTS**

Activity 1: Reflective learners

AT 3.4 | PLTS

**1 Lee las conversaciones. Copia y rellena la tabla.**

Students use the information in the conversations to complete the table.

*Answers:*

***1*** *Figueres; single; first class; 22:50; 13; 10:20; 64.60€;* ***2*** *Huelva; return; second class; 18:05; 11; 21:52; 84€*

AT 4.4

**2 Escribe las conversaciones.**

Students use the prompts to write their own conversations. They should refer back to Activity 1 for support if necessary.

KAL 4.4

**3 Complete these sentences using an appropriate adverb.**

There is more than one option in same cases so accept any sensible answers.

*Answers:*

***1*** *tranquilamente;* ***2*** *tarde;* ***3*** *tristemente;* ***4*** *completamente*

## 2B.8 Prueba

página 82

**Resources**
Student Book, page 82
CD 2, track 10
Assessment OxBox, Unit 2B

**Renewed Framework references**
L&S 1.1, 1.2, 1.4; R&W 2.2, 2.4; LLS 5.4

**PLTS**
All activities: Reflective learners

### Escuchar

AT 1.4–5 | L&S 1.1, 1.2 | PLTS

**Listen. True or false?**
This activity tests listening skills using the language covered in this unit.

**CD 2, track 10** — **página 82, actividad 1**

**1**

No me gusta demasiado el arte pero fui al museo a ver el *Guernica* de Pablo Picasso. Llegué al museo en metro y por suerte ese día el museo era gratis. El museo es muy grande y lo recomendaría sólo si te gusta mucho el arte. Yo prefiero pasear por la ciudad y ver monumentos.

**2**

Creo que es el mejor museo de España. Siempre voy al Prado cuando estoy en Madrid porque siempre hay nuevas exposiciones de arte. Todas las obras tienen una pequeña explicación lo cual es muy educativo. Me gusta mucho este museo.

**3**

Yo prefiero la escultura a la pintura. Lo que me gusta del museo es que no sólo hay cuadros, también hay esculturas. Ir al Prado en metro o autobús es muy fácil, yo recomendaría ir temprano para disfrutarlo más tranquilamente.

*Answers:* ***1*** *false;* ***2*** *true;* ***3*** *false;* ***4*** *true;* ***5*** *true;* ***6*** *false*

### Hablar

AT 2.4–5 | L&S 1.4 | PLTS

**Imagine last Saturday you went to Madrid. The pictures represent a snapshot of your day in the city. Tell your teacher about your weekend. Speak for as long as you can, trying to mention all the pictures featured.**
This activity tests speaking skills using the language covered in this unit.

### Leer

AT 3.4–5 | R&W 2.2 | LLS 5.4 | PLTS

**Read and answer the questions.**
This activity tests reading skills using the language covered in this unit.

*Answers:*
***1*** *between Toledo, Embajadores and Ronda de Toledo roads;*
***2*** *(one of) an entertaining walk, a surprise with every step;*
***3*** *it's fast and convenient;* ***4*** *'La Latina' as the market is in front of it;* ***5*** *(any three of) shoe shops, florist's, new and used clothes shops, electrical shops*

### Escribir

AT 4.4–5 | R&W 2.4 | PLTS

**Imagine you are on holiday in a foreign country. Write a blog entry about what you did yesterday.**
This activity tests writing skills using the language covered in this unit.

*Answers: Students' own answers*

## 2B Leer

página 152

**Resources**
Student Book, page 152

**Renewed Framework references**
LLS 5.4

**PLTS**
Activity 2: Reflective learners

LLS 5.4 AT 3.3 **1 Empareja las preguntas en español con las en inglés.**
Students match the Spanish and the English.

*Answers:*
***1** c; **2** h; **3** b; **4** i; **5** e; **6** g; **7** d; **8** a; **9** j; **10** f*

PLTS **2 How many questions can you answer without help?**
Students will have worked out what all of the questions mean in Activity 1, so this tests their knowledge of Madrid.

LLS 5.4 **3 ¿Cómo se dice en español?**

*Answers:*
***1** el atentado terrorista; **2** equipo de fútbol; **3** destaca; **4** carreteras*

LLS 5.4 **4 Empareja las respuestas con las preguntas de la actividad 1.**

*Answers:*
***1** 1819; **2** Nueva York; **3** 191; **4** Más o menos 2800; **5** Madrileños; **6** el Rayo Vallecano; **7** Barajas; **8** Es la capital a más altitud; **9** La Puerta del Sol; **10** El Barça*

### Follow-on

Students make up their own quiz about a town or city of their choice. The quiz can be as long as their ability allows and the questions, as difficult. With less able groups, work through some possible questions first. Once students have compiled their quiz, they can swap with a partner and answer the questions.

## Foundation Workbook

### Página 40 2B.1 ¿Vamos en bici?

- Use with Student Book, pages 68–69

AT 3.1 **1 Write the Spanish for these five places and five methods of transport. Then find them in the wordsearch. The words can be horizontal, vertical or diagonal.**

*Answers:*

| | | | | | | | | | | | | |
|---|---|---|---|---|---|---|---|---|---|---|---|---|
| | | C | I | N | E | | | | | | | |
| P | | | N | | | | | | | | | |
| | O | | S | | | | | | | | | |
| | | L | T | | M | E | T | R | O | A | | |
| | | | I | | U | | | | Z | | | |
| | | | T | D | S | | | A | | | | |
| | | | U | | E | | L | | | | | |
| | | | T | | O | P | | | | | | |
| | | N | O | I | V | A | O | | | | | |
| | | | | | | P | | R | | | | B |
| | | | | | | I | | | T | | | A |
| | | C | O | C | H | E | | | | I | | R |
| | | | | | | | | | | | V | C |
| | | | | | | | | | | | | O |

***a** school **instituto**; **b** cinema **cine**; **c** sports centre **polideportivo**; **d** museum **museo**; **e** square in a town **plaza**; **f** plane **avión**; **g** car **coche**; **h** underground **metro**; **i** on foot **a pie**; **j** boat **barco***

KAL 4.3 **2 Fill in the blanks with one of the following: *a*/*al*/*a la*/*a los*/*a las*.**

*Answers:*
***a** al; **b** a; **c** a las; **d** al; **e** a la; **f** a los*

AT 3.2 **3 Draw lines to match up the sentence halves.**
Remind students to think about grammar as well as meaning when matching the sentence halves.

*Answers:*
***1** d; **2** e; **3** a; **4** f; **5** b; **6** c*

AT 1.2 **4 Listen and check your answers to Activity 3.**

**CD 3, track 41 (Workbook 21)** **página 40, actividad 4**

1 Vivo en una ciudad que está en la costa.
2 Mis abuelos tienen un perro que es muy juguetón.
3 No me gustan los profesores que son aburridos.
4 Tenemos un coche que es bastante grande.
5 Lo que menos me gusta es hacer deberes.
6 Lo que más me gustó fue ir de compras.

## Página 41 2B.2 Planes para mañana

- Use with Student Book, pages 70–71

AT 3.1 **1 Write the correct caption next to each picture.**
Practice of places to visit vocabulary.

*Answers:*
***a** el museo; **b** el parque de atracciones; **c** el parque; **d** el centro comercial; **e** el zoo; **f** el estadio; **g** la playa; **h** la plaza de toros*

AT 1.3–4 L&S 1.1, 1.2 **2 Listen and tick the places that Marta is going to visit.**

**CD 3, track 42 (Workbook 22)** **página 41, actividad 2**

Vamos a ver … ¿Qué es lo que voy a hacer durante mis vacaciones? El lunes por la mañana voy a ir al Museo de Ciencias y por la tarde voy a ir de compras. El martes no voy a hacer nada, voy a descansar. El miércoles voy a ir al zoo todo el día porque me encantan los animales y el jueves, si hace sol, voy a ir a la playa por la tarde y por la mañana … voy a ir al estadio. No voy a ir a la plaza de toros porque no me gustan las corridas. Yo pienso que las corridas de toros son crueles.

*Answers:*
***a** museum; **d** shopping centre; **e** zoo; **f** football stadium; **g** beach*

KAL 4.5 **3 Fill in the blanks with a verb in the immediate future.**

*Answers:*
**a** ***Voy a comer*** en el restaurante. **b** ***Vamos a vivir*** en el campo. **c** ***Voy a alquilar*** un apartamento en Tenerife.

## Página 42 2B.3 Billetes de viaje

- Use with Student Book, pages 72–73

AT 3.1 AT 4.1 **1 Solve the clues by finding the correct Spanish word. Write the Spanish words in the grid to find the mystery phrase.**

*Answers:*

**C**
a **L**LEGA
b DE ID**A** Y VUELTA
c CLA**S**E PREFERENTE
d D**E** IDA
**T**
e **U**NABONO
**R**
f UNB**I**LLETE
g **S**ALE
**T**
h EL **A**NDÉN

AT 1.4 L&S 1.2 **2 Listen to the dialogues and fill in the table with the missing information.**
This practises the vocabulary needed to buy train tickets.

**CD 3, track 43 (Workbook 23)** **página 42, actividad 2**

**1**
– Hola, buenos días. ¿Qué desea?
– Dos billetes a San Sebastián, por favor.
– ¿De ida sólo o de ida y vuelta?
– De ida y vuelta.
– ¿Qué clase?
– Clase turista. Perdone, ¿a qué hora sale?
– Sale a las once y media del andén número 5.
– Y ¿a qué hora llega a San Sebastián?
– Llega a la una y cuarto.
– ¿Cuánto es?
– Son 42 euros.
– Aquí tiene.

**2**
– Hola, buenos días. ¿Qué desea?
– Un billete a Málaga.
– ¿De ida o de ida y vuelta?
– De ida. ¿A qué hora sale?
– Sale a las diez y cinco del andén número 4.
– Y ¿a qué hora llega a Málaga?
– Llega a las doce y veinticinco.
– ¿Cuánto es?
– Son 26 euros.
– Gracias, aquí tiene. Adiós.

**3**
– Buenas tardes, ¿qué desea?
– Tres billetes de ida a Valencia, por favor. Perdone, ¿A qué hora sale?
– Sale a las cuatro menos cinco.
– Y ¿a qué hora llega?
– Llega a las siete y veinte.
– ¿De qué andén sale?
– Del número 8.
– ¿Cuánto es?
– A ver, tres billetes de ida a Valencia. Son 54 euros.
– Aquí tiene.

*Answers:*

| | No. of tickets | Type | Departure time | Platform | Arrive time | Cost |
|---|---|---|---|---|---|---|
| 1 | 2 | Return | 11:30 | 5 | 1:15 | 42€ |
| 2 | 1 | Single | 10:05 | 4 | 12.25 | 26€ |
| 3 | 3 | Single | 15:55 | 8 | 19:20 | 54€ |

KAL 4.4 AT 3.3 **3 Unscramble the words to make correct sentences.**
Further practice of train station vocabulary.

*Answers:*
***a*** *Quiero un billete de ida y vuelta a Bilbao.* ***b*** *¿A qué hora sale el tren para Santiago?* ***c*** *El tren sale del andén número siete.* ***d*** *¿Cuánto cuesta un billete de ida a Alicante?* ***e*** *Tiene que cambiar en la próxima parada.*

## Página 43 2B.4 ¿Qué hiciste?

- Use with Student Book, pages 74–75

AT 3.2 **1 Write the correct caption under each picture in column 2.**

*Answers:*
***1*** *Hice ciclismo.* ***2*** *Jugué al baloncesto.* ***3*** *Di un paseo.* ***4*** *Vi leones.* ***5*** *Saqué fotos.* ***6*** *Visité un museo.*

KAL 4.6 AT 1.3 AT 2.3–4 **2 Listen to an example. Then listen to the questions, roll the dice and answer them. Your answers will be whatever you get from rolling the dice. Remember, you need to roll the dice four times.**

**CD 3, track 44 (Workbook 24)** **página 43, actividad 2**

Ejemplo
– ¿Qué hiciste?
– Más tarde jugué al baloncesto.
– ¿Qué tiempo hizo?
– Hizo mucho calor.
– ¿Qué tal lo pasaste?
– Lo pasé fenomenal.

– ¿Qué hiciste?
– ¿Qué tiempo hizo?
– ¿Qué tal lo pasaste?

**3 Play the game until you get to *Fue un desastre*.**

## Página 44 2B.5 ¿Dónde está?

- Use with Student Book, pages 76–77

AT 3.1 AT 4.1 **1 Where can you buy the following products? Write the name of the shop under each picture.**

*Answers:*
***a*** *carnicería;* ***b*** *floristería;* ***c*** *panadería;* ***d*** *pescadería;* ***e*** *tienda de electrodomésticos;* ***f*** *zapatería;* ***g*** *frutería*

AT 3.2 **2 Draw lines to match up each picture to the correct directions in Spanish.**

*Answers:*
***1*** *b;* ***2*** *d;* ***3*** *f;* ***4*** *g;* ***5*** *a;* ***6*** *c;* ***7*** *e*

AT 1.3 L&S 1.2 **3 Listen and write the letters of the directions given to each place.**

**CD 3, track 45 (Workbook 25)** **página 44, actividad 3**

**a**
– ¿Por dónde se va a la zapatería?
– Sigue todo recto, toma la primera calle a la izquierda y cruza el puente.

**b**
– ¿Por dónde se va al mercado?
– Cruza la calle, sigue todo recto y toma la tercera calle a la derecha.

**c**
– ¿Por dónde se va a la panadería?
– Tuerce a la izquierda, toma la segunda a la izquierda y sigue todo recto.

**d**
– ¿Por dónde se va a la pescadería?
– Sigue todo recto, cruza el puente y tuerce a la izquierda.

*Answers:*
***a*** *zapatería – b, a, f;* ***b*** *mercado – g, b, e;* ***c*** *panadería – d, c, b;* ***d*** *pescadería – b, f, d*

## Página 45 2B.6A Labolengua

- Use with Student Book, pages 78–79

KAL 4.5 **1 Draw lines to match up the English with the Spanish, then find the Spanish verbs in the wordsearch.**
Practice of the preterite.

*Answers:*
***1*** *e;* ***2*** *h;* ***3*** *g;* ***4*** *b;* ***5*** *c;* ***6*** *f;* ***7*** *a;* ***8*** *d*

| | | | | | | | | | |
|---|---|---|---|---|---|---|---|---|---|
| | | | | | | H | I | C | E |
| | | | | F | U | I | | | |
| | | | | | | C | | | |
| | | | | O | Z | I | H | | |
| | F | | | | | E | | | |
| T | U | V | E | | | R | | | |
| | I | | D | I | M | O | S | | |
| | M | | U | | | N | | | |
| | O | | P | | | | | | |
| | S | | | | | | | | |

KAL 4.5 **2 Complete the sentences using the verbs in Activity 1.**
Further practice of using the preterite tense.

*Answers:*
***a** hizo; **b** hicieron; **c** dimos, fuimos; **d** pude; **e** fui; **f** hice; **g** tuve*

LLS 5.1 **3 Work out how to say the adverbs in Spanish.**

*Answers:*

| | *Adjective* | *Adverb* | |
|---|---|---|---|
| 1 | *rápido (fast)* | ***rápidamente*** | *quickly* |
| 2 | *lento (slow)* | ***lentamente*** | *slowly* |
| 3 | *amable (kind)* | ***amablemente*** | *kindly* |
| 4 | *desgraciado (unfortunate)* | ***desgraciadamente*** | *unfortunately* |
| 5 | *triste (sad)* | ***tristemente*** | *sadly* |

### Página 46 2B.6B Técnica

- Use with Student Book, pages 78–79

**1 Read the paragraph below. Can you find the following things in it? Write them down.**

*Answers:*
***2 present tense verbs:** voy; vamos; dura; juego; escucho*
***2 past tense verbs:** fuimos; fui; hice; pasé; comí; cenamos; estaba; monté; fue; era; andaba; hicimos; me gustó; hizo; descansamos*
***2 future tense verbs:** voy a ir; voy a ver; voy a montar*
***2 adverbs that tell us 'how':** relajadamente; lentamente*
***2 adverbs that tells us 'when':** después; luego*
***2 connectives:** porque; pero; aunque*
***2 opinions:** estaba muy rica; fue un desastre*
***2 reasons:** no me gustó porque hizo mucho calor; fue un desastre porque el caballo era perezoso y andaba muy lentamente*

## Higher Workbook

### Página 40 2B.1 ¿Vamos en bici?

- Use with Student Book, pages 68–69

AT 3.1 **1 Write the Spanish for these five places and five methods of transport. Then find them in the wordsearch.**

*Answers:*

| | | | | | | | | | | | | |
|---|---|---|---|---|---|---|---|---|---|---|---|---|
| | | C | I | N | E | | | | | | | |
| P | | | N | | | | | | | | | |
| | O | | S | | | | | | | | | |
| | | L | T | | M | E | T | R | O | A | | |
| | | | I | | U | | | | Z | | | |
| | | | T | D | S | | | A | | | | |
| | | | U | | E | | L | | | | | |
| | | | T | | O | P | | | | | | |
| | | N | O | I | V | A | O | | | | | |
| | | | | | | P | | R | | | | B |
| | | | | | | I | | | T | | | A |
| | | C | O | C | H | E | | | | I | | R |
| | | | | | | | | | | | V | C |
| | | | | | | | | | | | | O |

***a** school **instituto**; **b** cinema **cine**; **c** sports centre **polideportivo**; **d** museum **museo**; **e** square in a town **plaza**; **f** plane **avión**; **g** car **coche**; **h** underground **metro**; **i** on foot **a pie**; **j** boat **barco***

AT 3.3 KAL 4.4 **2 Unscramble the words to make correct sentences.**
Remind students to think about grammar as well as meaning.

*Answers:*
***a** Vivo en una ciudad que está en la costa. **b** Mis abuelos tienen un perro que es muy juguetón. **c** No me gustan los profesores que son aburridos. **d** Tenemos un coche que es bastante grande. **e** Lo que menos me gusta es hacer deberes. **f** Lo que más me gustó fue ir de compras*

AT 1.2 **3 Listen and check your answers to Activity 2.**

**CD 4, track 22** **página 40, actividad 3**

**a** Vivo en una ciudad que está en la costa.
**b** Mis abuelos tienen un perro que es muy juguetón.
**c** No me gustan los profesores que son aburridos.
**d** Tenemos un coche que es bastante grande.
**e** Lo que menos me gusta es hacer deberes.
**f** Lo que más me gustó fue ir de compras.

## Página 41 2B.2 Planes para mañana

- Use with Student Book, pages 70–71

AT 4.2

**1 Write a caption for each picture.**
Practice of places to visit vocabulary.

*Answer:*
***a** el museo; **b** el parque de atracciones; **c** el parque; **d** el centro comercial; **e** el zoo; **f** el estadio; **g** la playa; **h** la plaza de toros*

AT 1.4–5 | L&S 1.1, 1.2

**2 Listen to Marta's plans and fill in the table in English.**

**CD 4, track 23** — **página 41, actividades 2 y 3**

Vamos a ver ... ¿Qué es lo que voy a hacer durante mis vacaciones? El lunes por la mañana voy a ir al Museo de Ciencias y por la tarde voy a ir de compras. El martes no voy a hacer nada, voy a descansar. El miércoles voy a ir al zoo todo el día porque me encantan los animales y el jueves, si hace sol, voy a ir a la playa por la tarde y por la mañana ... voy a ir al estadio. No voy a ir a la plaza de toros porque no me gustan las corridas. Yo pienso que las corridas de toros son crueles.

*Answers:*

| | Morning | Afternoon |
|---|---|---|
| Monday | *science museum* | *shopping* |
| Tuesday | / | / |
| Wednesday | *zoo* | *zoo* |
| Thursday | *stadium* | *beach* |

AT 1.4–5 | L&S 1.1, 1.2

**3 Listen again. Why is she not going to go to the bullring?**

*Answer: because she thinks bull fights are cruel*

AT 4.3–4 | KAL 4.5

**4 Write three more sentences saying what you are going to do next week in the evenings.**
Students should refer to pages 70 and 71 of the Student Book for ideas and support if necessary.

## Página 42 2B.3 Billetes de viaje

- Use with Student Book, pages 72–73

AT 4.2

**1 Fill in the Spanish translations of these verbs in the grid to find a mystery phrase.**

*Answers:*

C
**a** L L E G A
**b** D E I D A Y V U E L T A
**c** C L A S E P R E F E R E N T E
**d** D E I D A
T
**e** U N A E O N O
R
**f** U N B I L L E T E
**g** S A L E
T
**h** E L A N D É N

AT 1.4 | L&S 1.1, 1.2

**2 Listen to the dialogues and fill in the table with the missing information.**
This practises the vocabulary needed to buy train tickets.

**CD 4, track 24** — **página 42, actividad 2**

**1**

- Hola, buenos días. ¿Qué desea?
- Dos billetes a San Sebastián, por favor.
- ¿De ida sólo o de ida y vuelta?
- De ida y vuelta.
- ¿Qué clase?
- Clase turista. Perdone, ¿a qué hora sale?
- Sale a las once y media del andén número 5.
- Y ¿a qué hora llega a San Sebastián?
- Llega a la una y cuarto.
- ¿Cuánto es?
- Son 42 euros.
- Aquí tiene.

**2**

- Hola, buenos días. ¿Qué desea?
- Un billete a Málaga.
- ¿De ida o de ida y vuelta?
- De ida. ¿A qué hora sale?
- Sale a las diez y cinco del andén número 4.
- Y ¿a qué hora llega a Málaga?
- Llega a las doce y veinticinco.
- ¿Cuánto es?
- Son 26 euros.
- Gracias, aquí tiene. Adiós.

**3**
- Buenas tardes, ¿qué desea?
- Tres billetes de ida a Valencia, por favor. Perdone, ¿A qué hora sale?
- Sale a las cuatro menos cinco.
- Y ¿a qué hora llega?
- Llega a las siete y veinte.
- ¿De qué andén sale?
- Del número 8.
- ¿Cuánto es?
- A ver, tres billetes de ida a Valencia. Son 54 euros.
- Aquí tiene.

*Answers:*

| | *No. of tickets* | *Type* | *Departure time* | *Platform* | *Arrive time* | *Cost* |
|---|---|---|---|---|---|---|
| *1* | *2* | *Return* | *11:30* | *5* | *1:15* | *42€* |
| *2* | *1* | *Single* | *10:05* | *4* | *12.25* | *26€* |
| *3* | *3* | *Single* | *15:55* | *8* | *19:20* | *54€* |

KAL 4.4 AT 3.3 **3 Unscramble the words to make correct sentences.**
Further practice of train station vocabulary.

*Answers:*
***a** Quiero un billete de ida y vuelta a Bilbao. **b** ¿A qué hora sale el tren para Santiago? **c** El tren sale del andén número siete. **d** ¿Cuánto cuesta un billete de ida a Alicante? **e** Tiene que cambiar en la próxima parada*

## Página 43 2B.4 ¿Qué hiciste?

- Use with Student Book, pages 74–75

AT 4.3 **1 Write a caption under each picture in column 2 to say what you did.**

*Answers:*
***1** Hice ciclismo. **2** Jugué al baloncesto. **3** Di un paseo. **4** Vi leones. **5** Saqué fotos. **6** Visité un museo.*

AT 2.3 **2 First listen to an example.**

KAL 4.6 AT 1.3 AT 2.3–4 **3 Now listen to the questions and roll the dice to get the answers. Remember, you will need to roll the dice four times. Play the game until you get to "*Fue un desastre*".**

**CD 4, track 25** **página 43, actividades 2 y 3**

Ejemplo
- ¿Qué hiciste?
- Más tarde jugué al baloncesto.
- ¿Qué tiempo hizo?
- Hizo mucho calor.
- ¿Qué tal lo pasaste?
- Lo pasé fenomenal.

- ¿Qué hiciste?
- ¿Qué tiempo hizo?
- ¿Qué tal lo pasaste?

## Página 44 2B.5 ¿Dónde está?

- Use with Student Book, pages 76–77

AT 4.2 **1 Where can you buy the following products? Write the name of the shop under each picture.**

*Answers:*
***a** carnicería; **b** floristería; **c** panadería; **d** pescadería; **e** tienda de electrodomésticos; **f** zapatería; **g** frutería*

AT 3.2 **2 Draw lines to match up each picture to the correct directions in Spanish.**

*Answers:*
***1** b; **2** d; **3** f; **4** g; **5** a; **6** c; **7** e*

AT 1.3 L&S 1.1, 1.2 **3 Listen and complete the directions given to each place.**

**CD 4, track 26** **página 44, actividad 3**

**a**
- ¿Por dónde se va a la zapatería?
- Sigue todo recto, toma la primera calle a la izquierda y cruza el puente.

**b**
- ¿Por dónde se va al mercado?
- Cruza la calle, sigue todo recto y toma la tercera calle a la derecha.

**c**
- ¿Por dónde se va a la panadería?
- Tuerce a la izquierda, toma la segunda a la izquierda y sigue todo recto.

**d**
- ¿Por dónde se va a la pescadería?
- Sigue todo recto, cruza el puente y tuerce a la izquierda.

*Answers:*
***a** zapatería: go straight ahead, take the first on the left and cross the bridge; **b** mercado: cross the street, go straight ahead and take the third on the right; **c** panadería: turn left, take the second on the left and go straight ahead; **d** pescadería: go straight ahead, cross the bridge and turn left*

## Página 45 2B.6A Labolengua

- Use with Student Book, pages 78–79

KAL 4.5 **1 Write the verbs in Spanish next to the English. Then find the Spanish verbs in the wordsearch.**
Practice of the preterite tense.

*Answers:*
***a** fui; **b** hicieron; **c** hice; **d** dimos; **e** pude; **f** tuve; **g** fuimos; **h** hizo*

| | | | | | | | | | |
|---|---|---|---|---|---|---|---|---|---|
| | | | | | | H | I | C | E |
| | | | | F | U | I | | | |
| | | | | | | C | | | |
| | | | | O | Z | I | H | | |
| | F | | | | | E | | | |
| T | U | V | E | | | R | | | |
| | I | | D | I | M | O | S | | |
| | M | | U | | | N | | | |
| | O | | P | | | | | | |
| | S | | | | | | | | |

KAL 4.5 **2 Complete the sentences using the verbs in Activity 1.**
Further practice of using the preterite tense.

*Answers:*
***a** hizo; **b** hicieron; **c** dimos, fuimos; **d** pude; **e** fui; **f** hice; **g** tuve*

LLS 5.1 **3 Fill in the column of adjectives. Then work out how to say the adverbs in Spanish.**

*Answers:*

| | ***Adjective*** | ***Adverb*** | |
|---|---|---|---|
| *1* | *rápido (fast)* | ***rápidamente*** | *quickly* |
| *2* | *lento (slow)* | ***lentamente*** | *slowly* |
| *3* | *amable (kind)* | ***amablemente*** | *kindly* |
| *4* | *desgraciado (unfortunate)* | ***desgraciadamente*** | *unfortunately* |
| *5* | *triste (sad)* | ***tristemente*** | *sadly* |

## Página 46 2B.6B Técnica

- Use with Student Book, pages 78–79

**1 Read the paragraph below. Can you find the following things in it? Write them down.**

*Answers:*
***10 present tense verbs:** voy – I go; me encanta – I love; vamos – we go; dura – it lasts; juego – I play; me gusta – I like; tengo – I have; es – it is; escucho – I listen; tiene – it has*
***11 past tense verbs:** (11 of) fuimos – we went; fui – I went; hice – I did; pasé – I spent; comí – I ate; cenamos – we had dinner; estaba – it was; monté – I rode; fue – it was; era – it was; hicimos – we did; me gusto – I liked; hizo – it was; descansamos – we relaxed*
***3 future tense verbs:** voy a ir – I am going to go; voy a ver – I am going to see; voy a montar – I am going to ride*
***2 adverbs that tell us 'how':** relajadamente – relaxing; lentamente – slowly*
***2 adverbs that tells us 'when':** después – afterwards; luego – then*
***3 connectives:** porque – because; pero – but; aunque – although*
***2 opinions:** estaba muy rica – it was very nice; fue un desastre – it was a disaster*
***2 reasons:** (2 of ) no me gustó porque hizo mucho calor – I did not like it because it was very hot; no me gusta ir en avión porque a veces es muy aburrido – I don't like going by plane because sometimes it is boring; ... porque me encanta la comida italiana – ... because I like Italian food; ... porque el caballo era perezoso y andaba may lentamente – ... because the horse was lazy and travelled very slowly; ... porque el hotel es de cinco estrellas y tiene una piscina enorme – because it is a five-star hotel and has an enormous swimming pool.*

# 3A Bienestar

## Unit Objectives

**Contexts and cultural focus:** health and wellbeing
**Grammar:** question words and frequency words; reflexives in the past and present tenses; the verb *doler*; impersonal 'se' constructions *se juega, se necesita, se puede;* the imperfect and preterite
**Language learning:** practising memorising skills; adapting previously learnt language in a new context; understanding instructions; listening for detail; revising and extending language already covered

- *Aim*: To learn to talk about healthy/unhealthy lifestyles and different sports
- Each unit has an associated video which will feature throughout the unit. Below is the transcript of the video for this unit.

**Video clip: Unit 3A (CD 2, tracks 20 and 21)**

**Part 1**

*Juan and Roberto are running in the park.*

Juan: Te gusta correr, ¿a que sí Roberto?
Roberto: En Colombia voy a correr tres o cuatro veces a la semana.
Juan: Yo voy a escalada cinco veces a la semana. Me gustaría ir 7, pero es que no hay curso.
Roberto: Es lo bueno de correr, no tienes que hacer curso. Puede hacerlo uno solo.
Juan: Pues, el primo de un amigo mío es un atleta, y es campeón de Cross. Está en la selección española.
Roberto: ¿De verdad?
Juan: Sí. ¿Te gustaría conocerle?
Roberto: ¡Pues claro!
Juan: ¿Y qué me compras a cambio?
Roberto: Un helado.
Juan: No, tienes que comprarme un helado todos los días.
Roberto: Pero un helado todos los días no es muy bueno para la salud.
Juan: Bueno, si no quieres conocer a Javier Guerra Polo…
Roberto: De acuerdo, de acuerdo, te compro un helado todos los días….

**Part 2**

*At the sports ground Javier is working out. The boys now come up to him.*

Juan: Hola Javier.
Javier: Hola. Encantado.
Juan: Este es mi primo Roberto.
Javier: Encantado. Juan me ha dicho que te gusta correr.
Roberto: Sí, me gusta pero no soy ni muy bueno ni muy rápido. ¿Cuánto tiempo llevas tú corriendo?
Javier: Pues bueno yo, yo llevo ya once años entrenando al máximo nivel, y la verdad es que estoy encantado hacer el deporte que hago.
Roberto: ¿Cuántos años tienes, ya?
Javier: Pues, tengo veintisiete y en noviembre hago veintiocho.
Roberto: ¿Cuántas veces a la semana tienes que entrenar?
Javier: Entreno todos los días, de lunes a domingo, y luego hay tres o cuatro días que entreno por la mañana y por la tarde.
Roberto: ¿Y cuántas horas al día se necesitan de entrenamiento para ser un atleta internacional como tú?
Javier: Pues bueno, eh, por las mañanas entrenamos de once a una y media y luego por las tardes de seis a ocho.
Roberto: ¿Y qué haces en los entrenamientos?
Javier: Pues bueno, me hablo con mi entrenador y él tiene una planificación. Normalmente hacemos dos días de correr y más luego fortalecimiento en el gimnasio para prevenir lesiones. Y luego, dos o tres días hacemos entrenamiento en la pista para mejorar la velocidad y el fondo. ¿Quieres hacer un poco de entrenamiento conmigo?
Roberto: Sí, por favor.
Javier: Juan, y tú también.
Juan: Bueno, lo primero de todo, pones las manos detrás de la línea. Ponte bien las pies, levantamos el cuerpo, ¡y salimos! Y ahora vamos a hacer unos abdominales. ¡Vamos, venga!
Juan: ¡Venga!
Roberto: Es muy intenso, me duele de todo. Es muy duro.
Javier: La vida del atleta es muy sacrificada y hay que estar muchas horas entrenando para conseguir el máximo nivel. Hay que hacer muchos ejercicios y sufrir mucho para poder conseguir lo máximo.
Roberto: ¿No tienes miedo de lesionarte?
Javier: Sí, la verdad es que es muy difícil porque hay que cuidarse mucho, hay que ir al masajista, y para no lesionarse hay que fortalecer mucho el cuerpo. Entonces, hay que entrenar muy duro.

Roberto: ¿Qué es lo más difícil de ser atleta?

Javier: Pues, ahora mismo lo más difícil es el entrenar todos los días a la semana, una o dos horas al día o cuatro como te he dicho antes. Y sobre todo, por luego, el entrenamiento invisible que es cuidarte mucho, ir al fisio, comer bien y sobre todo, pues, no salir por la noche porque para los deportistas no es bueno.

Roberto: ¿Y cuáles son tus ambiciones para el futuro?

Javier: Pues, ahora mismo me estoy preparando en la prueba de maratón para intentar acudir a los juegos olímpicos del año que viene de Londres 2012. Y bueno, es un reto difícil pero tengo mucha ilusión y a ver si puedo conseguirlo.

Roberto: ¿Y cuáles son tus consejos para mantenerse en forma?

Javier: Bueno chicos, pues, lo primero de todo es que llevéis una buena alimentación. Luego, también, pues salir tres o cuatro días a correr por semana. Y luego es intentar descansar por la noche lo máximo posible para llevar un buen ejerció.

Roberto: Entonces ¿comer helados todos los días no es muy bueno para la salud?

Javier: Claro que no.

Juan: Pero de vez en cuando está bien ¿no?

Javier: De vez en cuando, sí. Bueno chicos, voy a continuar con el entrenamiento. Hasta luego. *Runs off.*

Juan & Roberto: Hasta luego.

Juan: Bueno, si solo puedo tomar helado de vez en cuando tiene que ser uno superbueno y supergrande.

Roberto: ¡Eres imposible!

Juan: ¡Venga Roberto, voy a ganar otra vez!

**Punto Lengua**

En Colombia voy a correr tres o cuatro veces a la semana.
Hay que hacer muchos ejercicios…
Es muy intenso, me duele de todo.
Entonces ¿comer helados todos los días no es muy bueno para la salud?

As a starter activity to introduce the unit and familiarise students with the language they will meet, view the video as a whole. Are there any words or phrases that they have recognised from this single viewing? What do they think it is about? You might like to explain what 'el cross' is or see if student can deduce it. Play Part 1 again a couple of times, as this sets the scene. Do students recognise any of the sports mentioned? What opinions are given? This starts students thinking about the video and will help them understand it better when you return to look at it in more detail later in this unit.

*Synopsis:*

Juan offers to introduce Roberto to Javier, an athlete he knows – but for a price! Roberto must buy him an ice-cream every day. Juan and Roberto go to meet and talk to Javier about his lifestyle and training. Juan has kept his promise, but with all the talk about healthy eating decides that eating ice-cream every day is not really a good idea!

| Unit 3A Bienestar Overview grid | | | | | | |
|---|---|---|---|---|---|---|
| **Page reference** | **Contexts and objectives** | **Language learning** | **Grammar** | **Key language** | **Framework** | **AT level** |
| Pages 84–85 **Vida sana** | • talk about what you have to/ must do to maintain a healthy lifestyle | • practise memorising skills | • revise question words and frequency words | *en forma; vago/a; gordo/a; la rutina; cambiar; sano/a; malsano/a; el polideportivo; acostarse(ue); las chucherías; siempre; a veces; cada; a menudo; casi nunca; rara vez; nunca; seguir; dormir; perder peso; saludable* | L&S 1.1, 1.2, 1.4; R&W 2.2; KAL 4.4, 4.6; LLS 5.2 | 1.4–5, 2.3, 3.1 3.3–4, 4.3–4 |
| Pages 86–87 **Cuerpo sano** | • identify parts of the body and discuss keeping fit | • adapt previously learnt language in a new context | • use reflexives in past and present tenses | *la cabeza; el cuerpo; la mano; el brazo; el dedo; el dedo gordo; la espalda; el estómago; los ojos; el ombligo; la oreja; la nariz; la pierna; la rodilla; el tobillo; el corazón; encima de; por delante; por detrás; doblar; poner; fumar; beber* | L&S 1.1, 1.2, 1.4; R&W 2.4; KAL 4.5 | 1.2–3, 1.5, 2.1, 3.4, 4.1, 4.4–5 |
| Pages 88–89 **Malestar** | • talk about illnesses and injuries | • understand instructions | • use the verb *doler* | *doler (ue); un dolor; los dientes; una fiebre; la garganta; romper (roto); torcer (torcido); sentirse mal; caer(se); hacer (hecho); una crema; una pastilla; un jarabe; una tirita/ venda; la farmacia* | L&S 1.2, 1.4; R&W 2.4, 2.5; IU 3.1 | 1.3–5, 2.4, 4.4–6 |
| Pages 90–91 **Nos encanta el deporte** | • discuss sports and how you play them | • listen for detail | • the impersonal se *(se juega, se necesita, se puede)* | *la natación; la escalada; el baloncesto; el voleibol; el cross; el judo; el skate; el fútbol; excepto; incluso; patinar; un casco; una tabla; un equipo; unas zapatillas; unas ruedas* | L&S 1.2; R&W 2.4; IU 3.2; KAL 4.4, 4.5; LLS 5.1 | 1.4–5, 3.2, 3.4, 4.3–4 |
| Pages 92–93 **Deporte y salud** | • talk more about sport and sporting accidents | • revise and extend language already covered | • use the imperfect | | L&S 1.1, 1.2, 1.4, 1.5; R&W 2.2, 2.4, 2.5; KAL 4.5 | 1.3, 2.4–6, 3.5, 4.2–6 |
| Pages 94–95 **Labolengua** | • review language and grammar from the unit | | | | KAL 4.5; LLS 5.1, 5.2 | |

| Unit 3A Bienestar Overview grid | | | | | | |
|---|---|---|---|---|---|---|
| **Page reference** | **Contexts and objectives** | **Language learning** | **Grammar** | **Key language** | **Framework** | **AT level** |
| Pages 96–97<br>**Extra Star**<br>**Extra Plus** | • differentiated extension/ homework material | • revise and consolidate all vocabulary and grammar covered in the unit | • revise and consolidate all vocabulary and grammar covered in the unit | | R&W 2.2, 2.4, 2.5;<br>KAL 4.4, 4.5,<br>LLS 5.2 | 3.1, 3.3–5, 4.2, 4.4–5 |
| Page 98<br>**Prueba** | • end-of-unit test | | | | L&S 1.1, 1.2, 1.4;<br>R&W 2.2;<br>KAL 4.4;<br>LLS 5.4 | 1.4, 2.4, 3.4, 4.3 |
| Page 99<br>**Vocabulario** | • a summary of the key language covered in each core spread of this unit | | | | | |
| Page 153<br>**Leer 3A** | • practice of longer reading texts based on the theme of the unit | | | | R&W 2.1, 2.2;<br>KAL 4.5 | 3.4, 3.6, 4.4 |

| **Week-by-week overview**<br>**(Three-year KS3 Route: assuming six weeks' work or approximately 10–12.5 hours)**<br>**(Two-year KS3 Route: assuming four weeks' worth or approxmately 6.5–8.5 hours)** | | | | | |
|---|---|---|---|---|---|
| **About Unit 3A, *Bienestar:*** Students work in the context of health and wellbeing. They talk about what you have to/ought to do to maintain a healthy lifestyle, identify parts of the body and discuss keeping fit and talk about illnesses and injuries. They also discuss which sports they like doing and how you play them. Students revise question words and frequency words, they use reflexives in the past and present tenses, the verb *doler*, the reflexive constructions: *se juega, se necesita, se puede,* and the imperfect and preterite. The unit also provides tips on language learning techniques. | | | | | |
| **Three-Year KS3 Route** | | | **Two-Year KS3 Route** | | |
| **Week** | **Resources** | **Objectives** | **Week** | **Resources** | **Objectives** |
| **1** | **3A.1 Vida sana**<br>**3A.6 Labolengua D**<br>(p.95) | talk about what you have to/must do to maintain a healthy lifestyle<br>practise memorising skills<br>revise question words and frequency words | **1** | **3A.1 Vida sana**<br>(Omit activities 1, Think, 6 & Challenge)<br>**3A.6 Labolengua D**<br>(p.95) | talk about what you have to/must do to maintain a healthy lifestyle<br>practise memorising skills revise question words and frequency words |
| **2** | **3A.2 Cuerpo sano** | identify parts of the body and discuss keeping fit<br>adapt previously learnt language in a new context<br>use reflexives in past and present tenses | **2** | **3A.2 Cuerpo sano**<br>(Omit activities Think, 4 & Gramática) | identify parts of the body and discuss keeping fit<br>adapt previously learnt language in a new context<br>use reflexives in past and present tenses |
| **3** | **3A.3 Malestar**<br>**3A.6 Labolengua A**<br>(p.94) | talk about illnesses and injuries<br>understand instructions<br>use the verb *doler* | **3** | **3A.3 Malestar**<br>(Omit Gramática & Challenge)<br>**3A.6 Labolengua A**<br>(p.94) | talk about illnesses and injuries<br>understand instructions<br>use the verb *doler* |
| **4** | **3A.4 Nos encanta el deporte**<br>**3A.6 Labolengua C**<br>(p.95) | discuss sports and how you play them<br>listen for detail<br>the impersonal *se (se juega, se necesita, se puede)* | **4** | **3A.4 Nos encanta el deporte**<br>(Omit Think, Activity 7 & Challenge)<br>**3A.6 Labolengua C**<br>(p.95)<br>**3A.8 Prueba** (p.98)<br>**Vocabulario** (p.99) | discuss sports and how you play them<br>listen for detail<br>the impersonal *se (se juega, se necesita, se puede)*<br>Prepare and carry out assessment in all four skills<br>Recapping on vocabulary of the unit |

| Three-Year KS3 Route | | | Two-Year KS3 Route | | |
|---|---|---|---|---|---|
| **Week** | **Resources** | **Objectives** | **Week** | **Resources** | **Objectives** |
| **5** | **3A.5 Deporte y salud**<br>**3A.6 Labolengua B** (p.94) | talk more about sport and sporting accidents<br>revise and extend language already covered<br>use the imperfect and preterite | | | |
| **6** | **3A.7 Extra (Star)** (p.96)<br>**3A.7 Extra (Plus)** (p.97)<br>**3A.8 Prueba** (p.98)<br>**Vocabulario** (p.99)<br>**Leer** (p.153) | Further reinforcement and extension of the language of the unit.<br>Prepare and carry out assessment in all four skills<br>Recapping on vocabulary of the unit<br>Further reading to explore the language of the unit and cultural themes | | | |

## 3A.1 Vida sana

páginas 84–85

# *Planner*

### Objectives
- talk about what you have to/must do to maintain a healthy lifestyle
- revise question words and frequency words
- practise memorising skills

### Skills:

### Resources
Student Book, pages 84–85
CD 2, tracks 11–12
Foundation Workbook, page 48
Higher Workbook, page 48
Foundation Workbook audio, CD 3, track 46 (Workbook 26)
Higher Workbook audio, CD 4, track 27
Interactive OxBox, Unit 3A
Copymasters 66–73

### Key language
*en forma; vago/a; gordo/a; la rutina; cambiar; sano/a; malsano/a; el polideportivo; acostarse(ue); las chucherías; siempre; a veces; cada; a menudo; casi nunca; rara vez; nunca; seguir; dormir; perder peso; saludable*

### Renewed Framework references
L&S 1.1, 1.2, 1.4; R&W 2.2; KAL 4.4, 4.6; LLS 5.2

### PLTS
Think: Self-managers; Independent enquirers
Gramática: Reflective learners
Challenge: Team workers; Effective participators; Reflective learners

### Starters
- Display the key language and give students a time limit to write the English for each item. They have come across all of this language before and so this should be a revision exercise. Once the time is up, check answers as a class.
- Go round the class asking each student to use at least one of the words from the key language list in a sentence. More able students should be able to produce extended sentences incorporating some of the grammar and vocabulary from previous spreads.

### Plenaries
- Once students have worked through the Grammar explanation, ask them to analyse the example sentences. What part of the verb follows *debes, tienes que* and *necesitas?* Once they have decided on a rule they tell a partner and check if he or she has the same rule. Once the whole class has agreed on a rule, ask students to translate 'One must eat fruit every day'.
- Following Activity 9, students write six resolutions saying what they are going to do/eat to stay healthy.

### Homework/Self-study
Think Activity, page 84
Gramática – students come up with their own sentences using the expressions from the Grammar box

LLS 5.2 | KAL 4.6 | AT 3.1

**1 Busca las palabras en inglés en la culebra. Emparéjalas con las palabras en español a–h.**
All of these question words have been used by students frequently in *Zoom español* 1 and in the previous units of *Zoom español* 2. This spread serves to consolidate this language and encourage students really to try to learn them by heart.

*Answers:*
*how – g; where – e; when – a; what – c; who – h; which – d; how many – b; what time – f*

PLTS | KAL 4.6

**Think**
Keeping this in mind will be help students write and speak better Spanish and will help in their understanding of written and spoken Spanish.

AT 1.4 | L&S 1.1, 1.2 | KAL 4.6

**2 Escucha y escribe las partículas interrogativas en orden.**
Students listen and put the question words into the order they hear them. They can write just the letters from Activity 1 as an answer but it would be more beneficial if they wrote each question word out on a learning card to make sure they have the correct spelling/meaningand that they know exactly where to place the written accent

**CD 2, track 11** — **página 84, actividades 2 y 3**

- ¿Cuándo tienes clase de deporte en el insti?
- Tenemos deporte en el insti todas las semanas pero a menudo le digo al profe que estoy enfermo.
- ¿Cómo pasas tu tiempo libre?
- Siempre escucho música o veo la tele.

- ¿Cuántas horas pasas delante de la tele?
- A menudo paso tres horas en el sofá viendo la tele o escuchando música.
- ¿A qué hora te acuestas normalmente?
- Todas los días me acuesto muy tarde, pasada la medianoche.
- ¿A quién admiras como deportista?
- No admiro a ningún deportista. Prefiero las estrellas de cine.
- ¿Sabes dónde está el polideportivo?
- A ver … casi nunca voy al polideportivo.
- Qué deporte practicas?
- Rara vez practico deporte.
- ¿Qué comes para llevar una vida sana?
- Todos los días como chucherías. No me interesa la comida sana.
- ¿Cómo podemos ayudarte a cambiar de rutina y ponerte en forma?
- Mire usted, no me interesa estar en forma. Prefiero ser un vago y estar gordo. Por favor no traten de cambiar mi rutina.

*Answers:*
*¿Cuándo?; ¿Cómo?; ¿Cuántas?; ¿A qué hora?; ¿Quién?; ¿Dónde?; ¿Cuál?; ¿Qué?; ¿Cómo?*

AT 1.4 | L&S 1.1, 1.2 | KAL 4.6

**3 Escucha la entrevista otra vez y pon las preguntas en orden.**
Students listen again and this time, put the questions into the correct order.

*Answer: 3, 2, 5, 4, 6, 1*

AT 3.3–4 | R&W 2.2 | KAL 4.6

**4 Lee las respuestas de abajo y empáréjalas con una pregunta de la actividad 3. ¿Es una vida sana?**
Students match the answers with the questions from Activity 3.

*Answers:* ***a** 4; **b** 2; **c** 6; **d** 3; **e** 1; **f** 5*

AT 4.3–4 | L&S1.4

**5 Ahora contesta tú a las preguntas.**
Students now answer the questions for themselves.

AT 2.3 | L&S1.4 | KAL 4.6

**6 Practica el diálogo con un compañero.**
This is a good opportunity for students to practise using the correct intonation when asking and answering questions. Ensure that students swap roles once they have been through the dialogue once so that they practise both asking and answering questions.

PLTS

**Gramática**
As a class, revise these expressions. Once students have looked at the examples given you could ask them to come up with some examples of their own to ensure that they understand how to use these terms.

AT 1.4–5 | L&S1.2 | KAL 4.4

**7 Lee las respuestas. Luego escucha y decide quién, Roberto o Elena, dice…**
Students listen carefully to Roberto and Elena talk about how healthy they are and decide who says each of the statements listed.

**CD 2, track 12** — **página 85, actividades 7 y 8**

- Vamos a ver Elena, yo creo que llevo una vida más saludable que tú.
- Pues yo no lo creo. Yo estoy mil veces más sana que tú.
- Vale pues a ver entonces… ¿Qué comiste ayer?
- Bueno, lo que pasa es que quiero perder peso …
- De modo que no comiste nada, ¿verdad?
- Comí cereales y fruta y fui al gimnasio.
- En cambio yo jugué dos horas a baloncesto.
- A mí no me gusta el baloncesto.
- ¿A qué hora te levantaste?
- Como siempre, me levanté temprano a las seis y media.
- ¿Qué desayunaste?
- Pues fruta porque …
- ¿Te acostaste con hambre, ¿verdad?
- Pues sí; vale vale, tienes razón pero …

*Answers:*
***1** Roberto; **2** Roberto; **3** Elena; **4** Elena; **5** Elena; **6** Roberto; **7** Roberto; **8** Elena; **9** Elena; **10** Elena*

AT 1.4–5

**8 Escucha otra vez y verifica.**
Students listen again to check their answers to Activity 7.

AT 3.3

**9 Lee el quiz y contesta a las preguntas.**
A fun way to try and learn the vocabulary of the spread.

AT 4.4 | PLTS

**Challenge**
**Write five pieces of advice for people who get between 13 and 18 points in the quiz.**
An alternative to this would be for partners to exchange their quiz papers and for each one to check the other's work and give them a verdict/ assessment on their lifestyle.

## 3A.2 Cuerpo sano

páginas 86–87

# Planner

### Objectives

- identify parts of the body and discuss keeping fit
- use reflexives in past and present tenses
- adapt previously learnt language in a new context

### Resources

Student Book, pages 86–87
CD 2, tracks 13–15
Foundation Workbook, page 49
Higher Workbook, page 49
Interactive OxBox, Unit 3A
Copymasters 66–73

### Key language

*la cabeza; el cuerpo; la mano; el brazo; el dedo; el dedo gordo; el hombro; la espalda; el estómago; el ombligo; la nariz; la pierna; la rodilla; el tobillo; el corazón; encima de; por delante; por detrás; doblar; poner; fumar; beber*

### Renewed Framework references

L&S 1.1, 1.2, 1.4; R&W 2.4; KAL 4.5

### PLTS

Think (1): Reflective learners
Think (2): Reflective learners
Activity 6: Reflective learners
Challenge: Creative thinkers; Reflective learners

### Starters

- To revise parts of the body, play a class game. Call out a part of the body, e.g. *la cabeza*. Students point to their head. Carry on with other parts of the body. Once students are confident with this, point to e.g. your head and ask them to say what it is in Spanish.
- Revise frequency words as a class. Display a list of activities on the theme of the spread, e.g. *ir al polideportivo; levantaba pesas en el gimnasio,* etc. and a list of frequency words, e.g. *siempre; todos los días; los lunes; tres veces a la semana,* etc. Students work with a partner to say how often they do each activity. Compare answers as a class.

### Plenaries

- Challenge students to write five sentences using reflexive verbs. Compare answers as a class. More able students should be able to produce sentences using different persons.
- Following Activity 7, students produce their own list of advice on how to stay/get fit.

### Homework/Self-study

Gramática, page 86
Activity 9, page 87

AT 1.2 L&S 1.2 **1 Escucha la clase de yoga. Repite e indica la parte del cuerpo mencionada.**
Students point to the body part on the drawing or on themselves. Repeating the names for the parts of the body after hearing then will also help the learning/memorising process. This activity also revises prepositions.

**CD 2, track 13** **página 86, actividades 1 y 2**

Primero vamos a poner las manos sobre la cabeza durante un minuto. Eso nos ayudará a descansar el cuerpo entero.
Luego hay que tocarse los hombros y girar los brazos hacia adelante y después hacia atrás.
Después vamos a doblar el cuerpo, ¡y tocarnos el ombligo con la nariz!
Luego, con las piernas rectas vamos a tocarnos el dedo gordo con la palma de la mano.
Finalmente levantaremos la rodilla izquierda primero y luego la rodilla derecha hasta tocarnos el estómago.

*Answers:*
***1** cabeza; manos; cuerpo; **2** hombros; brazos; **3** cuerpo; ombligo; nariz; **4** piernas; dedo gordo; mano; **5** rodilla; estómago*

AT 1.3 L&S1.2 **2 Escucha otra vez. ¿Cuáles no se mencionan?**
Students listen again and this time note down which body parts aren't mentioned.

*Answers:*
*el tobillo; los dientes; los dedos; la espalda; el corazón*

PLTS **Think**
Students should notice that the definite article is used.

AT 2.1 L&S 1.4 **3 ¡Contrarreloj! A jugar por turnos.**
This activity serves to help students memorise parts of the body.

AT 4.1 **4 Escribe una "sopa de letras" para diez partes del cuerpo – 10 letras por 10 letras. Cámbiala con un compañero.**
Further practice of parts of the body.

PLTS KAL 4.5 **Gramática**
Revision of reflexive verbs. To ensure that students have fully understood how these are formed, ask them to use *levantarse* in a sentence in the present, preterite and imperfect tense.

AT 1.3 L&S 1.1, 1.2 **5 Escucha la entrevista y anota las partes del cuerpo mencionadas.**
Students listen and note down the parts of the body that are mentioned.

**CD 2, track 14** **página 87, actividades 5 y 6**

- Cuando tenía tu edad quería ser atleta olímpico así que iba al polideportivo todos los días.
- ¿Y qué hacía?
- Pues los lunes siempre levantaba pesas en el gimnasio para reforzar los brazos.
- ¿Qué más?
- Tres veces a la semana iba a la piscina y nadaba unos quinientos metros para reforzar las piernas.
- ¿Eso es todo?
- Pues corría en el parque todas las mañanas para respirar aire limpio y tener fuerte el corazón.
- ¿Y nunca se relajaba?
- Claro que sí. Me relajaba haciendo yoga todas las noches en mi dormitorio así tranquilizaba la cabeza.

*Answers: brazos; piernas; corazón; cabeza*

PLTS KAL 4.5 **Think**
Students should be able to tell you that the older person is speaking about the past. They should also recognise that they are using the imperfect tense as they are talking about what used to happen.

AT 1.5 PLTS L&S 1.2 **6 Escucha otra vez. Copia y completa la tabla.**
Students met the imperfect tense in Unit 1B and have practised using it in each unit since then so shouldn't have any problems completing the table.

*Answers:*
*ejercicio; en el polideportivo; todos los días*
*levantaba pesas; en el gimnasio; los lunes*
*nadar unos quinientos metros; a la piscina; tres veces a la semana*
*corría; en el parque; todas las mañanas*
*haciendo yoga; en mi dormitorio; todas las noches*

AT 1.5 L&S 1.2 **7 Escucha la parte final de la entrevista. Anota los cinco consejos en inglés.**
Students listen and translate the advice into English.

**CD 2, track 15** **página 87, actividad 7**

- ¡Entonces llevaba una vida muy sana!
- Sí, no fumaba ni bebía alcohol en exceso.
- Me imagino que se levantaba temprano, ¿verdad?
- Claro. Cada mañana me levantaba a las seis en punto pero siempre dormía ocho horas.
- ¿Y qué comía?
- Pues comía platos saludables: ¡no comía chucherías como tú!

*Answers:*
*don't smoke; don't drink; get up early (at 6am); sleep 8 hours; eat healthy food*

AT 3.4 KAL 4.5 **8 Lee el texto y anota los nueve verbos reflexivos.**
This encourages students to read the text in detail in order to find the reflexive verbs.

*Answers:*
*me levanto; me pongo; me voy; me ducho; me lavo; me pongo; me relajo; me acuesto; me duermo*

AT 4.4–5 KAL 4.5 **9 Escribe los verbos en pasado para explicar lo que hiciste.**
This is an ideal homework activity, although you may want to go through it orally in class first.

AT 4.4–5 R&W 2.4 PLTS **Challenge**
**Write a paragraph about how you keep fit. Say what you did in the last week. Include healthy and unhealthy things!**
Remind students that they will need to use more than one tense in order to obtain a level 5.

## 3A.3 Malestar

páginas 88–89

### Planner

**Objectives**
- talk about illnesses and injuries
- use the verb *doler*
- understand instructions

**Resources**
Student Book, pages 88–89
CD 2, tracks 16–18
Foundation Workbook, page 50
Higher Workbook, page 50
Interactive OxBox, Unit 3A
Copymasters 66–73

**Key language**
*doler (ue); un dolor; las muelas/los dientes; una fiebre; la garganta; romper (roto); torcer (torcido); sentirse mal; caer(se); hacer (hecho); una crema; una pastilla; un jarabe; una tirita/venda; la farmacia*

**Renewed Framework references**
L&S 1.2, 1.4; R&W 2.4, 2.5; IU3.1

**PLTS**
Activity 5: Team workers; Effective participators
Challenge: Creative thinkers; Self-managers

**Starters**
- Work through the *Gramática* Activity on page 88 to revise parts of the body before students start work on the spread.
- Explain to students that you are going to practise talking about illnesses and injuries. Start by calling out an injury/illness, e.g. *Me duelen los dientes.* Students must point to their teeth, and so on. Once students are confident with doing this, swap roles so that you point to your head, teeth, knee, etc. and a volunteer must say in Spanish what the injury/illness is. So, if you point to your head, *Me duele la cabeza.* More able students could also use the third person singular.

**Plenaries**
- Challenge students to write five sentences in the preterite saying what they hurt. Depending on the level of the class, ask students to extend these sentences to say how they hurt themselves, which could also provide practice of the imperfect tense.
- Have a class quiz based on Activity 6. Once students have listened to the recording and completed the table, split them into teams and quiz them on the transcript, e.g. *Me duele la garganta: tengo que tomar este* ________ ________ *veces al día.* The team that gets the most points wins. It is up to you what type of questions you set. You may want to ask questions in English to test their comprehension of the Spanish

**Homework/Self-study**
Activity 7, page 89

### Gramática

Read through the grammar explanation with students before they attempt Activity 1. Quickly revise the parts of the body from page 86 3A.2.

AT 1.3 | L&S 1.2

**1 Escucha. Empareja lo que dice cada persona con su dibujo. No se necesitan todos los dibujos.**
Students listen and match the speakers to the pictures. Point out that they won't need all of the pictures and so must listen carefully. Give them a moment to look at the pictures and think about the vocabulary they are likely to hear.

**CD 2, track 16** — **página 88, actividades 1 y 2**

1 Ay doctor, me siento mal pero que muy mal. Me duelen los dientes. Comí demasiados caramelos.
2 Mira, mamá – me duele mucho el tobillo. Creo que me lo torcí cuando me caí en el patio.
3 A ver, a ver ese dedo – me corté el dedo y me duele mucho.
4 Me caí y mira, tengo el brazo roto.
5 Tengo fiebre y me duele la garganta; creo que tomé demasiado sol en la playa.
6 La espalda me duele bastante. Me parece que me la doblé mientras hacía gimnasia en el insti.

*Answers:* ***1** c; **2** b; **3** d; **4** f; **5** h, e; **6** g*

AT 1.4–5
L&S 1.2

**2 Escucha otra vez e indica porqué tiene el problema. Luego busca las frases en inglés en la casilla.**
Students listen again, this time for details in order to note down why each speaker is suffering. Note: there is more information on the use of the preterite and imperfect tense on page 94, *Labolengua*.

*Answers:*
***1** d – I ate too many sweets.; **2** f – I twisted my ankle.; **3** e – I cut my finger.; **4** c – I fell over.; **5** b – I spent too much time in the sun.; **6** a – I strained my back.*

AT 1.4
AT 3.4
L&S1.2
IU 3.1

**3 Roberto está en la farmacia. Escucha y lee la conversación.**
Before they listen to the recording, explain to students that chemist's in Spain offer excellent provision and advice.

**CD 2, track 17** **página 89, actividad 3**

- Buenos días. ¿En qué puedo ayudarte?
- Es que tengo mucha fiebre y me duele la cabeza.
- ¿Qué hiciste ayer?
- Ayer pasamos horas en la piscina. Hizo mucho sol.
- Me parece que tienes una insolación grave.
- ¿Qué debo hacer entonces? ¿Qué me recomienda usted?
- Tienes que quedarte en casa y beber mucha agua. También puedes toma estas pastillas tres veces al día.
- Gracias – le agradezco mucho.
- De nada. ¡Hay que tener más cuidado con el sol!

AT 1.4–5

**4 Contesta a las preguntas.**
Students listen again and this time answer the questions.

*Answers:*
***1** He has a high temperature and a headache. **2** He has bad sunstroke. **3** Stay at home, drink lots of water and take the tablets three times a day. **4** to be more careful in the sun*

AT 2.4
L&S 1.4
PLTS

**5 Practica la conversación de la actividad 3.**
Remind students to pay attention to pronunciation and try to sound as Spanish as possible. They should swap roles once they have practised the conversation once so that they get to practise both parts.

AT 1.4
L&S 1.2

**6 Escucha las instrucciones y copia y completa la tabla.**
Students listen and then copy and complete the table.

**CD 2, track 18** **página 89, actividad 6**

**1**
- Ay, mamá, me duele la garganta.
- Ah, pobrecito. Tienes que tomar este jarabe tres veces al día.

**2**
- Ay, doctor, tengo un dolor de espalda terrible.
- Bueno, vamos a ver. Tienes que quedarte en la cama todo el día y tomar dos de estas pastillas dos veces al día.

**3**
- Ay, ay – señora dentista, me duelen los dientes – es un dolor horrible.
- Vale, vale, no es para tanto. Tienes que ponerte esta crema sobre el diente afectado y tomar una pastilla para el dolor – una pastilla nada más.

**4**
- Ay, me corté la rodilla y me duele mucho.
- A ver, a ver. Ah sí, te has cortado. Tienes que ponerte una tirita y pasar el día en casa. Toma una pastilla en seguida y otra a la noche cuando te acuestes.

**5**
- Ay, me duele el dedo gordo. No sé lo que tengo pero me duele mucho.
- Bueno, bueno – me parece que no es algo grave. Tienes que ponerte esta crema cuatro veces al día durante cinco días a ver si se reduce la inflamación. Y además, toma dos de estas pastillas ahora y dos todas los días durante los próximos cinco días.

*Answers:*
***1** me duele la garganta; jarabe; tres veces al día; **2** tengo un dolor en la espalda; quedarse en la cama/tomar dos pastillas; todo el día/dos veces al día; **3** me duelen los dientes; crema/una pastilla; una pastilla nada más; **4** me corté la rodilla; una tirita/el día en casa/una pastilla; en seguida y en la noche; **5** me duele el dedo; crema/dos pastillas; cuatro veces al día durante cinco días/ahora y dos cada día durante los cinco días*

AT 4.4

**7 Escribe una conversación en la farmacia. Usa las frases en la actividad 6.**
This activity consolidates what students have learnt so far in this spread. It also practises different tenses.

PLTS
AT 4.4–6
R&W 2.4, 2.5

## Challenge

**Make up a new conversation in a pharmacy. Use the past tense to get a higher level (say what happened to you). Use the immediate future to get an even higher level (say what you are not going to do in the future – perhaps, for Roberto, not stay in the sun so long!).**
Encourage students to draw upon the vocabulary and grammar they have met in this spread.

## 3A.4 Nos encanta el deporte

páginas 90–91

# Planner

### Objectives

- discuss sports and how you play them
- the impersonal *se* (*se juega, se necesita, se puede*)
- listen for detail

### Resources

Student Book, pages 90–91
CD 2, tracks 19–21
Foundation Workbook, page 51
Higher Workbook, page 51
Foundation Workbook audio, CD 3, track 47 (Workbook 27)
Higher Workbook audio, CD 4, track 28
Interactive OxBox, Unit 3A
Copymasters 66–73

### Video

Video clip, Unit 3A

### Key language

*la natación; la escalada; el baloncesto; el voleibol; el cross; el judo; el skate; el fútbol; excepto; incluso; un casco; una tabla; un equipo; unas zapatillas; unas ruedas*

### Renewed Framework references

L&S 1.2; R&W 2.4; IU 3.2; KAL 4.4, 4.5; LLS 5.1

### PLTS

Activity 3: Creative thinkers
Activity 6: Reflective learners
Activity 7: Reflective learners
Challenge: Self-managers; Creative thinkers

### Starters

- Display the key language and, depending on the level of the class, either give students a time limit to write the English for each item, or display the English translations in jumbled order and ask students to match them to the Spanish. Check answers as a class.
- Play a quick-fire memory game to revise sports. Start by saying, *Me gusta la natación*. The next student continues, *Me gusta la natación y el voleibol*. and so on around the class. When students run out of sports, they could start using negatives, e.g. *Me gusta la natación, el voleibol, etc. pero no me gusta la escalada.*

### Plenaries

- Students write five sentences on the theme of the spread using reflexive constructions.
- Students work in pairs to invent a new sport. They should have fun thinking up the most bizarre sport possible using as many of the reflexive constructions as possible to explain how it is played and what equipment is needed. Once each pair has invented their sport, they should come up with a name for it. Each pair then presents their sport to the class who judges who has invented the most unusual one.

### Homework/Self-study

After reading through the Think box, students write some sentences in Spanish saying what sports they do.
Gramática, page 91

AT 3.4 | R&W 2.2

**1 Empareja los dibujos con las palabras de la casilla.**
Students note down the number of the picture and the sport in Spanish.

*Answers:*
***a** el fútbol;* ***b** el skate;* ***c** la natación;* ***d** el judo;* ***f** el baloncesto;* ***g** el cross*

AT 1.4 | L&S 1.2

**2 Escucha y copia y completa la tabla.**
Students listen again and this time copy and complete the table.

**CD 2, track 19** — **página 90, actividad 2**

Muy buenos días. El polideportivo municipal le informa del nuevo programa de verano.
Las clases de natación para los menores de diez años comienzan los lunes a las dos de la tarde y se repiten los jueves a las diez de la mañana.
Si le interesa usar las facilidades de escalada el muro está disponible los cinco días de la semana desde el mediodía hasta las cuatro de la tarde.
Hay nuevas instalaciones para los jóvenes que quieren practicar skate. Están abiertas todos los días, incluido sábados y domingos de diez de la mañana a diez de la noche.
Para los entusiastas del judo tenemos clases de todos los niveles los sábados por la mañana desde las nueve y media hasta las once y media.

*Answers:*
***1** natación; lunes/14h y jueves/10h; dos veces; **2** escalada; lunes a viernes; 12–16h; cinco veces; **3** skate; todos los días; 10–22h; siete veces; **4** judo; sábados; 9:30h–11:30h; una vez*

AT 4.3–4 | PLTS | R&W 2.4

**3 Inventa información para tres clases más. Usa tus apuntes de la actividad 2 para ayudarte.**
Students use what they have done in Activities 1 and 2 to invent three more sports classes. Encourage students to make the classes as interesting as possible.

AT 1.4–5 | L&S 1.2 | IU 3.2

**4 Mira el video (primera parte) y contesta a las preguntas en inglés.**
Students watch part 1 of the video clip for Unit 3A. Allow them to watch it as many times as necessary. Depending on the level of the class, you may choose to break it in smaller sections, pausing it to ensure that students understand the plot. Students then answer the questions.

**Video clip: Unit 3A (CD 2, track 20)**

**Part 1**
*Juan and Roberto are running in the park.*
Juan: Te gusta correr, ¿a que sí Roberto?
Roberto: En Colombia voy a correr tres o cuatro veces a la semana.
Juan: Yo voy a escalada cinco veces a la semana. Me gustaría ir 7, pero es que no hay curso.
Roberto: Es lo bueno de correr, no tienes que hacer curso. Puede hacerlo uno solo.
Juan: Pues, el primo de un amigo mío es un atleta, y es campeón de cross. Está en la selección española.
Roberto: ¿De verdad?
Juan: Sí. ¿Te gustaría conocerle?
Roberto: ¡Pues claro!
Juan: ¿Y qué me compras a cambio?
Roberto: Un helado.
Juan: No, tienes que comprarme un helado todos los días.
Roberto: Pero un helado todos los días no es muy bueno para la salud.
Juan: Bueno, si no quieres conocer a Javier Guerra Polo…
Roberto: De acuerdo, de acuerdo, te compro un helado todos los días….

*Answers:*
***a** running and climbing; **b** Roberto runs three or four times a week and Juan climbs five times a week; **c** you don't need to attend a class*

## Gramática

Read through the explanation and look at the examples. Ask students to look through the reading passages to find other examples of the impersonal *se*. You could also make copies of the transcripts for them so that they can also look through these.

**5 Empareja los dibujos con la palabra adecuada. de la casilla**
Students match the pictures with the correct words.

*Answers:*
***a** un casco; **b** unas ruedas; **c** unas zapatillas; **d** una tabla (de surf); **e** un equipo*

AT 3.4 | PLTS

**6 Lee las descripciones y emparéjalas con una foto.**
Students read the descriptions and match each one to the appropriate photo.

*Answers: **1** b; **2** a; **3** c*

AT 3.4 | PLTS | LLS 5.1

**7 Anota todas las expresiones impersonales.**
Students look again at descriptions in Activity 6 and note down any occurences of the impersonal *se*.

AT 4.4

**8 Sigue los ejemplos de la actividad 6 y escribe un párrafo para la foto que sobra.**

AT 1.5 | L&S 1.2 | IU 3.2

**9 Mira el video y escoge la respuesta adecuada.**
Students watch the second part of the video and then answer the questions.

**Video clip: Unit 3A (CD 2, track 21)**

**Part 2**
*At the sports ground Javier is working out. The boys now come up to him.*
Juan: Hola Javier.
Javier: Hola. Encantado.
Juan: Este es mi primo Roberto.
Javier: Encantado. Juan me ha dicho que te gusta correr.
Roberto: Sí, me gusta pero no soy ni muy bueno ni muy rápido. ¿Cuánto tiempo llevas tú corriendo?
Javier: Pues bueno yo, yo llevo ya once años entrenando al máximo nivel, y la verdad es que estoy encantado hacer el deporte que hago.

Roberto: ¿Cuántos años tienes, ya?
Javier: Pues, tengo veintisiete y en noviembre hago veintiocho.
Roberto: ¿Cuántas veces a la semana tienes que entrenar?
Javier: Entreno todos los días, de lunes a domingo, y luego hay tres o cuatro días que entreno por la mañana y por la tarde.
Roberto: ¿Y cuántas horas al día se necesitan de entrenamiento para ser un atleta internacional como tú?
Javier: Pues bueno, eh, por las mañanas entrenamos de once a una y media y luego por las tardes de seis a ocho.
Roberto: ¿Y qué haces en los entrenamientos?
Javier: Pues bueno, me hablo con mi entrenador y él tiene una planificación. Normalmente hacemos dos días de correr y más luego fortalecimiento en el gimnasio para prevenir lesiones. Y luego, dos o tres días hacemos entrenamiento en la pista para mejorar la velocidad y el fondo.
¿Quieres hacer un poco de entrenamiento conmigo?
Roberto: Sí, por favor.
Javier: Juan, y tú también.
Juan: Bueno, lo primero de todo, pones las manos detrás de la línea. Ponte bien las pies, levantamos el cuerpo, ¡y salimos!
Y ahora vamos a hacer unos abdominales. ¡Vamos, venga!
Juan: ¡Venga!
Roberto: Es muy intenso, me duele de todo. Es muy duro.
Javier: La vida del atleta es muy sacrificada y hay que estar muchas horas entrenando para conseguir el máximo nivel. Hay que hacer muchos ejercicios y sufrir mucho para poder conseguir lo máximo.
Roberto: ¿No tienes miedo de lesionarte?
Javier: Sí, la verdad es que es muy difícil porque hay que cuidarse mucho, hay que ir al masajista, y para no lesionarse hay que fortalecer mucho el cuerpo. Entonces, hay que entrenar muy duro.
Roberto: ¿Qué es lo más difícil de ser atleta?
Javier: Pues, ahora mismo lo más difícil es el entrenar todos los días a la semana, una o dos horas al día o cuatro como te he dicho antes. Y sobre todo, por luego, el entrenamiento invisible que es cuidarte mucho, ir al fisio, comer bien y sobre todo, pues, no salir por la noche porque para los deportistas no es bueno.
Roberto: ¿Y cuáles son tus ambiciones para el futuro?
Javier: Pues, ahora mismo me estoy preparando en la prueba de maratón para intentar acudir a los juegos olímpicos del año que viene de Londres 2012. Y bueno, es un reto difícil pero tengo mucha ilusión y a ver si puedo conseguirlo.
Roberto: ¿Y cuáles son tus consejos para mantenerse en forma?
Javier: Bueno chicos, pues, lo primero de todo es que llevéis una buena alimentación. Luego, también, pues salir tres o cuatro días a correr por semana. Y luego es intentar descansar por la noche lo máximo posible para llevar un buen ejercicio.
Roberto: Entonces ¿comer helados todos los días no es muy bueno para la salud?
Javier: Claro que no.
Juan: *Throwing a look at Roberto.* Pero de vez en cuando está bien ¿no?
Javier: De vez en cuando, sí. Bueno chicos, voy a continuar con el entrenamiento. Hasta luego. *Runs off.*
Juan & Roberto: Hasta luego.
Juan: Bueno, si solo puedo tomar helado de vez en cuando tiene que ser uno superbueno y supergrande.
Roberto: ¡Eres imposible!
Juan: ¡Venga Roberto, voy a ganar otra vez!

*Answers:*
***a** 27 (28 in November); **b** 11; **c** todos los días; **d** nacional*

AT 1.5 | L&S 1.2 | IU 3.2

**10 Write down in English three pieces of advice Javier gives about keeping fit.**

*Answers:*
*eat well, go running 3 or 4 times a week, get as much rest as possible at night*

AT 1.5 | L&S 1.2 | IU 3.2

**11 What is his ambition?**

*Answers:*
*to take part in the 2012 Olympic Games*

AT 4.4 | PLTS | R&W 2.4 | KAL 4.4, 4.5

## Challenge

**Choose an unusual sport and write a brief paragraph about it. Explain how, where, and when (how often) it is played; what equipment you need; why you think it is interesting or different. Use words such as *muy, bastante, un poco and demasiado* to add emphasis to your writing.**

Once students have finished this, you could pool all work and then see if class can guess which sport each person has written about. Explain to students that to obtain a level 5 or 6, they will need to use a variety of tenses, e.g. say when the sport began, where it used to be played, if they will go and watch/ play this sport in the near future, etc. They will also need to give opinions as well as describe the sport.

## 3A.5 Deporte y salud

páginas 92–93

# Planner

### Objectives
- talk more about sport and sporting accidents
- use the imperfect
- revise and extend language already covered

### Resources
Student Book, pages 92–93
CD 2, tracks 22–23
Foundation Workbook, page 52
Higher Workbook, page 52
Interactive OxBox, Unit 3A
Copymasters 66–73

### Renewed Framework references
L&S 1.1, 1.2, 1.4, 1.5; R&W 2.2, 2.4, 2.5; KAL 4.5

### PLTS
Activity 2: Creative thinkers
Activity 6: Self-managers; Independent enquirers
Activity 8: Reflective learners
Activity 11: Reflective learners; Creative thinkers; Self-managers
Challenge: Reflective learners; Team workers; Effective participators

### Starters
- Recap on how to form the imperfect and preterite tenses. Can students remember the ending for each verb type? Once you have come up with a class rule, ask students to write two sentences and in preterite and two in the imperfect tense on the theme of the spread. Compare answers as a class.
- Revise sports in Spanish. Ask students to list as many sports as they can. You could give them a time limit. Compare answers as a class. Has anyone managed to list a sport that no one else has? Once the list is complete, ask students to use two of these sports in sentences.

### Plenaries
- Play a class game on healthy/unhealthy lifestyles. Split the class into two teams. Call out an activity, e.g. *El otro día jugaba al baloncesto*. Each team must decide if it is healthy or unhealthy. Then change it around and call out *sana* or *insana*. Each team must give you an appropriate healthy or unhealthy activity.
- Ask students to change Teresa's speech bubble from Activity 10 so that her lifestyle is completely healthy.

### Homework/Self-study
Activity 4, page 92
Activity 11, page 93

AT 1.3 | L&S 1.2

**1 Escucha y anota lo que hacía la persona y la parte del cuerpo que le duele.**
Students listen and note down what sport each speaker was doing and what part of the body they have hurt.

**CD 2, track 22** — **página 92, actividad 1**

1 El otro día jugé al baloncesto y ahora me duele la rodilla.
2 El invierno pasado esquiaba con mis amigos cuando me caí y me rompí el brazo.
3 Ayer mientras montaba a caballo me caí y ahora me duele la cabeza.
4 Esta mañana cortaba el pan para el desayuno cuando me corté el dedo.
5 Corría por el parque cuando un perro me atacó y me caí y ahora tengo la pierna rota.

*Answers:* ***1*** *4, d;* ***2*** *3 b;* ***3*** *1 c;* ***4*** *6 a;* ***5*** *2 e*

PLTS | AT 4.2–3

**2 Inventa una parte del cuerpo que te duele para la acción que sobra.**
Following Activity 1, students decide on a part of the body for the picture that is left over (football) over and then write a sentence in Spanish.

AT 2.4–5 | L&S1.4

**3 Por turnos con un compañero pregunta y contesta. Usa los dibujos de la actividad 1.**
Students work with a partner. They follow the example to ask and answer questions based on the information in Activity 1.

AT 4.4–5 | L&S1.4

**4 Escribe una frase para cada respuesta de la actividad 3.**
This practises writing sentences in the third person singular.

AT 3.5

**5 Lee el texto y contesta a las preguntas.**
Students read the Internet profile and answer the questions.

*Answers:*
***1*** *el ciclismo;* ***2*** *todos los días si no llueve;* ***3*** *en un club – una vez a la semana (los jueves);* ***4*** *Con un grupo de amigos;* ***5*** *piensa aprender a boxear*

AT 2.4 | PLTS | L&S 1.4, 1.5

**6 Sondeo en clase: El deporte preferido.**
Students can present their findings orally or graphically.

AT 1.6 | L&S 1.1, 1.2

**7 Escucha y completa las respuestas de Julio.**
Students listen and complete Julio's answers.

**CD 2, track 23** **página 93, actividad 7**

- ¡Hola, Julio! Dime, ¿cuál es tu deporte preferido?
- Para mí el mejor deporte es el baloncesto. Sí, prefiero el baloncesto a los demás deportes.
- ¿Y qué otros deportes practicas entonces?
- Pues me gusta la natación y también practico el cross y el karate.
- Bastante, ¿verdad? Y ¿cuándo haces todos estos deportes?
- Bueno, hago baloncesto cuatro veces a la semana y corro en el parque los sábados y domingos. Tengo clases de karate los viernes por la noche y voy a la piscina con mis amigos durante las vacaciones.
- ¡Entonces usas todas las partes del cuerpo! A ver, ¿qué partes se usan para el baloncesto?
- Bueno, se usa la cabeza para pensar; los brazos para tirar la pelota y las manos para cogerla y se usan las piernas para correr… ¿No es así?
- ¡Así es! ¿Te gusta ver deporte en la tele?
- No mucho. Sólo veo el Barça contra el Real – ¡lo mejor del fútbol español!
- Te levantas temprano, ¿verdad? ¿A qué hora?
- Normalmente me levanto a las siete menos cuarto.
- ¿Y tomas un buen desayuno?
- Claro, me gusta un buen plato de fruta con cereales y zumo de naranja. El desayuno es la comida más importante del día.
- ¿A qué hora te acuestas durante la semana?
- Me acuesto a las diez y media todas las noches, incluidos los sábados y los domingos.
- ¿Qué hiciste ayer por la tarde, por ejemplo?
- Bueno, descansé un poco de tanto deporte y pasé la tarde en el cine viendo una película de terror.
- ¿Y este fin de semana tienes planes? ¿Qué vas a hacer?
- Pues, el sábado voy a correr por la mañana y el domingo voy a ir a nadar a la piscina con mis amigos.

*Answers: as in audio script*

AT 4.5–6 | PLTS | L&S 1.4

**8 Ahora contesta tú a las preguntas.**
Students answer the questions from Activity 7 for themselves.

AT 4.5–6 | AT 2.5 | L&S 1.4

**9 Practica la entrevista con un compañero.**
Following Activity 8, students practise the interview with a partner.

AT 3.5 | R&W 2.2

**10 Lee y anota en inglés cinco cosas sanas y cinco malsanas.**
Students read Teresa's speech bubble and note down five healthy and five unhealthy things. They will be familiar with the language and just need to recognise it in context.

*Answers:*
***healthy:*** *went to bed early; slept nine hours; got up at 7am; played volleyball; drank a glass of milk*
***unhealthy:*** *ate an unhealthy breakfast; drank strong coffee; went to school in the car; skipped lunch; ate ice-cream and drank lemonade after school*

AT 4.4–5 | PLTS | KAL 4.5

**11 Escribe en tu agenda la lista de actividades sanas para la semana que viene.**
This brings together the language that students have covered in this and previous spreads. With less able class, work through some examples first. Encourage more able students to be as creative as possible.

AT 4.5–6 | R&W 2.4, 2.5 | L&S 1.4 | PLTS

## Challenge

**Write a brief description of a famous sports personality: their sport and one or two more details about them. Include two or more tenses. Read out what you have written to a partner and see if they can guess who it is you are describing.**
Students should draw upon the vocabulary and grammatical structures they met earlier in the unit. With less able classes work through an example first.

## 3A.6 Labolengua

páginas 94–95

### Planner

**Objectives**

- review language and grammar from the unit

**Resources**

Student Book, pages 94–95
CD 2, track 24
Foundation Workbook, pages 53–54
Higher Workbook, pages 53–54
Foundation Workbook audio, CD 3, track 48 (Workbook 28)
Higher Workbook audio, CD 4, track 29
Interactive OxBox, Unit 3A
Copymasters 74–75

**Grammar**

- *doler* and past tenses

**Renewed Framework references**

KAL 4.5; LLS 5.1, 5.2

**PLTS**

All activities: Reflective learners/Self-managers
Activity 6: Team workers; Effective participators

**Homework/Self-study**

Activities 1, 2 and 3, page 94

### Comprender – *doler* and past tenses

#### A How to use the verb *doler(ue)* to say what hurts

KAL 4.5 PLTS

**1 Translate these examples.**
Practice of verbs commonly used in the third person only.

*Answers:*
***1** I like music. **2** I like art. **3** I enjoy the cinema; **4** I like science. **5** I like toffees; **6** I enjoy films about nature.*

KAL 4.5 LLS 5.1 PLTS

**2 How do you say the following in Spanish?**
Practice of the verb *doler(ue).*

*Answers: **1** Me duelen los pies; **2** Tengo dolor de garganta/ me duele la garganta; **3** Tengo dolor de muelas/me duelen las muelas; **4** Me duele la rodilla; **5** Tengo dolor de estómago/me duele el estómago*

#### B Past tenses: using a mix of preterite and imperfect

KAL 4.5 PLTS

**3 Read these examples and write down the verb and the tense used. Think about why each tense has been used.**
Practice of using the past tense in Spanish.

*Answers: **1** tenía – imperfect (went on over a longer period of time), me gustaba – preterite (action began and ended in the past); **2** quise and pude – preterite (action began and ended in the past), estaba – imperfect (went on over a longer period of time); **3** esquiaba – imperfect (what used to happen), me caí, me rompí, me quedé – preterite (action began and ended in the past); **4** era, teniamos, éramos – imperfect (what used to happen); **5** comía – imperfect (what used to happen); decidí, comencé – preterite (action began and ended in the past)*

### Aprender – listening skills

#### C Listening for detail

**Note:** Activities 4–8 all provide practice of preparing to do a listening test.

PLTS

**4 Write out a shopping list of as many items as you can think of.**

**5 Write down the different quantities people might ask for in the market.**

**6 Write down school subjects and a list of areas in school.**

**7 Think about the opinions you might express about school and subjects studied.**

**8 How do you say the following in Spanish?**

*Answers: **at about** – sobre las; **just past** – justo después de; **on the dot** – en punto*

### Hablar – pronunciation

#### D j/g sounds, plus how to memorise

PLTS LLS5.2

**9 Work with a partner and write down two more ways you find helpful when you need to remember things – for example, writing learning cards for vocabulary and verbs.**
Practice of finding strategies to memorise useful vocabulary and verbs.

**CD 2, track 24** — **página 95, Hablar**

Jorge Jiménez el gigante gulo jugaba al ajedrez mientras comía jamón y jugo.

## 3A.7 Extra Star

página 96

### Planner

**Objectives**
- talk about sports and healthy living
- use past and present tenses
- practise memory games

**Resources**
Student Book, page 96
Copymaster 76

**Renewed Framework references**
R&W 2.4, 2.5; KAL 4.5; LLS 5.2

**PLTS**
Activity 1: Reflective learners
Activity 5: Creative thinkers

PLTS | LLS5.2 | AT 4.2

**1 Mira la foto y escribe en español las partes del cuerpo de memoria. ¿Cuántas escribiste correctamente?**
Students practise writing words from memory. They label the parts of the body in Spanish and check to see how many they got right.

AT 3.1

**2 Escribe correctamente los nombres de los deportes.**
Students unjumble the sports.

*Answers:*
***1** baloncesto; **2** natación; **3** karate; **4** yoga; **5** ciclismo; **6** voleibol*

AT 4.3–4 | AT 3.3–4 | KAL 4.5

**3 Completa el texto con los verbos adecuados de la casilla.**
Students complete the text with the appropriate verbs from the box. Note that first person reflexive pronouns have been added to help students.

*Answer:*
***1** me levanto; **2** me visto; **3** me desperté; **4** fui; **5** hacía; **6** leí; **7** bebí; **8** llegó; **9** fuimos; **10** queríamos*

AT 4.4 | R&W 2.4 | KAL4.5

**4 Escribe por lo menos cinco cosas que haces para mantenerte en forma.**
This brings together what students have learnt in previous spreads. It also practises the future tense.

AT 4.4–5 | PLTS | R&W 2.4, 2.5

**5 Escribe cinco preguntas que quieres hacer a tu deportista preferido/a.**
Elicit from students that to get a level 5 or 6 they will need to include a variety of tenses and extend sentences to give reasons and opinions.

## 3A.7 Extra Plus

página 97

### Planner

**Objectives**
- talk about sport
- use a variety of tenses
- practise memory games

**Resources**
Student Book, page 97
Copymaster 77

**Renewed Framework references**
R&W 2.2, 2.4, 2.5; KAL 4.5, 4.6; LLS 5.2

**PLTS**
Activity 1: Reflective learners
Activity 3: Reflective learners; Creative thinkers
Activity 4: Reflective learners; Creative thinkers

AT 4.2 LLS 5.2 PLTS **1 De memoria, ¿cuántos deportes puedes nombrar que se juegen…?**
This practises sports vocabulary. Students do this from memory and should then look back at previous units to check their answers and add any sports they have forgotten.

AT 3.5 R&W 2.2 **2 Lee el texto y contesta a las preguntas en inglés.**
Students read the text and answer the questions in English.

*Answers:*
***1** depends on which year question is asked!; **2** Argentina; **3** he was diagnosed with a growth deficiency problem; **4** they funded his treatment; **5** works on behalf of disadvantaged children in Argentina and around the world.*

AT 4.5 PLTS R&W 2.4, 2.5 KAL 4.5, 4.6 **3 Prepara diez preguntas para hacer una entrevista a Lionel Messi. Usa los verbos subrayados del texto para ayudarte.**
Remind students to think about the question words they have learnt and to use the verbs underlined in the text to help them. They also need to think about the tenses used.

*Possible answers:*
***1** ¿En qué año naciste? **2** ¿Cuándo empezaste a jugar al fútbol?/¿Cuántos años tenías cuando…. **3** Qué le pasó a los once años?/¿Cuántos años tenías cuando el m´dico te diagnosticó con…; **4** ¿Quién quería contratarte? **5** ¿Qué dicidieron hacer?; **6** ¿Cuándo/en qué año se fue a vivir en Barcelona? **7** Cuándo/en qué año empezaste a jugar con los mayores?; **8** ¿Cuántos hermanos y hermanas tienes?; **9** ¿Cuántos títulos has ganado? **10** ¿A qué se dedica tu Fundación?*

AT 4.5 PLTS R&W 2.4, 2.5 KAL 4.5 **4 Escribe un artículo similar sobre tu deportista preferido/a.**
Students should refer back to the article n Activity 2 for support. Remind them that for their work to be a level 5 or 6 they will need to use a variety of tenses and grammatical structures. They should also extend sentences using descriptive language and giving opinions if possible.

## 3A.8 Prueba

página 98

**Resources**
Student Book, page 98
CD 2, track 25
Assessment OxBox, Unit 3A

**Renewed Framework references**
L&S 1.1, 1.2, 1.4; R&W 2.2; KAL 4.4; LLS 5.4

**PLTS**
All activities: Reflective learners

### Escuchar

AT 1.4 L&S 1.1, 1.2 PLTS **Listen to the interview and choose a, b or c to complete the sentence.**
This activity tests listening skills using the language covered in this unit.

**CD 2, track 25** **página 98, actividad 1**

- Leonor, ¿tú crees que eres una persona que hace mucho deporte?
- Pues en realidad el deporte no me gusta mucho pero lo hago de vez en cuando.
- ¿Qué deporte haces?
- Bueno, voy al polideportivo todos los días después del insti porque me encuentro con un grupo de amigos.
- ¿Qué hacen tus amigos?
- Normalmente juegan al pingpong en dos equipos pero yo les miro nada más.
- ¿Por qué no juegas con ellos?
- Porque no me gusta competir; prefiero hacer escalada y sólo puedo hacerlo los fines de semana con mi padre porque es bastante difícil y peligroso.

*Answers: **1** b; **2** a; **3** b; **4** b; **5** c; **6** a; **7** b; **8** b*

## Hablar

AT 2.4 | L&S 1.4 | PLTS

**Prepare the answers to the questions.**
This activity tests speaking skills using the language covered in this unit.

## Leer

AT 3.4 | R&W 2.2 | LLS 5.4 | PLTS

**Read the text and answer the questions.**
This activity tests reading skills using the language covered in this unit.

*Answers:*
***1** it is quite fashionable but you need to be tall; **2** he likes to do solo sports; **3** in the street or skatepark; **4** during the 90's; **5** helmets, knee and elbow protectors, wide trousers. **6** a half pipe is a u turn on a ramp and a Mactwist is a full jump of 360 degrees.*

## Escribir

AT 4.3 | KAL 4.4 | PLTS

**Reorder the fridge magnets to make complete sentences.**
This activity tests writing skills using the language covered in this unit.

*Answers:*
***1** La natación es el deporte más saludable de todos. **2** Es muy importante saber nadar. **3** Usas muchas partes del cuerpo cuando nadas.*

# Leer 3A

página 153

### Resources
Student Book, page 153

### Renewed Framework references
R&W 2.1, 2.2; KAL 4.5

### PLTS
Activity 2: Team workers
Activity 4: Creative thinkers
Activity 6: Creative thinkers; Effective participators

AT 3.6

**1 Lee los textos y busca las frases en español.**

*Answers:*
***1** ahora que soy mayor; **2** lo alto de las montañas; **3** la punta más al sur de España; **4** el viento me empuja hacia arriba como una cometa; **5** Lo mejor … es; **6** nos animan; **7** cuesta bastante; **8** el campeonato del mundo*

PLTS

**2 Escribe una lista de las nuevas palabras.**
Once students have compiled their list, they could work with a partner to try and work out what the words mean.

AT 3.4 | R&W 2.1, 2.2

**3 Busca las expresiones del tiempo.**
Students note down any expressions to do with the weather.

*Answers:*
*cuando el viento me empuja; hace demasiado viento; lo puedes hacer tanto si llueve como si hace sol*

AT 4.4 | PLTS

**4 ¿Qué haces si llueve? ¿Y si hace sol, viento o nieva?**
This provides the opportunity for students to revise weather phrases and to be creative.

KAL 4.5

**5 Identifica los tiempos de los verbos.**
Students write all the verbs down and say what they mean.

AT 4.4 | PLTS

**6 Escribe seis preguntas sobre los textos. Contesta a las preguntas de tu compañero.**
Students write six questions on the text and answer a friend's questions.

### Follow-up
Students could look on the Internet to find out more about one of the sports mentioned. They could also find out which sports they tend to do in different areas of Spain.

# Foundation Workbook

## Página 48 3A.1 Vida sana

- Use with Student Book, pages 84–85

KAL 4.1, 4.6 | AT 4.1 | AT 3.1

**1 Fill in the missing vowels in the Spanish question words, then draw lines to match them up with the English.**
Remind students that these question words all have accents.

*Answers:*
***1** ¿Cuándo? – When?; **2** ¿Cómo? – How?; **3** ¿Quién? – Who?; **4** ¿Cuál? – Which?; **5** ¿Qué? – What?; **6** ¿Dónde? – Where?; **7** ¿Cuántos? – How many?; **8** ¿A qué hora? – At what time?; **9** ¿Por qué? – Why?*

AT 3.2

**2 Complete the sentences with the missing frequency words.**

*Answers:*
***a** …a menudo. **b** … todos los días. **c** …dos veces a la semana. **d** …cada día. **e** Siempre….*

AT 1.4 | L&S 1.2

**3 Listen to Javier and circle the things he does to keep fit.**

**CD 3, track 46 (Workbook 26)** **página 48, actividad 3**

Me llamo Javier y tengo 14 años. Soy bastante deportista y por eso hago muchos deportes durante la semana, juego al rugby dos veces a la semana, al tenis una vez al mes y practico la natación los fines de semana. Para estar en forma debo comer mucha fruta y ensaladas todos los días. A veces cuando hay un torneo necesito seguir una dieta. Normalmente me acuesto temprano. Hago ejercicio cuatro veces a la semana así que no tengo que perder peso porque no estoy gordo. No me gusta ir al gimnasio porque creo que es aburrido.

*Answers:*
***a** Eat a lot of fruit and salads; **d** Play rugby; **f** Go on a diet; **g** Do exercise; **h** Swim; **j** Go to bed early; **k** Play tennis*

## Página 49 3A.2 Cuerpo sano

- Use with Student Book, pages 86–87

AT 3.1 | AT 4.1 | L&S 4.3

**1 Label the parts of the body. Write the masculine words (*el/los*) in blue and the feminine words (*la/las*) in red.**

*Answers:*
*la cabeza (head); la oreja (ear); los ojos (eyes); la nariz (nose); la boca (mouth); los dientes (teeth); las muelas (back teeth); el pelo (hair); la garganta (throat); la espalda (back); el brazo (arm); la mano (hand); el estómago (stomach); la pierna (leg); la rodilla (knee); el tobillo (ankle); el pie (foot)*

**2 How many parts of the body can you say in one minute? Point to the part of the body and say the words in Spanish.**
A fun way to practise parts of the body in Spanish.

## Página 50 3A.3 Malestar

- Use with Student Book, pages 88–89

AT 3.1

**1 Write the correct word(s) under each picture.**
Students can refer back to pages 88 and 89 of the Student Book for support, if necessary.

*Answers:*
***a** las pastillas; **b** una tirita; **c** la crema; **d** las aspirinas; **e** el jarabe*

AT 3.2

**2 Pedro is not feeling well. Follow the word snake to find out what is wrong and write it down. The snake can go up, down or across, but not diagonally.**

*Answers:*
*Me duele mucho la cabeza y también me duelen las muelas. Y tengo dolor de garganta. ¡Qué mal!*

R&W 2.4 | AT 3.3

**3 Draw lines to match up the questions to the answers.**

*Answers:*
***1** d; **2** a; **3** c; **4** b*

## Página 51 3A.4 Nos encanta el deporte

- Use with Student Book, pages 90–91

AT 1.4 | L&S 1.2

**1 Listen to Roberto and tick the sports he says he does.**
Practice of sports vocabulary.

**CD 3, track 47 (Workbook 27)** **página 51, actividades 1 y 3**

¿Cuánto deporte hago? Pues, hago muchos deportes. Los lunes juego al baloncesto con el equipo del instituto. Los martes voy al club de tenis y juego durante una hora más o menos y los miércoles suelo practicar un poco la natación con mi hermano. Los jueves corro por el parque antes de ir al instituto y los viernes juego al rugby. Los sábados me gusta hacer ciclismo así que el domingo estoy muy cansado.

*Answers:*
***a** cross; **b** tenis; **d** baloncesto; **e** natación; **f** ciclismo; **h** rugby*

AT 3.2 **2 Unscramble the words to make correct phrases.**

*Answers:*
***a** los lunes; **b** con el equipo del instituto; **c** durante una hora más o menos; **d** suelo practicar un poco; **e** antes de ir al instituto; **f** así que estoy muy cansado*

AT 1.4 **3 Now listen to Roberto again and check your answers to Activity 2.**

## Página 52 3A.5 Deporte y salud

- Use with Student Book, pages 92–93

AT 3.2 R&W 2.4 **1 Try to match up the sentence halves.**

*Answers:*
***1** e; **2** c; **3** g; **4** h; **5** a; **6** b; **7** f; **8** d*

KAL 4.5 **2 Write the sports from Activity 1 in the correct column.**
Practice of recognising the preterite, imperfect and present tenses.

*Answers:*
***Preterite:** Hice natación. Jugué al baloncesto. Hice gimnasia.*
***Imperfect:** Hacía escalada. Jugaba al tenis. Montaba a caballo.*
***Present:** Juego al fútbol. Hago atletismo.*

**3 Roll dice and see how quickly you can say the sports using the following verbs.**

*Answers:*
***1** jugué al fútbol; **2** hago natación; **3** juego al baloncesto; **4** hice escalada; **5** jugaba al tenis; **6** hacía gimnasia*

## Página 53 3A.6A Labolengua

- Use with Student Book, pages 94–95

KAL 4.5 **1 Fill in the missing verb endings.**

*Answers:*
***a** Me duel**e** la garganta. **b** Me duel**en** los ojos. **c** Me duel**e** la espalda. **d** Me duel**en** las manos. **e** Me duel**en** las piernas.*

KAL 4.5 **2 Underline the verbs in the preterite in blue and the ones in the imperfect in red.**

*Answers:*
***a** Cuando **tenía (imperfect)** doce años **jugaba (imperfect)** al tenis con mi padre todos los días.*
***b** Ayer **comí (preterite)** mucha fruta y ahora me duele el estómago.*
***c** Cuando **vivía (imperfect)** con mis padres **comía (imperfect)** verduras pero no me **gustaban (imperfect)**.*
***d** Antes mi padre **fumaba (imperfect)** bastante pero hace un año lo **dejó (preterite)** y ahora no fuma nada.*
***e Tomé (preterite)** mucho el sol mucho y ahora tengo insolación.*

KAL 4.5 **3 Preterite or imperfect? Circle the correct verb.**

*Answers:*
***a** Cuando **jugaba** al tenis, me **rompí** la pierna. **b** Ayer **jugué** al baloncesto y mi equipo **ganó**. **c** Cuando **tenía** catorce años **bailaba** mucho en una fiesta. **d** El año pasado **fui** de vacaciones a Valencia y **comí** paella. **e** Antes **solía** comer muchos pasteles pero **engordé** mucho y ahora no como nada dulce.*

## Página 54 3A.6B Técnica

- Use with Student Book, pages 94–95

**1 Decide whether the following adjectives are positive (P) or negative (N).**
Suggested answers are given below, but in many cases there is no definitive answer, so encourage discussion amongst students.

*Answers:*
***a** aburrido (N); **b** cortés (P); **c** agradable (P); **d** antipático (N); **e** divertido (P); **f** grosero (N); **g** perezoso (N); **h** limpio (P); **i** emocionante (P); **j** rápido (P); **k** trabajador (P); **l** sucio (N); **m** simpático (P); **n** lento (N); **o** amable (P); **p** sano (P)*

AT 1.3 **2 Listen and decide whether the opinions are positive (P), negative (N) or positive and negative (P + N).**

**CD 3, track 48 (Workbook 28)** **página 54, actividad 2**

**a** El cuarto de baño estaba muy sucio, no voy a volver a ese hotel nunca más.
**b** Yo creo que los camareros eran muy amables aunque la comida era bastante cara.
**c** Los trabajadores de la fábrica son muy lentos.
**d** Todos los estudiantes del instituto eran muy agradables pero me parece que algunos profesores son un poco perezosos.
**e** ¡Qué programa más emocionante hay en la tele!

*Answers: **a** N; **b** P+N; **c** N; **d** P+N; **e** P*

KAL 4.1 **3 Read the following words out loud. Circle the odd one out in each group.**

*Answers: **a** gemelos; **b** gasolina; **c** gente; **d** guante*

# Higher Workbook

## Página 48 3A.1 Vida sana

- Use with Student Book, pages 84–85

KAL 4.1–4.6 | AT 4.1 | AT 3.1

**1 Fill in the missing vowels in the question words. The write the English translations.**
Remind students that all question words have accents.

*Answers:*
***a** ¿Cuándo? – When?; **b** ¿Cómo? – How?; **c** ¿Quién? – Who?; **d** ¿Cuál? – Which?; **e** ¿Qué? – What?; **f** ¿Dónde? – Where?; **g** ¿Cuántos? – How many?; **h** ¿A qué hora? – At what time?; **i** ¿Por qué? – Why?*

AT 3.2

**2 Complete the sentence with the missing frequency words.**

*Answers:*
***a** ...a menudo. **b** ...todos los días. **c** ...dos veces a la semana. **d** ...cada día. **e** Siempre.... **f** A veces....*

AT 1.4 | L&S 1.2

**3 Listen to Javier and circle the tings he does to keep fit. Write how often ne does these things.**

**CD 4, track 27** **página 48, actividad 3**

Me llamo Javier y tengo 14 años. Soy bastante deportista y por eso hago muchos deportes durante la semana, juego al rugby dos veces a la semana, al tenis una vez al mes y practico la natación los fines de semana. Para estar en forma debo comer mucha fruta y ensaladas todos los días. A veces cuando hay un torneo necesito seguir una dieta. Normalmente me acuesto temprano. Hago ejercicio cuatro veces a la semana así que no tengo que perder peso porque no estoy gordo. No me gusta ir al gimnasio porque creo que es aburrido.

*Answers:*
***a** Eat a lot of fruit and salads – every day; **d** Play rugby – twice a week; **f** Go on a diet – sometimes, (when there is a tournament); **g** Do exercise – four times a week; **h** Swim – at the weekends; **j** Go to bed early – normally; **k** Play tennis – once a month*

## Página 49 3A.2 Cuerpo sano

- Use with Student Book, pages 86–87

AT 3.1 | AT 4.1 | KAL 4.3

**1 Label the parts of the body. Write the masculine words (*el/los*) in blue and the feminine words (*la/las*) in red.**

*Answers:*
*la cabeza (head); la oreja (ear); los ojos (eyes); la nariz (nose); la boca (mouth); los dientes (teeth); las muelas (back teeth); el pelo (hair); la garganta (throat); la espalda (back); el brazo (arm); la mano (hand); el estómago (stomach); la pierna (leg); la rodilla (knee); el tobillo (ankle); el pie (foot)*

AT 4.3

**2 Describe a monster using the parts of the body from Activity 1.**
Students should be as inventive as possible. The most able could use adjectives to describe the body parts. Volunteers could present their description to the class.

## Página 50 3A.3 Malestar

- Use with Student Book, pages 88–89

AT 4.1–2

**1 Unscramble the words and write the correct one under each picture.**
Students can refer back to pages 88 and 89 of the Student Book for support, if necessary.

*Answers:*
***a** las pastillas; **b** una tirita; **c** la crema; **d** aspirinas; **e** el jarabe*

AT 3.2

**2 Pedro is not feeling well. Follow the word snake to find out what is wrong with him and write it down. The snake can go up, down or across, but not diagonally.**

*Answers:*
*My head hurts a lot and I also have toothache. And I've got a sore throat. How awful!*

R&W 2.4 | AT 3.3

**3 Fill in the blanks and match up the questions to the answers to complete the dialogue at the chemist's.**

*Answers:*
***1** (tardes) d; **2** a (Me, tengo, de); **3** c (duele); **4** b (Muchas)*

## Página 51 3A.4 Nos encanta el deporte

- Use with Student Book, pages 90–91

AT 1.4 | AT 3.1 | L&S 1.2

**1 Write the names of the sports under the pictures. Then listen to Roberto and tick the ones he says he does.**
Practice of sports vocabulary.

**CD 4, track 28** **página 51, actividades 1 y 3**

¿Cuánto deporte hago? Pues, hago muchos deportes. Los lunes juego al baloncesto con el equipo del instituto. Los martes voy al club de tenis y juego durante una hora más o menos y los miércoles suelo practicar un poco la natación con mi hermano. Los jueves corro por el parque antes de ir al instituto y los viernes juego al rugby. Los sábados me gusta hacer ciclismo así que el domingo estoy muy cansado.

*Answers:*
***a*** *el cross ✓;* ***b*** *el tenis ✓;* ***c*** *la escalada;* ***d*** *el baloncesto ✓;* ***e*** *la natación ✓;* ***f*** *el ciclismo ✓;* ***g*** *el patinaje sobre hielo;* ***h*** *el rugby ✓*

AT 3.2 **2 Unscramble the words to make correct phrases.**

*Answers:*
***a*** *los lunes;* ***b*** *con el equipo del instituto;* ***c*** *durante una hora más o menos;* ***d*** *suelo practicar un poco;* ***e*** *antes de ir al instituto;* ***f*** *así que estoy muy cansado*

AT 1.4 **3 Now listen to Roberto again and check your answers to Activity 2.**

## Página 52 3A.5 Deporte y salud

- Use with Student Book, pages 92–93

R&W 2.4 AT 4.2 **1 Fill in the missing letters in the Spanish sentences. Then match them up with their translations.**

*Answers:*
***1*** *Juego al fútbol. e;* ***2*** *Hice natación. c;* ***3*** *Hacía escalada. g;* ***4*** *Jugaba al tenis. h;* ***5*** *Jugué al baloncesto. a;* ***6*** *Hago atletismo. b;* ***7*** *Hice gimnasia. f;* ***8*** *Montaba a caballo. d*

KAL 4.5 **2 Write the sports from Activity 1 in the correct column.**
Practice of recognising the preterite, imperfect and present tenses.

*Answers:*
***Preterite:*** *Hice natación. Jugué al baloncesto. Hice gimnasia.*
***Imperfect:*** *Hacía escalada. Montaba a caballo. Jugaba al tenis.*
***Present:*** *Juego al fútbol. Hago atletismo.*

**3 Roll dice and see how quickly you can say the sports using the following verbs.**
*Answers:*
***1*** *jugué al fútbol;* ***2*** *hago natación;* ***3*** *juego al baloncesto;* ***4*** *hice escalada;* ***5*** *jugaba al tenis;* ***6*** *hacía gimnasia*

## Página 53 3A.6A Labolengua

- Use with Student Book, pages 94–95

KAL 4.5 **1 Fill in the missing verb endings and the body parts.**

*Answers:*
***a*** *Me duel**e la garganta**.* ***b*** *Me duel**en los ojos**.* ***c*** *Me duel**e la espalda**.* ***d*** *Me duel**en las manos**.* ***e*** *Me duel**en las piernas**.*

KAL 4.5 **2 Underline the verbs in the preterite in blue and the ones in the imperfect in red.**
*Answers:*
***a*** *Cuando **tenía (imperfect)** doce años **jugaba (imperfect)** al tenis con mi padre todos los días.*
***b*** *Ayer **comí (preterite)** mucha fruta y ahora me duele el estómago.*
***c*** *Cuando **vivía (imperfect)** con mis padres **comía (imperfect)** verduras pero no me **gustaban (imperfect)**.*
***d*** *Antes mi padre **fumaba (imperfect)** bastante pero hace un año lo **dejó (preterite)** y ahora no fuma nada.*
***e Tomé (preterite)*** *mucho el sol y ahora tengo insolación.*

KAL 4.5 **3 Complete the sentences with the verbs in the preterite or imperfect tense.**

*Answers:*
***a*** *Cuando **jugaba** al tenis, me **rompí** la pierna.* ***b*** *Ayer **jugué** al baloncesto y mi equipo **ganó**.* ***c*** *Cuando **estaba** en España mi amigo y yo **bailamos** mucho en la discoteca.* ***d*** *El año pasado **fui** de vacaciones a Valencia y **comí** paella.* ***e*** *Antes **solía** comer muchos pasteles pero **engordé** mucho y ahora no como nada dulce.*

## Página 54 3A.6B Técnica

- Use with Student Book, pages 94–95

**1 Match up the adjectives in Spanish with the English. Are they positive (P) or negative (N)?**
Suggested answers are given below, but in many cases there is no definitive answer, so encourage discussion amongst students.

*Answers:*
***a*** *aburrido (N);* ***b*** *divertido (P);* ***c*** *emocionante (P);* ***d*** *simpático (P);* ***e*** *cortés (P);* ***f*** *grosero (N);* ***g*** *rápido (P);* ***h*** *lento (N);* ***i*** *agradable (P);* ***j*** *perezoso (N);* ***k*** *trabajador (P);* ***l*** *amable (P);* ***m*** *antipático (N);* ***n*** *limpio (P);* ***o*** *sucio (N);* ***p*** *sano (P)*

AT 1.3 **2 Listen and decide whether the opinions are positive (P), negative (N) or positive and negative (P+N).**

**CD 4, track 29** **página 54, actividad 2**
**a** El cuarto de baño estaba muy sucio, no voy a volver a ese hotel nunca más.
**b** Yo creo que los camareros eran muy amables aunque la comida era bastante cara.
**c** Los trabajadores de la fábrica son muy lentos.
**d** Todos los estudiantes del instituto eran muy agradables pero me parece que algunos profesores son un poco perezosos.
**e** ¡Qué programa más emocionante hay en la tele!

*Answers:*
***a*** *N;* ***b*** *P+N;* ***c*** *N;* ***d*** *P+N;* ***e*** *P*

KAL 4.1 **3 Read the following words out loud. Circle the odd one out in each group.**
*Answers:* ***a*** *gemelos;* ***b*** *gasolina;* ***c*** *gente;* ***d*** *guante*

# 3B Mi futuro

## Unit Objectives

**Contexts and cultural focus:** future plans
**Grammar:** the future tense including irregular verbs; the conditional tense; revision of past tenses
**Language learning:** differentiating between the future and the immediate future; understanding what qualities are necessary for different jobs; thinking of unusual ways to earn pocket money; talking about choosing options/subjects; finding out and describing how somebody got their dream job

- *Aim*: To learn to talk about future plans
- Each unit has an associated video which will feature throughout the unit. Below is the transcript of the video for this unit.

**Video clip: Unit 3B (CD 2, track 32)**

**Part 1**

*Elena, Roberto and Juan are in the garden at home.*

Roberto: Mi madre me pregunta si he elegido las optativas para el año que viene.
Juan: ¿Y qué vas a elegir?
Roberto: Aún no lo sé. Voy bien en ciencias pero mi asignatura favorita es el arte.
Elena: Bueno. ¿Y qué quieres hacer en el futuro?
Roberto: Todavía no lo sé. Quería ser artista pero mis padres dicen que es importante tener un buen trabajo.
Juan: ¡Ser artista es un buen trabajo!
Roberto: Sí, pero mis padres dicen que es mejor ser médico o ingeniero.
Elena: ¿Irás a la universidad?
Roberto: Supongo. ¿Y tú Elena? ¿Irás a la universidad más adelante?
Elena: Aún no lo sé. Pero tengo tiempo, decidiré el año que viene. Depende de los exámenes.
Juan: Bueno, yo seré campeón de escalada y para hacer esto no iré a la universidad, pero tendré que hacer mucha práctica.
Roberto: Pero ¿Qué contestaré a mis padres?
Elena: Seguro que no somos los únicos que no sabemos lo que haremos en el futuro.
Juan: Mira, vamos al centro y hacemos un sondeo a ver qué les gusta estudiar a los jóvenes y a ver qué les gustaría hacer en el futuro.

**Part 2**

*The three of them are in the street with clipboards stopping various young passers-by.*

Elena: *To camera.* Vosotros nos podéis ayudar. Anotad cuáles son las asignaturas preferidas y qué quieren hacer en el futuro.
Juan: Hola, buenos días. Perdona, ¿te puedo hacer una pregunta?
G1: Dime.
Juan: ¿Cuál es tu asignatura preferida?
G1: Mi asignatura preferida es matemáticas – es muy útil.
Juan: ¿Y por qué es tu asignatura preferida?
G1: Porque saco buenas notas.
Juan: ¿Y qué piensas en hacer en el futuro?
G1: Estudiaré matemáticas porque mi intención es ser profesora de matemáticas en el futuro.
Juan: Vale, muchas gracias.
Roberto: Buenos días.
B1: Buenos días.
Roberto: ¿Te podría hacer unas preguntas?
B1: Claro.
Roberto: ¿Vas al instituto?
B1: Sí, estoy en cuarto de la ESO.
Roberto: ¿Y cuál es tu asignatura preferida?
B1: Pues, la informática porque es muy divertida y en el futuro quisiera ser creadora de videojuegos. Trabajaré en una empresa que crea videojuegos para aprender.
Roberto: Y ¿Cuál es la asignatura que no te gusta?
B1: La historia porque saco malas notas.
Roberto: Vale, muchas gracias.
B1: Hasta luego.
Elena: Hola, perdona. ¿Te puedo hacer una pregunta?
G2: Claro que sí.
Elena: ¿Qué quieres ser en el futuro?
G2: Quisiera ser médico. Estudiaré medicina en la universidad de Salamanca. Son muchos años de estudio.
Elena: Muchas gracias.
G2: De nada.
B2: Voy al insti y mi asignatura preferida es el inglés. Es muy útil porque en el futuro viajaré por todo el mundo.
Juan: ¡Qué guay! Yo también viajaré por todo el mundo porque voy a ser campeón de escalada.
Roberto: ¿Y qué te gustaría ser en el futuro?
G3: Espero ser actriz pero mis padres dicen que no.
Roberto: Yo igual. Me gustaría ser artista pero mi madre dice que es mejor ser médico.
G3: Esta tarde voy a ir a una exposición de arte. ¿Te gustaría venir conmigo?
Elena: *Before Roberto gets a chance to reply.* No estará libre, está trabajando.

| | |
|---|---|
| G3: | Hasta luego, entonces…. |
| Juan: | ¿Vas a ser médico? ¡Qué bien! Yo voy a ser campeón de escalada. Voy a ser un muy famoso. |
| Elena: | Por favor chicos. Estamos aquí para hacer un sondeo serio y no para ligar. |
| Roberto: | De acuerdo. Veamos. ¿Cuáles son los resultados? |
| Juan: | No sé. |
| Elena: | ¿Roberto? |
| Roberto: | Yo tampoco lo sé. |
| Juan: | *Talking direct to camera*. ¿Y vosotros? ¿Habéis apuntado los resultados? ¿Sí? A ver. ¿Cuáles son las asignaturas preferidas de los jóvenes de Segovia? Y ¿Qué les gustaría hacer en el futuro? |

**Punto Lengua**

Voy bien en ciencias pero mi asignatura favorita es el arte.
Quería ser artista.
Decidiré el año que viene, depende de los exámenes.
Mi asignatura preferida es matemáticas – es muy útil.

As a starter activity to introduce the unit and familiarise students with the language they will meet, view the video as a whole. Are there any words or phrases that they have recognised from this single viewing? What do they think it is about? Play Part 1 again a couple of times, as this sets the scene. Do students recognise any of the careers mentioned? Do the plans and opinions of the characters reflect their plans and opinions? This starts students thinking about the video and will help them understand it better when you return to look at it in more detail later in this unit.

*Synopsis:*
Juan, Roberto and Elena and talking about what they would like to do in the future... and what their parents would like them to do. None of them is really sure what to do. Sure that they aren't the only ones, they decide to carry out a survey in the town centre to see what other young people enjoy studying and what they plan to do in the future.

| Unit 3B Mi futuro Overview grid | | | | | | |
|---|---|---|---|---|---|---|
| **Page reference** | **Contexts and objectives** | **Language learning** | **Grammar** | **Key language** | **Framework** | **AT level** |
| Pages 100–101 **Lo que haré** | • talk about what you will do in the future | • differentiate between the future and the immediate future | • use the future tense | *Estaré muy contento/a. Estudiaré. Ganaré mucho dinero. Seré muy famoso/a. Tendré un buen trabajo. Volveré a Colombia.* | L&S 1.2, 1.4; R&W 2.2; KAL 4.5; LLS 5.1 | 1.3, 2.5, 3.3, 4.5 |
| Pages 102–103 **Trabajaré como ...** | • talk about what job you will, would like to, or hope to do in the future | • understand what qualities are necessary for different jobs | • practise using the future tense including irregular verbs | *actor/actriz; cantante; deportista; director(a) de empresa; diseñador(a) de videojuegos; guía turístico/a; informático/a; periodista; piloto; ambicioso/a; comunicativo/a; organizado/a; serio/a; trabajador(a); espero trabajar como; espero ser; al aire libre* | L&S 1.2, 1.4; R&W 2.2, 2.4; KAL 4.4, 4.5 | 1.4, 2.4–5, 3.5, 4.5 |
| Pages 104–105 **¿Cómo ganar dinero ahora?** | • talk about how you earn pocket money now | • think of unusual ways to earn pocket money | • say who gives you money | *dar; ganar; cada mes; cada semana; de 3h a 6h; mensualmente; semanalmente; ayudar en casa; hacer de canguro; repartir periódicos* | L&S 1.2, 1.4, 1.5; R&W 2.2 | 1.4–5, 2.3–5, 3.4–5 |
| Pages 106–107 **Lo que estudiaré** | • talk about choosing options/ subjects | • give reasons for your choices | • recognise some phrases in the conditional | *El profe es muy simpático. Es mi asignatura preferida. Soy bueno/a en...; Me interesa. Mi padre dice que es importante. Mis amigos lo estudiarán. claro; no me digas; optativas; súper simpático* | L&S 1.1, 1.2, 1.4, 1.5; R&W 2.2; IU 3.1, 3.2; KAL 4.5 | 1.3, 1.5, 2.4–5, 3.4–5, 4.5–6 |
| Pages 108–109 **Mi trabajo de sueño** | • find out and describe how somebody got their dream job | • produce a piece of extended writing | • use a variety of tenses (past, present, future) | | L&S 1.2, 1.4; R&W 2.2, 2.4, 2.5; KAL 4.5; LLS 5.4 | 1.5–6, 3.6–7, 4.6–7 |
| Pages 110–111 **Labolengua** | • review language and grammar from the unit | | | | KAL 4.1, 4.3, 4.4, 4.5; LLS 5.8 | |

| Unit 3B Mi futuro Overview grid | | | | | | |
|---|---|---|---|---|---|---|
| **Page reference** | **Contexts and objectives** | **Language learning** | **Grammar** | **Key language** | **Framework** | **AT level** |
| Pages 112–113<br>**Extra Star**<br>**Extra Plus** | • differentiated extension/ homework material | • revise and consolidate all vocabulary and grammar covered in the unit | • revise and consolidate vocabulary and grammar covered in the unit | | R&W 2.2, 2.4, 2.5;<br>KAL 4.3, 4.4, 4.5 | 3.5–6, 4.4–5 |
| Page 114<br>**Prueba** | • end-of-unit test | | | | L&S 1.1, 1.2, 1.4;<br>R&W 2.2;<br>KAL 4.5;<br>LLS 5.4 | 1.5, 2.5, 3.5, 4.6 |
| Page 115<br>**Vocabulario** | • a summary of the key language covered in each core spread of this unit | | | | | |
| Page 154<br>**Leer 3B** | • practice of longer reading texts based on the theme of the unit | | | | R&W 2.1, 2.2 | 3.6 |

**Week-by-week overview**
**(Three-year KS3 Route: assuming six weeks' work or approximately 10–12.5 hours)**
**(Two-year KS3 Route: assuming four weeks' worth or approxmately 6.5-8.5 hours)**

**About Unit 3B, *Mi futuro:*** Students work in the context of future plans. They talk about what they will do in the future including what job they will, would like to, or hope to do. They also talk about how they earn pocket money and choosing options/subjects. They find out and describe how somebody got their dream job. Students use the future tense including irregular verbs and they also learn to recognise some verbs in the conditional tense. Students practise using a variety of tenses in their writing.The unit also provides tips on language learning techniques.

| Three-Year KS3 Route | | | Two-Year KS3 Route | | |
|---|---|---|---|---|---|
| **Week** | **Resources** | **Objectives** | **Week** | **Resources** | **Objectives** |
| **1** | **3B.1 Lo que haré**<br>**3B.6 Labolengua A** (p.110) | talk about what you will do in the future<br>differentiate between the future and the immediate future<br>use the future tense | **1** | **3B.1 Lo que haré** (Omit Challenge)<br>**3B.6 Labolengua A** (p.110) | talk about what you will do in the future<br>differentiate between the future and the immediate future<br>use the future tense |

| | | | | | |
|---|---|---|---|---|---|
| 2 | **3B.2 Trabajaré como ...**<br>**3B.6 Labolengua C**<br>(p.111) | talk about what job you will, would like to, or hope to do in the future<br>understand what qualities are necessary for different jobs<br>practise using the future tense including irregular verbs | 2 | **3B.2 Trabajaré de ...**<br>(Omit Activity 3 & Challenge)<br>**3B.6 Labolengua C**<br>(p.111) | talk about what job you will, would like to, or hope to do in the future<br>understand what qualities are necessary for different jobs<br>practise using the future tense including irregular verbs |
| 3 | **3B.3 ¿Cómo ganar dinero ahora?** | talk about how you earn pocket money now<br>think of unusual ways to earn pocket money<br>say who gives you money | 3 | **3B.3 ¿Cómo ganar dinero ahora?**<br>(Omit Activity 3) | talk about how you earn pocket money now<br>think of unusual ways to earn pocket money<br>say who gives you money |
| 4 | **3B.4 Lo que estudiaré**<br>**3B.6 Labolengua B**<br>(p.110) | talk about choosing options/ subjects<br>give reasons for your choices<br>recognise some phrases in the conditional | 4 | **3B.4 Lo que estudiaré**<br>(Omit Think, & Challenge)<br>**3B.6 Labolengua B**<br>(p.110)<br>**3B.8 Prueba** (p.114)<br>**Vocabulario** (p.115) | talk about choosing options/subjects<br>give reasons for your choices<br>recognise some phrases in the conditional<br>Prepare and carry out assessment in all four skills<br>Recapping on vocabulary of the unit |
| 5 | **3B.5 Mi trabajo de sueño**<br>**3B.6 Labolengua D**<br>(p.111) | find out and describe how somebody got their dream job<br>Produce a piece of extended writing<br>use a variety of tenses (past, present, future) | | | |
| 6 | **3B.7 Extra (Star)** (p.112)<br>**3B.7 Extra (Plus)** (p.113)<br>**3B.8 Prueba** (p.114)<br>**Vocabulario** (p.115)<br>**Leer** (p.154) | Further reinforcement and extension of the language of the unit.<br>Prepare and carry out assessment in all four skills<br>Recapping on vocabulary of the unit<br>Further reading to explore the language of the unit and cultural themes | | | |

## 3B.1 Lo que haré

páginas 100–101

# Planner

### Objectives
- talk about what you will do in the future
- use the future tense
- differentiate between the future and the immediate future

### Resources
Student Book, pages 100–101
CD 2, track 26
Foundation Workbook, page 56
Higher Workbook, page 56
Interactive OxBox, Unit 3B
Copymasters 79–86

### Key language
*Estaré muy contento/a. Estudiaré. Ganaré mucho dinero. Seré muy famoso/a. Tendré un buen trabajo. Volveré a Colombia.*

### Renewed Framework references
L&S 1.2, 1.4; R&W 2.2; KAL 4.5; LLS 5.1

### PLTS
Activity 2: Reflective learners
Activity 4: Independent enquirers
Activity 5: Team workers; Effective participators
Challenge: Team workers; Effective participators; Creative thinkers

### Starters
- Quickly recap the immediate future tense. Go round the class asking them all what they are going to do after school.
- Ask students to write down the future tense endings. Check answers as a class. Write these down and keep them to use in Plenary Activity 2.

### Plenaries
- Students work in pairs and play a simple guessing game to practise the future tense. Once they are confident with the phrases from Activity 1, partner B closes the book. Partner A says a phrase and B tries to remember which picture it is. The most able and confident can then reverse the game:
  *A Número 6*
  *B Ganaré mucho dinero.*
  They then swap roles.
- Display the list of future tense endings from Starter Activity 2. Then ask students to write a sentence using the future tense. Depending on the level of the class, you may want to display verbs they could use and a model sentence for support. More able students could write a sentence for each person rather than just the 1st person singular.

### Homework/Self-study
Activity 3 – students write a sentence in the immediate future and one in the future.
Activity 4, page 101

AT 1.3 | L&S 1.2

**1 Escucha y completa las frases de arriba.**
Students listen and complete the speech bubbles. First give them the opportunity to read through the speech bubbles as they are and to look at the list of words.

**CD 2, track 26** **página 100, actividad 1**

- ¿Qué harás el año que viene, Roberto?
- Pues, primero, el mes que viene **volveré** a Colombia. **Estaré** muy contento de ver a mi familia otra vez. Luego, el año que viene, **estudiaré** en el colegio con mis amigos.
- Más tarde **tendré** un buen trabajo y claro **ganaré** mucho dinero. Naturalmente **seré** muy, muy famoso...
- Vaya, Roberto, ¡qué egoísta eres!

*Answers: as in the transcript*

AT 3.3 | R&W 2.2 | PLTS

**2 Empareja los dibujos de la actividad 1 con las frases en inglés.**
Students match the pictures and speech bubbles from Activity 1 to the English sentences. Once students have done this, ask them what the *I will* words in Spanish have in common. Go on to explain in detail how to form the future tense as explained in the *Gramática* box.

*Answers:*
***1** I will return to Colombia. **2** I will be very happy. **3** I will study. **4** I will have a good job. **5** I will earn a lot of money. **6** I will be very famous.*

KAL 4.5 LLS 5.1

**Gramática**

Following Activity 2, explain to students how the future tense is formed. Look at the example given and work through a few more examples as a class. Finally, give students a verb to put into the future tense themselves.

KAL 4.5 LLS 5.1

**Gramática**

Students start to think about the difference between the immediate future and future tense. Read through the examples as a class. Remind students that there is further information on this on page 164 of the Student Book.

PLTS KAL 4.5

**3 Completa las frases con los verbos de la casilla. Identifica el tiempo del verbo.**

Students practise differentiating between the immediate future and future tense.

*Answers:*

***1** voy a ir; **2** voy a comprar; **3** iré; **4** trabajaré; **5** voy a ir*

KAL 4.5 LLS 5.1

**Gramática**

Students look at the future of irregular verbs. They should learn these by heart.

AT 4.5 PLTS KAL 4.5

**4 Completa las frases con el verbo correcto en el futuro.**

Further practice of differentiating between the future and immediate future tense.

*Answers:*

***1** ganaremos; **2** estará; **3** estudiarán; **4** volverás; **5** seréis; **6** tendrá*

AT 2.5 L&S1.4 KAL 4.5 PLTS

**5 Habla con tu compañero. ¿Qué harás el año que viene?**

Students work with a partner to practise using the future tense. They can use the verbs listed to get them started, or can use their own ideas. This activity could be extended into a class survey, and more able students could feed back in the 3rd person singular – *Natasha escuchará mucha música rap.*

AT 4.5 PLTS

**Challenge**

**In a group, work out your plans for next year. How imaginative can you be?**

Less able students can stick to writing in the 1st person, but working in a group should provide support for writing. The most able groups could feedback to the class in the 3rd person plural, taking about the rest of the group.

## 3B.2 Trabajaré como ...

páginas 102–103

### *Planner*

#### Objectives

- talk about what job you will, would like to, or hope to do in the future
- practise using the future tense including irregular verbs
- understand what qualities are necessary for different jobs

#### Resources

Student Book, pages 102–103
CD 2, track 27
Foundation Workbook, page 57
Higher Workbook, page 57
Interactive OxBox, Unit 3B
Copymasters 79–86

#### Key language

*actor/actriz; cantante; deportista; director(a) de empresa; diseñador(a) de videojuegos; guía turístico/a; informático/a; periodista; piloto; ambicioso/a; comunicativo/a; organizado/a; serio/a; trabajador(a); espero trabajar como; espero ser; al aire libre*

#### Renewed Framework references

L&S 1.2, 1.4; R&W 2.2, 2.4; KAL 4.4, 4.5

#### PLTS

Activity 1: Reflective learners
Activity 2: Reflective learners
Activity 3: Effective participators
Activity 4: Self-managers
Gramática: Self-managers
Activity 5: Self-managers

## Starters

- Display the key language and next to this, the English translations in jumbled order. Give students a time limit to match the English to the Spanish. When the time is up, get volunteers to come to the front and match one of the English translations to its Spanish equivalent. The class can say whether or not they think it is correct.
- Display the list of jobs and ask students which personal traits they think you would need to do each one. There is no right answer here, so encourage some discussion. Remind students to think about adjective endings as well. With less able students, display a list of personal traits for them to match to the jobs.

## Plenaries

- After working through the first Grammar box, display the list of key language including the different ways of referring to future plans. Go round the class, asking each student what they plan to do in the future. Explain that they can't refer to the future in the same way as the student before them, e.g. if one student says *Quiero ser piloto*. the next student can't use *Quiero ser ...* again. More able students could give a reason why they want to do a particular job, e.g. ... *porque soy inteligente y serio*.
- Students work in pairs and take it in turns to interview each other about their future plans using the vocabulary and grammatical structures from the spread. Volunteers could act out their interviews in front of the class.

## Homework/Self-study

Activity 4, page 103
Gramática, page 103

AT 1.4 | PLTS | L&S 1.2

**1 Escucha y escoge la letra correcta.**
Students listen and match the pictures to the speakers.

**CD 2, track 27** — **página 102, actividades 1 y 2**

1 En el futuro trabajaré como piloto. Viajaré en avión por todo el mundo. Será un buen trabajo para mí porque soy inteligente y serio.
2 En el futuro espero ser actriz. Es un trabajo muy interesante, y me gustaría ser famosa. Soy extrovertida y comunicativa. Creo que sería una buena actriz.
3 Me interesan mucho los ordenadores, así que mi trabajo ideal sería ser informático. Es un buen trabajo para mí porque soy un poco tímido, pero muy trabajador.
4 Soy paciente y organizada, y me encanta viajar y conocer gente. En el futuro trabajaré como guía turística y ayudaré a los turistas por todo el mundo.
5 Espero trabajar como periodista en el futuro. Es necesario ser ambicioso y comunicativo.
6 En el futuro quiero ser diseñador de videojuegos. Es un trabajo interesante y variado, y perfecto para mí porque soy inteligente y creativo.
7 Espero ser cantante en el futuro. Me encanta la música. Soy extrovertida e impaciente – ¡quiero ser famosa!
8 Soy ambiciosa y organizada. En el futuro seré la directora de mi propia empresa y ganaré mucho dinero.
9 No soy perezoso. Me encantan todos los deportes. También soy muy trabajador. En el futuro seré deportista profesional.

*Answers:*
***1** d; **2** a; **3** e; **4** i; **5** f; **6** c; **7** b; **8** h; **9** g*

AT 1.4 | PLTS | L&S1.2

**2 Escucha otra vez. Anota las cualidades personales de cada persona.**
Before listening again, get students to work in small groups to brainstorm all the personal qualities they can remember, and to look up a few more. Award points to groups for each new quality another group doesn't have. Less able students can select the "job qualities" listed on the page.

*Answers:*
***1** inteligente y serio; **2** extrovertido y comunicativo; **3** tímido y trabajador; **4** paciente y organizada; **5** ambicioso y comunicativo; **6** inteligente y creativo; **7** extrovertida y impaciente; **8** ambiciosa y organizada; **9** no perezosa y trabajadora*

KAL 4.4, 4.5

### Gramática

Explain to students that learning and using the different ways of talking about the future will help them to make their written and spoken work more interesting.

*Answers:*
*Trabajaré de informático/a. Espero trabajar de periodista. Me gustaría ser actor. Espero ser guía turístico/a. Quiero ser cantante.*

AT 2.4–5 | PLTS | L&S 1.4

**3 Con un compañero, juega a tres en raya con los dibujos de arriba. Tienes que decir lo que harás en el futuro.**
Less able students should stick to using the future *I will work as....* More able students should use a selection of sentences to place their nought or cross; the most able should use a different sentence each time. It is best to photocopy this section, or play it on OHP or interactive whiteboard.

AT 3.5 | PLTS | R&W 2.2

**4 Lee los textos de la página 103. Who ...?**
Students read the descriptions on page 103 and answer the questions. This provides the opportunity to see the various ways of referring to the future in context.

*Answers:*
***1** Miguel; **2** Alicia; **3** Pepe; **4** Pepe; **5** Sofía; **6** Miguel; **7** Sofía; **8** Miguel*

PLTS | KAL 4.5

### Gramática

Look at the examples of other verbs that are irregular in the future as a class. This would be an ideal homework or self-study activity.

AT 3.5 | PLTS | KAL 4.5

**5 Lee y completa los planes de Elena. Elige la forma correcta del verbo.**
Further practice of referring to future events and plans.

*Answers:*
***1** haré; **2** gustaría; **3** viajar; **4** viviré; **5** ser; **6** podré; **7** viajaré; **8** volaré*

AT 4.5 | R&W 2.4 | KAL 4.5

### Challenge

**What will you do in the future? Write a short paragraph about your future job and hopes.**
Students can either write a realistic paragraph about their future plans, or can make up some far-fetched, fantastic plans. Either way, they should try to include as many ways of referring to the future as possible and should also include opinions when they can.

## 3B.3 ¿Cómo ganar dinero ahora?

páginas 104–105

### Planner

#### Objectives

- talk about how you earn pocket money now
- say who gives you money
- think of unusual ways to earn pocket money

#### Resources

Student Book, pages 104–105
CD 2, tracks 28–29
Foundation Workbook, page 58
Higher Workbook, page 58
foundation Workbook audio, CD 3, track 49 (workbook 29)
Higher Workbook audio, CD 4, track 30
Interactive OxBox, Unit 3B
Copymasters 79–86

#### Key language

*dar; ganar; cada mes; cada semana; de 3h a 6h; mensualmente; semanalmente; ayudar en casa; hacer de canguro; repartir periódicos*

#### Renewed Framework references

L&S 1.2, 1.4, 1.5; R&W 2.2

#### PLTS

Activity 1: Independent enquirers
Activity 3: Effective participators
Activity 4: Reflective learners
Activity 6: Self-managers
Challenge: Creative thinkers; Reflective learners

## Starters

- As a class, brainstorm different ways of earning pocket money in Spanish. Students should already be familiar with much of the vocabulary in different contexts, e.g. *Hago las compras*. Keep the list and add to it as you work through the spread.

## Plenaries

- Play a memory game based on Activities 1 and 2. Split the class into teams and explain that you will read statements from the transcript for Activity 2 and they must try to remember which of the young people it refers to, e.g. *Mis padres me dan €40 cada mes*. refers to Elena. You can either ask teams to 'buzz' in or you can give each team in turn a statement. Teams score one point for each correct answer and the team with the most points at the end wins.
- Students interview a partner to find out if, and how, they earn pocket money. As students have made up interesting ways of earning pocket money for the Challenge Activity, they may prefer to make their answers more realistic here. As in the audio for Activity 4, students should try to give opinions on the jobs they have to do. If there is time, students could move around the classroom, interviewing more than one person.

## Homework/Self-study

Activity 3, page 104: students write out their conversations.

AT 3.4 | PLTS | R&W 2.2

**1 Empareja los dibujos con los textos 1–4.**
Students read the questionnaire and then match each person with the appropriate picture. On this reading, they just need to get the gist of the text.

*Answers:*
***1** c, **2** d, **3** a, **4** b*

AT 1.4 | L&S 1.2

**2 Escucha y empareja a los jóvenes con la información de la actividad 1.**
Students listen and identify which piece of information relates to which of the young people.

**CD 2, track 28** **página 104, actividad 2**

- ¿Cuánto dinero te dan, Elena?
- Bueno, mis padres me dan 40€ cada mes.
- ¿Tienes un trabajo?
- No, pero tengo que ayudar en casa. Hago las compras, a veces preparo la cena, y tengo que recoger mi dormitorio.
- ¿Cuántas horas trabajas?
- ¡Muchas! Por lo menos una hora cada día.
- Y ¿qué opinas?
- Me gustaría más trabajar en un café o una tienda, pero no es posible. Me siento como una esclava del hogar ...

- ¿Cuánto dinero te dan, Roberto?
- Pues, me dan 15€ semanalmente.
- ¿Tienes un trabajo?
- No, mi mamá me lo manda desde Colombia.
- Y ¿qué opinas?
- Parece bastante, pero siempre necesito más...

- ¿Cuánto dinero te dan, Pilar?
- Pues, es difícil de decir exactamente, pero más o menos 65€ mensualmente.
- ¿Tienes un trabajo?
- Sí. Como tengo una familia grande con muchos hermanos menores, trabajo como canguro para mis padres y a veces para mis vecinos.
- ¿Cuántas horas trabajas?
- Depende mucho, pero a veces por la tarde y los fines de semana.
- Y ¿qué opinas?
- Pues, a veces está bien, pero otras no me gusta demasiado. Depende mucho de la familia y los niños, ¿sabes?...

- ¿Cuánto dinero te dan, Ben?
- Gano £15 cada semana.
- ¿Tienes un trabajo?
- Sí. Reparto periódicos.
- ¿Cuántas horas trabajas?
- Normalmente trabajo de 6 a 7 de la mañana. No trabajo los domingos.
- Y ¿qué opinas?
- Está bien. El trabajo es interesante pero duro. Me parece que gano bastante dinero.

*Answers:*
***1** Roberto; **2** Elena; **3** Ben; **4** Pilar*

AT 2.3–4 | PLTS | L&S 1.4

**3 Habla con tu compañero. ¿Quién eres?**
Students work in pairs and use the information from the questionnaire and the key language box to have a conversation as Roberto, Elena, Ben or Pilar. More able students can use all the questions.

AT 3.5 | PLTS

**4 Lee el chat y empareja a las personas con los dibujos.**
Point out to students that it is absolutely true that with a licence, children in this country can act for money from the age of 12, with certain restrictions on their hours and stipulations regarding their continuing education.

*Answers:*
***a** PacoX; **b** Carlota23; **c** Ricky; **d** Ángel*

L&S 1.2 | AT 1.5

**5 Escucha la entrevista.**
Students listen to the recording.

**CD 2, track 29** — **página 105, actividades 5 y 6**

- ¿Tus padres te dan dinero, Gema?
- Bueno, mis padres me dan 30€ mensualmente.
- ¿Tienes que ayudar en casa?
- Desde luego. Hago mucho. Primero, paseo al perro, eso cada día por supuesto. También tengo que recoger mi dormitorio: ¡qué horror! Está siempre súper desordenado. Además de eso tengo que poner la mesa para la cena todas las tardes.
- Y ¿qué opinas?
- Es muy aburrido, y no me gusta mucho ayudar en casa, pero es necesario. Tenemos una familia grande y todo el mundo hace algo.
- ¿Y tus hermanos?
- Sí, ayudan, y mi padre también. Él prepara la cena a veces, y mis hermanos tienen que sacar la basura y hacer sus camas. Mamá les da 3€ cada semana.
- Entonces, ¿tienes un trabajo a tiempo parcial?
- Pues sí. Como tengo 16 años, puedo ser camarera. Trabajo en un pequeño restaurante del barrio, no muy lejos de mi casa de 4 a 9 los sábados por la tarde. Es bastante interesante.
- Y ¿cuánto ganas?
- 25€ a la semana. No está mal. Tengo una amiga inglesa que reparte periódicos a las 6 de la madrugada. ¡Imagina!
- ¿Qué harás en el futuro?
- Bueno, claro que me gustaría tener más dinero, pero con el instituto de momento no es posible trabajar más. Después de mis estudios tendré un trabajo muy bueno, y ganaré mucho dinero ...

PLTS | L&S 1.2 | AT 1.5

**6 Escucha otra vez y completa el texto siguiente.**
Students listen again and complete the text with the correct words. First, give students time to read through the text. What kind of word are they expecting to hear for each gap?

*Answers:*
***1** mes; **2** paseo; **3** dormitorio; **4** mesa; **5** aburrido; **6** basura; **7** semana; **8** tarde; **9** 9h; **10** tendré; **11** ganaré*

PLTS | AT 4.4–5 | L&S 1.4, 1.5

**Challenge**
**Imagine you have a surprising way of earning extra pocket money. Write a paragraph about it.**
Encourage students to have fun lying outrageously about their amazing fantasy part-time jobs/ways of earning pocket money. They should try to include two tenses. Students can also write down the description, and circulate it round the class, who have to decide who has written it.

## 3B.4 Lo que estudiaré

páginas 106–107

### Planner

**Objectives**
- talk about choosing options/subjects
- recognise some phrases in the conditional
- give reasons for your choices

**Resources**
Student Book, pages 106–107
CD 2, tracks 30–32
Foundation Workbook, page 59
Higher Workbook, page 59
Foundation Workbook audio, CD 3, track 50 (Workbook 30)
Higher Workbook audio, CD 4, track 31
Interactive OxBox, Unit 3B
Copymasters 79–86

**Video**
Video clip, Unit 3B

**Key language**
*El profe es muy simpático. Es mi asignatura preferida. Soy bueno/a en ... Me interesa. Mi padre dice que es importante. Mis amigos lo estudiarán. claro; no me digas; optativas; súper simpático*

## Renewed Framework references

L&S 1.1, 1.2, 1.4, 1.5; R&W 2.2; IU 3.1, 3.2; KAL 4.5

## PLTS

Activity 2: Self-managers
Activity 5: Effective participators
Think: Independent enquirers; Reflective learners
Activity 6: Independent enquirers
Challenge: Effective participators; Creative thinkers; Team workers

## Starters

- Activity 1, page 106, is an ideal starter activity which provides revision of school subjects.
- Display the school subjects and the adjectives from Activity 1 in a jumbled order. Students make a list of the subjects they study and allocate each subject one or more adjective according to their opinion of it. Compare answers as a class to see which are the most popular and unpopular subjects. You could present this information as a graph.

## Plenaries

- Think (2), page 107. Students make a note of any difference between British and Spanish schools that they can remember. Compare answers as a class.
- Following the Challenge Activity, students write five sentences saying what they will study next year. If possible, provide them with a copy of the transcript for Activity 2 for support. They should give reasons why they want to study these subjects, use a variety of ways to refer to the future and use the conditional tense.

## Homework/Self-study

Think box (1), page 107: Ask students to use each of the useful phrases listed in sentences of their own. Less able students could just choose one of the phrases.
Gramática, page 106: Students note down the conditional endings and learn them by heart. More able students could write a sentence in the conditional using the example verb, *estudiar*.

AT 1.3 | L&S 1.2

**1 Escucha. Anota la asignatura y la opinión.**
Students use this simple listening task to revise school subjects.

**CD 2, track 30** — **página 106, actividad 1**

1 Me gustan mucho las matemáticas. Son muy interesantes.
2 Para mí el español es muy fácil.
3 La educación física es mi asignatura preferida. ¡Es muy divertida!
4 No me gusta nada el inglés. Es demasiado difícil.
5 ¿La geografía? ¡Ni hablar! ¡Qué aburrida!
6 Para mí las ciencias son interesantes pero difíciles.
7 La historia es interesante pero no es útil.
8 No me gusta nada la informática. Es difícil y aburrida.

*Answers:*
***1** matemáticas – interesantes; **2** español – muy fácil; **3** educación física – muy divertida; **4** inglés – difícil; **5** geografía – aburrida; **6** ciencias – interesantes pero difíciles; **7** historia – interesante pero no útil; **8** informática – difícil y aburrida*

AT 1.5 | PLTS | L&S 1.2

**2 Escucha a los jóvenes y anota las letras correctas.**
Students listen and for each speaker, note down which cartoons illustrate why he/she wants to study a certain subject.

**CD 2, track 31** — **página 106, actividades 2 y 3**

**1**
Hola, soy Marisa. El año que viene creo que estudiaré música. Me encanta la música porque el profe es muy simpático. También estudiaré historia. No me gusta mucho porque voy mal en historia, pero mi padre dice que es muy importante.
**2**
Me llamo Carmen, y no me gustan ni la historia ni las lenguas. Prefiero las asignaturas más prácticas como el deporte o la tecnología. El deporte es mi asignatura preferida, y soy muy buena en tecnología.
**3**
Soy Nuria, y prefiero las asignaturas creativas como el arte, la literatura y la música. El año que viene estudiaré matemáticas y arte. ¡Todos mis amigos estudiarán arte! El profe de matemáticas no es muy simpático – qué lástima –, pero es una asignatura útil.

**4**
Me llamo Alberto. A mí me gustan los temas científicos. El año que viene estudiaré informática. Es mi asignatura preferida. Mi padre dice que el inglés es muy importante y útil, pero no quiero estudiarlo. Preferiría estudiar ciencias.
**5**
Soy Eugenio, y el año que viene creo que estudiaré inglés porque mi padre dice que es muy importante. También estudiaré música: ¡es mi asignatura preferida!
**6**
Yo soy Pablo. A mí también me interesan mucho las ciencias y la informática, pero no estudiaré informática. Mi padre dice que el inglés y las matemáticas son más importantes. Así que estudiaré ciencias, matemáticas e inglés.

*Answers:*
***1** f, d; **2** a, b; **3** a, e; **4** a, d; **5** d, a; **6** c, d*

AT 1.5 | L&S 1.2

**3 Escucha otra vez. ¿Verdad o mentira?**
Students listen again and decide whether each of the statements is true (V) or false (M).

*Answers:*
***1** V; **2** M; **3** V; **4** M; **5** V; **6** M*

AT 2.5 | L&S 1.4

**4 Habla con un compañero. ¿Qué estudiarás el año que viene? ¿Por qué? Usa las frases de las actividades 2 y 3 para ayudarte.**
Less able groups can take it in turns to say what they will do as you go round the class. More able groups can ask a partner and then report back what that person will do, changing the person of the verb.

KAL 4.5

## Gramática
Read through the explanation of the conditional tense and get students to make a note of the endings. Refer them also to the Grammar section, page 165 where there is more about this tense.

AT 3.5 | PLTS | R&W 2.2 | IU 3.1, 3.2

**5 Lee el chat (página 107). Elena chatea por Internet con su prima Laura. Laura vive en Londres porque su madre es inglesa.**
Students read the dialogue and answer the questions. Questions 2 and 3 can be reserved for more able students if you prefer.

*Answers:*
1. *Laura will study Maths, English and Science because they are compulsory, Spanish because she's very good at it, History or Geography because her father says it's important. Geography interests her and the teacher is really nice.*
2. *She would like to drop English because she doesn't get good marks, but can't as it's compulsory. She would like to study music because her friends will study it.*
3. *In Spain they don't have options; Elena will study 12 subjects while Laura will study only 8.*

PLTS

## Think
Students should make a note of these phrases to use in their speaking and writing.

*Answers:*
*¡claro!; No me digas; muy simpático; optativas*

PLTS | IU 3.1

## Think
Following Activity 5, students try to remember any other differences between Spanish and British schools from *Zoom español 1*?

AT 3.4–5 | PLTS | R&W 2.2

**6 ¿Qué razones de la actividad 2 son buenas razones para escoger una asignatura? ¿Cuáles son malas?**
Encourage more able students to adapt the given phrases for more reasons, e.g. *me interesa – no me interesa; el profe es simpático – el profe es antipático*. Students may disagree on what are good and bad reasons, so it could be interesting to compare answers.

AT 1.5 | L&S 1.1, 1.2 | IU 3.2

**7 Mira la primera parte del video y contesta a las preguntas en inglés.**
Allow students to watch the first part of the video as many times as necessary and then ask them to answer the questions.

**Video clip: Unit 3B (CD 2, track 32)**

**Part 1**
*Elena, Roberto and Juan are in the garden at home.*
Roberto: Mi madre me pregunta si he elegido las optativas para el año que viene.
Juan: ¿Y qué vas a elegir?
Roberto: Aún no lo sé. Voy bien en ciencias pero mi asignatura favorita es el arte.

Elena: Bueno. ¿Y qué quieres hacer en el futuro?
Roberto: Todavía no lo sé. Quería ser artista pero mis padres dicen que es importante tener un buen trabajo.
Juan: ¡Ser artista es un buen trabajo!
Roberto: Sí, pero mis padres dicen que es mejor ser médico o ingeniero.
Elena: ¿Irás a la universidad?
Roberto: Supongo. ¿Y tú Elena? ¿Irás a la universidad más adelante?
Elena: Aún no lo sé. Pero tengo tiempo, decidiré el año que viene. Depende de los exámenes.
Juan: Bueno, yo seré campeón de escalada y para hacer esto no iré a la universidad, pero tendré que hacer mucha práctica.
Roberto: Pero ¿Qué contestaré a mis padres?
Elena: Seguro que no somos los únicos que no sabemos lo que haremos en el futuro.
Juan: Mira, vamos al centro y hacemos un sondeo a ver qué les gusta estudiar a los jóvenes y a ver qué les gustaría hacer en el futuro.

*Answers:*
***a*** *He would like to choose art as an option as it's his favourite subject and he want to be an artist.* ***b*** *His parents say his should get a good job, such as a doctor or an engineer.*

AT 1.5
L&S 1.1, 1.2
IU 3.2

**8 Mira el video y completa la tabla.**
The other information column can be used an extension activity for more able pupils. They could complete the grid in Spanish or English according to their ability.

**Video clip: Unit 3B (CD 2, track 32)**

**Part 2**
*The three of them are in the street with clipboards stopping various young passers-by.*

Elena: *To camera*. Vosotros nos podéis ayudar. Anotad cuáles son las asignaturas preferidas y qué quieren hacer en el futuro.
Juan: Hola, buenos días. Perdona, ¿te puedo hacer una pregunta?
G1: Dime.
Juan: ¿Cuál es tu asignatura preferida?
G1: Mi asignatura preferida es matemáticas – es muy útil.
Juan: ¿Y por qué es tu asignatura preferida?
G1: Porque saco buenas notas.
Juan: ¿Y qué piensas en hacer en el futuro?
G1: Estudiaré matemáticas porque mi intención es ser profesora de matemáticas en el futuro.
Juan: Vale, muchas gracias.
Roberto: Buenos días.
B1: Buenos días.
Roberto: ¿Te podría hacer unas preguntas?
B1: Claro.
Roberto: ¿Vas al instituto?
B1: Sí, estoy en cuarto de la ESO.
Roberto: ¿Y cuál es tu asignatura preferida?
B1: Pues, la informática porque es muy divertida y en el futuro quisiera ser creadora de videojuegos. Trabajaré en una empresa que crea videojuegos para aprender.
Roberto: Y ¿Cuál es la asignatura que no te gusta?
B1: La historia porque saco malas notas.
Roberto: Vale, muchas gracias.
B1: Hasta luego.
Elena: Hola, perdona. ¿Te puedo hacer una pregunta?
G2: Claro que sí.
Elena: ¿Qué quieres ser en el futuro?
G2: Quisiera ser médico. Estudiaré medicina en la universidad de Salamanca. Son muchos años de estudio.
Elena: Muchas gracias.
G2: De nada.
B2: Voy al insti y mi asignatura preferida es el inglés. Es muy útil porque en el futuro viajaré por todo el mundo.
Juan: ¡Qué guay! Yo también viajaré por todo el mundo porque voy a ser campeón de escalada.
Roberto: ¿Y qué te gustaría ser en el futuro?
G3: Espero ser actriz pero mis padres dicen que no.
Roberto: Yo igual. Me gustaría ser artista pero mi madre dice que es mejor ser médico.
G3: Esta tarde voy a ir a una exposición de arte. ¿Te gustaría venir conmigo?
Elena: *Before Roberto gets a chance to reply*. No estará libre, está trabajando.
G3: Hasta luego, entonces ….
Juan: ¿Vas a ser médico? ¡Qué bien! Yo voy a ser campeón de escalada. Voy a ser un muy famoso.
Elena: Por favor chicos. Estamos aquí para hacer un sondeo serio y no para ligar.
Roberto: De acuerdo. Veamos. ¿Cuáles son los resultados?
Juan: No sé.
Elena: ¿Roberto?
Roberto: Yo tampoco lo sé.
Juan: *Talking direct to camera*. ¿Y vosotros? ¿Habéis apuntado los resultados? ¿Sí? A ver. ¿Cuáles son las asignaturas preferidas de los jóvenes de Segovia? Y ¿Qué les gustaría hacer en el futuro?

*Answers:*
***Girl 1**: maths; to study maths in order to become a maths teacher; thinks maths is useful and gets good marks in it*
***Boy 1**: ICT; wants to design video games; thinks ICT is fun; will work for a company that makes video games to learn about it, doesn't like history as he gets bad marks*
***Girl 2**: wants to study medicine at the University of Salamanca; wants to be a doctor; many years of study*
***Boy 2**: English; wants to travel the world; thinks English is useful, Juan will also travel the world as he wants to be a climbing champion*
***Girl 3**: wants to be an actress; her parents say she can't; she invites Roberto to an art exhibition, Elena steps in and refuses the invitation*

AT 4.5 | KAL 4.5 | IU 3.2

**9 ¿Cuáles son las asignaturas preferidas de los jóvenes de Segovia? ¿Qué les gustaría hacer en el futuro?**
Students should answer in Spanish. This provides practice in using the 3rd person singular and plural. They already have the information to hand from their answers to Activity 8.

AT 4.5–6 | PLTS | L&S 1.4, 1.5

### Challenge
**Write an email to a friend explaining your study choices for next year (three subjects). Use the future and try to use the conditional.**
This could be as simple or as complicated as ability allows. Students could swap emails at the end and more able students could comment on the reasons given.

## 3B.5 Mi trabajo de sueño

páginas 108–109

## *Planner*

### Objectives
- find out and describe how somebody got their dream job
- use a variety of tenses (past, present, future)
- produce a piece of extended writing

### Resources
Student Book, pages 108–109
CD 2, track 33
Foundation Workbook, page 60
Higher Workbook, page 60
Foundation Workbook audio, CD 3, track 51 (Workbook 31)
Higher Workbook audio, CD 4, track 32
Interactive OxBox, Unit 3B
Copymasters 79–86

### Renewed Framework references
L&S 1.2, 1.4; R&W 2.2, 2.4, 2.5; KAL 4.5; LLS 5.4

### PLTS
Activity 1: Independent enquirers
Activity 2: Independent enquirers
Activity 3: Reflective learners
Gramática: Independent enquirers
Challenge: Reflective learners; Creative thinkers

### Starters
- Revise how to form the past, present and future tenses. Give students a regular *ar, er* and *ir* verb and ask them to write these verbs out in the preterite, imperfect, present, immediate future and future tenses. Check answers as a class.

### Plenaries
- Students answer the questions for the two celebrities featured in this spread:
  ***1** ¿Cómo se llama? **2** ¿Dónde y cuándo nació? **3** ¿Cuál fue su primer trabajo? ¿Cuántos años tenía? **4** ¿Qué pasó durante los años siguientes? **5** ¿Ganó premios o títulos? **6** ¿Qué hace ahora? **7** ¿Qué hará en el futuro?*
- Challenge students to write five sentences, each on the theme of the spread, using the tenses listed in the Grammar box. Provide less able students with model sentences to adapt.

### Homework/Self-study
Gramática, page 109: Ask students to note down other examples of these tenses they can find in the biographies.
Challenge Activity

AT 3.6–7 | PLTS | R&W 2.2 | LLS 5.4

**1 ¿Verdad o mentira?**
Students read the text about Antonio Banderas and then answer the true/false questions.

*Answers:*
***1** V; **2** M; **3** M; **4** M; **5** M*

AT 3.6–7 | PLTS | R&W 2.2 | LLS 5.4

**2 Elige las palabras correctas para terminar las frases.**
Students choose the correct word to complete the sentences.

*Answers:*
***2** 18; **3** Toyota; **4** 2010; **5** Volkswagen*

AT 1.5–6 | PLTS | L&S 1.2

**3 Escucha. ¿Hablan de Banderas o de Sainz?**
Students listen and note down if each speaker is referring to Banderas or Sainz. Before they start listening, remind them to think about the vocabulary they are likely to hear for each of these people.

**CD 2, track 33** **página 109, actividad 3**

**1**
Nació en Madrid y siempre le gustó el deporte. Fue campeón nacional de squash, y hizo pruebas de selección para el Real Madrid.
**2**
Fue campeón mundial dos veces y todo el mundo le llama El Matador porque es un piloto maravilloso y muy trabajador.
**3**
Nació en Málaga y su trabajo de ensueño era ser futbolista, pero cuando tenía 14 años se rompió el pie.
**4**
Después de jubilarse, ganó el rally Paris Dakar, y en el futuro conducirá más para Volkswagen.
**5**
Antes de irse a Hollywood, fue actor de películas en España durante 10 años.
**6**
Le encanta el fútbol y le interesan el vino español y el perfume.

*Answers:*
***1** Sainz; **2** Sainz; **3** Banderas; **4** Sainz; **5** Banderas; **6** Banderas*

PLTS | KAL 4.5

## Gramática

Revise the preterite, imperfect, present and immediate future and future tenses. Elicit from students that:

- the **preterite** (past) tense describes what **happened** in the past, and is finished
- the **imperfect** (past) tense describes what **used to happen** over a longer period of time, or **was interrupted** by something else that happened
- the **present** tense describes what **happens** now, or regularly
- the **immediate future** tense describes what is definitely **going to happen** not very far in the future
- the **future** tense describes what **will happen** in the future – something further off, and less certain.

AT 4.6–7 | PLTS | R&W 2.4, 2.5

## Challenge

**Interview an older friend, relative, or local celebrity, about the work they do. How did they start? What was their first job? What happened next? Is this their dream job? What will they do next? Conduct your interview in English, and write up the biography of your chosen person in Spanish.**
This is an extended piece of writing, which can be tailored in length to suit ability, but more able students should aim for two paragraphs of 6–8 sentences each, with multiple tenses.

## 3B.6 Labolengua

páginas 110–111

### Planner

**Objectives**
- review language and grammar from the unit

**Resources**
Student Book, pages 110–111
CD 2, track 34
Foundation Workbook, pages 61–62
Higher Workbook, pages 61–62
Interactive OxBox, Unit 3B
Copymasters 87–88

**Grammar**
- the future and the conditional

**Renewed Framework references**
KAL 4.1, 4.3, 4.4, 4.5; LLS 5.8

**PLTS**
All activities: Reflective learners/Self-managers
Activity 3: Independent enquirers

**Homework/Self-study**
Activities 1 and 2, page 110 and 3, page 111

### Comprender – the future and the conditional

#### A The future

KAL 4.5 | PLTS

**1 Complete these sentences with the correct part of the verb.**
Practice of conjugating verbs in the future tense.

*Answers:*
***1** estudiarán; **2** ayudaré; ganaré; **3** será, viajará; **4** seremos, seremos, viviremos*

#### B The conditional

PLTS | KAL 4.3, 4.4

**2 Are these sentences in the future or the conditional?**
Practice of recognising the conditional tense in Spanish.

*Answers: 1 & 2 – conditional; 3 & 4 – future*

### Aprender – checking your work critically

#### C Improving your written work

LLS 5.8 | PLTS

**3 How many mistakes can you find in this text? Which of the points above do they match? Can you correct them?**
Practice of evaluating and improving written work.

*Answers:*
*En el **futur** (spelling – futuro) me gustaría mucho ser actriz. Soy **extrovertido** (extrovertida – agreement) y ambiciosa, y **espera** (espero – verb) ganar un premio oscar. Viajaré por el mundo, y **vivo** (viviré – tense) en Nueva York. Mi **preferida asignatura** (asignatura preferida – sentence structure) en el instituto es el teatro porque soy muy buena en eso, y es interesante y divertido. No me gustan las ciencias porque **no soy buena en ellas y no son interesantes** (interest – same reasons given as in the previous sentence). No me gustaría trabajar en una oficina, en mi opinión sería muy aburrido.*

### Hablar – accents

#### D Using accents when speaking, pronouncing accurately

**Students listen to the examples.**

**CD 2, track 34** — **página 111, Hablar**

Trabajo, Trabajé, Trabajó, Trabajaré

PLTS | KAL 4.1

**4 Add the missing accent, or underline the emphasised letter of these verbs.**
Practice of using accents.

*Answers:*
vi<u>a</u>jo – I travel (present); via**<u>jó</u>** – he travelled (preterite); ayu**<u>dé</u>** – I helped (preterite); ayuda**<u>ré</u>** – I will help (future)

## 3B.7 Extra Star página 112

### Planner

**Objectives**
- explain what you will study next year
- practise using the future tense
- write about future plans

**Resources**
Student Book, page 112
Copymaster 89

**Renewed Framework references**
R&W 2.4; KAL 4.3, 4.4, 4.5

**PLTS**
Activity 4: Creative thinkers

AT 3.3

**1 Imagina que entrevistas a estas personas cuando eran jóvenes. ¿Qué harán más tarde en la vida? Empareja las dos partes de las frases.**
Students match the sentence halves to say what the people will do later in life.

*Answers:*
***1** c; **2** d; **3** a; **4** e; **5** b*

AT 3.3

**2 Empareja las frases con los dibujos a–e.**
Students match the sentences they have made in Activity 1 with the pictures.

*Answers:*
***1** e; **2** c; **3** b; **4** d; **5** a*

AT 3.3 KAL 4.3, 4.4

**3 Completa las frases con las palabras de la casilla.**
Students complete the sentences with the appropriate words from the box.

*Answers:*
***1** interesa; **2** amigos; **3** importante; **4** simpático; **5** fuerte; **6** asignatura*

AT 4.5 PLTS R&W 2.4 KAL 4.5

**4 Escribe dos o tres frases para explicar qué estudiarás el año que viene y por qué.**
This brings together what students have learnt in previous spreads. It practises the future tense and other ways of referring to future plans.

## 3B.7 Extra Plus página 113

### Planner

**Objectives**
- understand what qualities are necessary for different jobs; talk about how you earn money now
- practise using the future tense
- find out about some famous Spanish people, past and present

**Resources**
Student Book, page 113
Copymaster 90

**Renewed Framework references**
R&W 2.2, 2.4, 2.5; KAL 4.5

**PLTS**
Activity 1: Independent enquirers
Activity 3: Reflective learners; Creative thinkers

AT 3.5 | R&W 2.2 | PLTS

**1 Empareja los anuncios de empleo con las personas.**
As an extension students could look these people up and find out more about them.

*Answers: **1** Cristóbal Colón; **2** Salvador Dalí; **3** Miguel Indurain*

AT 3.5–6 | R&W 2.2

**2 Lee los anuncios otra vez y completa la tabla.**
Students read the adverts again and fill in the table.

*Answers:*
***1** Cristóbal Colón: valiente, extrovertido; ganará mucho dinero; geografía*
***2** Salvador Dalí: creativo, inteligente, egoísta, distinto; será muy, muy famoso; arte*
***3** Miguel Indurain: ambicioso, trabajador, súper-sano; no ganará mucho dinero, pero lo conocerá mucha gente*

AT 4.4–5 | PLTS | R&W 2.4, 2.5 | KAL 4.5

**3 ¿Cómo ganas dinero? ¿Cuánto te dan? Escribe un párrafo.**
Students draw upon the vocabulary and the grammatical structures they have met in this unit to write their paragraph. Encourage more able students to use as many tenses as possible (What did they used to do to help? What did they do last week? What will they do tomorrow, etc.) and to give opinions.

## 3B.8 Prueba

página 114

**Resources**
Student Book, page 114
CD 2, track 35
Assessment OxBox, Unit 3B

**Renewed Framework references**
L&S 1.1, 1.2, 1.4; R&W 2.2; KAL 4.5; LLS 5.4

**PLTS**
All activities: Reflective learners

### Escuchar

AT 1.5 | L&S 1.1, 1.2 | PLTS

**Listen and answer the questions.**
This activity tests listening skills using the language covered in this unit.

**CD 2, track 35** — **página 114, actividad 1**

**1 Roger**
De momento reparto periódicos para el estanco de mi barrio. Me dan £15 cada semana, y trabajo de 6 y media a 8 cada día por la mañana. Me gusta mucho, pero en el futuro no haré eso. Quiero ser un hombre de negocios y tener mi propia empresa.

**2 Arancha**
Pues, no tengo trabajo, pero ayudo a mi madre en casa. Me da 10€ cada semana, y tengo que recoger mi dormitorio, ayudar con mis hermanos pequeños, y cocinar tres veces por semana. En el futuro seré una cantante muy famosa y viajaré por todo el mundo.

**3 José**
Pues, Conchi y yo ayudamos a mi abuelo que es diseñador de videojuegos. Es un trabajo fascinante. Trabajamos con un ordenador, y nuestro abuelito nos da 10€ todos los domingos. En el futuro seré diseñador de videojuegos como mi abuelo.

**4 Conchi**
Pero yo no. Es interesante, pero no quiero trabajar en una oficina. En el futuro quiero ser deportista olímpica.

*Answers:*
***Roger:** delivers newspapers, £15 weekly, businessman; **Arancha:** helps her mum at home, €10 weekly, famous singer; **José:** helps his grandad design videogames, €10 every Sunday, videogame designer; **Conchi:** helps her grandad design videogames, €10 every Sunday, (like José), Olympic sportswoman*

## Hablar

AT 2.5 | L&S 1.4 | PLTS

**Take it in turns with a partner to interview each other. Ask the questions and give answers.**
This activity tests speaking skills using the language covered in this unit.

## Leer

AT 3.5 | R&W 2.2 | LLS 5.4 | PLTS

**Read what Eugenia writes. Decide if the sentences are true or false.**
This activity tests reading skills using the language covered in this unit.

*Answers:* ***1*** *false;* ***2*** *true;* ***3*** *false;* ***4*** *true;* ***5*** *true;* ***6*** *true*

## Escribir

AT 4.6 | KAL4.5 | PLTS

**Write an email to your Spanish penfriend explaining what you will study next year and why. What did you like this year? What do you plan to do in the future? Write a short paragraph.**
This activity tests writing skills using the language covered in this unit.

# Leer 3B

página 154

**Resources**
Student Book, page 154

**Renewed Framework references**
R&W 2.1, 2.2

**PLTS**
Activity 3: Creative thinkers; Reflective learners; Self-managers

AT 3.6 | R&W 2.1, 2.2

**1 Lee lo que dicen Laura y su padre. Contesta a las preguntas.**

*Answers:*
***1*** *art, music, drama;* ***2*** *history, geography, ICT and languages;* ***3*** *actress or singer;* ***4*** *teacher or translator*

AT 3.6 | R&W 2.1, 2.2

**2 ¿Verdad o mentira?**

*Answers:*
***1*** *V;* ***2*** *M,* ***3*** *M,* ***4*** *M,* ***5*** *V,* ***6*** *V*

## Follow-up

Ask students to make a list, in Spanish, of all the subjects they study. For each subject, they should note their opinion (do they find it easy, hard, interesting, useful, etc.), whether they get good marks and if they would like to continue to study this subject. They should refer to the reading texts for ideas and support.
What do students think Laura should study next year? Do they think that her father will change his mind about what is important? Encourage discussion and ask students to give reasons for their views.

# Foundation Workbook

## Página 56 3B.1 Lo que haré

- Use with Student Book, pages 100–101

AT 3.2 **1 Match up the sentences and the pictures.**

*Answers:*
***1** e; **2** c; **3** a; **4** d; **5** b*

AT 3.4–5 R&W 2.2 **2 Read the text. Are the sentences below true (T) or false (F)?**
Students should refer back to pages 100 and 101 of the Student Book for support, if necessary.

*Answers:*
***a** F; **b** F; **c** F; **d** T*

R&W 2.4 AT 3.4 **3 Fill in the blanks with a verb from the box.**

*Answers:*
***a** viviré; **b** compraré; **c** nadaré; **d** tendré; **e** haré*

## Página 57 3B.2 Trabajaré como ...

- Use with Student Book, pages 102–103

AT 3.1 **1 Fill in the grid with the Spanish for these jobs and find out the word for a new job: lawyer.**

*Answers:*

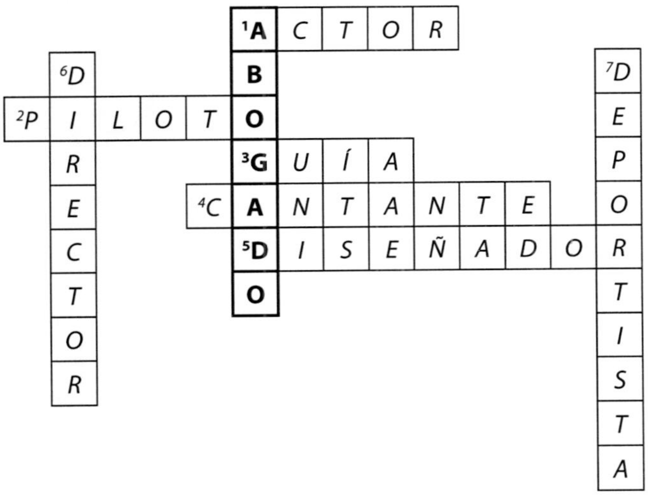


AT 3.2 **2 Draw lines to match up the descriptions to the jobs.**

*Answers:*
***1** c Electricista; **2** d Piloto; **3** e Profesor; **4** a Dependiente; **5** b Dentista*

R&W 2.4 AT 4.3 **3 Put the words in these sentences in order so that they make sense.**
Practice of referring to the future.

*Answers:*
***a** En el futuro viajaré mucho. **b** Espero encontrar un buen trabajo en una compañía. **c** Me gustaría ser más organizado. **d** Quiero trabajar como periodista para un periódico. **e** Ganaré mucho dinero y podré comprar una granja.*

## Página 58 3B.3 ¿Cómo ganar dinero ahora?

- Use with Student Book, pages 104–105

AT 3.2 AT 4.2 **1 Write what the teenagers do to earn money.**

*Answers:*
***a** Lavo el coche. **b** Lavo los platos. **c** Hago de canguro. **d** Hago la compra. **e** Paseo al perro. **f** Saco la basura. **g** Paso la aspiradora. **h** Recojo mi dormitorio.*

AT 1.3 **2 Listen to the five teenagers and circle the correct information.**

**CD 3, track 49 (Workbook 29)** **página 58, actividad 2**

**a** Ayudo a mi padre en el jardín los fines de semana y gano 5 euros.
**b** Los sábados hago las compras para una señora mayor. No gano mucho, sólo 4 euros.
**c** Para ganar dinero paso la aspiradora. Mi madre me da 12 euros al mes.
**d** Bueno, no hago mucho pero mis padres me suelen dar 3 euros cuando lavo el coche.
**e** A veces hago de canguro para los amigos de mis padres y gano bastante, me dan 15 euros.

*Answers:*
***a** I **help my father in the garden** at the weekends and I earn **5€**. **b** On Saturdays I **do the shopping** for an elderly lady. I don't earn much, only **4€**. **c** To earn money I **do the hoovering**. My mother gives me **12€** per month. **d** Well, I don't do much, but my parents usually give me **3€** when I wash **the car**. **e** Sometimes I **babysit** for my parents' friends and I earn quite a lot, they give me **15€**.*

AT 4.3 R&W 2.4 **3 Write three things that you sometimes do to help at home.**
Students should refer back to pages 104 and 105 of the Student Book, if necessary.

## Página 59 3B.4 Lo que estudiaré

- Use with Student Book, pages 106–107

KAL 4.3, 4.5

**1 Complete the words with the correct endings.** Practice of conjugating verbs in the present and adjectival agreement.

*Answers:*
***a** Me encant**an** las ciencias porque son fácil**es**. **b** Odio la informática porque me parece muy aburrid**a**. **c** A mi amigo le gust**an** mucho los idiomas porque son important**es** y quiere ser periodist**a**. **d** Creo que estudiaré química en la universidad porque me gust**a** hacer experimentos. **e** No me interes**a** nada la historia, a mi parecer es muy aburrid**a**. **f** Ojalá no tuviéramos que hacer deportes en el instituto, no me gust**an** nada.*

AT 3.4–5

**2 Read what Miguel says about his plans for the future. Can you unscramble the words in bold.**

*Answers:*
***1** dice; **2** informática; **3** trabajo; **4** estudiaré; **5** pasó; **6** haré; **7** año; **8** aprender; **9** espera; **10** quiere*

AT 3.4–5

**3 Now listen to Miguel talking about his plans for the future and check your answers to Activity 2.**

**CD 3, track 50 (Workbook 30)** **página 59, actividad 3**

Mi madre dice que es importante estudiar informática porque es necesario para cualquier trabajo pero yo creo que estudiaré historia porque me encanta saber lo que pasó en el pasado. No sé muy bien lo que haré el año que viene, quizás tenga un año sabático. Y me gustaría mucho aprender a hablar otro idioma. Mi mejor amigo espera estudiar alemán en la universidad porque quiere vivir en Alemania en el futuro.

## Página 60 3B.5 Mi trabajo de sueño

- Use with Student Book, pages 108–109

AT 3.4–5
R&W 2.2

**1 Read Javier's email about his job and find the Spanish for the phrases below.**

*Answers:*
***a** cuando era pequeño; **b** quería ser; **c** mi sueño; **d** (viajar) por todo el mundo; **e** conseguí; **f** muy bien pagado*

AT 3.4–5
R&W 2.2

**2 Read the email again and fill in the details.**

*Answers:*
***a** Dream job when he was little: fireman; **b** Work experience: International company; **c** After university: job in Madrid; **d** Dream: travel round the world; **e** Job: very well paid; **f** Why it is his ideal job: travel to many countries*

AT 1.4–5
L&S 1.2

**3 Listen to the five teenagers and complete their plans for the future.**

**CD 3, track 51 (Workbook 31)** **página 60, actividad 3**

1. En el futuro me gustaría trabajar en una oficina con mucha gente. Me gusta trabajar en equipo.
2. Yo quiero viajar por todo el mundo porque me encanta conocer sitios y gente nueva.
3. Cuando termine la universidad, quiero hacer una película de aventuras. Yo quiero disfrutar de mi trabajo.
4. No sé, espero tener mi propio negocio y ganar mucho dinero. Para mí es importante tener responsabilidad.
5. Bueno, pues quiero trabajar en producciones de teatro. Pienso que es importante hacer un trabajo que te guste.

*Answers:*

| | ***Plans for the future*** | ***What is important*** |
|---|---|---|
| *1* | *Work in an office with a lot of people* | *Likes working in a team* |
| *2* | *Travel round the world* | *Know new places and meet new people* |
| *3* | *Make an adventure film* | *Enjoy her job* |
| *4* | *Have his own business* | *Having responsibility* |
| *5* | *Work in theatre productions* | *To do a job that you like* |

## Página 61 3B.6A Labolengua

- Use with Student Book, pages 110–111

KAL 4.5 **1 Complete the verbs with the correct future tense endings. Then find them in the wordsearch.**

*Answers:*
***a** comer**é**; **b** estudiar**é**; **c** vivir**é**; **d** viajar**é**; **e** har**é**; **f** ganar**é**; **g** ayudar**á**; **h** trabajar**ás**; **i** visitar**emos**; **j** dormir**emos***

**2 Circle the odd one out in each group.**

*Answers:*
***a** compré – past not future; **b** comeremos – no accent; **c** estudiarás – only verb in you form (tú') not 'I'; **d** buscaría – conditional tense not future*

KAL 4.5 **3 Complete each sentence with the correct verb.**

*Answers:*
***a Ganaré** mucho dinero. **b Lavaré** el coche más tarde. **c Iré** de vacaciones al extranjero. **d Trabajaré** dos días a la semana. **e** Mi casa **estará** en el campo.*

## Página 62 3B.6B Técnica

- Use with Student Book, pages 110–111

**1 & 2 The following sentences have all got mistakes in them. The words that are wrong are in bold. Can you see why they are wrong? Write out the sentences from Activity 1 without the mistakes.**

*Answers: (Corrections are shown in bold)*
***a** El año que viene trabajar**é** en la oficina de una compañía pequeña en el extranjero. **b** El mes que viene **haré** prácticas laborales en una tienda. **c** El año pasado **fui** a España para trabajar. **d** Mañana mi hermano y yo **vamos** a salir.*

**3 Complete the Spanish sentences. Read the advice given for each one to avoid making any careless mistakes.**

*Answers:*
***a** El año que viene **viajaré** a España en tren. **b** El año pasado **fuimos** a **una** ciudad **muy bonita.** **c** Me **gustaría estudiar matemáticas** porque **son fáciles.***

## Higher Workbook

### Página 56 3B.1 Lo que haré

- Use with Student Book, pages 100–101

AT 3.2 AT 4.2 **1 Copy the correct sentence under each picture.**

*Answers:*
***a** Trabajaré en España. **b** Viajare por todo el mundo. **c** Tendré una familia. **d** Viviré en una casa en el campo. **e** Aprenderé a montar a caballo.*

AT 3.5 R&W 2.2 **2 Read the text. Are the sentences below true (T) or false (F)?**
Students should refer back to pages 100 and 101 of the Student Book for support, if necessary.

*Answers:*
***a** F; **b** F; **c** F; **d** T*

AT 4.4–5 R&W 2.5 **3 Write about what you will do in the future.**
Students use the verbs given as prompts. Encourage them to refer back to pages 100 and 101 and the previous activities for ideas.

### Página 57 3B.2 Trabajaré como ...

- Use with Student Book, pages 102–103

AT 4.2 **1 Fill in the grid with the Spanish for these jobs and find out the word for a new job: lawyer.**

*Answers:* **new job:** abogado

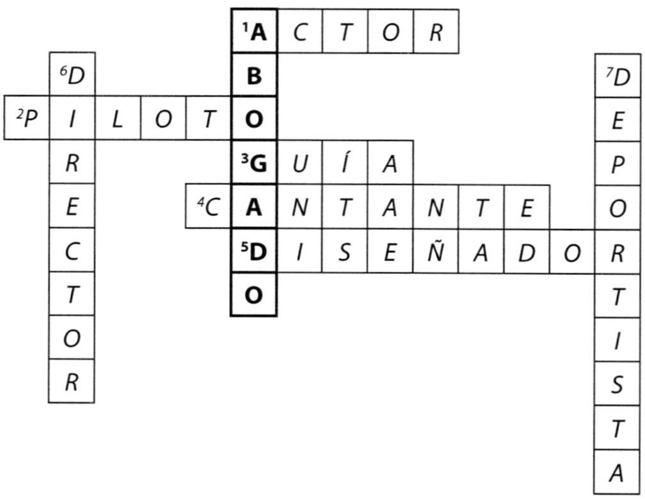


AT 3.2 **2 Draw lines to match up the descriptions to the jobs.**

*Answers:*
***1** c Electricista; **2** d Piloto; **3** e Profesor;*
***4** a Dependiente; **5** b Dentista*

AT 4.3–4 R&W 2.4 **3 Translate the following sentences into Spanish, using the expressions in the Recuerdo box.**

*Answers:*
***a** En el futuro viajaré mucho. **b** Espero encontrar un buen trabajo en una compañía. **c** Me gustaría ser más organizado. **d** Quiero trabajar como periodista para un periódico nacional. **e** Ganaré mucho dinero y podré comprar una granja.*

### Página 58 3B.3 ¿Cómo ganar dinero ahora?

- Use with Student Book, pages 104–105

AT 1.3 **1 Listen to the five teenagers and write down in English what they do to earn money and how much they earn.**

**CD 4, track 30** **página 58, actividad 1**

**a** Ayudo a mi padre en el jardín los fines de semana y gano 5 euros.
**b** Los sábados hago las compras para una señora mayor. No gano mucho, sólo 4 euros.
**c** Para ganar dinero paso la aspiradora. Mi madre me da 12 euros al mes.
**d** Bueno, no hago mucho pero mis padres me suelen dar 3 euros cuando lavo el coche.
**e** A veces hago de canguro para los amigos de mis padres y gano bastante, me dan 15 euros.

*Answers:*
***a** Juan: helps (dad) in the garden, 5€; **b** Susana: does the shopping (for elderly woman), 4€; **c** Pedro: does the hoovering, 12€ (per month); **d** Isabel: washes the car, 3€; **e** Javier: babysits, 15€*

AT 3.4 R&W 2.1, 2.2 **2 Read what Marta says she does to earn money and answer the questions in English.**

*Answers:*
***a** She cooks dinner. **b** Tidying her room and hoovering. **c** Because her parents go to an Italian course from 7 till 9pm. **d** No, because they behave well/are well-behaved. **e** On Saturdays she delivers newspapers. **f** Because she has to get up very early. **g** She buys a fashion magazine and she saves up the rest of the money (to buy a laptop).*

## Página 59 3B.4 Lo que estudiaré

- Use with Student Book, pages 106–107

KAL 4.5 **1 Complete the words with the correct endings.**

*Answers:*
***a** Me encant**an** las ciencias porque son fácil**es**. **b** Odio la informática porque me parece muy aburrid**a**. **c** A mi amigo le gust**an** mucho los idiomas porque son important**es** y quiere ser periodist**a**. **d** Creo que estudiaré química en la universidad porque me gust**a** hacer experimentos. **e** No me interes**a** nada la historia, a mi parecer es muy aburrid**a**. **f** Ojalá no tuviéramos que hacer deportes en el instituto, no me gust**an** nada. **g** Mi padre dice que es importante estudiar Económicas pero yo creo que es la asignatura más aburrid**a** de todas. **h** Voy a elegir geografía como una optativa porque pienso que la profesora es muy simpátic**a**.*

AT 3.4–5 **2 Read what Miguel says about his plans for the future. Can you unscramble the words in bold?**

*Answers:*
***1** dice; **2** informática; **3** trabajo; **4** estudiaré; **5** pasó; **6** haré; **7** año; **8** aprender; **9** espera; **10** quiere*

AT 1.4–5 **3 Now listen to Miguel talking about his plans for the future and check your answers to Activity 2.**

**CD 4, track 31** — **página 59, actividad 3**

Mi madre dice que es importante estudiar informática porque es necesario para cualquier trabajo pero yo creo que estudiaré historia porque me encanta saber lo que pasó en el pasado. No sé muy bien lo que haré el año que viene, quizás tenga un año sabático. Y me gustaría mucho aprender a hablar otro idioma. Mi mejor amigo espera estudiar alemán en la universidad porque quiere vivir en Alemania en el futuro.

AT 4.4 **4 Finish the sentences with information about yourself.**
Students should refer back to pages 106 and 107 of the Student Book as well as the previous activities for ideas and support.

## Página 60 3B.5 Mi trabajo de sueño

- Use with Student Book, pages 108–109

AT 3.3 **1 Draw lines to match up the sentence halves to complete the information about Javier's job.**

*Answers:*
***1** d; **2** f; **3** b; **4** a; **5** c; **6** e*

AT 3.4–5 **2 Find the Spanish for the following words in the sentences in Activity 1.**

*Answers:*
***a** cuando era pequeño; **b** por todo el mundo; **c** mi sueño; **d** conseguí; **e** muy bien pagado; **f** quería ser*

AT 1.4–5 L&S 1.2 **3 Listen to the five teenagers and complete their plans for the future.**

**CD 4, track 32** — **página 60, actividad 3**

1 En el futuro me gustaría trabajar en una oficina con mucha gente. Me gusta trabajar en equipo.
2 Yo quiero viajar por todo el mundo porque me encanta conocer sitios y gente nueva.
3 Cuando termine la universidad, quiero hacer una película de aventuras. Yo quiero disfrutar de mi trabajo.
4 No sé, espero tener mi propio negocio y ganar mucho dinero. Para mí es importante tener responsabilidad.
5 Bueno, pues quiero trabajar en producciones de teatro. Pienso que es importante hacer un trabajo que te guste.

*Answers:*

| | *Plans for the future* | *What is important* |
|---|---|---|
| 1 | *Work in an office with a lot of people* | *Likes working in a team* |
| 2 | *Travel round the world* | *Know new places and meet new people* |
| 3 | *Make an adventure film* | *Enjoy her job* |
| 4 | *Have his own business* | *Having responsibility* |
| 5 | *Work in theatre productions* | *To do a job that you like* |

## Página 61 3B.6A Labolengua

- Use with Student Book, pages 110–111

KAL 4.5 **1 Put the 10 verbs below into the future tense, and then find them in the wordsearch.**

*Answers:*
***a** comer**é**; **b** estudiar**é**; **c** vivir**é**; **d** viajar**é**; **e** har**é**; **f** ganar**é**; **g** ayudar**á**; **h** trabajar**ás**; **i** visitar**emos**; **j** dormir**emos***

KAL 4.5 **2 Circle the odd one out in each group.**

*Answers:*
***a** compré – past not future; **b** comeremos – no accent; **c** estudiarás – only verb in you form (tú') not 'I'; **d** buscaría – conditional tense not future*

R&W 2.4 **3 Translate the sentences using the words from the box. Careful! You don't need all the words. Only use each word once.**

*Answers:*
***a*** *Ganaría mucho dinero.* ***b*** *Lavaría el coche, pero no tengo tiempo.* ***c*** *Iría de vacaciones al extranjero.* ***d*** *Trabajaría dos días a la semana.*

## Página 62 3B.6B Técnica

- Use with Student Book, pages 110–111

**1 Read the following sentences. Tick the ones that are correct and cross any with mistakes. There are 10 mistakes in total.**

*Answers:*
***a*** *El año que viene trabajar**é** en la o**f**icina de una compañía pequeñ**a** en el extranjero. – ✗;* ***b*** *Me gustaría ganar mucho dinero. – ✓;* ***c*** *El mes que viene **haré** prácticas labora**les** en un**a** tienda. – ✗;* ***d*** *El año pas**a**do **fui** a España **para** trabajar. – ✗;* ***e*** *Cuando sea mayor, espero vivir en una casa grande en las afueras de la ciudad. – ✓;* ***f*** *Mañana mi hermano y yo **vamos** a salir. ✗*

**2 Write out correctly the sentences in Activity 1 that have mistakes in them.**

*Answers: See Activity 1.*

R&W 2.4 **3 Translate the following sentences being very careful about your accuracy. Look at the advice given for each sentence so that you don't make any careless mistakes.**

*Answers:*
***a*** *El año que viene **viajaré** a España en tren.* ***b*** *El año pasado **fuimos** a **una** ciudad **muy bonita.*** ***c*** *Me **gustaría estudiar matemáticas** porque **son fáciles.***

# 4A Mi mundo

## Unit Objectives

**Contexts and cultural focus:** your world: the environment; problems and solutions; your family environment
**Grammar:** opinions; superlatives; we can/must/have to; the imperative; words of frequency; negatives; *me permite(n)/ puedo*
**Language learning:** understanding and using very large numbers; carrying out and writing up a survey; making and referring to notes; reading skills; summarising and recounting; speaking and writing for different audiences using *tú* and *usted*

- *Aim*: To learn to talk about environmental problems and what we must/can do to protect the environment
- Each unit has an associated video which will feature throughout the unit. Below is the transcript of the video for this unit.

**Video clip: Unit 4A (CD 3, track 6)**

**Part 1**

*In the garden at Elena and Juan's house.*

Juan: Pero, mamá, nadie usa pesticidas hoy.
Mama: ¿Y qué se usa entonces?
Elena: Pues se pueden usar productos biológicos que ayudan a proteger el planeta.
Mama: Y ¿qué hago con los insectos que se comen los tomates?
Juan: Pues, no sé.
Roberto: He leído en el periódico que hay talleres en un huerto ecológico.
Mama: Excelente. ¡Iros al taller y luego me contáis!

**Part 2**

*Outside the Huerta.*

Juan: Ahora tenemos que trabajar toda la tarde en un huerto. Es culpa de Roberto.
Roberto: No es verdad. Es culpa tuya. *Direct to camera* Pero tenéis que ayudarnos. Anotad cómo un huerto ecológico ayuda a proteger el medio ambiente.
Elena: Bueno aquí estamos. Venid.

Charo: Hola chicos, bienvenidos a La Huerta. Aquí cultivamos todo tipo de frutas y verduras, pero eso sí, de manera ecológica.
Roberto: ¿Pero, qué significa trabajar de manera ecológica?
Charo: Pues, significa cultivar sin pesticidas sin herbicidas, todo con productos naturales. Pero controlando la calidad de los alimentos.
Juan: ¿Y qué podemos hacer con los insectos que se comen las verduras?
Charo: Vamos a la Huerta a ver cómo trabajamos.
Charo: ¿Qué creeis que es esto? ¿Qué puede ser?
Group: ¿Semillas? ¿Espárragos? ¿Cebollas?
Charo: ¿Espárragos? No. Una flor efectivamente. Una flor. En una huerta es muy importante recoger semillas, recoger las semillas de un año para otro. Esta es la semilla de la cebolla. Son muchas flores y de allí sale las semillitas para luego poner en el semillero, a volver a cultivar el siguiente año. Mira quién se come los insectos, los insectos malos. Las mariquitas son las mejores aliadas del hortelano. Mírala, cógela.
Juan: Se ha ido.
Charo: No la gustó tu mano. ¿Qué es esto?
Roberto: Una alcachofa
Charo: Muy bien muy bien, bueno. Hemos dicho que en la agricultura ecológica, no se usan pesticidas ni herbicidas para quitar las malas hierbas. Por lo tanto hay que quitarlas a mano. Y a la mano es, pues así. ¿Alguien quiere probar?
Roberto: Sí.
Charo: Venga, hombre. Ah, ¡tú sabes! Tú, sí que sabes. Ay, muy bien.
Elena: Voy a preguntar cuántas verduras diferentes crecen en el huerto. Anotad. ¿Charo?
Charo: Dime.
Elena: ¿Qué verduras crecen en el huerto?
Charo: Pues, tenemos calabacines, pepinos, tomates, judías, repollos, guisantes, acelgas.
Elena: ¿Todo ecológico?
Charo: Por supuesto.
Elena: ¿Por qué?
Charo: Porque al final es más barato, se protege el medio ambiente, y es algo que han hecho mis padres toda la vida.
Charo: Estupendo.
Juan: Perdona.
Charo: Dime
Juan: ¿Te puedo hacer una pregunta?
Charo: Claro.
Juan: ¿Qué se puede hacer con las verduras y con las hojas que no son buenas para cocinar?
Charo: Pues aquí no hay nada de basura con las hojas y con las verduras que no son buenas para cocinar se puede hacer abono, otras veces también con esas hojas se puede dar de comer a las gallinas o a las ovejas. Lo importante es reciclar y no hacer basura.
Juan: ¿Y qué podemos hacer en casa para ayudar al medio ambiente?
Charo: Reciclar. Reciclar papel, vidrio, ropa e incluso reciclar el aceite que usas para freír y con ello hacer jabón.

Juan: ¿Jabón con el aceite de freír las patatas fritas? No lo creo.
Charo: Sí, por supuesto. Se ha hecho toda la vida.
Charo: Hoy vamos a hacer la cosecha de calabacines. Notad que están cultivados junto a las lombardas y las patatas, especies totalmente distintas.
Roberto: ¿Qué hay que hacer para recoger el calabacín?
Charo: Pues, levantad el calabacín. Cortad así. Sin dañar la planta porqué allí hay más pequeñitos. Hay uno allí para cortar.
*Outside the Huerta.*
Elena: ¿Bueno, qué hemos aprendido hoy? ¿Por qué es importante trabajar de forma ecológica?
Juan: Es más barato.
Roberto: Ayuda a proteger el planeta.
Elena: ¿Y qué tenemos que hacer?
Juan: No usar pesticidas.
Roberto: Reciclar todo.
Elena: ¿Y vosotros qué opináis?
Juan: ¿Podemos hacer otro taller? Quiero aprender cómo se puede hacer jabón con el aceite de las patatas fritas.
Elena & Roberto: ¡Juan!

**Punto Lengua**
Hola chicos, bienvenidos a La Huerta.
Reciclar. Reciclar papel, vidrio, ropa…
¿Y qué tenemos que hacer?
No usar pesticidas.
Reciclar todo.

As a starter activity to introduce the unit and familiarise students with the language they will meet, view the video as a whole. Are there any words or phrases that they have recognised from this single viewing? What do they think it is about?
Play Part 1 again a couple of times, as this sets the scene. Can students find any cognates which will help them to understand the video? Ask students to think about things they do to protect the environment. Do they think any of these are mentioned in the video? This starts students thinking about the text and will help them understand it better when you return to look at it in more detail later in this unit.

*Synopsis:*
Juan, Roberto and Elena see Juan and Elena's mum spraying the tomatoes in the garden with pesticides. They tell her that she should be using environmentally friendly products instead. Mum isn't convinced – how will she get rid of all of the insects eating her tomatoes? Luckily, Roberto has read about some ecological workshops. They all decide to go so that Mum can make up her mind.

| Unit 4A Mi mundo Overview grid | | | | | | |
|---|---|---|---|---|---|---|
| **Page reference** | **Contexts and objectives** | **Language learning** | **Grammar** | **Key language** | **Framework** | **AT level** |
| Pages 116–117 **¿Cómo es tu mundo?** | • describe environmental problems and their causes | • give opinions with *para mí, en mi opinión* • understand and use very large numbers | • use superlatives *(el/la … más …)* | *la basura; la contaminación atmosférica; la destrucción de la naturaleza; la extinción de animales; el cambio climático; el sufrimiento humano; cien; doscientos; quinientos; setecientos; novecientos; mil; un millón; en peligro; agua limpia; los glaciares; la papelera; tirar basura; limpio/a; la selva; ganar dinero* | L&S 1.1, 1.2, 1.4; R&W 2.2, 2.4, 2.5; KAL 4.5; LLS 5.4, 5.5 | 1.3–4, 2.3–4, 3.2 3.4–5, 4.4–6 |
| Pages 118–119 **¿Qué podemos hacer?** | • talk about helping the environment | • carry out and write up a survey | • use expressions to say 'we can', 'we must', 'we have to'; use the imperative | *reciclar; usar transporte público; llevar tus propias bolsas al supermercado; apagar las luces; ahorrar agua; plantar árboles; comprar productos ecológicos; protestar; se puede; se debe; hay que; tener que; ahorrar; usar; ayudar* | L&S 1.2; R&W 2.2, 2.4; KAL 4.5 | 1.4, 2.3, 3.4–5, 4.4–6 |
| Pages 120–121 **Y tú, ¿cuidas del mundo?** | • talk about how you look after your world | • reading skills; make and refer to notes | • use negatives | *no; nada; ningún; ni ... ni ...; nadie; nunca; productos de comercio justo; proyectos medioambientales; trabajo de voluntariado* | L&S 1.1, 1.2, 1.3, 1.4, 1.5; R&W 2.2; IU 3.1, 3.2; KAL 4.6; LLS 5.4 | 1.3–6, 2.4–6, 3.3–5 |
| Pages 122–123 **Mi mundo familiar** | • talk about your world at home; what you are and aren't allowed to do | • summarise and recount | • use *(no) me permite(n)/ (no) puedo* | *llevar lo que quiero; poner mi música muy alta; acostarme cuando quiero; tener un trabajo a tiempo parcial; tener una televisión en mi habitación; invitar a mis amigos a mi casa; salir cuando quiero; tener piercings; estricto/a; indulgente; guay; sereno/a; anticuado/a; permitir; raro/a; no lo digas; en cambio* | LLS 5.1 | 1.4, 2.3–4, 3.2, 3.4, 4.4–6 |
| Pages 124–125 **Tenemos que ayudar** | • tell others how to care for the environment | • speak and write for different audiences – using *tú* and *usted* | • use the imperative to write rules | | L&S 1.2, 1.4, 1.5; R&W 2.2, 2.4, 2.5; KAL 4.5; LLS 5.4 | 1.5, 2.3–4, 3.3–4, 4.4–5 |

| | | | | | | |
|---|---|---|---|---|---|---|
| Pages 126–127<br>**Labolengua** | • review language and grammar from the unit | | | | KAL 4.5, 4.6;<br>R&W 2.4 | 4.4–5 |
| Pages 128–129<br>**Extra Star**<br>**Extra Plus** | • differentiated extension/ homework material | • revise and consolidate all vocabulary and grammar covered in the unit | • revise and consolidate all vocabulary and grammar covered in the unit | | R&W 2.2, 2.4, 2.5;<br>LLS 5.4 | 3.2–4,<br>4.4–6 |
| Page 130<br>**Prueba** | • end-of-unit test | | | | L&S 1.1, 1.2, 1.4;<br>R&W 2.2, 2.4;<br>LLS 5.4 | 1.4, 2.5,<br>3.4,<br>4.5–6 |
| Page 131<br>**Vocabulario** | • a summary of the key language covered in each core spread of this unit | | | | | |
| Page 155<br>**Leer 4A** | • practice of longer reading texts based on the theme of the unit | | | | R&W 2.1, 2.2 | 3.7 |

**Week-by-week overview**
**(Three-year KS3 Route: assuming six weeks' work or approximately 10–12.5 hours)**
**(Two-year KS3 Route: assuming four weeks' worth or approxmately 6.5–8.5 hours)**

**About Unit 4A, *Mi mundo*:** Students work in the context of the environment. They describe environmental problems and their causes, they also talk about protecting the environment and looking after their world. Students talk about their world at home and say what they are and aren't allowed to do at home and tell others how to look after the environment. Students give opinions with *para mí, en mi opinión* and use superlatives (*el/la … más …*). They use expressions to say, 'we can/must/have to', the imperative and negatives. They revise words of frequency and use *me permite(n)/(no) puedo*. The unit also provides tips on language learning techniques.

| Three-Year KS3 Route | | | Two-Year KS3 Route | | |
|---|---|---|---|---|---|
| **Week** | **Resources** | **Objectives** | **Week** | **Resources** | **Objectives** |
| 1 | **4A.1 ¿Cómo es tu mundo?**<br>**4A.6 Labolengua C** (p.127) | describe environmental problems and their causes<br>understand and use very large numbers<br>give opinions with *para mí, en mi opinión*<br>use superlatives (*el/la … más …*) | 1 | **4A.1 ¿Cómo es tu mundo?**<br>(Omit Think, Activity 6 & Challenge)<br>**4A.6 Labolengua C** (p.127) | describe environmental problems and their causes<br>understand and use very large numbers<br>give opinions with *para mí, en mi opinión*<br>use superlatives (*el/la … más …*) |
| 2 | **4A.2 ¿Qué podemos hacer?**<br>**4A.6 Labolengua B** (p.126) | talk about helping the environment<br>carry out and write up a survey<br>practise using the future tense; use expressions to say 'we can', 'we must', 'we have to'; use the imperative | 2 | **4A.2 ¿Qué podemos hacer?**<br>(Omit Gramática & Activity 2)<br>**4A.6 Labolengua B** (p.126) | talk about helping the environment<br>carry out and write up a survey<br>practise using the future tense; use expressions to say 'we can', 'we must', 'we have to'; use the imperative |
| 3 | **4A.3 Y tú, ¿cuidas de tu mundo?**<br>**4A.6 Labolengua A** (p.126) | talk about how you look after your world<br>reading skills; make and refer to notes<br>revise words of frequency, use negatives | 3 | **4A.3 Y tú, ¿cuidas de tu mundo?**<br>(Omit Activity 7 & Challenge)<br>**4A.6 Labolengua B** (p.126) | talk about how you look after your world<br>reading skills; make and refer to notes<br>revise words of frequency, use negatives |
| 4 | **4A.4 Mi mundo familiar** | talk about your world at home; what you are and aren't allowed to do<br>summarise and recount<br>use *(no) me permite(n)/(no) puedo* | 4 | **4A.4 Mi mundo familiar**<br>(Omit Think, & Challenge)<br>**4A.8 Prueba** (p.130)<br>**Vocabulario** (p.131) | talk about your world at home; what you are and aren't allowed to do<br>summarise and recount<br>use *(no) me permite(n)/(no) puedo* Prepare and carry out assessment in all four skills<br>Recapping on vocabulary of the unit |
| 5 | **4A.5 Tenemos que ayudar**<br>**4A.6 Labolengua D** (p.127) | tell others how to care for the environment<br>speak and write for different audiences using *tú* and *usted*<br>use the imperative to write rules | | | |
| 6 | **4A.7 Extra (Star)** (p.128)<br>**4A.7 Extra (Plus)** (p.129)<br>**4A.8 Prueba** (p.130)<br>**Vocabulario** (p.131)<br>**Leer** (p.155) | Further reinforcement and extension of the language of the unit.<br>Prepare and carry out assessment in all four skills<br>Recapping on vocabulary of the unit<br>Further reading to explore the language of the unit and cultural themes | | | |

## 4A.1 ¿Cómo es tu mundo?

páginas 116–117

# *Planner*

### Objectives
- describe environmental problems and their causes
- use superlatives *(el/la … más …)*
- give opinions with *para mí, en mi opinión*; understand and use very large numbers

### Resources
Student Book, pages 116–117
CD 3, tracks 2–3
Foundation Workbook, page 64
Higher Workbook, page 64
Foundation Workbook audio, CD 3, track 52 (Workbook 32)
Higher Workbook audio, CD 4, track 33
Interactive OxBox, Unit 4A
Copymasters 92–99

### Key language
*la basura; la contaminación atmosférica; la destrucción de la naturaleza; la extinción de animales; el cambio climático; el sufrimiento humano; cien; doscientos; quinientos; setecientos; novecientos; mil; un millón; en peligro; agua limpia; los glaciares; la papelera; tirar basura; limpio/a; la selva; ganar dinero*

### Renewed Framework references
L&S 1.1, 1.2, 1.4; R&W 2.2, 2.4, 2.5; KAL 4.5; LLS 5.4, 5.5

### PLTS
Think: Reflective learners
Activity 6: Team workers
Think: Independent enquirers
Activity 7: Self-managers
Activity 8: Independent enquirers
Challenge: Self-managers

### Starters
- Revise numbers as a class. Begin by playing a simple game of 'buzz', but in Spanish. Go round the class with each student saying a number, but every time they get to a multiple of five, they should replace the number with the word 'buzz' or a Spanish word of your choice, e.g. *hola*. So it would go, *uno, dos, tres, cuatro,* **hola**, *seis,* etc. Carry on as far as possible.
- To prepare for the Challenge, ask students to choose the issues that are relevant to their region. There could be a brief class/group discussion (probably in English) about which problems on this spread affect them and where they live, and which feel like less of a problem to them. They should now have enough language to equip them for the challenge.

### Plenaries
- As a follow-on activity from Activity 1, ask students to find the places mentioned on a map. They can then do some research into environmental problems in these places, e.g. *En Madrid también hay el problema de la contaminación del aire.*
- Following Activity 6, students write out the statements they discussed with a partner.

### Homework/Self-study
Activity 8, page 117
Challenge

AT 1.4
L&S 1.2

**1 Escucha e identifica de dónde vienen.**
Students listen and note down where each person comes from.

**CD 3, track 2** **página 116, actividades 1, 3 y 4**

**1**
Soy Conchita y vivo en las Islas Galápagos, que son parte de Ecuador. Para mí el problema más grave de mi país es la extinción de animales. En las islas hay más de 45 tipos de animales en peligro de extinción. En Ecuador hay más de 2.200 especies en peligro, y en el mundo más de 11.000.

**2**
Me llamo Imasu y soy de Bolivia. Para mí el problema más grave de mi país es el sufrimiento humano. Casi 7 millones de personas viven sin agua limpia ni electricidad.

**3**
Me llamo Quidel y vivo en Argentina. En mi opinión el problema más grave de mi país es el cambio climático. Los glaciares de las montañas – de los Andes – son más y más pequeños, porque la temperatura del planeta sube cada vez más. El agua de los glaciares es necesaria para los 40 millones de habitantes que viven en Argentina.

**4**
Soy Encarna y vivo en Madrid, la capital de España. Para mí el problema más grave que tiene mi ciudad es la basura de las calles. Se multa 750€ por tirar basura al suelo, y 3.000€ por pintar en las paredes, pero aún así ¡hay mucha basura y muchos grafitis!

5
Me llamo Felipe y soy de Ciudad de Méjico. En mi opinión el mayor problema los años noventa era la contaminación atmosférica. Mil personas morían cada año como consecuencia de la contaminación. Ahora, el aire está mucho más limpio.
6
Hola, soy Sinforosa y vivo en Guinea Ecuatorial en África. En mi opinión, el problema más grave de mi país es la destrucción de la naturaleza. La deforestación de la selva, afecta a más de 15.000 hectáreas por año, y eso es muy destructivo para los animales de la región.

*Answers:*
***1** Conchita – Islas Galápagos, Ecuador; **2** Imasu – Bolivia; **3** Quidel – Argentina; **4** Encarna – Madrid, España; **5** Felipe – Ciudad de Méjico, Méjico; **6** Sinforosa – la Guinea Ecuatorial, África*

AT 3.2 | R&W 2.2

**2 Empareja las frases de arriba (a–f) con las frases en inglés.**
Students look at the captions at the top of the page and match them to their English equivalents.

Answers:
*climate change – el cambio climático; destruction of nature – la destrucción de la naturaleza; extinction of animals – la extinción de animales; human suffering – el sufrimiento humano; pollution – la contaminación atmosférica; rubbish – la basura*

AT 1.4 | L&S1.1, 1.2

**3 Escucha otra vez e identifica el problema.**
Students listen again to the speakers from different countries describing which problem most concerns them (Activity 1). They identify which problem is being talked about by each person.

*Answers:*
***1** Conchita – la extinción de animales; **2** Imasu – el sufrimiento humano; **3** Quidel – el cambio climático; **4** Encarna – la basura; **5** Felipe – la contaminación atmosférica; **6** Sinforosa – la destrucción de la naturaleza*

PLTS

## Think

This is a useful revision activity that can be used, along with the vocabulary box before completing Activity 4.

AT 1.4 | L&S1.1, 1.2

**4 Escucha otra vez y anota todos los números y, si puedes, lo que significan.**
Students listen one more time to the recording from Activity 1 and this time make a note of all of the numbers they hear.

*Answers:*
***45** (tipos de animales en peligro de extinción en las Islas Galápagos); **2.200** (especies en peligro en Ecuador); **11.000** (especies en peligro en el mundo); **7 millones** (personas que viven sin agua limpia ni electricidad en Bolivia); **40 millones** (los habitantes de Argentina); **750€** (multa por tirar basura al suelo en Madrid); **3.000€** (multa por pintar en las paredes en Madrid); **mil** (personas que morían cada año como consecuencia de la contaminación en la Ciudad de Méjico); **15.000** (la deforestación de la selva afecta a más de 15.000 hectáreas por año en Guinea Ecuatorial en África)*

AT 1.3 | L&S1.1, 1.2

**5 Escucha y completa.**
Students listen and complete the short texts. They are the first parts of two speakers from Activity 1. This activity gives them the sentence structure they need for Activity 6.

**CD 3, track 3** **página 116, actividad 5**

– Me llamo Imasu y soy de Bolivia. Para mí, el problema más grave de mi país es el sufrimiento humano.
– Me llamo Quidel y vivo en Argentina. En mi opinión el problema más grave de mi país es el cambio climático.

*Answers:*
***1** soy; **2** mí; **3** más; **4** vivo; **5** opinión; **6** problema*

AT 2.3–4 | L&S1.4 | KAL 4.5 | PLTS

**6 Habla con tu compañero.**
Students make statements about the biggest problem in each country, drawing on the information gained from the previous activities, and using the example as a model. Their partner has to decide if the statement is true of false, and correct it if necessary. Use the Think box to make sure they can form the sentences.

AT 3.4–5 | PLTS | R&W 2.2 | LLS 5.4

**7 Lee el reportaje e corrige los errores. Usa tus respuestas de la actividad 4. Copia y completa la tabla.**
Make sure students have used the numbers *Vocabulario* box and done the activity in the Think box from the previous page before doing this activity. Students will also need to listen to the transcript from Activity 1 again to check the differences in the figures. Students can use English or Spanish here as appropriate to their ability.

*Answers:*

| *número en el reportaje* | *de …* | *número correcto* |
|---|---|---|
| *1 000* | *tipos de animales en peligro de extinción* | *11 000* |
| *700* | *personas que viven sin agua limpia o electricidad* | *7 000 000* |
| *60 000 000* | *habitantes de Argentina* | *40 000 000* |
| *570€* | *la multa para tirar basura* | *750€* |

| | | |
|---|---|---|
| *100* | *personas que morían cada año a causa de la contaminación atmosférica* | *1 000* |
| *5,000* | *hectáreas de la selva que deforestan cada año* | *15 000* |

AT 3.4 PLTS R&W 2.2 LLS 5.4, 5.5

**8 Empareja los dibujos con las frases subrayadas de la actividad 7.**
Students match the underlined phrases in the text to the pictures. Using the pictures, the context, the vocabulary list, a dictionary and logic, students work out what the phrases mean in English. Provide less able students with a list in English to match to the Spanish.

*Answers:*
***a** no usa las papeleras ([people] don't use bins);*
***b** el tráfico y las fábricas (traffic and factories); **c** para ganar dinero (to earn money); **d** destrucción de sus hábitats (the destruction of habitats); **e** calentamiento global (global warming); **f** pobreza (poverty)*

AT 4.4–6 R&W 2.4, 2.5 PLTS

**Challenge**
**Write a brief report about the environmental problems of your area. Use at least two tenses. If possible, include photos. What's the biggest problem in your opinion? Why? Use Activity 7 to help you.**
Students may also find it useful to look at the section on writing a formal letter and setting out an argument.

## 4A.2 ¿Qué podemos hacer? páginas 118–119

## *Planner*

### Objectives
- talk about helping the environment
- use expressions to say 'we can', 'we must', 'we have to'; use the imperative
- carry out and write up a survey

### Resources
Student Book, pages 118–119
CD 3, track 4
Foundation Workbook, page 65
Higher Workbook, page 65
Foundation Workbook audio, CD 3, track 53 (Workbook 33)
Higher Workbook audio, CD 4, track 34
Interactive OxBox, Unit 4A
Copymasters 92–99

### Key language
*reciclar; usar transporte público; llevar tus propias bolsas al supermercado; apagar las luces; ahorrar agua; plantar árboles; comprar productos ecológicos; protestar; se puede; se debe; hay que; tener que; ahorrar; usar; ayudar*

### Renewed Framework references
L&S 1.2; R&W 2.2, 2.4; KAL 4.5

### PLTS
Gramática: Self-managers
Activity 2: Reflective learners
Activity 4: Creative thinkers
Challenge: Effective participators

### Starters
- Play a class game to practise the imperative. Call out instructions to the class. They must act out the instructions, e.g. if you say, *comed* ... students pretend to eat something. Get faster and faster. You could also play a version of 'Simon says'.
- Activity 2, page 118.

### Plenaries
- Challenge students to write five sentences on the theme of the spread using imperatives. Depending on the level of the class, encourage them to use the *tú* and the *vosotros* forms.
- Following Activity 2, students write up some of the ideas they came up with.

### Homework/Self-study
Gramática, page 118
Activity 4, page 119

AT 1.4 AT 3.4 L&S 1.2

**1 Escucha y completa.**
Students listen to a report about how to help the environment and complete the text. They use the vocabulary from the pictures to fill the gaps.

**CD 3, track 4** **página 118, actividad 1**

Es muy importante proteger el medio ambiente, y no es difícil. En casa se puede **reciclar** las botellas, las latas y el papel para ayudar a reducir la basura que creamos. Se debe **apagar** las luces cuando salimos de la habitación para ahorrar energía. En el barrio se puede **usar** transporte público para **reducir** la contaminación. Cuando vas de compras, debes **llevar** tus propias bolsas al supermercado para no usar bolsas de plástico. Para ayudar más, se puede **comprar** productos ecológicos. En el campo hay que **ahorrar** agua, y para controlar el cambio climático se puede **plantar** árboles. Finalmente, para educar a la gente, ¡se puede **protestar**!

*Answers: in bold in the transcript*

PLTS

### Gramática

Students should familiarise themselves with these expressions before attempting Activity 2. Can they write an example sentence for each of the expressions listed?

AT 2.3 | PLTS | L&S 1.2

**2 ¿Cómo ayudar el medio ambiente en la casa, en la calle, en el supermercado y en el campo? Mira las fotos. Completa las ideas de tu compañero.**

Students play a game in pairs. Partner A starts a sentence about protecting the environment, partner B completes it, and vice versa.

KAL 4.5

### Gramática

Work through the Grammar box on the imperative as a class. Explain to students that they will see these in the next activity.

AT 3.5 | PLTS | R&W 2.2 | KAL 4.5

**3 Lee la nota de Elena. Busca los imperativos. ¿Tú o vosotros?**

Students find the imperatives in the text and note down whether they are in the *tú* or *vosotros* form.

*Answers: **Tú:** recicla, no uses, viaja, lleva, planta, **Vosotros:** apagad, no os bañeis, usad, comprad, protestad*

AT 4.5 | PLTS | KAL 4.5

**4 Lee la carta otra vez. Escribe lo que tienen que hacer los miembros de la familia.**

Students change the imperative form to the correct form of *tener que*.

*Answers:*

*Mamá tiene que reciclar. Papá tiene que usar transporte público. Roberto y Juan tienen que apagar las luces y usar la ducha. La abuela tiene que llevar sus propias bolsas al supermercado. La abuela y Mamá tienen que comprar productos ecológicos. El abuelo tiene que plantar árboles. Todos tienen que protestar.*

AT 4.4–6 | R&W 2.4 | PLTS

### Challenge

**Carry out a survey. Do your friends help the environment? What have they done recently? Write up your results, and say what people must do to help more.**

Students carry out a survey. Before they begin, agree on some questions to ask. Possible questions:

| | | |
|---|---|---|
| ¿Quién ... | ahorrará | energía? |
| | | agua? |
| | ayudará | a prevenir el cambio climático? |
| | contaminará | menos? |
| | producirá | menos basura? |
| | educará | a otra gente? |
| | usará | menos bolsas de plástico? |

More able students may be able to think of additional questions. The answers can be written up at different levels according to ability; the most able should produce statements like the example.

## 4A.3 Y tú, ¿cuidas del mundo?

páginas 120–121

### Planner

**Objectives**
- talk about how you look after your world
- use negatives
- reading skills; make and refer to notes

**Resources**
Student Book, pages 120–121
CD 3, tracks 5–6
Foundation Workbook, page 66
Higher Workbook, page 66
Interactive OxBox, Unit 4A
Copymasters 92–99

**Video**
Video clip, Unit 4A

**Key language**
*no; nada; ningún; ni ... ni ...; nadie; nunca; productos de comercio justo; proyectos medioambientales; trabajo de voluntariado*

**Renewed Framework references**
L&S 1.1, 1.2, 1.3, 1.4, 1.5; R&W 2.2; IU 3.1, 3.2; KAL 4.6; LLS 5.4

**PLTS**
Activity 3: Independent enquirers
Activity 4: Independent enquirers; Reflective learners
Activity 5: Effective participators
Challenge: Independent enquirers; Creative thinkers; Reflective learners

**Starters**
- Challenge students to list all of the frequency words and phrases they can remember. Share answers as a class and make a list of these on the whiteboard. Add any that students have forgotten. Ensure that students understand everything in the list by asking volunteers to translate each one. With less able classes, you could provide a list of English translations and ask them to match the English and Spanish.
- Display a list of things you can do to look after the environment. Depending on the level of the class, you can display these in the infinitive, e.g. *usar el transporte público* or in the 1st person singular, e.g. *Trabajo como voluntario*. Also display the list of frequency words from Starter Activity 1 and the negative forms, e.g. *no ... nunca, ni ... ni...*, etc. Go round the class asking students how often they do any of the measures listed.

**Plenaries**
- Students write negative sentences based on Grammar explanation...
- Following Activity 4, go round the class with students telling you which of the measures to help protect the environment they do/don't do, e.g. *Uso el transporte público en vez del coche, pero no compro productos ecológicos*. Encourage more able students to use frequency words and phrases as well as negatives.

**Homework/Self-study**
Activities 3 and 4, page 121

AT 1.3–4 | AT 3.3–4 | L&S1.2

**1 Escucha y completa la conversación.**
Students listen and complete the dialogue.

**CD 3, track 5** — **página 120, actividades 1 y 2**

Elena: El problema del medio ambiente es que nadie cuida del mundo. No se reciclan las botellas y el papel porque en el barrio no hay ningún contenedor de reciclaje.
Roberto: Mis amigos ni andan ni usan transporte público, van en coche a todas partes.
Juan: Es verdad, mis amigos tampoco hacen nada para ayudar al medio ambiente. Nunca llevan sus propias bolsas al supermercado...

*Answers:*
***1** se reciclan; **2** andan; **3** coche; **4** bolsas*

**Gramática**
Read through the Grammar box on negatives before students complete Activity 2. For more information on negatives, refer students to page 166 of the Grammar section.

AT 1.3–4 | L&S 1.2 | KAL 4.6

**2 Escucha y lee la conversación otra vez.**
Students listen to and read the conversation again. They then say who says each of the statements.

*Answers:*
***1** Juan; **2** Roberto; **3** Juan; **4** Elena; **5** Elena*

AT 3.5 | PLTS | KAL 4.6

**3 Lee el texto y anota todas las expresiones negativas.**
Students read the text and make a note of any negative expressions. For less able students, provide a list of the negatives they need to find so it is just a matter of them finding them in context.

*Answers:*
*nunca reciclamos nada; no vamos en autobús nunca; Ni compramos productos ecológicos ni llevamos nuestras propias bolsas al supermercado. no hay ningún voluntario; tampoco trabaja*

AT 3.5 | PLTS | R&W 2.2 | LLS 5.4

**4 Busca las frases en español. Escríbelas y anota en qué orden se mencionan.**
For less able students, this could be set up as a matching activity. By picking out information from this text, students are preparing themselves to write notes for the Challenge task. Before students start this activity, direct them to the Think box which gives some useful advice on understanding longer texts.

*Answers:*
*no recycling (nuna reciclamos nada); too much car use (no vamos en autobús nunca); taking baths not showers (nos duchamos raramente y nos bañamos a menudo); people not buying eco-products (ni compramos productos ecológicos ...); people don't use own shopping bags (... ni llevamos nuestras propias bolsas al supermercado); no volunteers (no hay ningún voluntario)*

AT 1.5–6 | PLTS | L&S 1.1, 1.2, 1.3 | IU 3.1, 3.2 | LLS 5.4

**5 Mira el video y contesta a las preguntas.**
Students watch the whole of the video and answer the questions. They will already have been introduced to this at the beginning of the unit and should now try to listen for more detail. The questions will help to focus their minds.

**Video clip: Unit 4A (CD 3, track 6)**

**Part 1**
*In the garden at Elena and Juan's house.*

Juan: Pero, mamá, nadie usa pesticidas hoy.
Mama: ¿Y qué se usa entonces?
Elena: Pues se pueden usar productos biológicos que ayudan a proteger el planeta.
Mama: Y ¿qué hago con los insectos que se comen los tomates?
Juan: Pues, no sé.
Roberto: He leído en el periódico que hay talleres en un huerto ecológico.
Mama: Excelente. ¡Iros al taller y luego me contáis!

**Part 2**
*Outside the Huerta.*

Juan: Ahora tenemos que trabajar toda la tarde en un huerto. Es culpa de Roberto.
Roberto: No es verdad. Es culpa tuya. *Direct to camera* Pero tenéis que ayudarnos. Anotad cómo un huerto ecológico ayuda a proteger el medio ambiente.
Elena: Bueno aquí estamos. Venid.

Charo: Hola chicos, bienvenidos a La Huerta. Aquí cultivamos todo tipo de frutas y verduras, pero eso sí, de manera ecológica.
Roberto: ¿Pero, qué significa trabajar de manera ecológica?
Charo: Pues, significa cultivar sin pesticidas sin herbicidas, todo con productos naturales. Pero controlando la calidad de los alimentos.
Juan: ¿Y qué podemos hacer con los insectos que se comen las verduras?
Charo: Vamos a la Huerta a ver cómo trabajamos.
Charo: ¿Qué creeis que es esto? ¿Qué puede ser?
Group: ¿Semillas? ¿Espárragos?
Charo: ¿Espárragos? No. Una flor efectivamente. Una flor. En una huerta es muy importante recoger semillas, recoger las semillas de un año para otro. Esta es la semilla de la cebolla. Son muchas flores y de allí sale las semillitas para luego poner en el semillero, a volver a cultivar el siguiente año. Mira quién se come los insectos ..., los insectos malos. Las mariquitas son las mejores aliadas del hortelano. Mírala, cógela.
...
Juan: Se ha ido.
Charo: No la gustó tu mano. ¿Qué es esto?
Roberto: Una alcachofa.
Charo: Muy bien muy bien, bueno. Hemos dicho que en la agricultura ecológica, no se usan pesticidas ni herbicidas para quitar las malas hierbas. Por lo tanto hay que quitarlas a mano. Y a la mano es, pues así. ¿Alguien quiere probar?
Roberto: Sí.
Charo: Venga, hombre. Ah, ¡tú sabes! Tú, sí que sabes. Ay, muy bien.
Elena: Voy a preguntar cuántas verduras diferentes crecen en el huerto. Anotad. ¿Charo?
Charo: Dime.
Elena: ¿Qué verduras crecen en el huerto?
Charo: Pues, tenemos calabacines, pepinos, tomates, judías, repollos, guisantes, acelgas.
Elena: ¿Todo ecológico?
Charo: Por supuesto.
Elena: ¿Por qué?
Charo: Porque al final es más barato, se protege el medio ambiente, y es algo que han hecho mis padres toda la vida.
Charo: Estupendo.

| | |
|---|---|
| Juan: | Perdona. |
| Charo: | Dime |
| Juan: | ¿Te puedo hacer una pregunta? |
| Charo: | Claro. |
| Juan: | ¿Qué se puede hacer con las verduras y con las hojas que no son buenas para cocinar? |
| Charo: | Pues aquí no hay nada de basura con las hojas y con las verduras que no son buenas para cocinar se puede hacer abono, otras veces también con esas hojas se puede dar de comer a las gallinas o a las ovejas. Lo importante es reciclar y no hacer basura. |
| Juan: | ¿Y qué podemos hacer en casa para ayudar al medio ambiente? |
| Charo: | Reciclar. Reciclar papel, vidrio, ropa e incluso reciclar el aceite que usas para freír y con ello hacer jabón. |
| Juan: | ¿Jabón con el aceite de freír las patatas fritas? No lo creo. |
| Charo: | Sí, por supuesto. Se ha hecho toda la vida. |
| Charo: | Hoy vamos a hacer la cosecha de calabacines. Notad que están cultivados junto a las lombardas y las patatas, especies totalmente distintas. |
| Roberto: | ¿Qué hay que hacer para recoger el calabacín? |
| Charo: | Pues, levantad el calabacín. Cortad así. Sin dañar la planta porqué allí hay más pequeñitos. Hay uno allí para cortar. |

*Outside the Huerta.*

| | |
|---|---|
| Elena: | ¿Bueno, qué hemos aprendido hoy? ¿Por qué es importante trabajar de forma ecológica? |
| Juan: | Es más barato. |
| Roberto: | Ayuda a proteger el planeta. |
| Elena: | ¿Y qué tenemos que hacer? |
| Juan: | No usar pesticidas. |
| Roberto: | Reciclar todo. |
| Elena: | ¿Y vosotros qué opináis? |
| Juan: | ¿Podemos hacer otro taller? Quiero aprender cómo se puede hacer jabón con el aceite de las patatas fritas. |
| Elena & Roberto: | ¡Juan! |

*Answers:*
***a** to a garden **b** how to be more eco-friendly; **c&d** see video script.*

AT 1.5–6 | L&S 1.1, 1.2, 1.3 | IU 3.1, 3.2 | LLS 5.4

**6 ¿Verdad o mentira?**
Students decide if each statement is true or false.

*Answers:*
***a** verdad; **b** mentira; **c** mentira*

AT 1.5–6

**7 ¿Y tu, qué opinas? Cómo podemos ayudar a proteger el planeta?**

PLTS | AT 2.4–6 | L&S 1.4, 1.5

### Challenge

**Give a report to the class about the state of your school or street. Include two or three tenses.**
Students should make notes first about the problems they wish to present; one problem for weaker students, several for the most able. Very confident students can speak straight from the notes, less confident ones should write out what they want to say, and then speak just from notes. If necessary, present an example report to show what is required, as many will find this quite a challenge. Students can then practise in pairs or small groups before producing and giving their own individual report.

## 4A.4 Mi mundo familiar

páginas 122–123

### *Planner*

**Objectives**
- talk about your world at home; what you are and aren't allowed to do
- use *(no) me permite(n)/(no) puedo*
- summarise and recount

**Resources**
Student Book, pages 122–123
CD 3, track 7
Foundation Workbook, page 67
Higher Workbook, page 67
Foundation Workbook audio, CD 3, track 54 (Workbook 34)
Higher Workbook audio, CD 4, track 35
Interactive OxBox, Unit 4A
Copymasters 92–99

## Key language

*llevar lo que quiero; poner mi música muy alta; acostarme cuando quiero; tener un trabajo a tiempo parcial; tener una televisión en mi habitación; invitar a mis amigos a mi casa; salir cuando quiero; tener piercings; estricto/a; indulgente; guay; sereno/a; anticuado/a; permitir; raro/a; no lo digas; en cambio*

## Renewed Framework references

L&S 1.2, 1.4; R&W 2.2, 2.4; IU 3.1, 3.2; KAL 4.5; LLS 5.1

## PLTS

Activity 1: Self-managers
Activity 2: Independent enquirers
Activity 3: Self-managers
Activity 4: Team workers
Activity 5: Effective participators
Activity 6: Reflective learners
Think Reflective learners
Activity 7: Self-managers
Challenge: Creative thinkers

## Starters

- Activity 1, page 122 is an ideal Starter Activity.
- Play a class game to practise the key language some more. If possible move the desks and make one area of the classroom the *puedo* area and another area, the no *puedo* area. Call out activities from the key language, e.g. ...*poner mi música muy alta*. Students go to the area that is applicable to them. So if they are allowed to play music loudly, they go to the *puedo* area, if they're not, they go to the *no puedo* area. Each time, elicit from students what the phrase means before calling out another one.

## Plenaries

- Have a class quiz to see who can remember the most differences between Roberto's life in Colombia and his life in Spain. Split the class into teams and ask each team in turn to tell you something that he is/isn't allowed to do in each place. Alternatively with less able classes, you could give each team a statement, e.g. *En Colombia, en suhabitación, puede poner sumúsica muy alta.* and ask them to tell you if it is true (*verdad*) or false (*falso*).
- Following Activity 4, do a class survey to find out what students can and can't do. Record the results and display them as a graph or piechart.

## Homework/Self-study

Following Activity 3, ask students to write out their lists as a full paragraph. More able students should also add opinions where possible as well as frequency words and phrases.
Students add the phrases from the Think box to their vocabulary list if they have one. Encourage them to add useful phrases every time they come across them as these will be useful to use in their own written and oral work.

AT 3.2 | PLTS | R&W 2.2

**1 Empareja las frases con los dibujos.**
As an introduction to the spread, students familiarise themselves with the key language by matching the phrases listed to the pictures.

*Answers:*
***1** h; **2** c; **3** f; **4** e; **5** g; **6** a; **7** b; **8** d*

AT 1.4 | PLTS | L&S 1.2 | IU 3.1, 3.2

**2 Escucha. ¿Qué puede hacer Roberto? ¿Es diferente en España y en Colombia? Copia y completa la tabla.**
Students listen to Roberto and note down how what he is allowed to do in Colombia differs from what he is allowed to do in Spain.

**CD 3, track 7** — **página 122, actividad 2**

Sabes, vivir en Segovia con mis tíos y mis primos es bastante diferente a vivir en Colombia con mamá. Mi madre es bastante despreocupada, y me permite invitar a mis amigos a casa cuando quiero, pero mi tía es más tradicional. Aquí puedo invitar a amigos a casa solamente los fines de semana, para comer con la familia o algo así.

En Colombia, en mi habitación, puedo poner mi música muy alta, pero aquí en Segovia eso rara vez es posible, y solamente cuando mis tíos no están en casa. Aquí mis tíos son bastante indulgentes y me permiten llevar más o menos lo que quiero. Mi madre tiene ideas muy anticuadas sobre qué ropa ponerse, y tengo que llevar lo que a ella le gusta. Además, mi madre es más estricta que mis tíos sobre lo de salir con mis amigos. En Colombia solamente puedo salir los fines de semana. En Segovia puedo salir cuando quiero, pero durante la semana tengo que estar en casa para las diez.

En Colombia, mi madre me permite acostarme cuando quiero – ¡qué guay! – pero mis tíos son más estrictos y entre semana, tengo que acostarme a las once en punto.

Mi madre no me permite tener un trabajo a tiempo parcial tampoco – dice que tengo que estudiar – pero mis tíos dicen que puedo buscar un trabajo si quiero.

Aquí en Segovia mis tíos no nos permiten tener una televisión en el dormitorio. Son muy anticuados y dicen que tenemos que ver la televisión en familia. ¡En Colombia tengo una televisión y un ordenador en mi habitación, y mi hermana también!

Hay una cosa que no puedo hacer ni en Segovia ni en Colombia. Ni mi madre ni mis tíos me permiten tener un piercing. ¡Es una lástima!

*Answers:*
***España:*** *(tíos); invitar a mis amigos a mi casa los fines de semana solamente; poner mi música muy alta solamente cuando mis tíos no están en casa; llevar más o menos lo que quiero; puedo salir cuando quiero (durante la semana tengo que estar en casa para las diez); acostarme a las once en punto entre semana; puedo buscar un trabajo; tenemos que mirar la televisión en familia; no me permiten tener un piercing*
***Colombia:*** *(madre); invitar mis amigos a mi casa cuando quiero; poner mi música muy alta; llevar lo que a Mamá le gusta; solamente puedo salir los fines de semana; acostarme cuando quiero; no me permite tener un trabajo a tiempo parcial; tengo una televisión y un ordenador en mi habitación; no me permite tener un piercing*

AT 4.4 | PLTS | LLS 5.1

**3 Escribe dos listas. ¿Qué te permiten hacer? ¿Qué no te permiten?**
Students write two lists, saying what they are, and are not, allowed to do. Before they start their lists, read through the Grammar box as a class to ensure that they understand how to use the verb *permitir*. Volunteers could share their lists with the class.

AT 2.3–4 | PLTS | L&S 1.4

**4 ¿Y tú? ¿Qué puedes hacer? Discute con un compañero.**
Students use what they have done in Activity 3 to discuss with a partner. They should try to use the verb *permitir* and *puedo*....

AT 2.4 | PLTS | L&S 1.4 | KAL 4.5

**5 Explica a otra persona.**
After speaking with a partner in Activity 4, students feed back to another student, or to the whole class. They could also write down the information to practise changing from the 1st person to the 3rd person. Before they attempt this activity, read through the second Grammar box to practise using *permitir* in the 3rd person. Also point out to students that they can use *puede*.

AT 3.4 | PLTS | R&W 2.2

**6 Completa el email con los verbos de la casilla.**
Students read the e-mail and fill in the gaps using the words from the box.

*Answers:*
***1*** *puede;* ***2*** *puede;* ***3*** *hacer;* ***4*** *puedo;* ***5*** *permiten;* ***6*** *permiten;* ***7*** *permiten;* ***8*** *tengo;* ***9*** *tenemos;* ***10*** *debo;* ***11*** *hago;* ***12*** *tienen;* ***13*** *tenemos*

PLTS

### Think
Students read the e-mail again and find the phrases listed. They should keep a note of phrases such as 'On the other hand', as it will come in useful in their speaking and writing.

*Answers:*
*Aquí todo es muy raro. ¡No lo digas a mamá! En cambio… Roberto is a disaster with the washing up because he always breaks something – three plates, four glasses last week.*

AT 4.4 | PLTS | R&W 2.4

**7 Escribe un resumen. ¿Qué puede, no puede, debe y tiene que hacer Roberto en Segovia?**
Students use what they have done in the previous activities to write a summary saying what Roberto can, can't and must do in Spain. Remind students that they will need to use the 3rd person singular.

AT 4.4–6 | PLTS | R&W 2.4

### Challenge
**Write a few sentences about what you can do at home, what you must do and what you would like to be able to do. You could also write about what you were not allowed to do when you were younger.**
This brings together everything that students have been learning in this spread. Encourage more able students to include phrases such as 'On the other hand...'.

## 4A.5 Tenemos que ayudar

páginas 124–125

# Planner

### Objectives
- tell others how to care for the environment
- use the imperative to write rules
- speak and write for different audiences – using *tú* and *usted*

### Resources
Student Book, pages 124–125
CD 3, tracks 8–9
Foundation Workbook, page 68
Higher Workbook, page 68
Foundation Workbook audio, CD 3, track 55 (Workbook 35)
Higher Workbook audio, CD 4, track 36
Interactive OxBox, Unit 4A
Copymasters 92–99

### Renewed Framework references
L&S 1.2, 1.4, 1.5; R&W 2.2, 2.4, 2.5; KAL 4.5; LLS 5.4

### PLTS
Activity 2: Team workers
Activity 4: Team workers; Effective participators
Activity 5: Creative thinkers; Effective participators
Activity 6: Self-managers
Gramática: Reflective learners
Activity 7: Team workers
Challenge: Creative thinkers

### Starters
- Before students start work on the spread, have a brainstorming session on the imperative, *tú* and *vosotros* forms. Can students remember how to form these in the positive and negative?

### Plenaries
- Students work in groups to practise giving each other instructions on the theme of protecting the environment.

### Homework/Self-study
Gramática, page 125: Students write their own polite instructions using using *usted* and *ustedes*
Challenge Activity

**1 Escucha a las normas de Doñana.**
Students listen to the rules.

**CD 3, track 8** — **página 124, actividad 1**

1 Recicla lata y papeles.
2 No tires basura.
3 Ahorra agua.
4 No caces animales.
5 Utiliza las papeleras.
6 Evita hacer ruido.
7 No hagas fuego.

AT 3.3–4 | PLTS | R&W 2.2

**2 Decide con tu compañero qué significan las normas. Escribe las normas en inglés.**
Students read the poster and write down what the rules mean in English.

*Answers:*
***1*** *Recycle tins and paper.* ***2*** *Don't drop litter.* ***3*** *Save water.* ***4*** *Don't hunt animals.* ***5*** *Use the bins.* ***6*** *Don't make a noise.* ***7*** *Don't make fires.*

AT 3.4 | LLS 5.4

**3 Empareja las dos partes de las frases.**
Students pick the correct words each time to finish the sentence. Remind students that they don't need to understand every word to work out the answers. They should already understand the rules, from Activity 1 and should look out for cognates and other words they know as well as at the vocabulary box in order to find the correct words each time.

*Answers:*
***1*** *b,* ***2*** *f,* ***3*** *d,* ***4*** *g,* ***5*** *c,* ***6*** *e,* ***7*** *a*

AT 2.3 | PLTS | L&S 1.4

**4 Trabaja en un grupo. Pon las normas en orden de importancia.**
This activity should encourage much discussion amongst members of each group, as there is no definite answer.

AT 2.4 | PLTS | L&S 1.2

**5 Presenta tu opinión a la clase.**
Once all groups have finished Activity 3, compare answers as a class. Do groups agree or does the order differ from group to group? More able students can use the Think box to present their opinions in the plural, e.g. *Para nosotros, utilizar los basureros es la norma más importante...*

AT 1.5 | PLTS | L&S 1.5

**6 Escucha. ¿Cuáles son las normas del Demonio del Desastre, y cuáles son normas ecológicas?**
Students refer back to the *Doñana* rules while they listen to help them. More able students can also note if the speaker uses a plural or singular instruction form.

**CD 3, track 9** **página 125, actividad 6**

1 No ahorres agua. No es necesario ni para los animales ni para las plantas tampoco. ¡Date un baño todos los días!
2 Mira, eso es muy importante: ¡tirad basura! ¡Tirad basura en las calles, en las montañas, en las playas! ¡Todo el planeta estará muy sucio!
3 Por favor, amigos míos, reciclad latas y papeles porque ayuda mucho al medio ambiente y habrá menos basura en las calles y en los parques.
4 Oye, no caces animales – es cruel, y muchos de ellos están en peligro de extinción. ¡Hay que protegerlos!
5 No utilicéis los basureros. No es necesario. No es importante tener una ciudad limpia, ¡será mejor tener una ciudad sucia!
6 Por favor, evitad hacer ruido porque asustará a los animales, y molestará a la otra gente que en ésta en el parque.
7 Haz fuegos. Puedes hacer fuego aquí si quieres. Es muy agradable charlar con los amigos alrededor de una hoguera, ¿verdad?

*Answers:*
*Answers here are just given in the singular to match the list in the Student Book, but more able students can write down the plurals they hear.*
***1*** *No ahorres agua – DD;* ***2*** *Tira basura – DD;* ***3*** *Recicla – NE;* ***4*** *No caces animales – NE;* ***5*** *No utilices basureros – DD;* ***6*** *Evita hacer ruido – NE;* ***7*** *Haz fuegos – DD*

PLTS
KAL 4.5
### Gramática
Read through the Grammar box on giving polite instructions using *usted* and *ustedes* and look at the examples.

PLTS
**7 ¿Tú, vosotros, usted o ustedes? Trabaja con un compañero y decide.**
Students work with a partner to decide which form each of the imperatives is in. This would also be a good time to look at the Think box on the verb *cazar* in the imperative.

*Answers:*
***1*** *usted;* ***2*** *vosotros;* ***3*** *tú;* ***4*** *usted;* ***5*** *ustedes;* ***6*** *ustedes;* ***7*** *ustedes*

AT 4.4–5
PLTS
R&W 2.4, 2.5
### Challenge
**Draw up rules for your school/home/town, e.g. *No tiréis chicle al suelo* (Don't throw chewing gum on the ground). Which type of instructions would you use? Can you give reasons? For example: *La calle estará muy sucia.***
Students can work in groups, and produce instructions for different situations. To extend the written work, they can add consequences or reasons, e.g. *No tiréis chicle al suelo – es peligroso para los animales y la calle estará muy sucia.*

## 4A.6 Labolengua

páginas 126–127

# Planner

### Objectives
- review language and grammar from the unit

### Resources
Student Book, pages 126–127
Foundation Workbook, pages 69–70
Higher Workbook, pages 69–70
Interactive OxBox, Unit 4A
Copymasters 100–101

### Grammar
- negatives and imperatives

### Renewed Framework references
KAL 4.5, 4.6; R&W 2.4

### PLTS
All activities: Reflective learners/Self-managers
Activity 7: Independent enquirers

### Homework/Self-study
Activities 1 and 2, page 126

### Comprender – negatives and imperatives

### A Nada, nunca, nadie

KAL 4.6
PLTS
**1 Make these sentences negative by adding the correct words.**
Practice of forming negatives.

*Answers:*
***1*** *No estudia nadie español.* ***2*** *No voy a comer ni un bocadillo ni una pizza.* ***3*** *No vamos nunca de vacaciones a España.* ***4*** *No hay nada que hacer por aquí.* ***5*** *Mi padre no tiene ningún coche.*

### B ¡No tires chicles al suelo! – instructions

KAL 4.5 PLTS **2 Complete these instructions.**
Practice of instructions in Spanish.

*Answers:*
***1** ¡Subid la escalera! **2** ¡Reciclen papel y cartón! **3** ¡No coma eso! **4** ¡No vivas aquí! **5** ¡Estudiad más!*

### Aprender – writing a formal letter and presenting an argument

### C Writing to the local newspaper

PLTS **3 Identify parts a, b and c of Ramón's letter.**

PLTS **4 How do you say 'Dear Sir' and 'Yours sincerely' in Spanish?**
Practice of formal letter vocabulary in Spanish.

*Answers:* Estimado señor; Atentamente

PLTS **5 How would you address a lady?**
Further practice of formal letter vocabulary in Spanish.

*Answers: Estimada señora*

PLTS AT 4.4–5 R&W 2.4 **6 Write a letter to a paper complaining about the state of your local park; there is a lot of litter, and kids have been lighting fires and making noise late at night. You can use this letter as a model.**
Practice of formal letter writing.

### Hablar – appropriate language

### D Saying the right thing

PLTS **7 Familiar or polite? Decide in what situation you might say these things.**
Practice of using appropriate language.

*Answers:*
***1** familiar – friend or sibling grabbing a bite from your sandwich; **2** polite – park warden telling adults not to bring dogs in; **3** familiar – teacher telling students where to write; **4** polite – asking a stranger in a cafe not to take your drink; **5** familiar – parent telling a child not to come in the house with dirty shoes; **6** polite – telling an adult stranger that what they're about to do is a really bad idea.*

## 4A.7 Extra Star

página 128

## *Planner*

### Objectives

- talk about environmental problems and their solutions
- practise *tú* imperatives
- write instructions

### Resources

Student Book, page 128
Copymaster 102

### Renewed Framework references

LLS 5.4

### PLTS

Activity 2: Reflective learners
Activity 3: Creative thinkers

AT 3.3 **1 Empareja las fotos con las frases. Completa las frases con las palabras de la casilla.**
Students match the photos to the sentences and then complete the sentences using the words in the box.

*Answers:*
***1** basura, f; **2** sufrimiento, d; **3** naturaleza, b; **4** exterminio, c; **5** contaminación, e; **6** climático, a*

AT 3.2 PLTS LLS 5.4 **2 Empareja las instrucciones en español con las en inglés.**
Practice of imperatives.

*Answers:*
***1** d; **2** e; **3** a; **4** c; **5** f; **6** b*

AT 3.3
PLTS

**3 Completa las soluciones a los problemas de la actividad 1.**
Students complete the solutions to the problems in Activity 1.

*Suggested answers:*
*__1__ ¡Usa las papeleras! __2__ ¡Protesta contra la pobreza! __3__ ¡Proteja los hábitats! __4__ ¡Proteja al medio ambiente! __5__ ¡No uses el coche! __6__ ¡Planta árboles!*

## 4A.7 Extra Plus

página 129

### *Planner*

**Objectives**
- understand environmental problems and their solutions
- practise using polite imperatives
- summarise a text

**Resources**
Student Book, page 129
Copymaster 103

**Renewed Framework references**
R&W 2.2, 2.4, 2.5; LLS 5.4

**PLTS**
Activity 1: Independent enquirers
Activity 3: Creative thinkers

AT 3.4
R&W 2.2
PLTS

**1 Completa los textos con las palabras de abajo, y empareja el texto con la foto del problema medioambiental.**
Students complete the texts and match them to the photos.

*Answers:*
*__1__ calentamiento global, b; __2__ cambio climático, d; __3__ destrucción de la naturaleza, a; __4__ contaminación, c*

AT 3.4
R&W 2.2
LLS 5.4

**2 ¿Qué describe cada texto? Escribe notas en inglés.**
This activity requires students to look at the texts in more detail. Remind them that they don't need to understand every word to be able to understand each text as a whole.

*Answers:*
*__1__ polar ice-cap melting – habitats disappearing – sea-levels rising; __2__ warm regions – climate change – less rain – hard to grow crops – more rain; __3__ destruction of nature – cutting down rainforest – need money – destruction of habitat for animals, birds, plants; __4__ lots of traffic, factories, rubbish – air pollution – health problems for inhabitants*

AT 4.4–6
PLTS
R&W 2.4, 2.5

**3 Escribe una frase para cada texto.**
Students can write various phrases to summarise each text. They may focus on one aspect that seems important to them.

AT 4.4–6
R&W 2.4, 2.5

**4 Escribe al director de tu instituto y sobre un problema medioambiental. ¿Cuál es el problema? ¿Y la causa? ¿Hay una solución?**
Students write appropriately to their ability, drawing on material from this unit, and adding their own ideas if they are able.

## 4A.8 Prueba

página 130

**Resources**
Student Book, page 130
CD 3, track 10
Assessment OxBox, Unit 4A

**Renewed Framework references**
L&S 1.1, 1.2, 1.4; R&W 2.2, 2.4; LLS 5.4

**PLTS**
All activities: Reflective learners
Hablar: Effective participators

## Escuchar

AT 1.4 | L&S 1.1, 1.2 | PLTS

**Listen and choose the correct picture for each instruction you hear.**
This activity tests listening skills using the language covered in this unit.

**CD 3, track 10** **página 130, actividad 1**

1 Hay demasiada basura en las calles de nuestra ciudad porque la gente ni usa las papeleras ni recicla tampoco. ¡Reciclad las latas y las botellas!
2 El parque nacional está aquí para proteger a los animales en peligro de extinción. ¡No cacen animales! La caza está prohibida.
3 El cambio climático es un problema muy grave, sobre todo en las regiones más calientes del planeta. ¡Ahorra agua! El agua es muy importante para la naturaleza y para los seres humanos.
4 ¡Todos tenemos que ayudar! Cuando vayas de compras, ¡lleva tus propias bolsas! Así usarás menos bolsas de plástico.
5 Chicos, hay que ahorrar energía. ¡Apagad la luz cuando salgáis de la habitación! Es muy importante.

*Answers:*
***1** d; **2** b; **3** a; **4** e; **5** c*

## Hablar

AT 2.5 | L&S 1.4 | PLTS

**Ask your partner what can be done to help the environment, and what they do.**
This activity tests speaking skills using the language covered in this unit. Students use the pictures as prompts to answer the questions as they wish.

## Leer

AT 3.4 | R&W 2.2 | LLS 5.4 | PLTS

**Read the text. Note down in Spanish three things we can do to help the environment, and three things we must not do.**
This activity tests reading skills using the language covered in this unit.

*Answers:*
***do:** shower; use public transport; travel on foot*
***don't:** throw litter on the ground; hunt endangered animals; use too much water*

## Escribir

AT 4.5–6 | R&W 2.4 | PLTS

**Write a short paragraph (about 4 or 5 sentences) about what you are allowed to do at home. Say what you were allowed to do when you were younger and what you will be able to do when you are 18.**
This activity tests writing skills using the language covered in this unit.

# Leer 4A

página 155

## Planner

### Resources
Student Book, page 155

### Renewed Framework references
R&W 2.1, 2.2

### PLTS
Activity 2: Self-managers

AT 3.7 | R&W 2.1, 2.2

**1 Read the reports and decide if the following statements are about the Mexican squirrels or the Amazon dolphins.**

*Answers:*
***1** Mexican squirrels; **2** Amazon dolphins; **3** Mexican squirrels **4** Amazon dolphins*

AT 3.7 | R&W 2.1, 2.2 | PLTS

**2 Completa las frases.**

*Answers:*
***1** ...tropical rainforests **2** ...look for food and water or to change trees. **3** The squirrels have between two and six babies at a time. **4** ...Peru. **5** ...they can damage fishermen's nets. **6** ...in a lagoon in the northwest of the country.*

### Follow-up
Students research other endangered species or other animals that live in Spain or Latin America. They should take notes in either Spanish or English to share with the class. This is also a good opportunity for them to find out more about the areas of Mexico and the Amazon.

# Foundation Workbook

## Página 64 4A.1 ¿Cómo es tu mundo?

- Use with Student Book, pages 116–117

AT 3.2 **1 Draw lines to match up the numbers with the words.**
Practice of higher numbers.

*Answers:*
***a** 3; **b** 6; **c** 5; **d** 2; **e** 4; **f** 1*

AT 1.2 **2 Listen and put the numbers into the order you hear them.**

**CD 3, track 52 (Workbook 32)** **página 64, actividad 2**

mil siete
siete mil trescientos
cuarenta y seis mil
noventa y tres millones
tres mil ochocientos
doce mil
seis millones
dos mil

*Answers:*
*1.007; 7.300; 46.000; 93.000.000; 3.800; 12.000; 6.000.000; 2.000*

AT 4.3–4 R&W 2.5 **3 Complete these sentences with your own opinions about the environmental problems.**
Students should refer back to pages 116 and 117 of the Student Book for ideas and support.

## Página 65 4A.2 ¿Qué podemos hacer?

- Use with Student Book, pages 118–119

AT 4.2 **1 Complete the phrases. Then match up each phrase to the correct picture.**

*Answers:*
***1** protestar; **2** apagar las luces; **3** plantar árboles; **4** ahorrar agua; **5** usar el transporte público; **6** comprar productos ecológicos; **7** reciclar plástico y vidrio; **8** llevar tus proprias bolsas al supermercado*

AT 1.4 L&S 1.1, 1.2 **2 Listen and look at the pictures again. Write the numbers of the things Isabel does to help the environment.**

**CD 3, track 53 (Workbook 33)** **página 65, actividad 2**

Bueno, pienso que es importante que cuidemos del medio ambiente. Se puede reciclar plástico y vidrio, apagar las luces cuando sales de las habitaciones, usar tus propias bolsas cuando vas de compras. También hay que usar el autobús o el metro siempre que se pueda. Otra cosa que se puede hacer es ducharse en vez de bañarse.

*Answers: 7, 2, 8, 5, 4*

**3 Use the code to work out what we can do to help the environment.**

*Answers:*
***a** Se puede ahorrar agua. **b** Se debe apagar las luces.*
***c** Hay que usar el transporte público. **d** Tienes que comprar productos ecológicos. **e** Se puede plantar árboles.*

## Página 66 4A.3 Y tú, ¿cuidas del mundo?

- Use with Student Book, pages 120–121

KAL 4.6 AT 3.1 **1 Draw lines to match up the negative words to their translations. Then find them in the wordsearch.**

*Answers: **1** e; **2** d; **3** a; **4** c; **5** b; **6** f*

| | | | | | | | | | |
|---|---|---|---|---|---|---|---|---|---|
| f | a | a | n | u | n | c | i | a | d |
| v | ~~t~~ | ~~a~~ | ~~m~~ | ~~p~~ | ~~o~~ | ~~c~~ | ~~o~~ | d | o |
| b | a | e | n | i | c | d | n | a | t |
| n | i | n | n | a | n | a | i | n | s |
| a | e | o | u | n | d | e | e | a | p |
| d | d | a | n | a | c | i | i | o | i |
| r | e | n | c | i | a | n | e | m | c |
| e | n | ~~n~~ | ~~a~~ | ~~d~~ | ~~a~~ | s | e | i | o |
| i | t | a | m | p | i | c | o | n | i |
| a | e | d | m | u | p | o | c | e | y |
| n | a | c | a | d | e | n | o | o | d |

AT 3.3 **2 Unscramble the words to make correct sentences.**
Students use the pictures as prompts to help them. They could also refer to pages 120 and 121 of the Student Book, if necessary.

*Answers:*
***a** Mi madre no compra productos ecológicos. **b** 1 Mis amigos nunca apagan las luces. **c** 4 Mis padres no llevan sus propias bolsas al supermercado. **d** 3 Nadie recicla nada.*
***e** 2 Mis amigos tampoco ahorran agua. **f** 5 Mi abuela no hace nada por el medio ambiente.*

## Página 67 4A.4 Mi mundo familiar

- Use with Student Book, pages 122–123

AT 3.2 **1 Read the list. Are they things that apply to you? Put a tick or a cross.**
Students could compare their answers with those of their classmates.

AT 1.4 L&S 1.1, 1.2 **2 Listen to Juan. What are his parents like?**

**CD 3, track 54 (Workbook 34)** **página 67, actividades 2 y 3**

Pues mis padres son bastante anticuados y estrictos así que hay muchas cosas que no puedo hacer. Por ejemplo, me gusta la ropa de color negro pero no la puedo llevar y mi madre me compra muchas camisas que son horribles. Me gusta mucho la música pero no puedo ponerla muy alta en mi dormitorio porque a mis padres no les gusta. Tampoco puedo acostarme cuando quiero. ¡Qué rollo! Pero sí puedo invitar a mis amigos a casa y tengo un trabajo a tiempo parcial los sábados. ¡Y ayer me hice un piercing! Pero mis padres no lo saben.

*Answers: old-fashioned and strict*

AT 1.4 L&S 1.1, 1.2 **3 Listen again. What is Juan allowed and not allowed to do? Fill in the grid in English.**

*Answers:*
***Juan is allowed to:** invite his friends to his house; have a part-time job*
***Juan is not allowed to:** wear black clothes; listen to loud music (in his room); go to bed when he likes*

L&S 1.5 AT 2.3–4 **4 Look at the table and say as many sentences as you can in one minute.**

## Página 68 4A.5 Tenemos que ayudar

- Use with Student Book, pages 124–125

AT 3.2 **1 Solve the clues to do the crossword.**

*Answers:*
***Horizontal:** **1** No hagas fuego. **2** Recicla latas. **3** No caces. **4** Miedo. **5** Utiliza papeleras. **6** animales*
***Vertical:** **1** No tires basura. **2** peligroso; **3** Ahorra agua. **4** se debe; **5** Evita hacer ruido. **6** sucio*

AT 1.4 L&S 1.1, 1.2 **2 Listen to the advice about helping the environment and put the pictures into the order you hear them. (There is one picture too many.)**

**CD 3, track 55 (Workbook 35)** **página 68, actividad 2**

Todos tenemos que ayudar a proteger el medio ambiente. No hagas ruido para no molestar y no hagas fuego en el campo. Recicla papel, latas y vidrio y ahorra agua, por ejemplo, dúchate en vez de bañarte. Cuida de tu ciudad o pueblo, no tires basura al suelo. Y no te olvides de usar las papeleras. Así todos tendremos una vida mejor.

*Answers:*
***a** 3; **b** 5; **c** 4; **d** –; **e** 6; **f** 1; **g** 2*

## Página 69 4A.6A Labolengua

- Use with Student Book, pages 126–127

KAL 4.6 **1 Fill in the blanks with a negative word.**

*Answers:*
***a** Mi abuela **no** recicla **nada.** **b** Mis padres **no** utilizan las papeleras **nunca**. **Tampoco** ahorran agua. **c** **Nunca** hago ruido por las noches. **d** **Nadie** recicla vidrio en el pueblo. **e** No reciclamos **ni** papel **ni** plástico.*

**2 Translate these sentences into English.**
Practice of imperatives.

*Answers:*
***a** Wash the dishes! **b** Don't make so much noise! **c** Clean the room! **d** Buy more green products! **e** Switch off the lights! **f** Have a shower in the morning!*

**3 Complete the instructions with one of the imperatives from the box.**

*Answers:*
***a** **¡Ahorra** agua! **b** ¡No **tire** basura al suelo! **c** ¡No **bebáis** tanta gaseosa! **d** **¡Comed** más verduras! **e** **¡Usa** el transporte público!*

## Página 70 4A.6B Técnica

- Use with Student Book, pages 126–127

**1 Read the letter and fill in the missing elements.**
Practice of writing a formal letter.

*Answers:*
***1** 12 enero 2012 **2** Estimado señor: **3** Le saluda atentamente*

R&W 2.1, 2.2 **2 Read the letter again. True (T) or false (F)?**

*Answers: **a** T; **b** F; **c** F; **d** T; **e** T; **f** F; **g** T; **h** T*

# Higher Workbook

## Página 64 4A.1 ¿Cómo es tu mundo?

- Use with Student Book, pages 116–117

AT 3.2 **1 Fill in the missing letters in the words and then draw lines to match them up with the numbers.**
Practice of higher numbers.

*Answers:* ***a*** *3 – ciento treinta y dos;* ***b*** *8 – quinientos veinte;* ***c*** *5 – tres mil ochocientos;* ***d*** *2 – mil setecientos;* ***e*** *4 – dos mil novecientos;* ***f*** *1 – seis mil doscientos;* ***g*** *7 – cinco millones;* ***h*** *6 – treinta y dos millones*

AT 4.2 **2 Write the following numbers in Spanish.**

*Answers: see Activity 3*

AT 1.2 **3 Now listen to the numbers and put them into the order you hear them.**

**CD 4, track 33** **página 64, actividad 3**

mil siete
siete mil trescientos
cuarenta y seis mil
noventa y tres millones
tres mil ochocientos
doce mil
seis millones
dos mil

*Answers:*

| | | |
|---|---|---|
| *2.000* | *dos mil* | *8* |
| *7.300* | *siete mil trescientos* | *2* |
| *3.800* | *tres mil ochocientos* | *5* |
| *1.007* | *mil siete* | *1* |
| *46.000* | *cuarenta y seis mil* | *3* |
| *12.000* | *doce mil* | *6* |
| *6.000.000* | *seis millones* | *7* |
| *93.000.000* | *noventa y tres millones* | *4* |

AT 4.4–5
R&W 2.5
**4 Write four more sentences about the environment.**
Students should refer back to pages 116 and 117 of the Student Book for ideas and support.

## Página 65 4A.2 ¿Qué podemos hacer?

- Use with Student Book, pages 118–119

AT 3.2 **1 Write the correct caption under each picture.**

*Answers:*
***1*** *h – protestar;* ***2*** *a – apagar las luces;* ***3*** *c – plantar árboles;* ***4*** *b – ahorrar agua;* ***5*** *g – reciclar;* ***6*** *d – usar el transporte público;* ***7*** *e – comprar productos ecológicos;* ***8*** *f – llevar tus propias bolsas al supermercado*

AT 1.4
L&S 1.1, 1.2
**2 Listen and look at the pictures again. Write the numbers of the things Isabel mentions.**

**CD 4, track 34** **página 65, actividad 2**

Bueno, pienso que es importante que cuidemos del medio ambiente. Se puede reciclar plástico y vidrio, apagar las luces cuando sales de las habitaciones, usar tus propias bolsas cuando vas de compras. También hay que usar el autobús o el metro siempre que se pueda. Otra cosa que se puede hacer es ducharse en vez de bañarse.

*Answers: 5, 2, 8, 6, 4*

AT 4.4
R&W 2.5
**3 Write five sentences saying what you do to help the environment and how often you do it.**
Students use the prompts given and should refer back to pages 118 and 119 of the Student Book for support, if necessary.

## Página 66 4A.3 Y tú, ¿cuidas del mundo?

- Use with Student Book, pages 120–121

KAL 4.6
AT 3.1
**1 Draw lines to match up the negative words to their translations. Then find them in the wordsearch.**

*Answers:* ***1*** *e;* ***2*** *d;* ***3*** *a;* ***4*** *c;* ***5*** *b;* ***6*** *f*

| | | | | | | | | | |
|---|---|---|---|---|---|---|---|---|---|
| f | a | a | n | u | n | c | i | a | d |
| v | t | a | m | p | o | c | o | d | o |
| b | a | e | n | i | c | d | n | a | t |
| n | i | n | n | a | n | a | i | n | s |
| a | e | o | u | n | d | e | e | a | p |
| d | d | a | n | a | c | i | i | o | i |
| r | e | n | c | i | a | n | e | m | c |
| e | n | n | a | d | a | s | e | i | o |
| i | t | a | m | p | i | c | o | n | i |
| a | e | d | m | u | p | o | c | e | y |
| n | a | c | a | d | e | n | o | o | d |

AT 3.3 **2 Unscramble the words to make correct sentences.**
Students should refer to pages 120 and 121 of the Student Book for support, if necessary.

*Answers:*
***a*** *Mi madre no compra productos ecológicos.* ***b*** *Mis amigos nunca apagan las luces.* ***c*** *Mis padres no llevan sus propias bolsas al supermercado.* ***d*** *Nadie recicla nada.* ***e*** *Mis amigos tampoco ahorran agua.* ***f*** *Mi abuela no hace nada por el medio ambiente.*

AT 4.4 R&W 2.4, 2.5 **3 Complete the following sentences about your family and friends**
Students should refer back to Activities 1 and 2 and to pages 120 and 121 of the Student Book for support, if necessary.

## Página 67 4A.4 Mi mundo familiar

- Use with Student Book, pages 122–123

AT 3.3 **1 Read the list. Are they things that apply to you? Put a tick or a cross.**
Students could compare their answers with those of their classmates.

AT 1.4–5 L&S 1.1, 1.2 **2 Listen to Juan and answer the questions in English.**

**CD 4, track 35** **página 67, actividad 2**

Pues mis padres son bastante anticuados y estrictos así que hay muchas cosas que no puedo hacer. Por ejemplo, me gusta la ropa de color negro pero no la puedo llevar y mi madre me compra muchas camisas que son horribles. Me gusta mucho la música pero no puedo ponerla muy alta en mi dormitorio porque a mis padres no les gusta. Tampoco puedo acostarme cuando quiero. ¡Qué rollo! Pero sí puedo invitar a mis amigos a casa y tengo un trabajo a tiempo parcial los sábados. ¡Y ayer me hice un piercing! Pero mis padres no lo saben.

*Answers:*
***a*** *Juan's parents are quite old-fashioned and strict.* ***b*** *He is allowed to invite his friends to his house and have a part-time job.* ***c*** *He is not allowed to wear black clothes, listen to loud music (in his room), go to bed when he likes.* ***d*** *Yesterday he had a piercing done.*

L&S 1.5 AT 2.3–4 **3 Look at the table and say as many sentences as you can in one minute.**

AT 4.4–5 R&W 2.5 **4 Write five sentences about what your parents are like and what you are and aren't allowed to do. Use the table in Activity 3 to help you.**
Students should also try to refer to what they used to be allowed/not allowed to do when they were younger as well, in order to increase the level of their Spanish.

## Página 68 4A.5 Tenemos que ayudar

- Use with Student Book, pages 124–125

AT 4.2 **1 Solve the clues to do the crossword.**

*Answers:*
***Horizontal:*** ***1*** *No hagas fuego.* ***2*** *Recicla latas.* ***3*** *No caces.* ***4*** *Miedo.* ***5*** *Utiliza papeleras.* ***6*** *animales*
***Vertical:*** ***1*** *No tires basura.* ***2*** *peligroso;* ***3*** *Ahorra agua.* ***4*** *se debe;* ***5*** *Evita hacer ruido.* ***6*** *sucio*

AT 1.4 L&S 1.1, 1.2 **2 Listen to the advice about helping the environment and put the pictures into the order you hear them. (There is one picture too many.)**

**CD 4, track 36** **página 68, actividades 2 y 3**

Todos tenemos que ayudar a proteger el medio ambiente. No hagas ruido para no molestar y no hagas fuego en el campo. Recicla papel, latas y vidrio y ahorra agua, por ejemplo, dúchate en vez de bañarte. Cuida de tu ciudad o pueblo, no tires basura al suelo. Y no te olvides de usar las papeleras. Así todos tendremos una vida mejor.

*Answers:* ***a*** *3;* ***b*** *5;* ***c*** *4;* ***d*** *–;* ***e*** *6;* ***f*** *1;* ***g*** *2*

AT 1.4 L&S 1.1, 1.2 **3 Listen again. What should we do to save water?**

*Answer:* We should have a shower instead of a bath.

KAL 4.5 **4 Fill in the missing verbs to complete the sentences.**

*Answers:*
***a*** *ahorra;* ***b*** *utiliza;* ***c*** *evita;* ***d*** *caces;* ***e*** *tires;* ***f*** *no hagas*

## Página 69 4A.6A Labolengua

- Use with Student Book, pages 126–127

KAL 4.6 **1 Fill in the blanks with a negative word.**

*Answers:*
***a*** *Mi abuela* ***no*** *recicla* ***nada.*** ***b*** *Mis padres* ***no*** *utilizan las papeleras* ***nunca. Tampoco*** *ahorran agua.* ***c Nunca*** *hago ruido por las noches.* ***d Nadie*** *recicla vidrio en el pueblo.* ***e*** *No reciclamos* ***ni*** *papel* ***ni*** *plástico.*

**2 Complete the instructions.**
Practice of imperatives.

*Answers:*
***a** ¡**Ahorra** agua! **b** ¡No **tire** basura al suelo! **c** ¡No **bebáis** tanta gaseosa! **d** ¡**Comed** más verduras! **e** ¡**Usa** el transporte público!*

KAL 4.5 **3 Write three positive and three negative instructions for a friend. Use the verbs in the box.**

## Página 70 4A.6B Técnica

- Use with Student Book, pages 126–127

**1 Some ink has been spilt on this formal letter. Find the correct missing words.**
Practice of writing formal letters.

*Answers:*
***1** enero; **2** estimado; **3** escribo; **4** problema; **5** donde; **6** jóvenes; **7** fiestas; **8** toda; **9** ruido; **10** ni; **11** dormir; **12** niño; **13** hace; **14** hablé; **15** llamé; **16** tanto; **17** contra; **18** atentamente*

# 4B ¡Aquí se habla español!

## Unit Objectives

**Contexts and cultural focus:** the Spanish-speaking world
**Grammar:** comparatives and superlatives; adjectives; idiomatic uses of *tener; soler* + infinitive when talking about the past; *lo* + adjective to express opinions; adjectival agreement
**Language learning:** carrying out research on the Internet; identifying false friends; pronouncing *ll*, *ñ* and *r/rr* correctly; using grammar knowledge to eliminate wrong answers in reading tasks; sounding Spanish when pronouncing cognates

- *Aim:* To learn more about Spanish-speaking countries and people
- Each unit has an associated video which will feature throughout the unit. Below is the transcript of the video for this unit.

**Video clip: Unit 4B (CD 3, track 14)**

**Part 1**

*Elena, Roberto and Juan are at home. Juan is on his laptop.*

Juan: Es tu último fin de semana aquí con nosotros. ¿Antes de irte, te gustaría hacer algo especial?
Roberto: Sí. ¿Pero, qué podemos hacer que no hemos hecho ya?
Juan: ¿Te gustaría ir al parque de atracciones?
Roberto: No. Prefiero hacer algo que no puedo hacer en Colombia.
Elena: ¿Te gustaría ir a la discoteca?
Roberto: No gracias. En Colombia tenemos discotecas. ¿No hay alguna fiesta española que podamos ver?
Juan: ¿Como los San Firmines o las Fallas de Valencia o la Tomatina?
Elena: Juan no es época de esas fiestas. Necesitamos algo que pase ahora y más cerca de casa.
Juan: Voy a ver en Internet. Mira, este sábado es el festival de las velas en Pedraza.
Roberto: ¿Y qué hacen en ese festival?
Juan: Mira. Lo pone aquí: "por la tarde los 480 habitantes del pueblo ayudados por los visitantes colocan miles de velas en cada rincón. Al caer la noche la suave luz de las velas lo invade todo"
Elena: Qué bonito ¿no? Y Pedraza es precioso, es un pueblo medieval amurallado y muy bien restaurado.
Roberto: Tiene que ser impresionante ver el pueblo solamente iluminado con la luz de las velas.
Juan: ¡Qué romantico! Entonces vamos el sábado a la noche de las velas.

**Part 2**

Elena: Esta es la única puerta del pueblo porque es un pueblo amurallado.
Roberto: Mi ciudad, Cartagena, también es una ciudad amurallada. Supongo que cuando los españoles fueron a las Américas también construyeron sus casas y sus pueblos como aquí.
Juan: A lo mejor es porque echaban de menos a sus familias.
Elena: ¿Tú echas de menos a tu familia, Roberto?
Roberto: Sí, un poco, pero está bien viajar por el mundo y conocer otros lugares.
Elena: Así conoces mejor otras culturas.
Juan: Sí, pero ahora lo que tenemos que conocer es cómo y dónde conseguimos las velas y qué hay que hacer.
Elena: Perdone.
Passerby: Sí, dígame.
Elena: ¿Dónde se pueden conseguir las velas?
Passerby: Mira, puedes encontrar las velas en la calle Mayor. ¿Quieres alguna?
Elena: Sí, por favor.
Passerby: Toma.
Elena: Gracias.
Juan: Mira, cómo está el pueblo.
Elena: Sí, qué de velas. Tenemos que buscar un sitio donde encontrar más. Ha dicho que en la plaza del pueblo.
Juan: ¿Es verdad?
Elena: Tenemos que preguntar por donde está.
Juan: Sí.
Roberto: Muy bonitas las velas.
Elena: Sí. Ay, ¡mira qué revelas!
Juan: Sí esta ventana está plagada.
Elena: ¿Encendemos alguna?
Juan: Vale.
Elena: Están muy altas. Ya está.
Roberto: Yo he encendido dos.

*Juan is chatting to someone.*

Juan: Hola, buenas. ¿Te gusta el festival?
Passerby 2: Sí, por supuesto. Es muy bonito y muy romántico ver todo el pueblo a la luz de velas.
Juan: ¿Y te gustaría verlo conmigo?

*Roberto with another passerby.*

Roberto: Hola, buenas. ¿Eres de aquí?
Passerby 3: No, soy de Málaga. Vine para el festival.
Roberto: ¿Y es la primera vez que vienes?
Passerby 3: No, suelo venir con mis amigos cada año.
Roberto: Pásalo bien.

Juan: ¿Viste la iglesia?
Elena: ¡Qué bonita!

| | |
|---|---|
| Elena: | ¿Bueno, y qué te ha parecido nuestro festival de las velas, Roberto? |
| Roberto: | A mí, me gustó muchísimo pero espero que en alguna otra ocasión podáis venir a ver alguno de los festivales en Colombia. |
| Juan: | ¿Y cómo son las chicas de allí? |
| Elena & Roberto: | ¡Juan, siempre lo mismo! |

**Punto Lengua**
¿No hay alguna fiesta española que podamos ver?
Mira, este sábado es el festival de las velas en Pedraza.
¿Tú echas de menos a tu familia, Roberto?
Sí, un poco, pero está bien viajar por el mundo y conocer otros lugares.
Así conoces mejor otras culturas.

As a starter activity to introduce the unit and familiarise students with the language they will meet, view the video as a whole. Are there any words or phrases that they have recognised from this single viewing? What do they think it is about? Teach students the word 'vela' so they'll recognise it in video.
Play Part 1 again a couple of times, as this sets the scene. Have students recognised any of the festivals mentioned? Some members of the class may have been to one of these festivals. Ask students if they have understood what Roberto wants to do on his last weekend in Spain? Would they have chosen this? This starts students thinking about the video and will help them understand it better when you return to look at it in more detail later in this unit.

*Synopsis:*
It's Roberto's last weekend with Elena and Juan in Spain and he wants to do something typically Spanish that he wouldn't be able to do in Colombia. It's not the right time for the big festivals, and anyway, they need something closer to home. Fortunately, Elena finds the perfect solution, the festival of candles in Pedraza – close by and at the weekend. What will Roberto think of the festival?

| Unit 4B ¡Aquí se habla español! Overview grid | | | | | | |
|---|---|---|---|---|---|---|
| **Page reference** | **Contexts and objectives** | **Language learning** | **Grammar** | **Key language** | **Framework** | **AT level** |
| Pages 132–133 **Países de habla hispana** | • give key facts about a country | • carry out research on the internet | • use comparatives and superlatives | *el expediente; el idioma principal; la moneda; la exportación; concurrido/a; desgraciadamente; un secuestro; más ... que; menos ... que; tan ... como; tanto ... como* | L&S 1.2, 1.5; R&W 2.2, 2.4; IU 3.1; LLS 5.4 | 1.4, 2.4, 3.3–4, 4.3–6 |
| Pages 134–135 **Sabor latino** | • revise describing people | • identify false friends | • revise use of adjectives and recognise idiomatic uses of *tener* | *la cantante; la actriz; un hombre; la pobreza; simpático/a; atender; soportar; actualmente; asistir; tener éxito* | L&S 1.2, 1.4; R&W 2.4 | 1.4–5, 2.2–4, 3.1, 3.5, 4.5–6 |
| Pages 136–137 **¡Vamos a celebrar!** | • find out about some Latin American festivals | • pronounce *ñ* correctly | • use *soler* + infinitive when talking about the past | *colorido/a; los muertos; el Festival de las Velas; El Día de la Raza; El Día de Todos los Santos; solía visitar; solía quedarme; solía venir; solíamos ver; solíamos asistir; no suelo ir* | L&S 1.1, 1.2, 1.3, 1.4; R&W 2.4, 2.5; IU 3.1, 3.2; KAL 4.5; LLS 5.4 | 1.3–6, 2.4, 3.4, 4.4 |
| Pages 138–139 **Lo mejor de los idiomas** | • talk about the importance of language learning | • use grammar knowledge to eliminate wrong answers in reading tasks | • use *lo* + adjective to express opinions | *la población mundial; la lengua materna; otro idioma; soy valiente; estoy seguro/a de mí mismo; soy consciente de otras culturas; estoy abierto/a a nuevas experiencias* | L&S 1.2, 1.4; R&W 2.4, 2.5; KAL 4.3, 4.5 | 1.4, 2.4, 3.4, 4.4 |
| Pages 140–141 **Hispanoamericanos** | • describe people's nationality and personality | • sound Spanish when pronouncing cognates | • revise adjectival agreement | | L&S 1.4, 1.5; R&W 2.2, 2.4, 2.5; KAL 4.3 | 1.5, 2.5–6, 3.3, 4.5 |
| Pages 142–143 **Labolengua** | • review language and grammar from the unit | | | | KAL 4.1, 4.4, 4.5 | |

| | | | | | | |
|---|---|---|---|---|---|---|
| Pages 144–145 **Extra Star** **Extra Plus** | • differentiated extension/ homework material | • revise and consolidate all vocabulary and grammar covered in the unit | • revise and consolidate all vocabulary and grammar covered in the unit | | IU 3.2; LLS 5.4 | 3.2, 3.4–6, 4.3–6 |
| Pages 146 **Prueba** | • end-of-unit test | | | | L&S 1.1, 1.2, 1.5; R&W 2.2, 2.4; LLS 5.4 | 1.5, 2.4–6 , 3.6, 4.5–6 |
| Page 147 **Vocabulario** | • a summary of the key language covered in each core spread of this unit | | | | | |
| Page 156 **Leer 4B** | | | | | R&W 2.1, 2.2 | 3.6–7 |

**Week-by-week overview**
**(Three-year KS3 Route: assuming six weeks' work or approximately 10–12.5 hours)**
**(Two-year KS3 Route: assuming four weeks' worth or approximately 6.5–8.5 hours)**

**About Unit 4B, ¡Aquí se habla español!:** Students work in the context of the Spanish-speaking world. They give key facts about Spanish-speaking countries and also revise describing people. They find out about some Latin American festivals, talk about the importance of language learning and describe people's personalities. Students also use comparatives and superlatives and adjectives, and recognise idiomatic uses of *tener*. They use *soler* + infinitive when talking about the past and *lo* + adjective to express opinions. They also revise adjectival agreement. The unit also provides tips on language learning techniques.

| **Three-Year KS3 Route** | | | **Two-Year KS3 Route** | | |
|---|---|---|---|---|---|
| **Week** | **Resources** | **Objectives** | **Week** | **Resources** | **Objectives** |
| **1** | **4B.1 Países de habla hispana** **4B.6 Labolengua A** (p.142) | give key facts about a country<br>carry out research on the Internet<br>use superlatives (*el/la … más …*)<br>use comparatives and superlatives | **1** | **4B.1 Países de habla hispana** (Omit Think, Gramática, Activity 5 & Challenge) **4B.6 Labolengua A** (p.142) | give key facts about a country<br>carry out research on the Internet<br>use superlatives (*el/la … más …*)<br>use comparatives and superlatives |
| **2** | **4B.2 Sabor latino** **4B.6 Labolengua B** (p.142) | revise describing people<br>identify false friends<br>use adjectives and recognise idiomatic uses of *tener* | **2** | **4B.2 Sabor latino** (Omit Activities 2, 5 & Gramática) **4B.6 Labolengua B** (p.142) | revise describing people<br>identify false friends<br>use adjectives and recognise idiomatic uses of *tener* |

| | | | | | |
|---|---|---|---|---|---|
| **3** | **4B.3 ¡Vamos a celebrar!**<br>**4B.6 Labolengua C** (p.143) | find out about some Latin American festivals<br>pronounce *ñ* correctly<br>use *soler* + infinitive when talking about the past | **3** | **4B.3 ¡Vamos a celebrar!**<br>(Omit Activity 5 & Challenge)<br>**4B.6 Labolengua C** (p.143) | find out about some Latin American festivals<br>pronounce *ñ* correctly<br>use *soler* + infinitive when talking about the past |
| **4** | **4B.4 Lo mejor de los idiomos**<br>**4B.6 Labolengua D** (p.143) | talk about the importance of language learning<br>use grammar knowledge to eliminate wrong answers in reading tasks<br>use *lo* + adjective to express opinions | **4** | **4B.4 Lo mejor de los idiomas**<br>(Omit Activity 1 & Challenge)<br>**4B.6 Labolengua D** (p.143)<br>**4B.8 Prueba** (p.146)<br>**Vocabulario** (p.147) | talk about the importance of language learning<br>use grammar knowledge to eliminate wrong answers in reading tasks<br>use *lo* + adjective to express opinions<br>Prepare and carry out assessment in all four skills<br>Recapping on vocabulary of the unit |
| **5** | **4B.5 Hispanoamer-icanos**<br>**4A.6 Labolengua E** (p.143) | describe people's personalities<br>revise adjectival agreement<br>sound Spanish when pronouncing cognates | | | |
| **6** | **4B.7 Extra (Star)** (p.144)<br>**4B.7 Extra (Plus)** (p.145)<br>**4B.8 Prueba** (p.146)<br>**Vocabulario** (p.147)<br>**Leer** (p.156) | Further reinforcement and extension of the language of the unit.<br>Prepare and carry out assessment in all four skills<br>Recapping on vocabulary of the unit<br>Further reading to explore the language of the unit and cultural themes | | | |

## 4B.1 Países de habla hispana

páginas 132–133

# Planner

### Objectives
- give key facts about a country
- use comparatives and superlatives
- carry out research on the internet

### Resources
Student Book, pages 132–133
CD 3, track 11
Foundation Workbook, page 72
Higher Workbook, page 72
Interactive OxBox, Unit 4B
Copymasters 105–112

### Key language
*el expediente; el idioma principal; la moneda; la exportación; concurrido/a; desgraciadamente; un secuestro; más ... que; menos ... que; tan ... como; tanto ... como*

### Renewed Framework references
L&S 1.2, 1.5; R&W 2.2, 2.4; IU3.1; LLS 5.4

### PLTS
Activity 3: Reflective learners
Activity 5: Self-managers
Activity 7: Independent enquirers; Self-managers
Challenge: Self-managers

### Starters
- Students study the map of Central and South America to get an idea of where the Spanish-speaking countries are. Play a class game by displaying the map and covering the country names. Students must say which country is which.

### Plenaries
- Following Activity 7 and the Challenge Activity, students could produce a brochure on the country they have chosen. They should include pictures if possible, and, depending on their level, longer chunks of text, or bullet points and captions for the pictures. Less able students can just include the information from the fact-file while more able students could find out more information from the Internet and also include this.
- Have a class quiz based on the information in the fact files. Split the class into two teams and ask each team in turn a question (in Spanish) on the texts, e.g. *Argentina es más o menos grande que Perú?* The teams should try to answer using full sentences. They score a point for each correct answer. The team with the most points at the end wins.

### Homework/Self-study
After reading the Think box, students find out the names inhabitants of other Spanish-speaking towns and make a note of these.
Gramática

AT 3.3–4 | R&W 2.2

**1 Lee los expedientes. ¿De qué país se trata?**
This activity introduces students to other Spanish-speaking countries. First, read through the fact-files as a class and elicit from students what all of the information means. Once you are satisfied that students understand the Spanish, ask them which country each files refers to. The map, which provides an overview of the Spanish-speaking countries, may be of some help.

*Answers:* ***1*** *Chile;* ***2*** *Argentina;* ***3*** *Peru*

IU 3.1

### Think
Students should make a note of these names – they may crop up in reading or listening texts. As a homework activity, ask students to find out the names of inhabitants of other Spanish-speaking cities and to list these. You could compare lists in class and make a definitive list for reference.

AT 3.4 | R&W 2.2

**2 Lee. ¿Verdad o mentira?**
Students use the information in the fact-files to decide whether the sentences are true or false.

*Answers:* ***1*** *verdad;* ***2*** *mentira;* ***3*** *verdad;* ***4*** *verdad;* ***5*** *verdad*

### Gramática
This is a good time to revise comparatives and superlatives. Can students remember how to say, 'more ... than', 'less ... than', 'the most ...' and 'the least ...'? Once you have elicited the correct answers, ask students to use these phrases in examples of their own. If necessary provide gapped sentences for them to complete.

AT 4.3 | R&W 2.2 | PLTS

**3 Corrige las frases falsas.**
Students now correct the false sentences from Activity 2.

*Answers:*
*El salario mínimo de los peruanos es **menos** alto que el de los chilenos.*

AT 3.4 | R&W 2.2

**4 Lee el informe de Roberto. Completa el expediente 4 sobre Colombia.**
Students use the information from the text to complete the fact-file on Colombia. Before they do this, read through the second Grammar box.

*Answers:*
*Nombre: Colombia*
*Habitantes: 46,3 millones*
*Capital: Bogotá*
*Extensión: 1.140.000 km$^2$*
*Idiomas principales: español*
*Moneda: peso*
*Exportación: petróleo, café, oro, plátanos, productos químicos, esmeraldas, productos de algodón, azúcar, ganado*
*Salario mínimo: 207€ por mes*

AT 3.4 | LLS 5.4 | PLTS

**5 Copia las frases subrayadas. ¿Qué significan en inglés?**
Students now copy out the underlined sentences and note down what they mean in English.

*Answers:*
***no es tan grande como Argentina:** it's not as big as Argentina*
***hay tantas lenguas indígenas como en los otros países sudamericanos:** there are as many indigenous languages as in the other South American countries*

AT 1.4 | L&S 1.2

**6 Escucha y rellena el expediente 5.**
Students listen and fill in fact-file 5.

**CD 3, track 11** **página 133, actividad 6**

Cuba es una isla caribeña de 109.886 km$^2$ situada al este de Méjico y al sur de los Estados Unidos. Su capital es La Habana donde viven más de dos millones de los 11.275.000 de habitantes que tiene la isla. Cuba fue territorio español desde el 1492 hasta el 1898 y aún hoy su lengua oficial es el español.

El peso cubano es la moneda oficial de este país. Es un país comunista así que el gobierno proporciona viviendas, educación e incluso algunos productos esenciales de comida son gratis. Por otro lado el salario mínimo, que varía según las ocupaciones, es de unos 6,25€ al mes. El mundo conoce Cuba por sus exportaciones de tabaco pero Cuba también exporta azúcar, marisco, limas y limones, y café.

*Answers:*
*Nombre: Cuba*
*Habitantes: 11.275.000*
*Capital: La Habana*
*Extensión: 109.886 km$^2$*
*Idioma principal: español*
*Moneda: peso cubano*
*Exportación: tabaco, azúcar, marisco, limas y limones, café*
*Salario mínimo: 6,25€ por mes*

AT 4.4–6 | PLTS | R&W 2.4

**7 Investigación. Crea tu propio expediente sobre otro país latinoamericano.**
Students create their own fact-file about another Latin American country. They can find information on the Internet. They should read the advice in the Think box before they begin their research.

AT 2.4–6 | L&S 1.5 | PLTS

## Challenge

**Prepare an oral presentation about the Spanish-speaking country you chose for activity 7. Try and use present, past and future tenses to reach level 6.**
Encourage more able students to include adjectives and connectives in their writing to make it more than just reading out a list. They should also compare their country to one or more of the other countries included using the comparatives and superlatives they have practised in the spread.

## 4B.2 Sabor latino

páginas 134–135

## *Planner*

### Objectives

- revise describing people
- revise use of adjectives and recognise idiomatic uses of *tener*
- identify false friends

### Resources

Student Book, pages 134–135
CD 3, track 12
Foundation Workbook, page 73
Higher Workbook, page 73
Foundation Workbook audio, CD 3, track 56 (Workbook 36)
Higher Workbook audio, CD 4, track 37
Interactive OxBox, Unit 4B
Copymasters 105–112

### Key language

*la cantante; la actriz; un hombre; la pobreza; simpático/a; atender; soportar; actualmente; asistir; tener éxito*

### Renewed Framework references

L&S 1.2, 1.4; R&W 2.4

### PLTS

Activity 1: Reflective learners
Activity 4: Self-managers
Challenge: Creative thinkers; Self-managers

### Starters

- Brainstorm adjectives that can be used to describe people. Make a list of these in their masculine and feminine forms. Explain that they will come in useful in this spread.
- Play a class game to practise using the adjectives listed in Starter Activity 1. Pick a volunteer who describes another member of the class or a famous person of their choice. The rest of the class must try to guess who he/she is describing. Alternatively, the volunteer could describe a person and the rest of the class have to draw what he/she describes. At the end, students all show their drawings. They should all look similar, but do they?

### Plenaries

- Challenge students use the verb *tener* idiomatically in at least three sentences of their own. More able students should be able to do this without support. With less able classes, brainstorm idiomatic uses of *tener* before asking students to put these into sentences.
- Following the Challenge Activity, students produce a written description of another celebrity.

### Homework/Self-study

Activity 6, page 135
Think, page 135: Students look at the text for Activities 5 and 6 again and list all words that look like English words. They should then note down the meaning of these words, being careful to watch out for false friends.

PLTS | L&S 1.2 | AT 3.1

**1 Clasifica las palabras. Escríbelas en la columna adecuada.**
Students classify the words. They will already be familiar with most of this vocabulary and this activity serves to refresh their memory.

*Answers:*
***Nacionalidad – Es…:*** *cubano/a, argentino/a, mejicano/a, puertorriqueño/a, uruguayo/a, colombiano/a*
***Profesión – Es…:*** *cantante, actriz, actor, futbolista, escritor(a), pintor(a), artista, productor(a) de cine*
***Descripción (pelo) – Tiene el pelo…:*** *corto, rubio, largo, moreno, ondulado, gris, rizado, castaño, pelirrojo, (Es) calvo, blanco, negro*
***Descripción (ojos) – Tiene los ojos…:*** *azules, verdes, marrones, negros, grises*
***Descripción (general): Es…:*** *guapo/a, feo/a, viejo/a, hombre, mujer, joven, simpático/a*

AT 2.2–3 | L&S 1.4

**2 ¿Quién es quién? Elige un famoso latinoamericano. Adivina el famoso de tu compañero: tu compañero sólo puede responder "sí", "no" o "no sé".**
Students work in pairs to play this game. Partner A chooses one of the famous Latin American people. Partner B asks questions to try to guess who A has chosen. Partner A can only answer *sí, no* or *no sé*. Once Partner B has guessed, they swap roles. You may decide to limit the number of questions each partner can ask.

### Gramática

Students will have been using adjectives throughout the previous units and should be aware of this. A quick recap would, however, be useful to ensure that students understand how to make adjectives agree and where to position them in a sentence.

AT 1.5 | AT 3.5 | L&S 1.2

**3 Escucha y lee. Luego completa las frases.**
Students listen, read and complete the sentences.

**CD 3, track 12** **página 135, actividades 3 y 4**

Consciente de la situación de su país, cuando tenía sólo dieciocho años la simpática cantante colombiana Shakira fundó la Fundación Pies Descalzos. La Fundación se dedica a atender a los niños pobres, particularmente a los niños que tienen que soportar una pobreza extrema.

Actualmente Pies Descalzos apoya a seis colegios colombianos. Más de cinco mil niños asisten a estos colegios donde, además de educación, también reciben comida y apoyo psicológico.

La Fundación de Shakira tiene mucho éxito pero muchos más niños colombianos necesitan ayuda.

*Answers:* ***1** 18 years old;* ***2** children living in poverty;* ***3** six Columbian schools;* ***4** five thousand*

AT 1.4 | L&S 1.2 | PLTS

**4 Escucha otra vez. ¿Qué significan estas palabras? Utiliza las frases de la actividad 3 para ayudarte.**
Students listen again and this time note down what the words listed mean. They must be aware of false friends and make sure that they translate the words correctly. The sentences from Activity 3 will help them.

*Answers:*
***1** kind/nice;* ***2** to look after;* ***3** suffer;* ***4** at present;*
***5** attend;* ***6** success*

### Gramática

Students should note down these phrases to use in their own written and spoken work. Including idioms will make their Spanish sound more natural and flow better.

*Answers:*
*tenía sólo dieciocho años; tienen que soportar una pobreza extrema; tiene mucho éxito*

AT 4.2–4

**5 Escribe seis frases usando las palabras de la actividad 4.**
Further practice of using 'false friends' correctly.

AT 4.5–6 | R&W 2.4 | PLTS

### Challenge

**Choose a celebrity from Activity 2 and write a detailed description of them. You should include his/her age, nationality, profession, a physical description, something about his/ her personality, a recent success, what they'll do in the future and your opinion of this celebrity. Use past, present and future tenses to reach level 6.**
This consolidates the work students have done in the spread.

## 4B.3 ¡Vamos a celebrar! páginas 136–137

## *Planner*

### Objectives

- find out about some Latin American festivals
- use *soler* + infinitive when talking about the past
- pronounce *ñ* correctly

### Resources

Student Book, pages 136–137
CD 3, tracks 13–15
Foundation Workbook, page 74
Higher Workbook, page 74
Interactive OxBox, Unit 4B
Copymasters 105–112

### Video

Video clip, Unit 4B

### Key language

*colorido/a; los muertos; el Festival de las Velas; El Día de la Raza; El Día de Todos los Santos; solía visitar; solía quedarme; solía venir; solíamos ver; solíamos asistir; no suelo ir*

### Renewed Framework references

L&S 1.1, 1.2, 1.3, 1.4; R&W 2.4, 2.5; IU 3.1, 3.2; KAL 4.5; LLS 5.4

### PLTS

Activity 3: Self-managers
Challenge: Creative thinkers; Reflective learners; Self-managers

# 4B.3 ¡Aquí se habla español!

## Starters

- Practice pronouncing words with *rr* and *ll*. Display a list of words containing these sounds and get students to practice pronouncing them in pairs. Volunteers could read the list to the class.

## Plenaries

- Following Activity 3, ask students to use the Internet to research one of these festivals further. They should makes notes, in English or Spanish according to ability.
- Challenge students to write five sentences using *soler* and the infinitive. Compare answers as a class.

## Homework/Self-study

Activity 3, page 136
Challenge, page 137

AT 1.3–4 | L&S 1.2

**1 Escucha. ¿En qué orden se mencionan estos festivales latinoamericanos?**
Students study the photographs of festivals. They then listen and note down the order in which the festivals are mentioned.

**CD 3, track 13** **página 136, actividades 1 y 2**

1 Los ciudadanos de la ciudad peruana de Cuzco celebran la fiesta de la Virgen del Carmen el 16 de julio.
2 Las Fiestas Patrias de Chile tienen lugar el 18 de septiembre.
3 La Semana Santa es el festival católico más importante de Sudamérica con celebraciones particularmente famosas en Perú, Chile, Colombia y Guatemala. Generalmente cae en el mes de abril.
4 El Día de la Raza se celebra el 12 de octubre en varios países latinoamericanos como Argentina, Chile, Costa Rica, Ecuador, Honduras, Méjico, Uruguay y Venezuela.
5 El Día de Todos los Santos se celebra en todos los países de tradición católica el primero de noviembre.

*Answers:* ***1** c; **2** e; **3** d; **4** b; **5** a*

AT 1.4 | L&S 1.2

**2 Escucha otra vez. ¿En qué país o países se celebran? ¿Cuándo?**
Students listen again, this time for more detail.

*Answers:*
*c – Perú, 16 de julio; e – Chile, 18 de septiembre; d – Perú, Chile, Colombia y Guatemala, el mes de abril; b – Argentina, Chile, Costa Rica, Ecuador, Honduras, Méjico, Uruguay y Venezuela, 12 de octubre; a – todos los países de tradición católica, el primero de noviembre*

AT 3.4 | PLTS | IU 3.2 | LLS 5.4

**3 Lee y empareja las frases en español con las en inglés.**
Students read the Spanish descriptions and match them to the English ones.

*Answers:*
***1** b; **2** d; **3** a; **4** c; **5** e*

AT 1.5–7 | L&S 1.1, 1.2, 1.3 | IU 3.1, 3.2 | LLS 5.4

**4 Mira el video y contesta a las preguntas en inglés.**
Students watch the whole of the video and answer the questions. They will now need to listen for more detail. The questions will help to focus their minds.

**Video clip: Unit 4B (CD 3, track 14)**

**Part 1**
*Elena, Roberto and Juan are at home. Juan is on his laptop.*

Juan: Es tu último fin de semana aquí con nosotros. ¿Antes de irte, te gustaría hacer algo especial?
Roberto: Sí. ¿Pero, qué podemos hacer que no hemos hecho ya?
Juan: ¿Te gustaría ir al parque de atracciones?
Roberto: No. Prefiero hacer algo que no puedo hacer en Colombia.
Elena: ¿Te gustaría ir a la discoteca?
Roberto: No gracias. En Colombia tenemos discotecas. ¿No hay alguna fiesta española que podamos ver?
Juan: ¿Como los San Firmines o las Fallas de Valencia o la Tomatina?

| | |
|---|---|
| Elena: | Juan no es época de esas fiestas. Necesitamos algo que pase ahora y más cerca de casa. |
| Juan: | Voy a ver en Internet. Mira, este sábado es el festival de las velas en Pedraza. |
| Roberto: | ¿Y qué hacen en ese festival? |
| Juan: | Mira. Lo pone aquí: "por la tarde los 480 habitantes del pueblo ayudados por los visitantes colocan miles de velas en cada rincón. Al caer la noche la suave luz de las velas lo invade todo" |
| Elena: | Qué bonito ¿no? Y Pedraza es precioso, es un pueblo medieval amurallado y muy bien restaurado. |
| Roberto: | Tiene que ser impresionante ver el pueblo solamente iluminado con la luz de las velas. |
| Juan: | ¡Qué romantico! Entonces vamos el sábado a la noche de las velas. |

**Part 2**

| | |
|---|---|
| Elena: | Esta es la única puerta del pueblo porque es un pueblo amurallado. |
| Roberto: | Mi ciudad, Cartagena, también es una ciudad amurallada. Supongo que cuando los españoles fueron a las Américas también construyeron sus casas y sus pueblos como aquí. |
| Juan: | A lo mejor es porque echaban de menos a sus familias. |
| Elena: | ¿Tú echas de menos a tu familia, Roberto? |
| Roberto: | Sí, un poco, pero está bien viajar por el mundo y conocer otros lugares. |
| Elena: | Así conoces mejor otras culturas. |
| Juan: | Sí, pero ahora lo que tenemos que conocer es cómo y dónde conseguimos las velas y qué hay que hacer. |
| Elena: | Perdone. |
| Passerby: | Sí, dígame. |
| Elena: | ¿Dónde se pueden conseguir las velas? |
| Passerby: | Mira, puedes encontrar las velas en la calle Mayor. ¿Quieres alguna? |
| Elena: | Sí, por favor. |
| Passerby: | Toma. |
| Elena: | Gracias. |
| Juan: | Mira, cómo está el pueblo. |
| Elena: | Sí, qué de velas. Tenemos que buscar un sitio donde encontrar más. Ha dicho que en la plaza del pueblo. |
| Juan: | ¿Es verdad? |
| Elena: | Tenemos que preguntar por donde está. |
| Juan: | Sí. |
| Roberto: | Muy bonitas las velas. |
| Elena: | Sí. Ay, ¡mira qué revelas! |
| Juan: | Sí esta ventana está plagada. |
| Elena: | ¿Encendemos alguna? |
| Juan: | Vale. |
| Elena: | Están muy altas. Ya está. |
| Roberto: | Yo he encendido dos. |

*Juan is chatting to someone.*

| | |
|---|---|
| Juan: | Hola, buenas. ¿Te gusta el festival? |
| Passerby 2: | Sí, por supuesto. Es muy bonito y muy romántico ver todo el pueblo a la luz de velas. |
| Juan: | ¿Y te gustaría verlo conmigo? |

*Roberto with another passerby.*

| | |
|---|---|
| Roberto: | Hola, buenas. ¿Eres de aquí? |
| Passerby 3: | No, soy de Málaga. Vine para el festival. |
| Roberto: | ¿Y es la primera vez que vienes? |
| Passerby 3: | No, suelo venir con mis amigos cada año. |
| Roberto: | Pásalo bien. |

| | |
|---|---|
| Juan: | ¿Viste la iglesia? |
| Elena: | ¡Qué bonita! |
| Elena: | ¿Bueno, y qué te ha parecido nuestro festival de las velas, Roberto? |
| Roberto: | A mí, me gustó muchísimo pero espero que en alguna otra ocasión podáis venir a ver alguno de los festivales en Colombia. |
| Juan: | ¿Y cómo son las chicas de allí? |
| Elena & Roberto: | ¡Juan, siempre lo mismo! |

*Answers:*
***a** going to theme park, going to disco; **b** He wants to do something he can't do in Colombia; he would like to see a Spanish festival. **c** He says it is good to travel and live in another country.*

IU 3.1, 3.2

**5 Do you think the festival was a nice way for Roberto to finish his stay in Segovia? Why?**
Students could do this either as a spoken, or a written activity. Encourage some discussion.

## Gramática

Read the grammar explanation before asking students to attempt Activity 6.

AT 3.5, 1.5
KAL 4.5

**6 Lee y escucha a Roberto. ¿Cómo dice ...?**
Students listen and answer the questions.

**CD 3, track 15** **página 137, actividad 6**

Roberto:
Recuerdo que cuando era pequeño solía visitar a mis abuelos en Medellín a principios de agosto. En Medellín mis abuelos, mi madre y yo solíamos ir a la Feria de las Flores donde solíamos ver el Desfile de los Silleteros que es un desfile muy bonito y colorido.

A mi madre le gustan mucho las flores, así que durante la feria solíamos pasear por las exposiciones de orquídeas y también solíamos ver los desfiles de autos antiguos ya que a mí me encantan los coches. Además, solíamos asistir a un espectáculo diferente cada noche.

Ahora no suelo ir tan frecuentemente como cuando era niño.

*Answers:*
***1** solía visitar; **2** solíamos ver; **3** solíamos pasear;*
***4** solíamos asistir a*

### Think
Read through the Think box as a class. Allow students time to practise pronouncing these sounds.

PLTS | AT 4.5–6 | R&W 2.4, 2.5

### Challenge
**Write about a celebration you used to go to when you were little. Do you still go? When will you go again? Include description and past and present opinions.**
Students should draw upon the vocabulary and grammatical structures they have met in this spread.

## 4B.4 Lo mejor de los idiomas

páginas 138–139

## *Planner*

### Objectives
- talk about the importance of language learning
- use *lo* + adjective to express opinions
- use grammar knowledge to eliminate wrong answers in reading tasks

### Resources
Student Book, pages 138–139
CD 3, track 16
Foundation Workbook, page 75
Higher Workbook, page 75
Foundation Workbook audio, CD 3, track 57 (Workbook 37)
Higher Workbook audio, CD 4, track 38
Interactive OxBox, Unit 4B
Copymasters 105–112

### Key language
*la población mundial; la lengua materna; otro idioma; soy valiente; estoy seguro/a de mí mismo; soy consciente de otras culturas; estoy abierto/a a nuevas experiencias*

### Renewed Framework references
L&S 1.2, 1.4; R&W 2.4, 2.5; KAL 4.3, 4.5

### PLTS
Activity 5: Reflective learners; Creative thinkers; Self-managers
Activity 6: Effective participators
Challenge: Creative thinkers

### Starters
- Activity 1, page 138
- After doing Starter Activity 1, ask student to guess which languages the rest of the famous people speak. The answers are as follows: *Gwyneth Paltrow – Spanish; Nick Clegg – Spanish, and 4 others; Gary Lineker – Spanish; Arnold Schwarzenegger – German (or English, as German is his 1st language); Eva Longoria – Spanish; Tony Blair – French; Emma Watson – French; Sandra Bullock – German*

### Plenaries
- Students act out their debates from Activity 6. What to most students think are the best and worst things about learning a language?
- Following Plenary Activity 1, students carry out a survey to find out what most of their peers think are the best and worst things about learning a language. They could then present the results in a graph or piechart.

### Homework/Self-study
Activities 4 and 5, page 139

**1 Mira las fotos de los famosos. Todos hablan más de una lengua. Adivina los cuatro que hablan español.**
As an introduction to the spread, students guess which four of the famous people pictured speak Spanish. All of the people pictured speak at least one foreign language and can be found online line doing so. If time permits, play one of these snippets to students.

*Answers:*
*Gwyneth Paltrow, Nick Clegg, Gary Lineker, Eva Longoria*

AT 3.4 | KAL 4.3, 4.5

**2 Lee. ¿Sabías que ...? Empareja las dos partes de las frases.**
Students match the sentence halves. To help them do this, they should first read the Think box. This illustrates the importance of grammar.

*Answers:*
***1** f; **2** a; **3** d; **4** c; **5** b; **6** e*

AT 1.4 | L&S 1.2

**3 Escucha. ¿Por qué estudian otro idioma? Escribe las letras correctas.**
Students listen to the reasons for studying another language and write the correct letter each time.

**CD 3, track 16** — **página 139, actividad 3**

1 Creo que es divertido, es creativo y es entretenido.
2 Elegí aprender otro idioma porque queda bien en tu currículum y te ayuda a entender otras culturas.
3 Te puedes comunicar con gente de otras nacionalidades.
4 Aprender idiomas es bastante difícil pero creo que te ayuda a tener más seguridad en ti mismo.
5 Pienso que si hablas otro idioma, eso dice que eres una persona con buena habilidad para la comunicación.
6 Hablar otro idioma demuestra respeto por otras culturas cuando vas al extranjero de vacaciones.
7 Ayuda tu memoria porque siempre estás aprendiendo cosas diferentes, así que te ayuda a ejercitar tu memoria.

*Answers:*
***1** c; **2** d; **3** g; **4** b; **5** e; **6** f; **7** a*

AT 3.4 | L&S 1.4

**4 ¿Qué dicen los idiomas sobre ti? Lee y empareja las frases con los dibujos.**
Students match the sentences to the pictures. This reinforces what they have listened to in Activity 3.

*Answers:*
***1** b; **2** c; **3** a; **4** d*

AT 4.4 | PLTS | R&W 2.4

**5 En tu opinión, ¿qué es lo mejor/peor de aprender un idioma? Haz una lista.**
Once students have compiled their lists, compare answers as a class to see how opinions vary. With more able classes, encourage some discussion with students using 'opinion words'. Also look at the Grammar box, as this structure will come in useful.

AT 2.4 | PLTS | L&S 1.4

**6 Debate con un compañero.**
This consolidates what students have done in this spread so far.

AT 4.4 | PLTS | R&W 2.4, 2.5

## Challenge

**Prepare a 60-second video sketch promoting language learning. Be as creative and original as possible. Try to use some of the language you have learnt on these two pages.**
This brings together everything that students have been learning in this spread.

## 4B.5 Hispanoamericanos

páginas 140–141

# Planner

### Objectives
- describe people's nationality and personality
- revise adjectival agreement
- sound Spanish when pronouncing cognates

### Resources
Student Book, pages 140–141
CD 3, tracks 17–18
Foundation Workbook, page 76
Higher Workbook, page 76
Interactive OxBox, Unit 4B
Copymasters 105–112

### Renewed Framework references
L&S 1.4, 1.5; R&W 2.2, 2.4, 2.5; KAL 4.3

### PLTS
Activity 3: Self-managers
Activity 4: Independent enquirers
Activity 6: Creative thinkers; Effective participators
Activity 7: Effective participators; Team workers
Challenge: Reflective learners; Self-managers

### Starters
- Have a quick fire quiz to practise nationalities. Split the class into two teams and call out, e.g. *Son de Venezuela*. The first team to give you the correct nationality, e.g. *Son venezolanos*. scores a point.
- Give students a time limit to write down as many personality adjectives as possible. Compare answers and compile a class list.

### Plenaries
- Activity 6, page 141
- Display the list from Starter Activity 2 and go round the class asking students to say the words out loud. Make sure that all students know how to pronounce these words correctly in Spanish.

### Homework/Self-study
Activity 4, page 141

KAL 4.3

**1 Escribe las frases: Es ... / Son ...**
This activity practises countries and nationalities. Draw students' attention to adjectival agreement. The Think box also reminds students that in Spanish, nationalities do not begin with a capital letter.

*Answers:*
***a** Son de la República Dominicana. Son dominicanas. **b** Es de Honduras. Es hondureña. **c** Son de Ecuador. Son ecuatorianos. **d** Son de Bolivia. Son bolivianos. **e** Es de Costa Rica. Es costarricense. **f** Son de Méjico. Son mejicanos.*

AT 3.3 R&W 2.2

**2 Lee, copia y rellena los espacios.**
Students read the text about Mexico and then fill in the gaps with the words from the box.

*Answers:*
*país; extensión; habitantes; capital; idioma principal; moneda; salario mínimo*

PLTS

**3 Categoriza los adjetivos. ¿Son positivos o negativos? Adivina su significado.**
Some adjectives may be viewed differently by different students. There are no right or wrong answers, except perhaps with aggressive, violent, adorable, responsible and intelligent.

### Think
Practise pronouncing some of the cognates as a class to ensure that students sound Spanish.

**CD 3, track 17** **página 141, Think**

ambicioso, ambiciosa; conservador, conservadora; cruel; honesto, honesta; modesto, modesta; introvertido, introvertida; extrovertido, extrovertida; generoso, generosa; responsable; moderno, moderna; inteligente; popular; serio, seria; agresivo, agresiva; violento, violenta; adorable

PLTS

**4 Escribe otros seis o más adjetivos de personalidad a tu lista.**
Compare answers as a class.

AT 1.5 L&S 1.5

**5 Escucha y escoge la respuesta correcta.**
Students listen and choose a, b or c each time.

**CD 3, track 18** **página 141, actividad 5**

Salma Hayek es la actriz mejicana con más éxito y más famosa del mundo. Nació el dos de septiembre de 1966 en Coatzacoalcos en Méjico. Sus padres estaban bastante bien acomodados: su padre era un empresario mejicano-libanés y su madre era una cantante de ópera mejicana. Cuando era joven, Salma practicaba la gimnasia pero decidió estudiar para ser actriz después de ver *Willy Wonka y la fábrica de chocolate* en el cine de su ciudad. Ahora, Salma es la actriz mejicana más famosa del mundo. Salma también es muy conocida por su belleza, audacia e inteligencia.

*Answers:*
***1** c; **2** b; **3** a; **4** b; **5** b; **6** c*

AT 2.5
PLTS
L&S 1.4

**6 Imagina que eres Salma Hayek. Contesta a las preguntas.**
Students answer the questions as if they were Salma Hayek.

AT 2.5
PLTS
L&S 1.4

**7 Entrevista a tu compañero utilizando las preguntas de la actividad 6. Toma notas de sus respuestas.**
Students use the questions from Activity 6 to interview a partner. Volunteers could perform their interview in front of the class.

AT 4.5
PLTS
R&W 2.4, 2.5

**Challenge**
**Use your partner's answers to Activity 7 to write a passage about him/her. Include at least two tenses.**
Remind students that they must now write in the 3rd, rather than the 1st person.

## 4B.6 Labolengua

páginas 142–143

### *Planner*

**Objectives**
- review language and grammar from the unit

**Resources**
Student Book, pages 142–143
CD 3, track 19
Foundation Workbook, pages 77–78
Higher Workbook, pages 77–78
Foundation Workbook audio, CD 3, tracks 58–59 (Workbook 38–39)
Higher Workbook audio, CD 4, tracks 39–40
Interactive OxBox, Unit 4B
Copymasters 113–114

**Grammar**
- comparatives and superlatives, *tener* and *soler*

**Renewed Framework references**
KAL 4.1, 4.4, 4.5

**PLTS**
All activities: Reflective learners/Self-managers
Activity 4: Creative thinkers

**Homework/Self-study**
Activity 2, page 142 and Activity 3, page 143

### Comprender – comparatives and superlatives

#### A Comparatives and superlatives

KAL 4.4
PLTS

**1 Look at the outfits. Write sentences about them using the structures given. You may want to use the adjectives in the box.**
Practice of comparatives and superlatives.

#### B Idiomatic uses of *tener*

KAL 4.5
PLTS

**2 Write the correct word.**
Practice of using the verb *tener* in idiomatic phrases.

*Answers:*
***1** tiene; **2** tengo; **3** sed; **4** suerte; **5** razón; **6** miedo*

#### C *Soler* + infinitive

KAL 4.5
PLTS

**3 Write these sentences in the imperfect.**
Practice of using *soler* and the infinitive.

*Answers:*
***1** Solía celebrar las Navidades en Méjico. **2** Solíamos ir en coche. **3** Mi abuela solía cocinar mucha comida. **4** En Navidad solía hacer bastante calor. **5** Solíamos comer excesivamente.*

### Aprender – vocabulary learning

#### D False friends

PLTS

**4 Write what these Spanish words look like. Then look them up in a dictionary and write the correct translation.**
Practice of recognising false friends in Spanish.

*Answers:*
*carpeta – carpet – folder; codo – code – elbow; contestar – contest – answer; éxito – exit – success; ganga – gang – bargain; molestar – molest – to annoy; revolver – revolver – to turn over; ropa – rope – clothing; suceso –success – event*

### Hablar – pronunciation

### E The sounds *ll, ñ* and *r/rr*

PLTS | KAL 4.1

**5 Practise pronouncing these words. Listen and check your pronunciation.**
Practice of pronouncing the sounds *ll, ñ* and *r/rr* in Spanish.

**CD 3, track 19** **página 143, actividad 5**

1. llora, llave, llueve, llama, lleno
2. niño, año, uña, baño, araña
3. raro, Enrique, rico, roto, carro
4. El perro de San Roque no tiene rabo porque Ramón Rodríguez se lo ha cortado.

## 4B.7 Extra Star

página 144

## Planner

### Objectives

- find out more about the Spanish-speaking world
- use comparatives
- work out the meaning of unfamiliar vocabulary

### Resources

Student Book, page 144
Copymaster 115

### Renewed Framework references

IU 3.2; LLS 5.4

### PLTS

Activity 1: Self-managers
Activity 2: Self-managers
Activity 5: Reflective learners

PLTS | AT 3.2

**1 Mira las fotos de las actrices de 'Betty la Fea' y lee las frases. ¿Qué opinas?**
Students study the photographs and decide if they think the statements are true or false. This is purely their opinion so you could encourage some discussion.

AT 4.3 | PLTS

**2 Escribe las frases en otra manera.**
Further practice of comparatives.

*Answers:*
***1*** *Ana Ortiz es menos guapa que América Ferrera.* ***2*** *Ana Ortiz es más baja/menos alta que América Ferrera.* ***3*** *América Ferrera es más gorda/menos delgada que Ana Ortiz.*
***4*** *América Ferrera es menos simpática que Ana Ortiz.*
***5*** *América Ferrera es menos inteligente que Ana Ortiz.*

AT 3.5 | IU 3.2 | LLS 5.4

**3 ¿Cuál es el origen de los sombreros mejicanos? Lee y contesta a las preguntas.**
Students read the text and answer the questions.

*Answers:*
***1*** *Because it was very sunny.* ***2*** *Because there were few trees and very little natural protection from the sun.* ***3*** *The mixed-race labourers.* ***4*** *Because the workers were wearing their own little bit of shade.*

AT 4.3 | PLTS

**4 Escribe frases comparando estos sombreros.**
Students write a few sentences comparing the hats. They can use the words from the box.

## 4B.7 Extra Plus

página 145

### *Planner*

**Objectives**
- describe someone in detail
- use comparatives; use the preterite
- complete gap-fill exercises

**Resources**
Student Book, page 145
Copymaster 116

**Renewed Framework references**
R&W 2.5; LLS 5.4

**PLTS**
Activity 1: Independent enquirers
Activity 4: Creative thinkers; Reflective learners

AT 4.3 | PLTS

**1 ¿Qué sabes de estos dos futbolistas latinoamericanos? Compáralos utilizando los adjetivos de la casilla.**
Not all students will know a lot about these footballers, so you may find it useful to have a quick brainstorming session in English first to find out more about each one. Alternatively, students could do this for homework. For most of the adjectives in the box, there are no right or wrong answers, it is purely students' opinion.

AT 3.5

**2 Lee el artículo sobre Maxi Rodríguez y completa su línea cronológica con la información del texto.**
Students read the text and complete the timeline.

*Answers:*
*1981 – nació; 1999 – La carrera futbolística de Rodríguez empezó. 2002 – Se trasladó a España. 2003 – Juega para su equipo nacional contra Japón. 2005 – Se trasladó al Atlético de Madrid 2007 – Fue el capitán del equipo. 2010 – Se traspasó al Liverpool.*

AT 3.4–5 | LLS 5.4

**3 Copia y completa las frases sobre Maxi Rodríguez con las palabras de la casilla.**
To ensure that they have understood the text, students copy out and complete the sentences.

*Answers:*
***1** futbolista, Liverpool, Argentina; **2** fue; **3** comenzó; **4** costó*

AT 4.4–5 | R&W 2.5 | PLTS

**4 Escribe una descripción completa de Maxi Rodríguez.**
Students now write a full description of Maxi Rodríguez.

## 4B.8 Prueba

página 146

**Resources**
Student Book, page 146
CD 3, track 20
Assessment OxBox, Unit 4B

**Renewed Framework references**
L&S 1.1, 1.2, 1.5; R&W 2.2, 2.4; LLS 5.4

**PLTS**
All activities: Reflective learners
Escribir: Creative thinkers

### Escuchar

AT 1.5 | L&S 1.1, 1.2 | PLTS

**Listen to the information about the Dominican Republic and answer the questions in English.**
This activity tests listening skills using the language covered in this unit.

**CD 3, track 20** — **página 146, actividad 1**

La República Dominicana, con una extensión de 47.072 km² comparte una isla del Caribe con Haití al este de Jamaica y Cuba. La ciudad más grande de la República Dominicana es su capital que se llama Santo Domingo y se encuentra en la costa sur de la isla.

En Santo Domingo viven unos 3 millones de los 10 millones de habitantes que tiene este país que consiguió la independencia de España en 1844 pero conserva el español como su lengua oficial.

Si te gustan el calor y la playa, te va a gustar este popular destino turístico.

*Answers:*
***1** 47,072 km$^2$; **2** on an island in the Caribbean together with Haiti, to the east of Jamaica and Cuba; **3** It's the biggest city, called Santo Domingo, and located on the south coast of the island. **4** 10 million; **5** Those who like heat and the beach.*

### Hablar

AT 2.4–6 | L&S 1.5 | PLTS

**Prepare a 90-second presentation about a period of time in your life when you were younger. You can choose up to 15 words from your presentation to have with you during your test.**
This activity tests speaking skills using the language covered in this unit.

### Leer

AT 3.6 | R&W 2.2 | LLS 5.4 | PLTS

**Read the passage. True or false?**
This activity tests reading skills using the language covered in this unit.

*Answers:*
***1** true; **2** false; **3** false; **4** false; **5** false*

### Escribir

AT 4.5–6 | R&W 2.4 | PLTS

**Imagine you are a Spanish teacher. Write an article for the school magazine about language learning.**
This activity tests writing skills using the language covered in this unit.

## Leer 4B

página 156

**Resources**
Student Book, page 156

**Renewed Framework references**
R&W 2.1, 2.2

**PLTS**
Activity 1: Self-managers

AT 3.7 | R&W 2.1, 2.2 | PLTS

**1 Contesta a las preguntas.**

*Answers:*
***1** El Día de la Raza – when Columbus arrived in 1492; **2** four; **3** 12th October 1492; **4** by ship; **5** he went back to Spain to recount his adventures; **6** spread Christianity and bring back riches; **7** four; **8** he was named the Governor General of the new colonies; **9** the multicultural and multiethnic society that has resulted from Spanish colonisation of the Americas.*

AT 3.6–7 | R&W 2.1, 2.2

**2 Lee el texto. ¿Cómo se dice en español?**

*Answers:*
***1** el día de la llegada de Cristóbal Colón; **2** fue el mayor de cinco niños; **3** la Tierra no era plana; **4** su pequeña flota de tres barcos; **5** ahora llamada Las Bahamas; **6** para contar sus aventuras; **7** a la gente en tierras lejanas; **8** después de su tercer viaje; **9** actualmente; **10** más de quinientos años más tarde*

### Follow-up

Students look on the Internet to find more information on *El Día de la Raza* – how exactly is it celebrated? Have any of the students taken part in such a celebration? Students could also find out more about the explorer Christopher Columbus. They should take notes in either Spanish or English to share with the class.

# Foundation Workbook

## Página 72 4B.1 Países de habla hispana

- Use with Student Book, pages 132–133

AT 3.1 **1 Match up each Spanish-speaking country with its capital.**

*Answers:*
***1** j; **2** g; **3** a; **4** b; **5** c; **6** e; **7** d; **8** i; **9** h; **10** f*

AT 3.4 **2 Read the information about Bolivia. Draw lines to match the words with their meaning.**

*Answers:*
***1** f; **2** e; **3** b; **4** a; **5** c; **6** d*

AT 3.4 R&W 2.1, 2.2 **3 Read the text in Activity 2 again. True (T) or false (F)?**

*Answers:*
***a** F; **b** T; **c** F; **d** T; **e** F*

## Página 73 4B.2 Sabor latino

- Use with Student Book, pages 134–135

AT 3.4–5 **1 Fill in the blanks with a word or phrase from the box.**

*Answers:*
***1** 5 de junio; **2** menor; **3** era; **4** problemas; **5** primero; **6** sus; **7** concurso; **8** tiene*

AT 1.5 L&S 1.1, 1.2 **2 Now listen and check your answers to Activity 1.**

**CD 3, track 56 (Workbook 36)** **página 73, actividades 2 y 3**

David Bisbal nació el 5 de junio de 1975, en Almería, en el sur de España. Es el menor de tres hermanos. Desde pequeño ya demostraba talento para la música cantando aunque era muy tímido.

Es sencillo, humilde y se preocupa por los problemas actuales que afectan al mundo. Para él, la familia es lo primero y también disfruta pasando tiempo con sus amigos.

Alcanzó la fama tras participar en el concurso de telerrealidad que se llama Operación Triunfo donde quedó en segundo lugar. Antes de participar en Operación Triunfo, era cantante del grupo 'Orquesta Expresiones' que actuaba en fiestas populares.

En la actualidad Bisbal es una gran estrella tanto en España como en América y tiene 30 Discos de Platino, 15 deOro y 2 de Diamante.

AT 1.5 L&S 1.1, 1.2 **3 Listen again and complete the sentences.**

*Answers:*
***a** He was very shy when he was little. **b** His family comes first. **c** He enjoys spending time with his friends. **d** He finished second in a TV programme called* Operación Triunfo. ***e** Bisbal has won 15 gold discs.*

## Página 74 4B.3 ¡Vamos a celebrar!

- Use with Student Book, pages 136–137

AT 3.4 R&W 2.2 **1 Read about the festival from Madrid and answer the questions.**

*Answers:*
***a** Carnival; **b** disfrazarse; **c** a sardine; **d** typical black suits/clothes; **e** tristemente; **f** in the streets (of the city)*

AT 3.4–5 R&W 2.2 **2 Read one of the possible origins of this tradition. Then match up each English word with its Spanish translation.**

*Answers:*
***1** century – **e** el siglo; **2** king – **f** el rey; **3** the people – **b** la gente; **3** it was hot – **c** hacía calor; **5** a smell – **a** un olor; **6** started crying – **d** empezó a llorar*

## Página 75 4B.4 Lo mejor de los idiomas

- Use with Student Book, pages 138–139

**1 Complete the sentences with *Lo bueno/Lo mejor/Lo malo/Lo peor/Lo difícil/Lo divertido*.**

*Answers:*

***a*** *Lo bueno/Lo mejor es que te ayuda a encontrar trabajo.*
***b*** *Lo malo/Lo peor es que no es fácil entender todo lo que dice la gente.*
***c*** *Lo bueno/Lo mejor es que lo puedes poner en tu Currículum.*
***d*** *Lo divertido/Lo difícil es hablar con gente de otros países.*
***e*** *Lo difícil es aprender el vocabulario.*
***f*** *Lo bueno/Lo mejor es que aprendes sobre otras culturas.*

AT 1.4–5 L&S 1.1, 1.2 **2 Listen to the five teenagers. Do they like languages: ☺ or ☹? Match up each person with the correct reason.**

**CD 3, track 57 (Workbook 37)** **página 75, actividad 2**

**1 Juan**
Pues a mí, me gustan muchísimo los idiomas, me encanta poder comunicarme con gente de otros países y otras culturas.
**2 Marisol**
No sé, no me gusta mucho aprender idiomas. ¡Me parece tan difícil aprender todo el vocabulario! ¡Sin embargo es importante aprenderlos!
**3 Eneko**
Bueno, pues a mí me encantan los idiomas. Estoy aprendiendo dos idiomas y en el futuro quiero trabajar en el extranjero.
**4 Nagore**
¿Si me gustan los idiomas? Pues, en general sí, son divertidos y aprendes a comunicarte mejor con los demás.
**5 Roberto**
Al principio me gustaba, pero ahora no me resulta nada fácil entender lo que dice la gente.

*Answers:*
***1** Juan ☺ d; **2** Marisol ☹ c; **3** Eneko ☺ a; **4** Nagore ☺ e;*
***5** Roberto ☹ b*

AT 4.4 **3 Use the phrases in the table to give your own opinion about languages.**
Students should give their own opinion, but can refer to Activities 1 and 2 for ideas and support.

## Página 76 4B.5 Hispanoamericanos

- Use with Student Book, pages 138–139

AT 3.1 **1 Find eight personality adjectives in the wordsearch.**
Students can refer back to pages 138 and 139 of the Student Book for support, if necessary.

*Answers:*

| | | | | | | | | | | |
|---|---|---|---|---|---|---|---|---|---|---|
| R | | G | E | N | E | R | O | S | O | |
| A | | A | M | B | I | C | I | O | S | O |
| L | E | | | | N | | R | | | |
| U | L | | | | T | | E | | | |
| P | B | | | | R | | S | | | |
| O | A | | | H | O | N | E | S | T | O |
| P | S | | | | V | | | | | |
| | N | | | | E | | | | | |
| | O | | | | R | | | | | |
| | P | | | | T | | | | | |
| | S | | | | I | | | | | |
| | E | | M | O | D | E | S | T | O | |
| | R | | | | O | | | | | |

AT 3.4–5 **2 Complete the text using the words from the box.**

*Answers:*
***1** nació; **2** precioso; **3** albañil; **4** concurso; **5** ganó;*
***6** puertas; **7** todo; **8** cuando*

AT 4.4 R&W 2.4, 2.5 **3 Complete the sentences about your own personality.**
Students can refer back to Activities 1 and 2 as well as pages 138 and 139 of the Student Book for support.

## Página 77 4B.6A Labolengua

- Use with Student Book, pages 142–143

**1 Complete the translations using *más* or *menos* to compare Luis, Alfredo and Esteban.**

*Answers:*
***a** Luis es **más alto que** Alfredo. **b** Alfredo es **más fuerte que** Luis. **c** Esteban es **más gordo que** Luis. **d** El coche de Luis es **el más caro**. **e** El coche de Esteban **es más barato** que el coche de Luis.*

**2 Match up the Spanish with the English.**

*Answers:*
***1** Tengo suerte – c; **2** Tengo miedo – e; **3** Tengo sed – a;*
***4** Tengo calor – b; **5** Tengo frío – d*

KAL 4.5 **3 Complete the sentences with the correct part of the verb *soler*.**

*Answers: **a** suelen; **b** suelo; **c** solía; **d** suele; **e** solemos*

## Página 78 4B.6B Técnica

- Use with Student Book, pages 142–143

KAL 4.1 **1 Listen and repeat the following words.**

**CD 3, track 58 (Workbook 38)** **página 78, actividad 1**

- cañón; castaña; antaño; quinceañero; pañal; pañuelo; peña; leña
- calle; cepillo; camello; lleno; rellenar; llover; callarse; camilla
- caro; carro; roto; puerro; pera; perro; cinturón; carretera

KAL 4.1 **2 Now it's your turn. Practise saying the following words aloud and then listen and check your pronunciation.**

**CD 3, track 59 (Workbook 39)** **página 78, actividad 2**

correr; rápido; llavero; piña; castillo; cero

**3 Be careful with these false friends. Match up each one with its real meaning.**

*Answers:*
***1** h; **2** f; **3** a; **4** g; **5** i; **6** b; **7** d; **8** c; **9** j; **10** e*

# Higher Workbook

## Página 72 4B.1 Países de habla hispana

- Use with Student Book, pages 132–133

AT 4.1 **1 Unscramble the 10 countries where Spanish is spoken; then match up each one with its capital.**

*Answers:*
***1** España – j; **2** Argentina – g; **3** Cuba – a; **4** México – b; **5** Colombia – c; **6** Venezuela – e; **7** Chile – d; **8** Perú – i; **9** Costa Rica – h; **10** Bolivia – f*

AT 3.4 **2 Read the information about Bolivia. Find the following words in the text.**

*Answers:*
***a** está situada; **b** el área; **c** el clima; **d** ropa abrigada; **e** las lluvias; **f** río*

AT 3.4 R&W 2.1, 2.2 **3 Read the text in Activity 2 again. True (T) or false (F)?**

*Answers:*
***a** F; **b** T; **c** F; **d** T; **e** F*

## Página 73 4B.2 Sabor latino

- Use with Student Book, pages 134–135

AT 3.4–5 **Fill in the blanks with a word or phrase from the box.**

*Answers: see transcript below*

AT 1.5 L&S 1.1, 1.2 **2 Now listen and check your answers to Activity 1.**

**CD 4, track 37** **página 73, actividades 2 y 3**

David Bisbal nació el 5 de junio de 1975, en Almería, en el sur de España. Es el menor de tres hermanos. Desde pequeño ya demostraba talento para la música cantando aunque era muy tímido.

Es sencillo, humilde y se preocupa por los problemas actuales que afectan al mundo. Para él, la familia es lo primero y también disfruta pasando tiempo con sus amigos.

Alcanzó la fama tras participar en el concurso de telerrealidad que se llama Operación Triunfo donde quedó en segundo lugar. Antes de participar en Operación Triunfo, era cantante del grupo 'Orquesta Expresiones' que actuaba en fiestas populares.

En la actualidad Bisbal es una gran estrella tanto en España como en América y tiene 30 Discos de Platino, 15 de Oro y 2 de Diamante.

AT 1.5 L&S 1.1, 1.2 **3 Listen again. True (T), false (F) or not mentioned (NM).**

*Answers:*
***a** T; **b** T; **c** F; **d** T; **e** T; **f** F; **g** T; **h** NM*

## Página 74 4B.3 ¡Vamos a celebrar!

- Use with Student Book, pages 136–137

AT 3.4 R&W 2.2 **1 Read about this festival from Madrid and answer the questions.**

*Answers:*
***a** febrero; **b** disfrazarse; **c** una sardina; **d** trajes negros típicos; **e** tristemente; **f** por las calles (de la ciudad)*

AT 3.4–5 R&W 2.2 **2 Read one of the possible origins of this tradition. Then find the words or expressions in the text.**

*Answers:*
***a** el siglo; **b** el rey; **c** el finale; **d** hacía calor; **e** el olor; **f** la gente empezó a llorar*

## Página 75 4B.4 Lo mejor de los idiomas

- Use with Student Book, pages 138–139

AT 3.2 **1 Write the sentences in the correct column.**

| *Lo bueno/Lo mejor es que …* | *Lo malo/Lo peor es que …* |
|---|---|
| ***a** te ayuda a encontrar trabajo.*<br>***c** aprendes a comunicarte mejor.*<br>***d** es divertido.*<br>***f** aprendes sobre otras culturas.* | ***b** no es fácil entender todo lo que dice la gente.*<br>***e** es difícil aprender el vocabulario.* |

AT 1.4–5 L&S 1.1, 1.2 **2 Listen to the five teenagers. Do they like languages: ☺ or ☹? Write the reason.**

**CD 4, track 38** **página 75, actividad 2**

**1 Juan**
Pues a mí, me gustan muchísimo los idiomas, me encanta poder comunicarme con gente de otros países y otras culturas.

**2 Marisol**
No sé, no me gusta mucho aprender idiomas. ¡Me parece tan difícil aprender todo el vocabulario! ¡Sin embargo es importante aprenderlos!

**3 Eneko**
Bueno, pues a mí me encantan los idiomas. Estoy aprendiendo dos idiomas y en el futuro quiero trabajar en el extranjero.

**4 Nagore**
¿Si me gustan los idiomas? Pues, en general sí, son divertidos y aprendes a comunicarte mejor con los demás.

**5 Roberto**
Al principio me gustaba, pero ahora no me resulta nada fácil entender lo que dice la gente.

*Answers:*
***1*** *Juan ☺ He loves being able to speak/communicate with people from other countries and other cultures.* ***2*** *Marisol ☹ She finds learning vocabulary difficult.* ***3*** *Eneko ☺ He enjoys languages and wants to work abroad.* ***4*** *Nagore ☺ They are fun and you learn to communicate better with others.* ***5*** *Roberto ☹ He finds it difficult to understand what people say.*

AT 4.4–5 **3 Use the phrases in the table to give your own opinion about languages.**
Students should give their own opinion, but can refer to Activities 1 and 2 for ideas and support.

## Página 76 4B.5 Hispanoamericanos

- Use with Student Book, pages 138–139

AT 3.1 **1 Find eight personality adjectives in the wordsearch.**
Students can refer back to pages 138 and 139 of the Student Book for support, if necessary.

*Answers:*

| | | | | | | | | | | |
|---|---|---|---|---|---|---|---|---|---|---|
| R | | G | E | N | E | R | O | S | O | |
| A | | A | M | B | I | C | I | O | S | O |
| L | E | | | | N | | R | | | |
| U | L | | | | T | | E | | | |
| P | B | | | | R | | S | | | |
| O | A | | | H | O | N | E | S | T | O |
| P | S | | | | V | | | | | |
| | N | | | | E | | | | | |
| | O | | | | R | | | | | |
| | P | | | | T | | | | | |
| | S | | | | I | | | | | |
| | E | | M | O | D | E | S | T | O | |
| | R | | | | O | | | | | |

AT 3.5 **2 Complete the text using words from the box.**

*Answers:*
***1*** *nació;* ***2*** *precioso;* ***3*** *albañil;* ***4*** *concurso;* ***5*** *ganó;* ***6*** *puertas;* ***7*** *todo;* ***8*** *cuando*

AT 4.5 R&W 2.4, 2.5 **3 Write sentences about your own personality. Use the phrases in the box.**
Remind students to pay attention to any adjective endings. Students could also mention what they used to be like when they were younger.

## Página 77 4B.6A Labolengua

- Use with Student Book, pages 142–143

**1 Translate the following sentences using *más* or *menos* to compare Luis, Alfredo and Esteban.**

*Answers:*
***a*** *Luis es* ***más alto que*** *Alfredo.* ***b*** *Alfredo es* ***más fuerte que*** *Luis.* ***c*** *Esteban es* ***más gordo que*** *Luis.* ***d*** *El coche de Luis es* ***el más caro.*** ***e*** *El coche de Esteban* ***es más barato*** *que el coche de Luis.* ***f*** *Alfredo es* ***más guapo*** *que Luis.*

**2 Unscramble the phrases; then match the Spanish with the English.**

*Answers:*
***1*** *Tengo suerte. – d I am lucky.* ***2*** *Tengo miedo. – f I am scared.*
***3*** *Tengo sed. – a I am thirsty.* ***4*** *Tengo calor. – c I am hot.*
***5*** *Tengo frío. – e I am cold.* ***6*** *Tengo hambre. – b I am hungry.*

KAL 4.5 **3 Translate the sentences into Spanish.**

*Answers:*
***a*** *Suelo comer fruta.* ***b*** *Suelo ir al cine los fines de semana.*
***c*** *No suelo leer libros.* ***d*** *Solía estudiar historia.*

## Página 78 4B.6B Técnica

- Use with Student Book, pages 142–143

KAL 4.1 **1 Listen and fill in the missing letters.**
Practice of the Spanish sounds, *ñ*, *ll* and *r* and *rr*.

**CD 4, track 39** **página 78, actividades 1 y 2**

- cañón; castaña; antaño; quinceañero; pañal; pañuelo; peña; leña
- calle; cepillo; camello; lleno; rellenar; llover; callarse; camilla
- caro; carro; roto; puerro; pera; perro; cinturón; carretera

KAL 4.1 **2 Now listen again and repeat the words in Activity 1.**

KAL 4.1 **3 Match up the Spanish and English words. Then practise saying the Spanish words aloud and then listen and check your pronunciation.**

**CD 4, track 40** **página 78, actividad 3**

correr; rápido; llavero; piña; castillo; cero

*Answers:*
***1** c; **2** e; **3** a; **4** f; **5** b; **6** d*

**4 Be careful with these false friends. Match up each one with its real meaning.**

*Answers:*
***1** h; **2** f; **3** a; **4** g; **5** b; **6** d; **7** c; **8** e*

# Gramática

## 1 Nouns and determiners página 158

**A Copy and complete the table. Follow the example.**

*Answers:*

| | | the (definite article) | | a/an/some (indefinite article) | | |
|---|---|---|---|---|---|---|
| **masc.** | **fem.** | **singular** | **plural** | **singular** | **plural** | |
| | ✓ | *la manzana* | *las manzanas* | *una manzana* | *unas manzanas* | *apple/apples* |
| ✓ | | *el perro* | *los perros* | *un perro* | *unos perros* | *dog/dogs* |
| | ✓ | *la casa* | *las casas* | *una casa* | *unas casas* | *house/houses* |
| ✓ | | *el hotel* | *los hoteles* | *un hotel* | *unos hoteles* | *hotel/hotels* |
| ✓ | | *el lápiz* | *los lápices* | *un lápiz* | *unos lápices* | *pencil/pencils* |
| | ✓ | *la araña* | *las arañas* | *una araña* | *unas arañas* | *spider/spiders* |
| ✓ | | *la canción* | *las canciones* | *una canción* | *unas canciones* | *song/songs* |
| ✓ | | *el jardín* | *los jardines* | *un jardín* | *unos jardines* | *garden/gardens* |
| | ✓ | *la piscina* | *las piscinas* | *una piscine* | *unas piscinas* | *pool/pools* |
| ✓ | | *el animal* | *los animales* | *un animal* | *unos animales* | *animal/animals* |

## 2 Adjectives página 158

**B How would you say these in Spanish?**

*Answers:*
***1*** *un abrigo verde;* ***2*** *los sombreros azules;* ***3*** *un vestido blanco;* ***4*** *las camisetas rojas;* ***5*** *unos calcetines amarillos;* ***6*** *las botas marrones;* ***7*** *los pantalones negros;* ***8*** *una camisa rosa*

## 3 Demonstrative adjectives página 159

**C Tell the shop assistant which item from this shop window you want using demonstrative adjectives.**

*Answers:*
***1*** *Quiero aquellas sandalias moradas.* ***2*** *Quiero esa camiseta amarilla.* ***3*** *Quiero estos vaqueros azules.* ***4*** *Quiero estas sandalias rojos.* ***5*** *Quiero esa falda morada.* ***6*** *Quiero ese bolso negro.* ***7*** *Quiero aquellos zapatos marrones.* ***8*** *Quiero esas sandalias blancas.*

## 4 Possessives página 159

**D Translate into Spanish.**

*Answers:*
***1*** *vuestros padres;* ***2*** *su casa;* ***3*** *sus primos/as;* ***4*** *mis amigos;* ***5*** *tu abuelo;* ***6*** *nuestra madre*

## 5 Prepositions página 160

**E Where is Don Quijote?**

*Answers:*
***1*** *Don Quijote está sobre el (or encima del) coche.* ***2*** *Don Quijote está dentro del coche.* ***3*** *Don Quijote está debajo del coche.* ***4*** *Don Quijote está entre dos coches.* ***5*** *Don Quijote está detrás del coche.* ***6*** *Don Quijote está a la derecha del coche.*

## 6 Pronouns página 160

**Information on spanish pronouns.**

## 7 Verbs páginas 161 –167

**F How would you say in Spanish...?**

*Answers:*
*__1__ terminamos; __2__ admite; __3__ vas; __4__ abren; __5__ creo; __6__ leemos; __7__ abrís; __8__ ha*

**G Complete these sentences with the verbs in the box.**

*Answers:*
*__1__ almuerza; __2__ siente, dice; __3__ sirven; __4__ juego; __5__ volamos*

**H Complete the sentences with the correct form of the preterite.**

*Answers:*
*__1__ cocinó; __2__ vi; __3__ dio; __4__ jugasteis; __5__ dormiste, bebiste; __6__ terminó; __7__ estudiaron; __8__ fueron*

**I Write in Spanish using the imperfect.**

*Answers:*
*__1__ llovía; __2__ llevaba; __3__ teníais; __4__ usaba; __5__ trabajaban; __6__ compraba; __7__ comían; __8__ hacíamos*

**J Preterite or imperfect? Rewrite the sentences with the correct verbs.**

*Answers:*
*__1 Estaba__ en la fiesta cuando me __llamaste__. __2__ La película __terminó__ mientras __hablábamos__ por teléfono. __3 Hacíamos__ los deberes cuando papá __llegó__. __4 Estaba__ enfermo cuando __empezaron__ las vacaciones. __5 Llevaba__ una falda roja cuando __fueron__ de compras. __6 Llamé__ a mi madre mientras __esperaba__ el autobús.*

**K Rewrite these sentences in the immediate future.**

*Answers:*
*__1__ Vamos a viajar por Madrid en metro. __2__ Voy a comer en el restaurante del museo. __3__ Van a alquilar una bicicleta para visitar el parque. __4__ Va a comprar recuerdos en el Rasto. __5__ Va a ir a la capital el fin de semana.*

**L Translate into Spanish.**

*Answers:*
*__1__ Iré a la universidad. __2__ Haré muchos amigos. __3__ Mis padres ganarán la lotería. __4__ Viajaré por el mundo. __5__ Tendré un buen trabajo. __6__ Mi padre comprará un Ferrari. __7__ Vivirán a orillas del mar. __8__ Seré rico/a y famoso/a.*

**M You have been granted five wishes. Write a sentence for each of the verbs in the box.**

*Answers: students' own*

**N Use the verbs in the box to translate these phrases.**

*Answers:*
*__1__ se enojó; __2__ se preocupa; __3__ nos acostamos; __4__ me afeitaré; __5__ te maquillaste; __6__ nos duchamos; __7__ me levanto; __8__ se despertó*

**O Write the correct form of the imperative to complete these sentences.**

*Answers:*
*__1__ Ahorra; __2__ visitad; __3__ viajen; __4__ coman; __5__ olvidéis*

**P Answer the questions using the structure *soler* + infinitive.**

*Answers: students' own*

**Q What do these sentences mean in English?**

*Answers:*
*__1__ You/One must not smoke. __2__ You/One can't smoke. __3__ We have to look after the environment. __4__ You/One must recycle. __5__ They must recycle rubbish. __6__ Here they live well.*

## 8 Negatives página 167

**R Complete the sentences with the appropriate negative word.**

*Answers:*
*__1__ no; __2__ nada; __3__ ni, ni; __4__ ninguno; __5__ nadie; __6__ nunca; __7__ nada; __8__ no, nunca*

## 9 Direct object pronouns
página 167

**S Identify and replace the direct objects in these sentences.**

*Answers:*
***1*** *Compro* ***flores*** *para mi madre. –* ***Las*** *compro para mi madre.* ***2*** *Comí* ***los mangos*** *ayer. –* ***Los*** *comí ayer.* ***3*** *Escribo* ***un email****. –* ***Lo*** *escribo.* ***4*** *Vendí* ***mi coche*** *a un amigo. –* ***Lo*** *vendí a un amigo.* ***5*** *Compraré* ***la camiseta*** *azul. –* ***La*** *compraré.* ***6*** *Marisa no entiende* ***inglés****. – Marisa no* ***lo*** *entiende.*

## 10 Asking questions
página 168

**T Complete the questions with an appropriate question word.**

*Answers:*
***1*** *Quién;* ***2*** *Cuándo;* ***3*** *Cuántos;* ***4*** *Dónde;* ***5*** *Cómo;* ***6*** *Por qué*

## 11 Opinions
página 168

**U How do you say in Spanish...?**

*Answers:*
***1*** *Le gustan las patatas fritas.* ***2*** *Me gusta la cultura;* ***3*** *Nos gustó la película.* ***4*** *Les gusta el arte.* ***5*** *No me gustó la comida.* ***6*** *No me gusta el ruido.*

## 12 Comparative and superlative
página 169

**V Compare the two neighbourhoods. Write at least six sentences. Use the words in the box.**

*Answers: students' own*

## 13 Adverbs
página 169

**W Complete these sentences with the adverb which comes from the adjective in brackets.**

*Answers:*
***1*** *felizmente;* ***2*** *verdaderamente;* ***3*** *tristemente;* ***4*** *rápidamente*